THE SECRET AGENT

INSIDE THE WORLD OF THE FOOTBALL AGENT

THE SECRET AGENT

INSIDE THE WORLD OF THE FOOTBALL AGENT

ARENA
SPORT

First published in Great Britain in 2014 by
ARENA SPORT
An imprint of Birlinn Limited
West Newington House
10 Newington Road
Edinburgh
EH9 1QS

www.arenasportbooks.co.uk

ISBN: 978-1-909715-24-0
eBook ISBN: 978-0-85790-815-5

British Library Cataloguing-in-Publication Data
A catalogue record for this book is available on request from the
British Library.

Designed and typeset by Polaris Publishing, Edinburgh

Printed and bound in Great Britain by
TJ International Ltd, Padstow, Cornwall

CONTENTS

PROLOGUE

I ALWAYS KNEW I wanted to do something in football, just like I always knew I wanted to be rich. The trouble was that, as a kid, I was pretty crap on the pitch, and when you come from an East London council estate with parents who both have to work for a living, then the odds are really stacked against you.

So, ruling out being the next David Beckham, or buying my own club, that left me with fairly limited choices. I was great with stats. But Jeff Stelling had the prime job in that area all tied up, and not being blonde, female and with great tits, I couldn't see a future for myself on Sky Sports. I thought about coaching, but that was a long and rocky road, and I knew that not having played the game at the highest level, or any level at all when it came to that (other than my school class second XI – and given that there were only twenty boys in my class that was no real achievement), I was at some disadvantage from the start.

But then I watched a programme that changed my life. Or at least made me make a life-changing decision. It was one of those fly-on-the-wall documentaries that was meant to uncover the dirt and corruption that lay beneath the world of football agents. You know the sort of thing, paying bungs to managers to make a deal happen, fitting up a rival to steal a player, lying through their teeth to parents to get the first run on looking after little Tommy and, worst of all (at least as far as the programme makers were concerned), making serious money.

Now, I know that to most people that would be a turn-off. Who wants to be a part of what seemed to be one of the most reviled groups of operators in the world? I was going to call it a profession, but clearly nobody on screen (apart from the agents protesting their innocence after having been caught fairly red-handed) actually used that word to describe the trade they plied. Yet, at twenty years of age, in my final year of a degree in media studies (well, I had to pick something or else face going out to work straight from school) it seemed more of an opportunity than a turn-off.

The main thing that the agents on show had in common, apart from greed and duplicity, was stupidity. They had all the contacts in the world (well, two of them were ex-pros so they ought to have) but they didn't have a brain cell between them. The fact that they'd all fallen for the TV network's sting proved it. So that was when I decided that I could do better than them.

It was an odd decision for me to make. I'd never done anything dishonest in my life, and in a way it felt like suddenly deciding to embark on a life of crime. I was never going to be one for armed robbery or even Bernie Madoff-type fraud (although I confess to having had a sneaking admiration for Bernie which was balanced by disappointment when he got caught), but the opportunity for taking on what seemed to be nothing other than a career for chancers did appeal to me. It didn't seem to be very different from what bankers and share dealers were doing, and a lot more fun.

There were drawbacks to my plan. I didn't know any footballers personally, although I knew an awful lot about them from my obsessive compilation of profiles and statistics of every single player in the UK, and I don't just mean the international stars either. I had them all nailed down: from the English Premier League to the Football Conference, and taking in all the Scottish divisions on the way. It's amazing what you can pull together using the internet coupled with the sports papers not to mention good old YouTube, Twitter and Facebook.

My first decision was to create a fairly inventive CV. I wasn't really looking for paid employment at one of the big accountancy or law firms, so I reckoned I was pretty safe from a close inspection and I was certain I'd impress if I could only get in front of somebody for an interview. That, in itself, was much harder than I thought it would be.

Every agent in England has to register with the Football Association (FA) who provide a list online of what they call 'Authorised Licensed Agents'. I spent a whole day trawling through the names. Some I'd heard of through the media, some were part of the big agencies and others were clearly just one-man bands operating from their front rooms. It hadn't occurred to me up to that point that I'd need to pass an exam to pursue my chosen career, but there were details of the next FA Agents' Exam posted on the website together with how to get the details of the syllabus. I'd never had any problem in passing exams so that was no obstacle either, but again, at that point, I didn't have a clue as to how hard the authorities made it. There were a lot of things I didn't have a clue about then, but over the next five years I unravelled them all, and more.

As I wrote my letters of application or fired off emails where I could, I felt this enormous sense of excitement. I could do this, I knew it. And I'd be good at it, of that I was certain. I just needed somebody to give me a chance.

GETTING STARTED

IT WAS MUCH harder than I thought. I wrote to all the mega agencies like WMG, Stellar, SEM, First Artist and James Grant, and although for the most part I got polite letters back saying they had no vacancies at the moment but wishing me luck for the future, I never got a sniff of an interview.

The breakthrough came when one of the guys, whose name I'd read about often in the paper, actually replied to my email and offered to meet me for a coffee. If I thought I was about to be invited to one of London's exclusive members' clubs then I was disappointed because the venue was a Starbucks not far from Oxford Circus.

I recognised him immediately. I knew he was over fifty, but he looked a good ten years younger. Smart casual clothing, hair impeccably groomed, dark glasses even though it was January and we were meeting indoors. That was one of my first lessons. The right image was important. If you were meeting a young player for the first time, there was no point in turning up in a suit and a shirt with a collar and a tie. He had to be able to gauge the value of what you were wearing to be able to decide if you were cool and sharp enough to represent him. Players are judged by their agents. They talk about them in the dressing room as if they're trophies.

'My man reps . . .' and then he lists a series of England internationals. No good saying you're somebody's only client. No street cred in that at all, and don't even think about turning up at the training ground in any vehicle worth less than £40k.

I extended my hand and – I'm going to call him 'R' – R nodded in the direction of the counter and said, 'Mine's an Americano. And a skinny muffin while you're at it.' Which was when I understood that an invitation to coffee did not extend to the actual purchase.

It didn't take me long in the industry to discover that most agents are intuitively tight-fisted. They're happy to shower gifts and freebies on their players because they're investing in them, but when it comes to anything else, then their wallets remain firmly folded, opening only to receive and not to give.

I brought the drinks over to the table and waited for him to open the conversation, but when nothing was forthcoming it dawned on me that he was waiting for me to try and impress him.

'Thanks for seeing me,' I said, an opening gambit that merely made him yawn and glance at his diamond-encrusted Rolex. I noted that he made sure that I saw it too and I automatically tugged down my sleeve to conceal the watch that I'd worn ever since my bar mitzvah.

'I see everybody that contacts me,' R said.

'That's good of you,' I replied.

He grunted, took a sip of his coffee and said, 'It's just to tell you that if you want to become an agent you're fucking delusional. Are you a gambler, son?'

'Not really,' I said.

'OK. Let me show you the odds then. There are ninety-two clubs in the League. Let's say they each have thirty or so professionals. That's two thousand, seven hundred players. And there are about four hundred agents not to mention all the others working the same patch – lawyers, close relations, foreign agents registered elsewhere. Then there are the unlicensed guys who do the same job and hide behind either a lawyer or a real agent. I couldn't begin to tell you how many of them there are but it probably runs into the hundreds. The top half-a-dozen agencies have about a hundred players each, including the pick of the crop. So that leaves about two thousand players divided amongst about five or six hundred agents, about three or four players each. Now, even if you're lucky and you manage to sign up your quota, let's say those players aren't the best. Let's say they only earn an average of thirty to fifty grand a year. You charge five per cent. So for a deal you might make fifteen hundred to two-and-a-half grand a year. Multiply that by the number of players you have and build in the probability that not every one of them will get a deal each year and what have you got? Eight, ten grand a year coming in? Still think it's worth it?'

'Yes,' I said. 'But I'm thinking you don't do deals for that level. And I'm also thinking from the value of that watch you're wearing and the cost alone of those shades that you don't just charge five per cent.'

For the first time I'd piqued his interest. He pushed back his glasses and I saw his eyes – so dark brown they were almost black – and I felt them drilling into me, seeming to reach right down into my deepest thoughts, and I wondered how anybody ever won any negotiations when he was sitting on the other side of a desk.

'So,' he said, almost to himself, 'the kid thinks. That's good because I have to tell you that most people in this game don't think at all. They're so busy chasing after deals that they don't even think about tying up their shoelaces, which means the minute they try to run they fall over. This,' he lifted my CV, 'it's a load of shit, isn't it?'

I nodded, thinking that the meeting was coming to an end, but suddenly there was a little smile on his face.

'You know what, you've got chutzpah at least, I'll give you that; and in this game, you need that in barrow loads. It's a bit like selling double glazing. You knock on a hundred doors but you only need one old lady to invite you in and you know your day has been worthwhile. Substitute footballers for old ladies and there you are. We trawl for them, we pick up what we can and we hope for the best. If they're no good we throw them back in the sea. But the ones we catch, the ones we want to keep, that's where the money is. It's hard to pick them, hard to reel them in and even harder to keep them. Don't suppose you're licensed, are you?'

'No, but I reckon I can pass that exam easily enough.'

R laughed out loud. 'That's what they all say, but the pass rate is less than twenty per cent. I've known blokes with first-class honours degrees fail a couple of times. What they ask you is totally obscure and if you really want to do this then it's also fucking useless. I tell you what. I like you. If you work with me then you won't need a licence anyway. So this is what I'll offer you. I'm going to give you three months to sign six players for me. I'm not going to pay you but if I earn anything out of those players I'll make sure you're looked after. I'll pay you your expenses as long as you clear them with me first, and whether you make the grade with me or not I promise you that at the end of those three months you'll have learned a fucking sight more than you ever got out of books at college or what you'd have stuffed into your head working for that FA exam.'

'Do I get anything in writing?' I asked.

'Listen, son, you've heard the old saying that a verbal contract isn't worth the paper it's written on?'

I nodded. That one was down to one of the old movie moguls.

'Well, in this sweet world of football the effort of chopping down the tree to make the paper to write a contract is also a total fucking waste of time. Now, do you want to do this or not? 'Cos if you do you can buy me another coffee, you can tell me the players you're going to target and I'm going to explain to you exactly how you're going to go about getting them.'

I reached towards him and extended my hand and, as somebody told me far too late, I should've counted my fingers when his grip relaxed.

PLAYER RECRUITMENT LESSON ONE: KNOW YOUR ENEMY

IT DIDN'T TAKE me too long to discover what I was in for working alongside R. To be fair to him, he did exactly what he'd promised. He even got me some business cards printed with his company name and logo and my name with the word 'Scout' beneath it.

That word covered a multitude of sins. The guys operating below the radar in the industry were either scouts or consultants. They seemed to fall into two distinct categories. There were wannabe agents like myself, all bright-eyed and bushy-tailed, getting to as many matches as we could during a week at all levels; and there were the seasoned ex-pros who'd never bothered to pass the exams but were still, to all intents and purposes, carrying on the business of a football agent.

As I realised from the off, the enemy was the FA. The challenge was to bypass their dreaded Agents' Regulations, which had been introduced some years previously to try to bring some order into what had been pretty much the Wild West. I've been to meetings of the Association of Football Agents (AFA) since and heard speakers say that they didn't want to return to the bad old days of 'the Wild West', but my experience is that those days never went away and for the people who made fortunes they were anything but the 'bad old days'.

The way the system was supposed to work was a civil servant's dream and a businessman's nightmare. Only 'Licensed Agents' could carry out what was described as 'Agency Activity' in the regs. That just about covered everything from making the first phone call to get the player, meeting him, signing him up and then finding him a club and negotiating his contract. What the FA had done was create a *War and*

Peace-scale document for every step of the process. You get the player to sign the contract and you have to get it signed in triplicate. You have to tell the player to get independent advice. You send it off to the FA who get one of their bean counters to check it and send it back if a comma is out of place. Then when they register it, the result is that only the agent named in the contract can deal with the club, and the club is supposedly obliged only to deal with that agent.

It simply didn't work like that, as I'll explain later when I get down to some of the sleazier deals I got involved with. The lodged contract also meant that if you did get to the point of agreeing terms with a club then all the forms that had to be signed were also multi-copied and signed by everybody: club, player and you. And when your payment was due, the club paid the FA, the FA eventually released the money to you and that was where it got interesting.

Only the actual agent involved was allowed to be paid and he was supposed to tell the FA if he was paying anybody else. Yeah, right. I suppose R could've got away with telling the FA he was paying his scouts some bonuses but I couldn't see him telling them about the payments that went to the managers and the parents (particularly the fathers) of the player concerned and sometimes the players themselves.

I made it my business to find out how a transaction was supposed to work as far as the FA was concerned. The reality when I finally got to meet a potential player was very different.

I'd been to see a few academy matches on my own. I flattered myself that I could tell a decent player from the dross, but the problem was that so could everybody else who was watching. It wasn't easy getting into some of the grounds to watch the games, as you either needed to be accredited from a club or else be a close relation. I soon learned to recognise the parents of the boys who were playing and realised that if I chatted them up outside the match venue and carried on my conversation as we went in, the stewards on the gate automatically assumed I was also related. It was a bit tricky with some of the black lads, so I tended to latch on to the white parents and pretend to be an older brother.

If you praised the kid during the match then it wasn't hard to keep the dialogue going. It was obvious, at whatever level I watched, that most of the parents thought their sons were only marking time before they joined Manchester United or Barcelona. If the kid had a stinker of a match then that was down to the coach playing him out of position. It was never the boy's fault, and I found that if I encouraged the parent by telling him that we had a real inside run at a major club then they'd be more than willing to supply their phone number to set up a meeting.

There was a tiny problem in that respect. The good old FA say that you can't sign a player up before his sixteenth birthday and, in fact, you can't even legally approach him before that. However, if you wait until then, the player, if he's any good, will almost certainly have been snapped up by another agency. There are players as young as ten or eleven who, if you ask them, will say they've got an 'agent'. Grooming on the net is nothing compared to the way agencies groom young players and their parents, so my ruse of getting the numbers and arranging a meeting was nothing compared to what was going on elsewhere – as I was to discover in spades at my first sit-down with a fifteen-year-old and his mum and dad.

PLAYER RECRUITMENT LESSON TWO: THIS IS WHAT WE WANT

IN EVERY GENERATION there are young footballers known as 'talking players'. Everybody knew about Joe Cole and Wayne Rooney from when they were about ten years old, and the agents who secured them when they were teenagers knew what they were doing. And they talked about them.

Nowadays there are far more agents, which means there's much more competition for those precious signatures. There are two problems. As I said, one is that they can't sign until they're sixteen and the other is that a parent has to sign off as their guardian. So, you have to get the parents to like and trust you, and you have to get the kid to buy into your style of representation.

I'd spotted a target at an academy match at a London Championship side. His dad was there, and I soon found out he'd been laid off from his job a few months back and that the mother had two jobs and was the sole breadwinner of the family. It didn't take long to figure out that his son – let's call him Ryan – was the guy's intended meal ticket for the rest of his life.

I could see the lad was a decent player. He was tall for his age and had a football brain on him, and playing in midfield he reminded me of a young Frank Lampard. He just had something about him. I went to watch him three or four times and then, when I could see other agents were also homing in on the father, I decided the time was right to make a move – and to my delight I managed to get the dad to agree to see R and me at his home one night.

I thought R was going to be delighted, but he was fairly cynical about the whole thing. 'Don't get too excited until you see what he wants,' he said, and in those early days I confess I didn't really understand what he meant.

I must have visited dozens of that type of house since then, and they're all remarkably alike. Terraced, a small front room dominated by a giant TV always locked on to Sky Sports, a wife stuck in the kitchen who is friendly but nervous, offering tea and biscuits from their best china, and a few younger siblings poking their heads around the door.

You have to relate to them all. Conversation with the boy's mother has to reassure her that you'll look after the apple of her eye and treat him as your own. Questions to the younger ones as to what they're up to. If there's a little girl you need to know something about the latest bands; if it's a boy then does he also want to be a footballer. It's all about making a good impression and leaving a positive memory behind. The thing is, though, there are others who will be leaving something more substantial behind.

Ryan's dad eased himself into his favourite chair. I looked at the TV, R looked at the TV, and we waited for the dad to turn it off or down. No chance. He was looking at it too and continued to do so for the whole of our meeting even when talking to us.

'OK,' he said, 'so what have you lot got to offer that the others haven't?'

R began to tell him about the players he'd represented, about all the club contacts he had, about his own career as a player, and how he had kids himself and would treat Ryan as if he were his own son.

I could see that the dad wasn't impressed or really interested.

'Well,' the dad said, 'that's all very well and good, but we've spoken to a few agents already. One of them sent a Roller to pick us up and take Ryan to his office, and when we left, my boy found a brand new Xbox and iPad on the seat. Good set-up. They had (he named a current England international) there to meet us and he really likes the way Ryan plays. Thinks he's going to be a real star.'

I have to say R handled it really well.

'They're a good agency. You can tell that from the number of players they have. But that's also the downside. They act for too many to give your Ryan the individual attention he deserves. We'd be hands-on all the time.' He pointed to me. 'My assistant will be like a brother to him, I promise you.'

The dad paused for a moment and took his eyes of the screen. He appraised me. 'I get that,' he said. 'It's a good point. But what about me?'

'You'll always be involved,' R said. 'Nothing will ever happen without us speaking to you first and getting your views.'

'Yeah, well that goes without saying,' the dad replied. 'But what are you going to do to help me out? I've not worked for months and I'm the one who ferries Ryan back and forwards to the club, to training, to matches. I'm the one who has to get him all the stuff he needs . . .'

I could see this bloke raiding his wife's purse for her hard-earned cash to do just that, but I kept my counsel.

'Boots won't be a problem. And I'm sure we can help you out with petrol and so on.'

I could see it was the 'and so on' which was going to be the thing for the father.

'The other lot offered that. And they also said that when I was watching Ryan I could do some scouting for them.'

R wasn't giving up. 'You can tip us off as well. We sign anybody, we'll pay you something and we'll look after you when we do a deal for the kid.'

'The thing is,' the dad continued, warming to his task, 'I need the money now.'

The gloves were off, the sparring was over. The mother had closed the door to the kitchen as if she knew exactly when the conversation would get to this point. The younger children were up in their bedrooms. This was man's talk now.

'How much did they offer you?' R asked.

'Twenty-five grand in cash and then a scouting deal for thirty grand a year.'

R looked long and hard as if assessing whether or not the man was telling the truth.

'And if we give you this as well, will Ryan sign? We'd have to leave the date blank in the contract and fill it in when he gets to sixteen.'

'Well, we like you, and Ryan likes your lad here, so I'm thinking we might well do that. The other lot were a bit flash, a bit up themselves, if you know what I mean?'

R nodded. Yes, he knew exactly what he meant. It was a gamble on R's part. The lad's career might come to nothing. He'd sign effectively at sixteen and by the time he was eighteen when the maximum two years of the contract had run out he might not even have got a meaningful contract that could recoup the investment. But R knew that the bigger risk was letting the opportunity pass. And so the deal was done.

As it happened it was a good move. The lad was playing in the first team just a few months after his sixteenth birthday and a year later had moved to a Premiership club. R's fee was in the region of three hundred grand for the two deals. Not a bad return for what was by then the eighty-five grand that he'd paid the dad.

But there was a sting in the tail. When the two years were up and the boy needed to re-sign with R, the dad had become a lot more streetwise and said he'd only allow it if R paid him half of all future fees. R had no choice but to agree. If he hadn't, then others would've, and half of something was better than one hundred per cent of nothing. If I learned nothing else from R then it was to be pragmatic.

GOT TO KEEP THE CUSTOMER SATISFIED

I NEVER ASKED where R got his cash from but it always seemed to be around. I knew he'd done a few favours for one or two managers when he'd effectively laundered some cash they'd made from a deal via another agent, but more about managers later. His other ploy was to charge a couple of per cent less than the normal five per cent, get more money into a player's contract to compensate for it and then get the player to give him one per cent back in cash. He reckoned everybody earned from that little scheme, but I doubted that HMRC would've seen it that way.

He wasn't the only one being a bag man for managers. There was an agent based abroad who kept huge stashes of cash for various managers and had an understanding with the local police who felt the need to make routine raids on his house just to appease their bosses. They'd call him an hour or so before they were coming and there would be a frantic packing-up operation. A car loaded with cash would then be taken to a lock-up garage and exchanged for another vehicle kept there just for that purpose, and the police would report back that nothing had been found.

There were always uses for cash. Players needed to be looked after in more ways than one. When one player came down from up north he asked for a guaranteed entry into a club of his choice and a hotel room booked for afterwards so he could take the girl (or girls) of his choice back there. That service paled into insignificance compared to one agent who actually maintained a flat in Central London with hookers on tap to accommodate the players' every needs as and when they were in town. I heard that he liked to test-drive the girls himself – so good clean healthy fun all round.

It wasn't just girls the players wanted their agents to provide. It was drugs as well. Obviously they were terrified of testing positive in a random post-match drug test, but when there was a good long gap between matches and they had a few days of R & R they were really into the substances, including the hard stuff.

I knew R's dealer because I used to have to collect from him occasionally, and once when we got chatting I was surprised to learn that he'd been a player himself at one time. He'd worked out that he could earn more off the pitch by supplying his teammates using the contacts he'd grown up with, and now he had a thriving business which was almost exclusively player-based.

Most of the players I met or represented came from really tough backgrounds and as schoolboys had been faced with few career opportunities. If you couldn't make it at football then a life of crime was a real alternative; and if you weren't into physical things like armed robbery or burglary, then drug dealing was an attractive career path. It offered not only big bucks but the chance of a base in somewhere like Spain, Portugal or Greece. R used to joke that you could tell the dealers by their perma-tans and the players by their dodgy knees. You could carry on dealing after you were in your mid-thirties, which was another plus, and a few players we knew went over to the dark side once their careers were over.

Footballers are naturally takers rather than givers, and any agent has to be prepared to invest money in them all the time. Most boot companies won't give boots for free any more to anybody apart from the top-flight players. Although they'll nearly always give an agent a discount, they still run a pretty price from a hundred quid right up to two-fifty. If you have more than a dozen players and they run through four pairs a year on average it's a sizeable hit on your income. It's not even tax deductible. Nor can you claim back the VAT as the Revenue don't regard it as an allowable expense and the FA look on it as a potential inducement to get a player to enter into a contract. But more about boots later. They're a commodity just like any other. The FA's attitude to their supply is a real joke. If you want to talk about inducements, then apart from the sex and drugs I've mentioned above, I've known agents give gifts such as cars, expensive holidays, Rolex watches, and even houses for the players' families. Agents are desperate not to miss out on an opportunity and once they've done one or two massive dodgy deals and amassed a slush fund then the sky is the limit to ensure they position themselves in a transaction.

If there's a deal in the offing and there's a six- or even a seven-figure commission to earn, then it's relatively small change to pay an inducement to a player's father to get him to persuade his son to get the player involved in the transaction. Now I know what you're thinking. Doesn't the player have to have had a contract? And you're right. But it often happens that, as far as the player's old agent is concerned, his client just goes AWOL. Every player has the right to represent himself even if he has a contract (welcome to the wild and wacky world of football). He tells the buying club he isn't using his agent but wants the club to use the agent who has looked after his dad. The club wants to sign the player and aren't really bothered as long as they only pay one lot of fees. The new agent represents the club and recoups his 'gift' to the player's dad in spades. And the added bonus is that the player doesn't have to pay any tax as he hasn't incurred any agents' fees for himself, which would normally have been paid for by the club and incurred a tax liability for the player as a benefit in kind. Sorted. Everybody's happy except the poor old agent who's been left out in the cold and our good friends at HMRC.

In the real world, rather than the parallel universe of football and agents, the wronged party would just sue his player-client. But it doesn't work like that. Reputation is everything as I'll go on to explain. Also one 'participant' in football can't sue another and that term includes players, agents and clubs. They have to proceed by way of what is called a Rule K Arbitration under FA Rules. The FA are so anal about keeping everything in-house that they won't even let outside justice in through the door, nor let us out to play in the courts. It's just another example of how agents are treated as a school class with rules and punishments to match. Every time I've been called in to see them I've been made to feel like a naughty schoolboy who has been found smoking behind the toilets. As for the Revenue, well, they move in mysterious ways. And they don't like agents. But then who does? We might just as well adopt the old Millwall song as our theme.

We are agents, super agents,
No one likes us,
We don't care.

Perhaps we should've printed up some T-shirts bearing that legend. No one likes us: not the clubs, the FA, the Leagues, the media and certainly not the PFA, the Professional Footballers' Association.

And to be perfectly honest, when we can make as much money as we can on any single transaction why should we give a flying fuck?

THE TRUTH, THE WHOLE TRUTH AND NOTHING BUT THE TRUTH

EVERY JOURNALIST LIKES to think he has one or more agent in his front pocket, whereas the truth is that every agent has a pet journalist in his back pocket. Not that the truth has anything to do with journalism of course. When I was at university I conducted a small experiment for a thesis I was writing. I took all the headlines from three tabloids for three months – November, December and January – those leading up to the transfer window and the window itself. Of all the headlines predicting this signing and that signing, less than twenty per cent turned out to be true. So let me tell you why that is.

Agents get called by their 'friendly' journos almost every day as the window gets near to closing. They want their cards marked in advance of an event happening. But a shrewd agent will ensure that's a two-way street. Let's assume Player X wants to leave his current club but the club is having none of it. It can be necessary to stir the waters a little and plant a story – and that has to be done very carefully.

You might say that Clubs Y and Z have expressed an interest in X, or that the manager of his current club is shopping for a player in exactly the same position (perhaps a bit younger) and that's because he doesn't fancy X much any more. Now, the club may well issue all sorts of denials, but the seeds are sown and one fact that's incontrovertible in football is that when a player wants to leave a club, he leaves. The only issue becomes how much the club gets for him. A brilliant operator like Daniel Levy at Spurs got the maximum figure for Gareth Bale because he knew exactly how to play the game. There was never ever any doubt that Bale was on his way out to Real Madrid, but Levy played it cool right to the very last moment. You have to admire clubs like Spurs for maximising income for players. Irving Scholar, one of Levy's predecessors, had the same talent. Newcastle got a crazy fee for Andy Carroll from Liverpool with similar tactics. But in each and every case the relevant agent also played a very clever hand with no little help from the media. There's nothing wrong with that whatsoever, and as I gained more experience I realised that the manipulation of the press was all part of the game.

There has to be care as to how you get the stories written. Most players will have signing-on fees payable in their contracts. That's a lump sum that the club pays when the player joins or his contract is renegotiated. Even though it's not paid in one hit, but spread over the term of the contract in equal instalments, agents like to have that in, not only because players are impressed by large capital sums even more than weekly salaries, but because it's guaranteed income and as such they're allowed to charge commission on it within the FA Rules. These say that commission can only be charged on guaranteed income and that is limited to salaries and signing-on fees. So things like appearance money, bonuses and loyalty payments (loyalty – such an inappropriate word when it comes to players and clubs) don't qualify for commissions. And we do so love our commissions.

The only problem with signing-on fees is that if a player asks for a transfer, then the club is entitled not to pay any outstanding signing-on fees. If they decided to sell him then the whole of the unpaid balance of the signing-on fee becomes due. As you can imagine, that can be a huge sum, so once a club realises it's going to lose a player it not only seeks to maximise the amount it gets from the buying club, but also to minimise anything it has to pay to the player and his agent.

Now, a written transfer request is one thing. That truly is a document of last resort. Once that's in, the die is cast and your player can forget all about whatever you (or your predecessor) may have negotiated for him by way of a signing-on fee. However, without anything in writing, the club may still try to prove that the player has, in effect, really asked for a transfer – and one excellent method of proof are quotes from his agent in a paper saying how unhappy his client is and how he's desperate to further his career at a club with European football guaranteed. The fact that the more successful club may well be doubling the player's salary (not to mention the agent's commission) is something that you really don't want mentioned. Anyway, once a club sees anything like that in a paper or hears words to that effect in an interview, they'll be on it like a dog with a bone saying that the player is asking for a transfer even though he hasn't put anything in writing. And you know what, they're right.

The challenge is finding a trustworthy journalist – and those words don't often go together. Now, I'm not suggesting that most journalists are dishonest. If you go to a bar with them you can safely leave your wallet on the table. I'm not so sure you can leave your girlfriend with them, but if they've got such crap taste as to be prepared to shag a journo would you really want to be with them anyway? It's not that sort of dishonesty that worries me or other agents. It's breaching trust. The magic words are 'off the record'. If you have a conversation with a journo and say it's off the record and find the next day he's written it up as a banner exclusive, then that's the last time you ever speak to him. But the damage has been done, and it may have meant the end of the relationship between you and your player, or you and a particular club.

It's a very short-term policy for journos to write up what you've told them in confidence but it's amazing how many of them do it. They have to fill a paper, they're under pressure from their editors; even their jobs can be on the line unless they deliver something sensational. The really experienced ones may try to pressurise you to go on the record but as long as you have the willpower to resist what can be daily (or even hourly) calls they'll keep schtum.

So why tell them anything confidential at all? Well, they need to feel loved for one thing. Maybe, more importantly, they want to be able to blow the story wide open as soon as you give them the go-ahead, and if they've written it up already then they get the jump on their rivals. The world of newspapers and sports media journalism is even more cut-throat than that of football agents, and that's really saying something.

You may also need a trade-off with a journalist. You give him a story and he kills another (damaging) story about your client. Believe me, that doesn't just happen in the world of Max Clifford, the once undisputed master of PR and press manipulation. A journalist may call you to tell you that he has a story and a photo of one of your star players stumbling out of a nightclub blind drunk with a wannabe footballer's wife on his arm who isn't actually his wife. It's going to take a big one to keep that out of the paper, but that biggie may be there in the shape of the player's proposed transfer which, until then, only you and the two clubs involved know about. You have to make the judgement call, because if you don't hush up the incident it may well affect the transfer itself. I told you being an agent isn't as easy as it looks. The rewards may be great, but so is the stress and effort.

Planting a story, whether in return for a favour or just because you need to plant it, is always a delicate operation. First, you don't want it traced back to you, and you want to be in a position to deny it even when you know full well it's true or is about to be true. The journalist concerned won't mind the denial and certainly not when he's proved to be one hundred per cent correct. Agreeing that he'll quote 'an unnamed source' or 'somebody close to' or 'a friend' is standard procedure for anonymity.

It's not difficult to get column inches when you have a star asset to sell in whom there's genuine interest. It gets more tricky when your player wants to move but you don't have a queue of suitors stretching around the block. Here you may have to move into a world of wishful thinking rather than reality. Pick a club that you'd like your player to join, preferably one where you think the club could do with somebody like him in his position. Get the story planted that the club is interested. That not only gives you a reason for calling the club you've named but may also get another club calling you who is suddenly reminded of the existence of the player.

And if nothing comes of it then all that's happened is that a paper has carried yet another article which turns out to be untrue and unfounded. That's probably how my statistic of twenty per cent true and eighty per cent false came about – and now here I am contributing to it. Not just watching fiction but playing a role in creating the script. Welcome to the dream factory.

THE BABY SITTER

IF ANYBODY HAS ever babysat for a niece of nephew and been told by the doting parent that he or she never wakes up – only to find that the little bugger just wants to play all night – then you kind of get the idea of what it's like to look after a footballer.

There are the odd ones who have married their childhood sweethearts, had their two or three kids by the time they reach their early twenties and never look at another woman. But they're the odd ones. Not just numerically odd but regarded as odd by their teammates. If a player doesn't shag around then all sorts of rumours get put about regarding his sexuality.

So, the control of these red-blooded young men becomes a challenge. Agents fall into two camps here. There are the ones who are only too happy to go out clubbing with their lads and partake in whatever frolics may follow. There is a girls' club who want to sleep with as many footballers as possible, notching up the bed-posts and exchanging notes. Sadly there isn't actually a similar fan club for agents. But if you're young and not too bad-looking and out on the town with your client then the odds are that you won't have to stay up all night to get lucky, as the song puts it.

Then there are the ones, usually a bit older and wiser and less rash, who have to clean up all the shit after it's hit the fan. That can come in all shades and thicknesses of brown, sometimes bordering on black.

I know one agent who has a slush fund dedicated to paying off predatory girls who either threaten to sell a story to a newspaper (often with pictures in which the pissed footballer has been a willing and laughing participant) or else want to be paid for an abortion or far worse – and this is when the picture turns really dark – belatedly cry rape.

In each and every case the player is faced with exposure not just to the media but a very angry and possibly vengeful wife or partner at home who will become a financial nemesis far worse than any one-night stand. You might be thinking, this is just blackmail so why not go straight to the police? The fact of the matter is that the police are no friends of footballers or agents, although sometimes there can be an uneasy alliance when they've also been dropped a few quid (not to mention a few tickets) to turn a blind eye to a speeding, drink-driving or minor drug offence. Generally speaking, footballers and their agents make more money in a week (sometimes a day) than some police officers earn in a year and, from the police perspective, this is the time to level the playing field a little.

So, when these girls come calling it's just easier to pay. They seem to know their value and their price and I've come to the conclusion that they may actually talk to each other to see which players are the easiest marks. But it's never the players who have to meet them in hotels or cafés. That's the agent's lot, and although he'll have had some kind of confidentiality agreement drawn up by a lawyer you can never be a hundred per cent certain that they won't come knocking on the door again for another handout when the first one is spent.

Sometimes it's not money. Sometimes your client has another souvenir from a liaison in the shape of an STD, and so the agent always has to have a friendly doctor on hand who is prepared to write out private prescriptions to solve the problem. Meanwhile, the player is left to find a way to explain to his spouse why he's suddenly gone off sex for a while. Oh, the hardships of wealth, success and fame.

It's not just the problem of predatory women that agents have to deal with. Gambling is a huge problem. One very famous player couldn't walk past a betting office without going in to have a bet, and it got so bad that that the agent actually had the player's salary paid into his account each week and then doled it out to the player and his family as he needed it. He was the lucky one. He had a good agent who became his friend. Sometimes an agent only finds out there's a problem when it's too late.

After working with R for about a year I finally got my FA licence and had gathered together my own roster of about ten players, most of them youngsters with real potential. One young lad called me at two in the morning to tell me he'd had a visit from masked men wielding baseball bats and iron bars threatening to break both his legs (his most valuable assets) unless he paid them the gambling debts he'd incurred. I rolled out of bed and called R who gave me the authority to make the payment. I felt that the player owed me and R forever, but I was wrong. The player started gambling again and found another agent willing to lend him money to bail him out and signed with him when his contract with me ran out. I was really upset, but R just shrugged. 'I've seen it all before, son. And so will you in due course.'

I think he felt it was all part of his investment in my learning curve.

We both had a good laugh when this same player had to be smuggled out of the back door of his club because a couple of loan sharks were waiting outside in a car with sawn-off shotguns.

It's one small step from racking up huge gambling debts to agreeing to throw a match or assist with spot or spread betting. When bookmakers pay out on all sorts of things – times of goals, the next throw-in, the number of yellow and red cards and so on – then the opportunities are there. Footballers sometimes can't arrange this sort of thing themselves, and there are one or two agents only too willing to help and take the risk of sharing the dock with their clients.

Drugs are rife in football – or at least in footballers' lives – and again there are several agents quite happy to provide them to their clients. We are talking about recreational drugs, usually, which is not to say there are no players who don't get involved in the harder stuff or that there are no agents with the capability of obtaining them and providing them to their clients.

It's all a question of timing. Players know there's a real chance of being asked to give samples before or after matches or occasionally at training. But if there's a match on a Saturday they may not train again until the Monday or sometimes even the Tuesday, and that means that whatever they've taken gets through their systems and is undetectable.

I know at least one agent who finds it hard to function unless he's high. He seems to work 24/7, is at a match every day when one is on (which is most days) and his only social life is going to clubs where he knows he'll be able to meet more players. And offer them drugs. And offer them girls.

Sometimes the line between player and agent becomes blurred. The agent so lives the life of his client that he fools himself into thinking that he's the client, forgetting that the client has a unique talent which he'll never have. Unless you count making money as a talent, which I suppose it is – although unlikely to draw crowds of over fifty thousand to watch.

I suppose somebody has to protect players from themselves and it might as well be us agents. Certainly their parents and their wives won't, as they're usually too busy feathering their own nests. Again, I'm not apologising for what we do or how players behave. I suspect musicians and movies stars are very much the same, only their agents charge them twenty per cent. So what we provide is a real bargain and you'd think they'd be grateful. You'd hope they'd be grateful. But not a bit of it. I've dealt with getting clients and looking after them and I'm about to look at how to keep them. Short of clamping them in chains (some of them might actually like that knowing their sexual predilections) and taking away their passports, it's a real challenge. Just as few players are one-club men, the number of one-agent players is also a minority. The grass is always greener and there's always a competitor waiting to pounce. Agents as brothers in arms? I don't think so.

LEARNING TO FLY

I'LL NEVER FORGET the first time R took me to a contractual negotiation.

'Look and learn, son, but keep your fucking mouth shut. You may have your own ideas, but believe me, I'm really not interested in them and nor is the bloke we're going to see.'

The club was a Championship club in the Midlands and we were meeting the CEO to effect the transfer of a player from a League Two club. It was unusual for R to bother with a player so far down the pecking order but he'd spotted something in this kid and, as usual, he'd been proved right.

There are agents who never venture above the lower Leagues when it comes to representation. It's almost as if they hit their own personal wall and just don't want to climb over it. I used to wonder how they made a living, but I suppose if, like some of them, you act for fifty players and earn two grand a deal it mounts up and can make it worthwhile. But that seemed like too much effort for too little reward to me, and certainly R was generally long past that stage.

R, to be fair to him, had shown me what he intended to ask for before we got there so none of it came as a surprise except the level of what he wanted. He saw me raise my eyebrows.

'Always ask for everything, son, 'cos then you might get something. Never start where you're prepared to end up and never accept it when the club says they've gone as far as they can go because they'll always go that bit further if you put it to them in the right way. And I've put stuff in there that I can give up to get what I want.'

The CEO clearly knew R and was on his guard.

'None of your fancy dan London tricks up here,' he said by way of greeting. 'We've not got fortunes to spend and I've given you my best shot.'

R totally ignored him and asked for a cup of tea.

'Didn't think you'd be staying that long but I'll get one for you. Does the lad want one too?'

'He's my assistant and he can speak for himself,' R replied and I really loved him at that moment for that, which made what I did to him later even worse.

Tea delivered, we got down to business and I realised just how professional R really was under all the mockney behaviour. There was no signing-on fee in the offer and R told the CEO he had to have one, but he'd accept less than he'd asked for if there was a loyalty payment tucked in at the end. Signing-on fees are capital payments made at the start of a contract to induce the player to sign, and if he leaves without asking for a transfer then the club has to pay them. Better still, they count as guaranteed income upon which agents can charge commission. A loyalty payment is kind of what it says on the tin: a payment after the player has been with the club for a while and isn't payable if the player leaves. That makes it non-guaranteed and so R was actually doing his best for the player to his own disadvantage. I could see that was why he kept his players, or at least those who were bright enough to understand what he was doing.

He didn't like the fact that the salary was the same right through the contract so he wanted uplifts to be guaranteed (again where he could charge) and uplifts to come after a certain number of appearances (where he wouldn't be charging). He wanted appearance money to which the CEO replied, 'Fucking hell, R, we're paying him a salary to play so why do we have to pay him more money to "appear"?'

R didn't miss a heartbeat. 'Because you're not paying him enough salary. If you want to pay him more then we can reduce the appearance money.'

And so it went on for most of the afternoon. The CEO got hotter and hotter as did the debate. R asked for goal bonuses, promotion bonuses, part of any future transfer fee for the player, relocation costs, a minimum of double salary on promotion, international cap bonuses, reviews of the contract after so many games, and if he'd thought that the player might have needed a new kitchen sink then doubtless he would've asked for that as well.

The CEO finally crumbled around seven in the evening. I figured it was either because he wanted to go home for his supper or because he just wanted R (and me, I suppose) out of his room and out of his life. He gave R a lot of what he wanted, far more than I'd ever have thought possible and then, just when he must have thought that he could get home for his egg and chips, R started in on his fees.

He had five per cent in his contract with the player and, to be fair to him, he hadn't tried to chip away at what he'd got for the player. I know now that there are some agents who go into a room and say, 'My fee is a million quid, so let's see what's left in the deal for the player.'

That wasn't R's style at all.

'OK,' he said, 'I've delivered to you a top-class player and one that quite a few clubs were after. So five per cent is cheap.'

The CEO didn't agree. 'I'll agree we can do it on duality, but that's it.'

What he meant was that the club would pick up 2.5 per cent and the player would only pay tax on the other half even though the club would pay the whole five per cent.

'Yes,' R concurred, 'duality is good. So let's call it five per cent from you and five per cent from the player.'

Ten per cent was a lot and I didn't understand then how R was going to square it with the player as it would cost him more tax. But he had a plan. R had a plan for everything.

At nine in the evening, when the CEO's dinner was probably already burned to a cinder and in the bin, R agreed on eight per cent. The two men shook hands and the player who had been patiently waiting outside was called in to sign off pending his medical in the morning.

R took the player aside and told him what the deal was. The player was delighted as R had achieved a package beyond his wildest dreams. R put his arm around him. 'I've agreed a bit more commission for me with the club. It might cost you a bit of tax. Most agents wouldn't tell you and just hope you wouldn't spot it when it gets taken out of your pay packet. But you know me. I always like to be up front and open with my players. Are you OK with that?'

Of course the player was OK with that. He was earning big bucks for the first time in his career. What did it matter if R took a little more? Later, when he had to pay the tax, he might think about it again but probably not. It was a masterclass in negotiation and client management – and one I never forgot.

CUTTING THE APRON STRINGS

IT TOOK ME nearly two years of working with R to believe that I'd learned all that he could teach me and it was time to move on. He wasn't happy when I told him I was leaving. In fact, he was incandescent and told me I was an ungrateful cunt and that he'd do his best to make sure that I never sign another client ever again. Nice. But I also knew R blew hot and cold, and I doubted he would ever actually do anything about it. He'd been very philosophical when players left so why should he be any more difficult with me?

However, he was even less impressed when he realised that I'd never signed a contract with him, mainly because in his caveman approach to business he'd never bothered to send me one. That would've meant paying his lawyer a fee to draw it up, and R was never one for spending money, only on raking it in. Anyway, the absence of a contract meant that I had no covenant not to compete and even more important than that, there was nothing to stop me taking 'my' players with me.

That doesn't seem fair, you may well say. Well, in football there's not a lot that's fair. It's every man for himself. Yet, in this instance, I was simply using the rules and regulations to help myself. The Football Association Agents' Regulations may be pretty restrictive, they may be rubbish when you're working for a company and trying to comply with them (or at least keeping up a pretence at compliance, as the good old FA doesn't realise that most agents drive a coach and horses through them), but when you're moving on, then, wow, can they be helpful!

This is the way it works. Neither FIFA (the world governing body of football – and I use the word 'governing' in its loosest sense) nor any of the domestic regulatory bodies recognise the existence of companies. To be an agent you have to be a warm and breathing human being. Not that many of the agents I've come across can be described as warm. Or even human if it comes to it.

But, although the FA only issues licences to individuals it still does its best to get its hooks into the companies through which many agents trade. It has a really odd rule which states that when an agent leaves a company, even if he was a director or shareholder, then any players who have signed representation contracts with him are automatically released and become free men with choices. The FA, in its generosity, gives them multiple choices (a bit of an intellectual challenge to some players), namely that they can either stay with the company and sign with another agent, sign with the departing agent whether he goes out on his own or joins a new company, or they can say a plague on both of them and simply do their own thing and represent themselves. What is it they say about lawyers? When they do their own work then they have a fool for a client? I'm thinking you could say exactly the same about footballers.

Against the background of that provision most prudent and sophisticated agencies (and, yes, there are quite a few of those around) try to tie up their employees every which way but loose. It's not as simple as it appears because covenants have to be reasonable and enforceable and, generally speaking, in this country at least, you can't make them so restrictive that a bloke can't earn a living. The situation is made even more complicated and fraught with danger (at least as far as the company operator and owner is concerned) by the fact that many agents working for companies aren't actually employed in the normal sense of the word. Agencies appoint them as self-employed consultants or, as is more likely when they're unlicensed, as scouts. The same rules don't quite apply to the self-employed, so it's a minefield, but in any event R did fuck all which gave me a licence to kill as well as a licence to be an agent.

It was as surprising to me as it was, eventually, to R that he took his eye off the ball in this instance because he was such a wheeler dealer and cunning operator in every other way. I think he was so upset because he was really angry with himself: a) for trusting me; b) for not putting anything into writing; and c) as it transpired not even knowing the bloody rules.

I confess I felt a bit bad about the whole thing. On the whole R had been good to me, if not exactly generous, and my conscience was salved when I thought about just how much money I'd actually made him. I'd come to like him a lot and I could never forget his leaping to my defence with the Midlands CEO or what he'd taught me. But nothing stays the same forever. I had to leave the nest now and learn to fly on my own.

As I've discovered since I left, so many of the bigger agents, the high rollers, not to mention the wildly successful footballers, are just not ones for detail when it comes to their own affairs. Which is, I guess, why so many deals end in tears and why so few player–agent relationships last for the whole career of the player. As I say, one-agent players are as rare a breed as one-club players, which is why you have to squeeze as much out of your representation of them as you can while the going is good.

So many of the big agencies have suffered in the same way as R. They've taken someone in, trained them up, allowed and even encouraged them to deal with the players directly (often because they can't be arsed themselves) and then suddenly one day, *whoosh*. The bomb drops, and the player and the agent are gone in a puff of smoke.

Without the right paperwork, and sometimes even with it, there's very little that can be done about it other than to lock the doors on an empty stable and vow not to make the same mistakes again.

It's hard to say if it all comes about because the older agents are mean or because the younger ones are just plain greedy. My thinking is that it's six of one and half a dozen of the other, because in this wonderful world of football there are very few innocents and those that exist soon get trampled underfoot.

I know of one young agent (and he's probably typical) who was supported and encouraged by his boss in everything he did. He was given a job, leads when he'd none of his own and even given a car to get him around. After a long wait, and a not inconsiderable investment on the part of his employer, he finally landed a Premiership player who was fast-tracked into the first team and then into the international squad. At that point the young agent went in to see his boss and told him that unless he got eighty per cent of all the deals for the player (instead of the ten per cent he was getting on top of his basic salary) then he was off. His boss, not known for a calm and measured approach to life, told him to fuck off – which he did and within days the player gave notice to leave the company complaining about the lack of service and the fact that he'd never even spoken to the head of the company let alone met him.

On that occasion you might have had a bit of sympathy for the boss (not me, I don't do sympathy except at funerals and even then not always as there are one or two people I know who are better off dead), but then you have to realise that the situation whereby the old guard don't want to give anything away always prevails. To invest to progress is not a motto that they work with. They keep their agents on low wages and low commissions and even delay in paying them when they've banked the fruits of their labours. And even when they begrudgingly shell out they try to deduct all the 'expenses' they've incurred off the top. Not just a percentage of them equal to what the agent gets, but all of them. Generous.

When they've finally written the cheque out with great reluctance they can hardly be surprised when they get a knife squarely between the shoulder blades. I get that because it's payback for the metaphorical (and in a few cases physical) kicking up the backsides they've delivered to their young protégés over the years.

Just like others before me, I'd planned my escape from R carefully. I spent a lot of time quietly whispering in the ears of all the players – both those I'd found and signed myself and those who'd been with R for a while but found my instant service more appealing than the distance R tended to keep from them – that I was thinking of moving on and setting up on my own. R had taught me that there was no loyalty in the game and I took that particular lesson to heart. There's gratitude for you, as they say. If I'd been honest with myself and had a good long hard look in the mirror I'd neither have recognised, nor liked, the person I'd become in just two short years.

What I'd also done was to get as many of the players as I could to sign with me personally to ensure that my departure triggered off their release and so they were able to sign with me all over again. I also let players' contracts run out and then got them to sign blank contracts so I could insert the name of my new business and date them when the time was right.

I was pleased, although not wildly surprised, when even some of the players who had been with R for years jumped ship. I knew he'd regarded them as friends as well as clients and that had made him smug and complacent. A big mistake in our industry. He'd been to their weddings and christenings, had held their hands during their divorces and tabloid exposures, but he'd also been a greedy bastard with a liking for cash who too often had gone for the short-term hit rather than playing the long game.

One of his favourite tricks was to be paid by the club through the FA, thus doubling the percentage that was in the contract on the duality principle (something I'll explain later) and then having the gall to go back to the player and plead that he should've got more and ask the player for a 'top-up' in cash. He'd explain that he could only be paid a commission on the basis of the basic salary and the signing-on fee (the guaranteed income) but he'd got the player all sorts of bonuses and loyalty payments that weren't guaranteed, and that the player should provide the brown-envelope money to compensate for that. He was utterly convincing when he explained to the players that he'd constructed the contract in a way that benefited them, and almost every player bought it. But only once. After that they'd talk to their teammates and get wise. That was a huge mistake by R, because he was giving the players and anybody they told power over him. Did he even think about that or did the colour of the money make him blind to the risks? Who knew? But it did play into my hands as I'll explain in a moment.

I played on that with the clients. I assured them they'd just be charged what was in the contract. No more, no less, and I'd make sure the club paid it all. I never mentioned that the player would pay tax on half (assuming I convinced the club to do the deal on duality) as the payment by the club would be a benefit in kind to the player. If and when they called me (and some wouldn't even notice it) to question why they'd had a tax deduction that month because of what the club had paid me, I'd have a ready answer. But that was a bridge I didn't need to cross, and as far as I was concerned tomorrow's problem wasn't a problem right now. My concern was to ensure that I had a business moving forward. My business. Even if it was one that I'd substantially nicked from R.

R's rage continued to grow. I received threatening texts and even more threatening phone calls which, under normal circumstances, one might have reported to the police. I didn't do that, of course. I just faced down the charging bull elephant by telling him that he should consider himself lucky that I didn't go to HMRC and give them the address where R had deposited his security box containing all his cash.

You may think that I was behaving badly, that I was the ungrateful cunt that he thought me to be, but I prefer to think of my actions as some kind of free education to him. He would never make those same mistakes again. As for me, I didn't intend making them even once. I was out there on my own in the big wild world and that was exactly where I wanted to be and wanted to stay. If you operate without partners and staff then you reduce the risks of anybody cheating on you. From now on I was going to be a lone wolf. Looking after Number One; and I'd make sure that there wasn't going to be a Number Two.

THE VULTURES CIRCLE

WHAT I DISCOVERED, just three months after branching out on my own, was that there were a fair number of sole operators out there who were just as unscrupulous as I'd been with R. You always know you have a problem with a player when he stops replying to your texts and then blanks your calls. It didn't take me long to find out what was happening. I was young. I seemed inexperienced. Just as I'd seemed like a breath of fresh air to R's players, now the vultures were circling to try to get to mine.

One of the lads to whom I'd become closest called me up and relayed the dialogue in such a way that I told him he might well have a career on the stage when his footballing days were over.

'I am X's agent [X being an established England international]. Gather you've left R and joined up with his young gofer. Nice lad, but not a player, if you get my drift. Has he told you that United have been watching you? No? I didn't think so. Well, I can tell you that they are interested, very interested indeed. I've got the manager there in the palm of my hand and I can tell you that nobody signs there unless I'm involved. If you want it to happen then I can make it happen – and I'm afraid your young man simply can't . . .'

And so on and so on, the poison dripping into the player's ear until, despite them wanting to stay with me, they'd truly believe I couldn't get them where they wanted to go while X's agent could.

I'd written contracts with the players all lodged according to the rules with the FA, so you would've thought that I'd be OK, but it's unbelievable the strokes players try to pull to get themselves out of a contract they were so keen to sign just a few months before, when you were the flavour of the day.

I've known them to claim that their signatures have been forged.

I've known them to claim that they didn't even sign anything.

But sometimes you get the total reverse of that. One player simply couldn't say no (certainly not to the inducements being offered to him) and signed with three different agents. One of the agents decided to be clever and didn't date his 'contract' so he could have the option to say he was acting for the club rather than the player he was really representing (I'll come back to the reason for that in due course). The only problem was that when he saw that wasn't going to happen and sent his contract into the FA for registration somebody else had got in before him and the FA had already received two 'signed' contracts, coincidentally signed on the same day, which was the day that news of the player's impending transfer had hit the papers.

Given that the two agents were at different ends of the country one had to wonder how the player could've been in two places at the same time. The truth, of course, was that he'd signed on different days and the other two agents had also held back (though not for as long as the third one) until the deal was imminent. That also extended the term of the contract (which could only be for two years under the rules – go figure the reason for that one), but the player, at least, remained consistent. He simply said he hadn't signed for any of them and on the actual day of the transfer ended up speaking to a fourth agent who then represented the buying club in the deal while the player completed the documentation by stating that he'd acted for himself. He almost dared the three agents who had lost out to sue but, of course, none of them did. They didn't want what they'd done to come out and they also didn't want the player bad-mouthing them in the dressing room and on the training pitches to all and sundry who would listen.

A slightly more sophisticated excuse, and one that seems to be becoming very popular where a lawyer is involved, whether as the wannabe agent or as a part of the company seeking to sign him, is that the player claims he wasn't told to take independent advice before he put pen to paper.

'This contract was just shoved in front of me and I was told there was nothing in it to worry about and if I didn't sign right away then the deal wouldn't happen.'

There's a clause at the end of the standard contract where the player acknowledges he's been told to take independent advice, but invariably says he's chosen not to. And you know what, generally speaking, he really doesn't need to because the FA will only register a contract if it's in the standard form with a few approved additions.

Yet I've known shrewd operators looking to get players out of contracts use the argument that while the player was an ill-educated professional footballer knowledgeable only in the art of kicking a ball around, the agent was a wily, sophisticated businessman who simply took advantage by telling his potential client to trust him as to what he was signing. And now the trust is gone. Because it suits him to say he didn't understand and doesn't trust his agent any longer. Footballers are very adept at reinventing history and providing a revisionist view of what actually occurred.

There are loads more examples of the my-hamster-ate-my-homework variety. 'I was told I'd only get a move to this club if I signed.' Or on a slight variation of the theme, 'I was promised a move to this club if I signed. And I didn't get it.' 'I was blackmailed into signing because my potential agent knew I'd been with a bird after a night on the town and threatened to tell my missus if I didn't.' 'I signed because the agent promised to give me back half of his commission.' Substitute 'my dad' for 'me' and that's another option. 'The agent said he'd buy my mum/dad a house/car/holiday of a lifetime.' Et cetera, et cetera. You get the picture.

The fact is that I've known all of these to be true in the case of some agents and some players, but whether or not they're true when a player is trying to wriggle out of his contract who on earth actually knows? That's one of the more exasperating aspects of being a football agent. The thin line between truth and fiction so often becomes blurred.

One agent developed a particular scam to perfection. In his impatience to get players signed up to him he seemed prepared to offer them a substantial signing-on fee. Sometimes it went to the player himself and sometimes to a parent, and the agent always weighed up the amount against what he thought he could earn. But he wasn't one for taking chances so what he did to cover all bases, was to slip a 'loan agreement' into the papers, and the players just blithely signed everything stuck in front of them. If the player's moves didn't recoup the loan or if the player dared to leave him then the lad would find himself faced with a lawyer's letter demanding repayment of the 'loan' with interest. The player couldn't deny he'd received the money and the agent would protest that he'd done nothing illegal but simply say that he tried to help the player who was desperate for money at the time. It didn't do a lot for agent–client relationships but it all helped to make this agent's wheels go round. That is until he came off the road when one player with whom he tried it on sent some heavies round to sort him out and after a few weeks in hospital he decided that enough was enough.

It can be pure fiction when an agent either tries to sign (or steal) a player by telling him that he's done a better job than his current agent and actually found him a club. But he can't actually tell him which club it is unless he can be sure that he's going to be involved. Usually, the agent on the make is winging it. He's just plucked the name of a club out of thin air and even if he doesn't disclose it at first he has it up his sleeve to produce, like a magician, when the player gives him the nod that he's buying into what he's offering. Then he'll try and put the two ends together. Namely, the player he didn't have and the club that didn't exist, and it's surprising just how many deals do come about in exactly that way.

In any event, there I was with my newly acquired (if somewhat illicitly acquired) clients, in my newly acquired business, trying to repel all boarders and knowing that at this stage in my career I was only as good as my next deal. Given that everything I'd done until then had been for R, I didn't really have a last deal to use as a calling card – just my youth, enthusiasm and dubious charm.

Players are notoriously impatient, blaming anybody but themselves if they don't get the deal they want either by way of a transfer or at their current club. Top of the blame list is invariably the poor old agent. Unfortunately, we're not equipped with magic wands and we can't turn a donkey into a thoroughbred or a crap player into a world beater. But you'll never find a player, even at the lower levels, admitting he's crap or a donkey.

I realised I couldn't just rely upon the fact that the players had liked me enough to abandon R and sign for me. I needed to have a few aces up my sleeve; the one that trumps them all is to have a manager as the wild card in your pack. That acquisition never comes cheap. I knew what R was paying, and he had deals going with at least half a dozen managers that I knew of. I was prepared to settle for just one to start with and once he was in the bag I could start to build up my collection.

Like in every other business, although more so in football, success brings success. And failure brings failure. Both winning and losing are habits that are hard to break once they get a hold. I'd come this far and I wasn't prepared to fail. I couldn't afford to fail. I wasn't trained to do anything else. I wasn't going to fail and my meeting with manager M was going to ensure that. Whatever price I had to pay.

THE BUNG

I WASN'T A stranger to managers. I'd met a few through R and just by listening to gossip at agents' meetings I was pretty much able to put together a list of managers who, how shall I put it, were approachable. And amenable once approached. Amenable, that is, to what in the bad old days would've been called a bung and now in these modern times is called – a bung. Or, if you're trying to police the business and want to be unkind, you might call it a bribe.

Nothing really changes in an industry such as ours. Except that my lawyer told me I had to be careful of something called the Bribery Act. (Yes, I'd also acquired a sharp West End legal eagle along the way to deal with some of the shit that was being chucked at me and advise me on some contracts to ensure no further shit was launched, unnecessarily, my way.) The Bribery Act did pretty much what it said on the tin. It worried me to the point that I actually went to a lecture on the subject but then I thought fuck it. Although what I had in mind seemed definitely to be a criminal offence I figured they'd have bigger fish in their sights than me and when I got so big as to be a target for the authorities then I might review the situation.

Meanwhile, some four months into my sole enterprise I decided to take my chances. Yes, it was reckless, but in this business if you didn't take your chances then you lost your opportunities. I had to balance the risk and work on the basis that the managers I'd be approaching had been on the take from others for so long that they were pretty much made of Teflon. Nothing was going to stick to them no matter what the authorities both within and outside football might think. After the

Harry Redknapp case collapsed in February 2012, you couldn't see the CPS rushing to bounce another manager into court, and they weren't going to knock off the agent without the manager. The dock would contain Punch but no Judy.

The thing about managers, well, the thing about most people in football, is that they can never get enough money. You kind of understand that philosophy when it comes to players. I mean, you wake up one day, you're thirty-five years old, your legs won't take you out of bed and into training, and you have to accept that it's over. Just like that. The money machine has stopped printing the fifty-pound notes that were so easy to come by. But managers in theory can go on forever and some of them seem to. If it's not one job then it'll be another.

I think the fact that the survival odds are a little bit longer than for those of a First World War infantryman or those of a bomber pilot in the Second World War may be a factor in a manager's desire to stockpile cash at every opportunity. They seem to grab at whatever is offered to them, particularly as they often feel that, compared to the players they manage, they're criminally underpaid. Which may explain in some part why they turn to crime and in some cases actively seek out agents to work with them.

One agent, whom I'll call 'the Bagman', acts for several managers, laundering their ill-gotten gains and making a very nice ancillary living out of it in addition to his own legitimate agency activities. The crazy thing is that everybody knows who this guy is and what he does, and yet nobody seems inclined to stop him. It may be because he runs with a rough crew and is a bit of a gangster himself, but you wouldn't think that would scare off the authorities; although rumour has it that he has one or two of the FA administrators on his payroll as well. Useful guy to know, but not a man to cross as he's not averse to threatening with a crowbar or a shotgun if the mood takes him. I've heard it whispered that he thinks everything belongs to him and therefore he's entitled to first dibs at it. So far, our paths haven't crossed, but I'm sure they will given time and an upsurge in my career and fortunes.

As I say, I wasn't new to this tame manager lark. When R had been starting out he told me about one high-profile manager whose fall from grace, although not unexpected, came from a most unusual direction. He would always ask for a 'sweetie'. This individual had huge balls, as he not only expected these backhander 'sweeties' from agents but from players as well. A player would be offered a new contract provided a proportion of the uplift found its way back into the pocket of the man who had graciously granted the right to the new deal. The odds were also on the player in question never having found his way into the club without his agent having also shared his commission with the manager. That gave the manager some comfort because if the player ever discussed his demands with his agent then the agent would reassure him by saying that there was nothing wrong or unusual about what was being asked. The player got a better deal, the manager got a rake-off, and the agent got a fee. Everybody was happy, including the club who didn't have a clue what was going on but had secured a player that its manager had said was decent on a long contract. The gravy train only stops occasionally and then just to spread the gravy around.

Now, the days of the brown paper bags have been well documented. They made an example of poor George Graham years ago, and while they were doing so there were quite a few who said, 'There but for the grace of God [or whatever divinity watches over football] go I.' But there are far more sophisticated ways of going about things. R used to explain to me that he'd never dream of making a payment directly to a manager. It would've been all too obvious from his records if the Revenue or the FA or even the police came calling. The trick was to get an invoice from somebody overseas for scouting fees and then to pay the money into an offshore account. That way it could be used as an allowable expense, but it also achieved the successful task of money laundering.

There are various schemes out there but the Bagman seems to be at the heart of most of them. Even if he's not involved at the start of the deal, somehow or other he worms his way into the loop and then earns some extra on top for the delivery on behalf of the manager. It does not even necessarily end with the money in a numbered account earning minimal interest, as properties get purchased abroad in the names of nominee companies and they make the money work to provide a pension for the day when the manager runs out of clubs. That can also be for any number of reasons: he's fucked it up on the pitch, the club's been sold and the new owner wants his own man in place, or, as was the case with one Premiership club, he'd tried it on once too often and had been rumbled.

Mind you, if the manager is successful on the pitch and if the bent agent delivers a steady stream of talented players then the road to departure can be a very long and lucrative one with all the dodgy dealings overlooked in the pursuit of honours.

However unpleasant the agent may be, if he gets a reputation as a man who delivers, then the club will use him. And if he gets a reputation for spreading the rewards around among the manager and his immediate staff then, for sure, the manager will make him his agent of choice. The corrupting influence can move all the way up the club hierarchy. Directors, CEOs, club secretaries and chairmen are not necessarily immune to the persuasive charms of a generous agent.

Whatever it takes to make the wheels go around, I suppose. All I knew was that I really needed to establish such a relationship – or relationships.

Sometimes dodgy managers come in the most unlikely of guises. They can appear smooth and sophisticated in the media, lovable, even well educated, often well groomed and softly spoken, but as old Bill Shakespeare said, a man may smile and smile and still be a villain. Or something along those lines. I just remember it because it was in my GCSE play.

Agents don't get time to go to the theatre or the cinema as a general rule. They stick to the drama of the football stadium. There's rarely such a thing as a social dinner and when it comes to entertainment the lines blur because a good night out is when you go to a match and land a new player, or spot a new talent that you make up your mind to land, or get or develop a new relationship with a manager.

That was how I came to invite manager M out to dinner, and as I watched him down a bottle of very expensive Merlot I also watched, and listened, for any tells that might suggest he'd be ripe for the plucking when it came to an 'arrangement'.

It was to take another bottle of wine before he relaxed enough to accept that I genuinely wanted to do business and wasn't a journalist with a recorder. So then he told me how it would work.

'You're a young agent, but if you look after me then I'll look after you.'

His looking after me would take the shape of his recommendation to some of his better young players. I asked what would happen if they already had an agent, and he just shrugged as if any such contractual attachment was a matter of insignificance.

'I'll tell them they'll do better at the club if they use you. And if they try to stay loyal to their old agents then I'll let them see that the players who come to you do better than them. Sometimes it may take a while, but I know a good player when I see one, and trust me, it'll be worth it for both of us in the end. You'll pay me [he named a figure] for each one I get signed to you and you'll give me half the commission you earn from him at this club or any other. I'll persuade the chairman to give our players the best deal possible and I'll also try and get you involved in any other club deals I can. Same terms.'

I knew it was highly unlikely that I was the only agent with whom he'd cut a deal, and I was pretty sure that some of the more experienced guys had secured better terms for themselves. But I've always known an opportunity when I see one and this was a chance for me to take a short cut into the grown-ups' tent. I'd been on my own for a while now and had come to realise that this could be a very lonely business. These sorts of arrangements of convenience were what so many seemed to be entering into, and so, after a brief wrestle with my conscience, which I won, I was committed.

I was beginning to realise I wasn't the same person I'd been when I'd started out so bright-eyed and bushy-tailed with R. I was becoming more and more like the 'others'. But was that such a bad thing when the others were successful, when the others made big money? Did it really matter that I was smashing my way through the rules and probably the laws of the land as well? Not really, I decided, and that would prove to be a decision that would change my life forever.

FOREIGN DEALINGS

A S IF DEALING with English or other home-grown UK players wasn't tough enough, representing a foreign player, particularly one from one of the African countries, is a total nightmare. And no, I'm not in the slightest bit racist, just a realist. For one thing, you're never sure that you're acting for the player, and then he may not actually be the player you thought he was.

Agents live or die by their reputations, and one of the great certainties in life is that if you persuade a manager to have a look at somebody who you claim to be the best thing since sliced bread and he turns out to be a cross between a plank and a Muppet then you can be fairly sure he won't take your word for anything again – even if he's sort of on your payroll.

I made that mistake very early on in my career with R when I was chasing each and every deal that came my way. I was contacted via Facebook by a player with some of the most impressive YouTube clips I'd ever seen. He looked like Pelé, Messi and Best all rolled into one package and seemed to have the looks of Beckham to go with it. With hindsight I should've asked myself why he was reduced to contacting the likes of me if he was such a brilliant player, and also why Real Madrid, Paris Saint-Germain, Barcelona and Bayern Munich hadn't fallen over themselves in the race to get his signature. Had I bothered to ask the questions and listened to the answers, it was very simple. The answer would've been the same to both questions. He was fucking crap.

I put him into a Championship side in the Midlands where R was close to the manager, and even persuaded them to fork out for his flight and accommodation – unheard of for an unknown triallist. If I tell you that the club booked him in for a whole week for a trial and then cancelled the booking after one night you get the picture. I knew something was wrong when R called me in as he'd had a call from the manager and said I needed to get to the Midlands by lunchtime and that I'd be picking up the cost of any speeding tickets I might gather en route.

When I arrived at the club's training ground I soon discovered the reason for the manager's call and R's response. The player who had looked so good in his videos did, at least, have one thing in common with David Beckham. He had tattoos. In fact he was so covered by them that he looked like the cover of a science fiction book I once saw my dad reading, Ray Bradbury's *The Illustrated Man*. He was also carrying a paunch that reminded me of the player in a betting company TV ad where the background music is 'Hey, fatty boom boom'. With his man breasts he looked nothing like the bloke in the clips and as he confessed to me . . . he wasn't the bloke in the clips.

When I pinned him up against the wall of the changing room and virtually choked the truth out of him I soon became aware that he had some serious mental problems of a delusional nature. The thing was, he really believed he had the talent of the bloke on YouTube but that if he sent footage of himself as others saw him (rather than as he saw himself) then he wouldn't be given a chance.

In fact R made it all right with the manager (not too tricky when the manager wasn't going to kill the goose regularly laying golden eggs for him). The manager saw the funny side and even when I'd left, R always asked me if I had any more tattooed, overweight players I wanted to send him. It was a good lesson for me and I was always more cautious after that, checking out any players with more than one source before I recommended them.

However, all agents are chasing the same dollars and the same dreams, so there is still the faint temptation when you get the chance to represent a player who looks good on paper and on film to take a chance. Yet, as I say, I still remind myself that football is played in the flesh, on grass and not on film or on paper – and that has stood me in good stead.

So, back to Africa. I was once in the States watching a Major League Soccer game and said, 'That black boy looks good,' and I was told that if I had said that to a non-white I was quite likely to have my lights punched out for my trouble. But this is the point I want to make. Players from different countries have a radically different approach to the game and to representation.

There are some great players around from Nigeria, Ghana, the Ivory Coast and Cameroon all playing at the highest level of the game, represented by some decent local agents who are usually working with influential agents in the UK. However, there's also a cottage industry of one-man bands out there trying to persuade you to work with them and sending you the names of players they can bring to the table, who, again, often look quite attractive on paper. Plus, they all claim to have access to so-called 'academies' dotted along the length and breadth of the African continent and from which they claim to have the pick of the crop of the emerging young talent.

I'm sure that some of these kids are talented, but the approach of some of the agents who do actually make a living out of them does smack a bit of a cross between human trafficking and the slave trade. Anyway, like a lot of other agents I get regular invitations to come out and visit and see for myself – and maybe I should just brave the vaccinations and do just that.

But there are all sorts of problems attached to representing these foreign players whether they're kids or adults anyway. The UK exercises tight work-permit controls outwith EU players, and even experienced players have to be regular internationals for their national side and sometimes, if the nation is only a small footballing country, even that isn't enough.

Apart from the fact that you're not supposed to move kids that young across borders and certainly shouldn't be earning from them, there was, for years, a scam of placing the kid in a convenient EU country and then applying in due course for a passport. R had great contacts in the likes of Spain and Italy in the shape of dubious immigration lawyers and other officials who seemed able to conjure up EU passports at the drop of a hat (or at least at the drop of five grand or so) for the least likely of candidates.

The other route was to place them temporarily – or 'park them' as the saying goes – in a Scandinavian or Benelux country who for a long time made that possible. Again, once the player had played there for a while, often gathering a local wife along the way, he could sneak into the UK under the radar having acquired a suitable passport.

However, when it came to South American players, what I soon discovered was that I was coming up against what the FA and FIFA call third-party ownership. It's commonplace in South America and some other jurisdictions, but the FA simply don't like it and have declared war on anything that even suggests it might be happening.

So, what does it mean and how does it work? I now know exactly how it works because like a lot of UK agents I've got myself a partner in South America and I'm not just dipping my finger into the honeypot. I'm plunging my whole hand in right up to the elbow.

Just examining the likes of Brazil and Argentina for the moment, where there's a heady mixture of young talented footballers, they almost invariably come from unbearably poor backgrounds, if not the *favellas* themselves, and are there for the taking by rich predatory agents. In fact, they're there for the taking by anybody – and by anybody I mean unlicensed individuals who seem to take a delight in putting two fingers up to the global football authorities as they continue their uninterrupted march towards multi-millionaire status. Forget *Twelve Years a Slave*. These kids can become slaves for their entire careers.

This is how it works. There's a talented youngster from a poor background. He can sometimes be as young as eight or nine. The agent comes to his family and offers to give him money or, more likely, give the family money. From that moment on, the player effectively belongs to the agent to do with as he wants – football wise, that is. I've come across a few gay agents in my time, but no paedophiles. We can be accused of everything else but not child molestation. We leave that to the TV stars, media celebs and politicians.

Anyway, some good does come out of the 'ownership'. The lads do get some education and generally keep out of the clutches of the gangs and the police, but from a very early age the focus is on turning them into money-spinning, football-playing machines. There's a Dickensian feel to the whole system. It's not toiling in the workhouse or being shoved up a chimney, and it's not the poor house either – whatever a footballer may earn he's unlikely to go to debtors' prison – but in many ways there's still something of the Oliver Twist about it with the agent cast as the wicked and manipulative Fagin.

As the kids grow up, the local agent will probably place them with a domestic club. He won't earn a fortune, but whatever the club pays for the youngster will end up in the agent's pocket. The agent may argue that he deserves that for his investment and ability to spot the talent, and it's hard to dispute that really.

When the kid starts earning there's a bit more payback as well, but the real jackpot is yet to come if and when the lad is good enough to move to a European club. As I've said, by then he may well be travelling on a passport of convenience, and the local agent will almost certainly have a European agent (or an agent from some exotic tax haven) with whom he'll be dividing the spoils, having made sure to recoup the investment he's made over the years.

If you have followed everything I've been telling you – sorry if that sounds condescending, but I've got so used to dealing with footballers – you may wonder how the agent can earn anything given that third-party ownership is frowned upon in so many jurisdictions and carries a penal sentence in the UK. Well, here's the plan. If there's any kind of fee paid by the European club to the player's home club then because the agent, rather than the club, owns the player, the agent takes the lion's share. If for any reason there's no fee then the payment for the player is concealed in the agency fees in acting for the buying club and the successful delivery of the player. What is a given is that until the player becomes a super star, the agent (or agents) will earn considerably more than him from his career. And even when he is a superstar they may earn just as much if a massive transfer and commercial opportunities come along.

Never mind that it's all against the rules. If a club wants a player, really wants a player, then the rule book goes out of the window along with the club's high moral stance. One thing I learned pretty early on was that clubs have totally different rules in different situations: when the agent has a player they really want, to the situation where they already have the player and it's simply a matter of renegotiation, or where they're prepared to be persuaded to sign a player but aren't all that bothered if they don't.

As my work in this business has gone on, I've realised that when it comes to hypocrisy, clubs take all the prizes. At the same time as its chairman/CEO/manager is going public slagging off some agent or other for easing a player out by unsettling him, then that same club is paying a barrow-load of money to another agent (or quite probably somebody unlicensed) for easing a player in and dishing out exactly the same amount of dirt to another club.

I've strayed off the subject of foreign players and ownership a bit, I know, but ownership can come in all shapes and sizes. One very high-profile player was totally controlled by his agent throughout his career. The agent managed to get media headlines by saying the player wanted away. The club went ballistic, not least its excitable and seemingly totally unforgiving manager. They said publicly they'd never deal with this agent again and all their other players were specifically warned not to deal with him, but however hard the club tried, it could not drive a wedge between the player and his agent. Within less than a year the club had been forced to grit its teeth, buy a very long spoon and sit down with the same agent who had been barred from coming anywhere near the stadium or the training ground to negotiate a brand new extended and much improved contract. Talk about expediency.

However, I think every agent in the country, many of whom intensely disliked the agent in question, was actually quite pleased when he made the club pay in spades for their actions by building in a penalty fee to compensate him for all the crap they'd thrown in his direction.

Now, when an agent controls a player like that, when he makes a fortune out of his commercial deals, isn't that really a kind of ownership? And is it any worse than taking a slice of a transfer fee in one way or another? Yet one is perfectly legitimate and the other totally illegal. Go figure.

It's a lovely business, isn't it? Such nice loyal people in it from top to bottom. But it's what I do and you know what? I love every minute of it.

SMOKE AND MIRRORS

I T MAY COME across as a bit xenophobic, but believe me, dealing with home-grown players and their agents is a doddle compared to dealing with foreign agents.

I've already explained how the overseas agent who controls the player interacts with his UK-based associate or partner. It's difficult enough dealing with somebody you know and trust; when you get involved in a transaction with somebody for the first time you have to watch your back. And your front. Not to mention your middle and any other vulnerable piece of your anatomy.

Somehow or other you have to sum up the other agents involved in a transaction and try to establish whether or not they're who they claim to be and if they really do act for the player they say they represent. None of which is helped when the player arrives with an entourage that may or may not include the actual agent with whom the English guy has been dealing. And may also not include anybody who speaks English. An interesting challenge.

When I'd been with R, I'd watched from the sidelines open-mouthed as he managed to get himself involved in a deal involving a South American agent who claimed to have a player wanted by a Premier League club. The player duly arrived, having demanded four first-class tickets, but there was no sign of the agent with whom R had arranged the transportation. The other three tickets had in fact been used by a trio, one of whom claimed in very limited English to be the player's mentor and/or guardian and/or representative depending upon the time of day R spoke to him and also depending on how much of what he said R actually understood.

The other two companions were even more sinister and incomprehensible, consisting of two burly South Americans who appeared to be related either to the player or his wife. R never did find out. The three of them created a major problem for R because they made it quite clear that all communications with the player had to be through them and there could be no direct conversations between the player and R. That might have been tricky anyway, as the player spoke only Spanish and R's grasp of that language was limited to two words: 'sangria' and 'paella'.

With everything being done via the 'representative', R had no idea what he was telling the player or even if the details of the deal were being correctly relayed to him. He had no idea what the player was really looking for, although it was certainly more than the club had to offer, as everything had to be 'net'.

R had explained to me early doors the concept of 'net' or 'netto'. If you told an English lad he'd be earning three grand a week he immediately understood he wouldn't be getting that amount into his bank account and that the Revenue would take their slice. But tell that to any player outside the UK and he assumes that the club (or some other beneficent being) will be paying the tax on his behalf and that what the gross salary is in his contract is exactly what he'll receive. Talk about cultural differences.

On the day of the transfer we all squeezed into the office of the club chairman who said he wanted to see the correct documentation to know he was dealing with somebody who actually had authority to represent the player. And, by the way, who are you all?

R phoned the player's original agent – who quite clearly hadn't been invited to the party – who expressed astonishment that the player was even in England let alone about to conclude a deal. So the chairman's question became highly relevant. Who the fuck were all these people? R never actually found out, but the player still insisted he wouldn't sign anything unless his 'representative' not only agreed to it all but was also paid a million pounds. Which was unlikely to leave very much for R.

The guys who were there with the player gave varying assurances: from saying the old agent had released him to claiming that the agreement had expired, had never been signed or had been induced to be signed pursuant to fraudulent representations and/or promises of payments which had never materialised. Take your pick basically. Who knew?

Eventually, R, by consummate negotiating, managed to get the club to agree that he could act for them and receive a comparatively modest fee. The club, having flatly refused to make any kind of illegal payment of one million quid to a bloke they'd never met before, then doubled the signing-on fee they were going to pay the player so that he could pay the representative directly. And for a while it appeared to have ended reasonably happily, although with a few bruised egos and damaged pockets.

But football is not the land of fairytales and is rarely filled with happy endings. The original agent simmered like a volcano for a while and then erupted. He sued the player for the commission he claimed to have lost because he'd been excluded from the transaction. He would've sued R as well, except that R actually gave him half of what he'd received, so he was off the hook.

The player audaciously counter-claimed against the agent, saying all the things that the 'representative' had said in the meeting with the chairman were false and then adding, for good measure, that the deal he'd secured was no good because he'd understood that the monies he would be paid would be 'netto' and not gross. How on earth the poor agent could've checked that, when he'd been excluded from the negotiations, heaven only knew.

Whether or not the 'representative' ever got paid, whether he'd even told the player accurately what the deal really was, R never discovered. R was never one to give up and did have a tilt at getting the player to sign with him as he'd been the only one who'd known what he was doing during the whole deal, but he was tainted by his relationship with the real agent and by then the player had already moved on to yet another agent, who had rampaged his way into the club to try to renegotiate the deal up to the level the player allegedly thought it should've been.

Anyway, the whole fiasco was a real eye-opener for me in the world of international transfers. I promised myself I'd never get involved even in lifting a phone unless I was satisfied the paperwork was airtight. That was easier said than done. At the risk of sounding like a potential UKIP parliamentary candidate – again – the worst confusion often arises in relation to players coming from African or South American countries. However, as a general rule in the world of football, and agents in particular, nothing is ever what it appears to be.

One international player, for example, appeared to be controlled totally by the owner of the club for which he played. The owner would decide if and when he'd play for his country, and despite any international regulations would simply send in a medical certificate to say the player was injured if his absence did not suit him. He was also determined to control the identity of any agent who might come to represent him. The player, somehow or other, came to sign for an English agent. The chairman did not approve and consequently decided to instruct his own tame agent to sell the player at the price he wanted – an inflated one at that (the price that is, not the tame agent – it has to be said that he was a bit overweight). The English agent, foolhardily, totally ignored the chairman and got the player a trial at an English club, omitting to tell them that: a) the chairman had appointed another agent; and b) that the price was one that no sane club would ever pay. Not that in my experience I've ever come across what you might call a sane club by normal standards.

The player did well on his trial. The club was interested and tried to make an offer to buy him, which fell so short of what the chairman had wanted as to be insulting, but probably reflected what he was really worth. The chairman ignored the club and demanded that the player return. Instead of increasing the offer, the English club cut its losses (having paid for the player to come over) and, deciding that this was never going to be a straightforward transaction, simply pulled out. The poor player, whose English wasn't great, did not know if he was coming or going, and was left in limbo. Which really is neither coming nor going.

The agent appointed by the chairman started phoning other clubs to get some interest, only to find that the player's English agent had got there before him, suggesting a price that was half of what he'd been delegated to obtain by the chairman. Not unsurprisingly, none of the clubs were interested.

The chairman became impatient, as chairmen tend to do. Imagine the Fat Controller in *Thomas the Tank Engine* and you get an idea of the temperament of the average club chairman anywhere in the world. His agent finally succeeded in finding another English club sufficiently interested to offer the player a trial. The chairman agreed but then told the English club that if they wanted to see his player in action – yes, he really did regard him as 'his' – then they had to pay his fare over. The club, not being entirely convinced and having only agreed to see the player because of the persuasive powers of the chairman's agent, declined to pay. The chairman's agent, being unwilling and scared to piss off the chairman, not to mention having spent an inordinate amount of time in trying to place the player, agreed to buy the ticket himself. In for a penny, in for several hundred pounds.

The player duly arrived, and the club promptly phoned the agent to ask him why he'd sent them a player carrying an injury. The agent called the chairman, only to be told that he'd had to make an unexpected business trip for an indefinite period of time but would call as and when.

The call did not come. The English club assessed the injury and was told recovery time would be at least a month, so back the player went. You wonder who got the air miles. Once he was back, calls to ascertain his fitness were stonewalled by the club and the chairman remained steadfastly uncontactable. Meanwhile, the player's own English agent refused to give up and reactivated his own efforts to place the player. Clubs, having been contacted by two different agents quoting conflicting prices became increasingly wary about the whole thing.

I've said it before and I'll say it again: football is a village. Everybody knows everybody else's business, and every club knew the player hadn't only been on trial twice but had collected an injury the second time around, and had two people punting him about. They also knew that even if he was given a trial and proved his fitness that the transfer fee was likely to be a great unknown.

At this stage, the chairman's agent and the player's agent hadn't even spoken to each other or considered pooling their resources. They each felt they were operating within their own individual bubbles and racing against time. In fact, there was a race but, as it proved, neither of them had even got to the starting blocks because, to their mutual astonishment, they awoke one fine morning to discover that the chairman had miraculously surfaced and bypassed them both. He'd personally flogged the player off to a club in a totally different country for a fee which bore no resemblance whatsoever to that which he'd demanded, nor even to that the English agent had optimistically quoted to get the attention of clubs.

Faced with the choice of either bringing an action against the chairman and his club in his own third-world territory or trying their chances with a complaint to FIFA (about which more later), they both decided to cut their losses and retire to lick their wounds, with interesting stories to relate to their grandchildren in the future.

As I say, nothing in the world of football is ever what it seems to be and although a contract may say 'contract' on its outside cover, it doesn't necessarily mean that when you open it up. I worked out fairly quickly that a deal is only done when the money you have earned finds its way into your bank account. Until then it's all potential, and potential doesn't pay the bills or impress bank managers.

PROMISES, PROMISES

I'D BEEN OUT on my own for over a year and had convinced myself I was doing pretty well. I hadn't made a lot of friends among the other agents mainly because I was picking up their players with alarming regularity. You're not supposed to approach a player who's contracted to another agent, but if you don't, how on earth are you ever supposed to find out if he's ripe for the picking?

The most valuable asset for a football agent is his phone book. Mobile numbers of players are pure gold. They tend to change them more often than they change their underwear or their women, but just to get the number of a player you have targeted puts you in with a chance. A text is a good way to start, either mentioning another player known to the target or a high-profile player you already represent, preferably an international. Some agents don't even bother with the nicety of representing the player they mention, and just hope the target doesn't check, and that they'll be able to blag their way through things right up to the point where the target signs a rep contract. Even if the text doesn't get a response, at least you have an excuse to call the player to see if he received it.

The conversation usually goes something like this (assuming he actually answers, although with some players you never really figure out if they're on the line or awake or not): 'Hi, hope you don't mind my calling but I've got something that may interest you.'

You either get a grunt in response or, if you're having a lucky day, 'How did you get my fucking number? I'm busy.'

To be honest, either of them could mean anything, and so you plough on into the unknown just hoping the player isn't shagging some bird while he's taking your call. And yes, I've known that to have happened more than once. Footballers always show such respect towards their women. I'm amazed they don't make them walk at least one pace behind them – when they let them out, that is.

'I hear you might be a bit unhappy,' you continue. He might well be if you've interrupted his sex life, but there you go. You're in hot pursuit and are you really going to let the odd orgasm get in your way? Anyway, your comment as to his happiness could refer to his situation with his agent or his club, and it's amazing how often he'll tell you. He tells you because, generally speaking, players are miserable bastards and greedy to boot, and they wouldn't want to miss any opportunity to put some money into their already well-lined pockets.

Now you've awoken their curiosity, you've got their attention and you're one step away from getting a meeting. Just as it is with double-glazing and insurance salesmen, once you have them eyeball-to-eyeball then you're in with a real chance. They'll have made a real effort and, trust me, for a footballer to get off his arse and come to a meeting is an effort, particularly when he could've been playing golf. And if you get the meeting then you need to make sure that you deliver.

So you need to find somewhere to meet where you won't be seen. Unauthorised meetings in public may be good for your ego and your profile, but if you're spotted, as one agent found out to his cost a few years back, it can prove to be a very expensive mistake. He met a player in a hotel with a view to tapping him up for a club who wanted a transfer, and although the agent in question may have stood to make a small fortune from the ultimate deal, he committed the ultimate transgression of being spotted – and hence found out – and received a not insubstantial fine and lengthy suspension from the FA. Not, I suspect, that either penalty cramped his style or really interfered with his business methods or acted as a genuine deterrent.

So, assuming you have found somewhere totally out of the way to meet, this is how the conversation goes. You offer them a drink. Sometimes they accept and, to be fair, it's usually just a juice rather than anything alcoholic. That comes when you're meeting the father of a young player. Be prepared for an endless evening of beers, shorts and boredom then. If the player you have come to meet doesn't accept a drink then he'll most likely just sit there, avoiding eye contact while checking for messages on whatever latest electronic gadget he's brought with him. The pressure is on you to make the running, to keep (what may well prove to be a one-sided) conversation going.

I've discovered that footballers never open conversations (well, at least not unless they want something), never make small talk and never show the slightest interest in who or how you are or what your personal family situation may be. All they care about is what you might be able to do for them, so it's best not to forget that. Although you need to sell yourself, you also need to have something that the player actually needs otherwise you might as well not bother to open your shop doors.

They don't even really care what you've done for other players, although if you have no track record you're probably wasting your time, unless you have a sister they might like to shag. However, a few calling cards of previous deals does at least set the scene even if it only leads to them asking you what sort of deals you got for the players in question. You can try and take the high moral ground and say it's confidential, but if you think they'll be impressed by that, heartened that you won't be exposing their financial secrets to others, then you're fooling yourself. They want to know because they want to make sure they're not earning anything less.

You have to put into the equation of your courtship that players have the attention span of a newt and the egos of a dictator of a medium-sized, troublesome Central American country. This means that the time of the audience you have been granted with them is limited, and so you have to speak quickly and make them realise as early on as possible in the conversation that the very universe revolves around their individual careers and that you'll devote your own life to ensuring that planetary state will continue.

First of all, you find out who their current agent is. Once they tell you, then you come right out with it and ask if they're happy with him (or her, and yes, there are more and more women coming into the industry). If they say they are, then you tell them you understand; you understand, that of course you don't want to drive a wedge between them and their current representatives, but that, he, the player, has a duty to look after himself. Loyalty is a great virtue, but the deal that you alone can offer has to be given some thought. You tell them that you also like their current agent. That he's a good bloke and that you're sure you can work something out with him, that you'll look after him, and as you'll get everybody more than he would then he, the agent, won't lose out. You say anything to keep the conversation going. Promises in football come cheaper than anywhere else. They're not just two a penny, they're a hundred a penny and they're nearly always broken.

If the player tells you he's not happy then you've hit the jackpot. You run the other agent down and then you run him over again and again until it looks like he's been hit by a steamroller. And by now you can be fairly sure that the player has given up texting, emailing, surfing the web, tweeting or posting on Facebook (or whatever by then is the current fad). He's no longer playing video games because he's now the central character in your game and you're the only one pushing the buttons.

He's the game. He's the prey and you're the hunter. He's in your sights but he's far too valuable a commodity to kill. You'll only use the stun gun, and when he comes round he simply won't know what has hit him.

You tell him that you're 'in' at a Premier League club. That you, and you alone, can get him a move there. You tell him all the other things that you can do for him that his current agent can't. And then, when he's almost in your grasp, there's just one small problem left to address. The fact that he's already contracted to somebody else.

As I've made clear, footballers are hardly queuing up to participate in *Mastermind*. They might even struggle to join the dots to make a picture in a kids' comic. So once you have their ear, they tend to believe whatever it is you have to tell them. That is, until somebody else gets their ear.

So, particularly when what you're telling them is something they really want to hear, they aren't going to be too bothered about something as mundane as a previous contract if you have already told them it's the only impediment to their getting the move of their dreams. You have them on the hook and you just have to reel them in until they're lying at your feet, fresh from the water and gasping for breath.

'Don't worry about a thing,' you say. 'Just leave it to me and it won't cost you a penny, because I'll act for the club and you'll represent yourself. Because you can, you know, and the beauty of it is that you don't even need to tell your agent until after the deal is done because that's what it says in the contract with him.'

You don't add: 'You remember the contract? That's the one I've just torn into shreds and put in the incinerator.'

'What if my agent has a go at me?' the player might ask, if he's not totally devoid of intelligence.

'Leave that to me as well,' you reply in honeyed, reassuring tones. By now you're his saviour, he wants to trust you and you are there for him. Almost over the line.

The fact of the matter is that his agent may well sue him for breach of contract somewhere along the line, but by then you'll have banked the hefty fee you've earned from delivering him and that then gives you several options. One is to get him a specialist sports lawyer who can pick all sorts of holes in the representation contract. Although the FA check through all the contracts before they register them, to ensure they comply with their regulations, what they don't do is dig any deeper into the circumstances which led to them being signed. Nor once it's signed and registered do they monitor the agent's due performance of it and whether or not he's fulfilling his obligations.

Another approach is to bankroll the player to a certain degree (obviously not to a huge one as you don't want to give away too much of what you have earned, otherwise what was the point of the whole exercise), so that he can offer it to his old agent as a consolation. He's not really the old agent anyway as the poor bastard still has a contract which he thought was watertight, but he might just take it as an easy alternative to bringing a claim against his player and having the player turn things around in the dressing room to make the agent look like the bad one and ruin his chances with anybody else at the club. And if he does take it, then you're even more of a hero to the player than you were for finding him the club and ensuring he got a great deal. So, your contribution is a very small price to pay.

The third course of action is, in fact, one of total inaction. You do nothing, take the short-term view that it was a good deal for you and just leave the player to his fate. If it gets really nasty, he has no proof of what he claims you said and all you've done is act for the club and you just move on, somewhat the richer.

I know quite a few agents for whom that third option would be the preferred choice, but to me it seems just plain silly – not to mention plain greedy and short-sighted. However attractive it might be not to give away any money, the fact of the matter is that players talk. They say good things when you've delivered (even though their memories of the good things may be cut short when a predatory agent comes along to offer the earth, as illustrated above) and they'll certainly say bad things when they've been shafted. In fact, my experience is that they'll say bad things even when they just perceive they've been shafted because they've had to lay out a bit of money by way of a fee or tax, but there you go. I acted for one player where the club had a thing about paying agents. So, what I did was to get them to add a few grand to the player's signing-on fee so he could pay me directly. I even worked out the tax on what he'd have to pay on the extra I got him and I invoiced him for a net sum after taking off that amount of tax. He did pay with a cheque in a grubby envelope and the wrong amount of postage so I had to pay extra when I went to collect it from the Post Office, but still. In the envelope there was just a cheque, not even a thank-you note, and then, as soon as he could he dumped me. And when I asked him why, he said it was because I'd charged him. I tried to explain that if the club had paid my fees on his behalf I'd still have, in effect, been charging him, but he wasn't having any of it.

The truth is, you can't carry on in this business for too long if bad things follow you around from deal to deal, leaving a nasty smell. There are one or two agents who specialise in foul-smelling deals, and because they deliver they're still allowed into the room, and I suppose you get to a point where you're so successful that nobody has the balls to talk about your BO.

Me, I give a bit away of what I get every time. The old agent might be left feeling a bit down, but something is better than nothing, and you know what, I'm starting to get agents I've taken a player off talking to me again and even wanting to work with me and tap into my connections. People tend to be pragmatic in this industry. You don't have to like the folks you work with. You just have to make money with them or out of them.

Going back to the sort of deal I was talking about where you nick a player by sweet talk, the odds are that many agents who do just that don't have a club ready and waiting, and certainly not the attractive club they mentioned. The player giving them the nod is the signal for them to put the two ends together to make fire. If they can, then great. If they can only do it with another club then they'll probably be able to substitute that club for the one that hooked the player. And if they can't find any club at all, well, all it's cost them is the juice they bought the player and a bit of time, and his old agent can have him back and is welcome to him because there's nothing to be made from him.

Anyway, I guess I must have been doing something right because I was being noticed. Not just by players, but agents as well, and not just the agents who couldn't help but notice me because I now had their players. And that was how I came to be having lunch with Agent B who had gone beyond the foul smells of reputation because he could afford to have his own deodorant and after-shave designed for him. So I took with me the longest spoon I could find, rolled up at the Mayfair restaurant he'd chosen, and crossed my fingers that he was picking up the bill. Which, indeed he did. In cash of course.

AGENT B

EVERYBODY IN THE business knew or knew of Agent B. His nickname was 'The Lizard', because every time he got the merest sniff of a deal he crawled out from beneath the nearest rock. B was not the most pleasant of individuals. In fact, let me put it another way, he was the sleaziest, greasiest man I'd ever met. Somebody described him as 'unctuous', and after I looked it up in a dictionary I had to agree. Charles Dickens would've smothered him in adjectives.

Yet, the one positive thing you could say about him was that he knew how to make a deal happen, and although he rarely directly recruited players of his own to represent, he was often sought out by a club to act for them when they wanted to source a particular player and needed to untangle the log jam.

As one fairly decent chairman told me when I asked him why he'd anything at all to do with B he said, very succinctly, 'He delivers. He may cost, but he delivers.'

He didn't add that B also had scant regard for any rules and regulations – which he truly believed had not been put in place with him in mind. He wasn't licensed out of England so unless he did something wrong here when he'd had to register for a particular transaction as an overseas agent, the English FA had a hard job pinning anything on him. He ducked in and he ducked out, bobbing and weaving like an overweight heavyweight boxer, but deliver he did, albeit at a price. And the price was often paid by an innocent agent who had thought he had a player or transaction in hand only to see B swoop down and take it out of his grasp.

It did not matter one jot to B that he was taking the bread out of the mouth of an agent who actually represented the player and who had worked very hard (sometimes for years) for that privilege. B was just focused. Show him an opportunity to make money and he was like a dog with a bone. Sometimes he would even move on to the next deal before the ink was dry on the paper of the last. He was a man obsessed.

There were many stories told about him, some of which seemed like pure fiction until people who were there or were involved confirmed their truth.

On one occasion, he actually kidnapped a player and quite literally wafted him off on false pretences to his remote, albeit palatial, home. The player in question had been with his agent for years, but the opportunity came along for him to move to a top club abroad. B had it all planned out. He convinced the player that his own agent just couldn't do a deal of this magnitude. He got himself a retainer from the buying club where he was well known, so that was all fine and dandy. He then approached the selling club and asked them what they wanted for the player. They named a price, and he said he'd try and get it for them, but anything above that would belong to him. So, having got control of both ends of the transaction all he now needed to do was to get the player as the last piece of this very remunerative transaction. But there was a problem. The player's agent was honest and reputable, and to see this deal through B had to control the player as well. Hence the drastic step of taking the player away from his loved ones and, in particular, from his agent.

This was in the days before representation contracts had to be registered, and the player had enjoyed a long relationship with his old agent which was so based upon trust that neither of them had felt the need for a written contract. Consequently, he was there for the taking, and take him B did, both metaphorically and physically.

It didn't take B too long to persuade the player that he, B, was the only one who could actually make the deal happen, and, I suppose, with him acting for all the parties, that was actually true. At first everything went swimmingly. For B. He added a million pounds to the asking price of the selling club. He then gave an even higher figure to the buying club and asked for an extra commission from them if he reduced it to what the selling club wanted (plus his million of course). Naturally he knew he could reduce it because the selling club were not expecting it.

He then asked the player what he wanted and applied the same technique, telling him he'd be charging a 'super commission' (payable in cash of course) on the excess he might obtain for him. It was all so terribly simple, as long as he could keep the parties from talking to each other – and why should they when good old honest B was there to enable them to communicate? Just like Hannibal in *The A-Team*, he was able to say he loved it when a plan came together.

I suppose, if you were taking a pragmatic view of the whole situation, you could say that nobody really lost out. One club sold a player and got the price it wanted. Another club acquired a player it really wanted (and who in fact helped them both to a domestic title and a tilt in Europe), and the player doubled his salary in the move – and with the tax-free advantages, he had no worries about life after his career ended. But the biggest winner of all was B, and here he was in the flesh (rather a lot of it after a life of expensive dinners and even more expensive booze) and he'd asked me out to lunch.

R had told me, quoting the old Hollywood adage, that there was no such thing as a free lunch, so I never really relaxed, told him I didn't drink when he offered me wine and never for a moment let my eyes move from his face. He wasn't one for eye contact, so that rather put him off as his eyes slid all over the place and ended up staring intently at the crisp white tablecloth.

He told me he liked my style, that I reminded him of his younger self, and after a few questions about my business and the level of my turnover he asked me if I'd like to work with him. And I have to say I was tempted. Despite everything I'd heard about him he came across as sincere, and much more pleasant than the reputation which preceded him. But I didn't fancy it. I'd heard too many stories.

Like when he dashed off to a transaction he'd set up very much like the one I described in detail before, only to find that the player had got there before him. In this case the player was very much his own man and told the buying club (which had been assured by B that he controlled the player) that he'd never actually met him. B arrived, breathless from his last killing, only to find the player sitting down with the club officials and his father, the terms already agreed. The only words that passed between B and the player were as follows:

PLAYER: 'Who the fuck are you?'

B: 'I'm B, your agent.'

PLAYER: 'No, you're not. Just fuck off.'

Some you win, some you lose, I guess, and B did not have a reputation for sensitivity or a thinness of skin.

On this occasion I trusted my instinct, told B I'd let him know (given that I didn't want to decline there and then in case I got lumbered with the lunch tab), and when I did let him know it was by text and read, thanks, but no thanks.

I knew I'd made an enemy, because he wasn't a man who was used to people saying no to him. Don't get me wrong. I'm not saying B was totally dishonest or dishonourable. In fact, if he agreed a deal with another agent he always kept to it. It was just that he tried very hard to avoid having to agree a deal. I'd heard that on one occasion he'd arrived in the middle of a transaction and grabbed it by the scruff of its neck even though he didn't act for any of the parties at its start. One startled agent suddenly realised that all the money in the deal was going to B, even though he was entitled to half a million pounds.

'Look,' he said, 'I don't really know you. In fact I've never met you before today.'

'Are you not trusting me, son?' B had said, pulling himself up to his full height and looming over the by now trembling agent.

The agent assured him that he'd trust him with his bank account, his child and the keys to his house while his wife was alone and naked in bed upstairs.

B rose and went over to his briefcase, which the agent noticed was full of cash. He pulled out a sheet of headed paper and signed it, and then handed it over to the agent.

'There you go, son. You just fill in the amount you think you're owed.'

And sure enough the money was paid over as soon as B received it, although if it hadn't been paid the agent would probably never have dared to sue B on the basis of the sheet of paper. Or, indeed, on any other basis, given his reputation.

I really wasn't prepared to give B the chance to show me what a good partner he could be even though, as it transpired in the future, it would cost me a deal. Quite frankly I had the feeling that if I'd gone in with him it might have cost me much more, including potentially my liberty. That particular asset of mine I managed, in due course, to fuck up all on my own, or at least just with a little help from someone I thought to be a friend. But meanwhile, let me tell you what the Lizard actually did to me.

I'd started to build up my own little network of contacts abroad, and one of them had introduced me to a player in one of the European leagues. He wasn't top class, but he scored goals consistently at his level and he was certainly good enough to play in the Championship.

I began to make some enquiries, although his current club was a bit reticent about the level of the fee it wanted; I eventually got a figure out of them which was fairly realistic. A few clubs showed a bit of interest, but none of them were sufficiently keen to make an offer, or even to pay up front to get the player across to have a look at him. But I soldiered on because that's what you do. You live in hope and you never give up: those are the two mottos that every football agent should have on his family crest.

Then, one day, I was sitting at home minding my own business when a friend called me and told me to switch on Sky Sports. My TV is permanently fixed on those channels, so I can keep up with everything that's going on, but on this occasion I was making myself one of the endless cups of coffee that keep me going through the day.

To my astonishment, there on the screen was B at Heathrow walking though with my European player, taking him to a club to which I'd already spoken, a club whose manager had told me he didn't fancy the player. As you can imagine, I got to the phone in a heartbeat and called the CEO of the club who expressed total ignorance of the transaction and thought it must be the manager winging it on his own.

This news did not surprise me, because there were already hot rumours in the industry that B and this particular manager were in cahoots. However, the CEO said he'd investigate and get back to me, and to be fair to him he actually did. He told me that the club were not proceeding because the price was too high. I asked him the price he'd been quoted, and he told me it was fifty per cent higher than the figure I'd quoted and that the player was heading home.

I let the dust settle and then got back to the player's European club who told me that B had contacted them and told them the price they'd quoted me was too high and had got them to agree to a lower figure, only then to ask the English club for even more than the original price to boost his own potential profit on the deal. Yes, B had been up to his old tricks again and had agreed with the club that whatever he got above the figure would belong to him. Only this time he'd been too greedy, and instead of making money the little jaunt had cost him the expense of bringing the player over (although I did hear that such was his nerve that he invoiced the English club for the costs of the flights).

Having got the selling club to see sense, I tried to resurrect the deal, but the buying club was now suspicious of the whole arrangement, and despite the player having done well in his trial, decided to pass. However, seeds of doubt had been sown about the manager and his relationship with B, and it wasn't too long before he got the sack. On the face of it, the dismissal may have seemed to be performance-based, but I knew the truth. You might have thought the club would look closely at all the players B had brought to the club in the past while this manager was there, but, not for the first time, the club didn't want to wash its dirty linen in public, didn't want to look foolish, and just closed its books on the whole sorry episode. It appointed a new manager in due course, but I knew that this guy was hand-in-glove with yet another agent, so I wondered how long that relationship might last – unless they were going to cut the CEO into their nefarious dealings, which was always a possibility at some clubs.

I'd like to say that justice caught up with B, that clubs kept their distance, that the Revenue was hot on his heels, that he became yesterday's man, but the fact was that he lived (and continues to live) happily and prosperously ever after, and even today as a veteran he's still in demand as the man who delivers where others fail.

Yet, as I say, he wasn't for me. I might have been losing my moral compass but I didn't feel ready to descend to his murky depths, however much money the association might make me. At least, not just yet.

THE FRONT

I HAD PLAYERS signed to me, decent ones at that; I had a couple of managers I was 'looking after'; and I had gained the grudging respect of some of the more experienced agents who could see by now that I was a young man on the up. But there was something missing from my armoury. The ex-footballer who could act as my scout, talk the talk and walk the walk with the young players because he had the experience, had done it all before.

It had become apparent that anybody who was anybody was utilising one or more of these ex-players to a certain degree. Sometimes they were on the payroll, sometimes on commission and sometimes it was hard to tell which of the operators at a company was actually the licensed agent. Indeed, as far as some companies were concerned, forget the 'ex', it was actually current players who were involved. Or, in a couple of cases, were the true owners hiding behind a fronting agent.

One international player was absolutely blatant – calling player after player and asking them to join 'his' agency. I didn't give a toss until he called one of mine and I hit back with a threat to report him both to his club and the FA, and after that it subsided for a bit. At least as far as I was concerned. I mean, the guy was on about eighty grand a week and here he was trying to take deals away from me worth about twenty grand at most. Greedy or what? Well, definitely not 'or what'.

Some of these players even went so far as to tap up players on the pitch or in the bar after a match. They'd butter up the player by telling him how well he'd played, how good they thought he was and then innocently ask how much they were earning and who was acting for them. They'd express surprise at what they called a low figure and then say that they weren't surprised at all given the identity of the agent who had negotiated the deal. Shortly thereafter electronic devices would be out to exchange information with a view to setting up a meeting, with the agency with which the player had a deal, or of which he owned a slice (or even sometimes a majority share).

I may have given you the wrong impression on occasion about the relationship between agents and the FA. They're definitely not our friends. They may offer small crumbs of kindness, in much the same way a prison warden might bring a prisoner a message from home, but generally speaking we're simply not on the same side. We're trying to make money. They're trying to stop us. Those at Wembley who have been, and are, responsible for the Agents' Regulations have to sit and watch some of us earn fortunes from our deals while they put in their nine-to-five shifts, overlooking a huge car park in which they've parked their modest family saloons, for a comparative pittance. Sometimes I kind of get why they might feel a bit peeved and why at times they seem to be creating and enforcing regulations just for the hell of it, but mostly I don't. I've seen too many of my fellow agents suffer at their hands. You'd think I might be pleased, but in fact all I generally do think is, who's next in line? And I guess it could be me with some of the business practices I've started to adopt. Not that I'm doing anything that anybody else doesn't. And I don't reckon I'm as blatant as most, but one of the things the FA seems to like least (and believe me there's quite a lot they don't like – usually things that earn us our living) is what they call 'fronting'.

Now, I don't call it fronting when an unlicensed guy who works for me finds a player, gets him to sign with me, finds him a club where he knows the manager, and virtually does the deal leaving me to come in and sign it off. I call that deploying staff to maximise income. Where's the harm in that? Indeed, FIFA seem to agree – which is why come 2015 they're doing away with our licences and bringing in a new breed of individuals to be called 'intermediaries'. I'll talk about them a bit later, because FIFA have been talking about it since time immemorial so who knows – it may still never happen. But if it does and any 'intermediary' chooses to write a book like this, then I can tell you it's going to be one hell of a sight juicier than anything I've come up with.

But I don't have a crystal ball so I'm looking at the hard facts of what the situation is now. Which is: the FA say that only a licensed agent can carry out what they, in their wisdom, have designated as 'Agency Activities'. Someone at HQ must have a real sense of humour (or sadistic nature) because they've made the definition so wide that if an unlicensed agent (i.e. your ex-pro) even meets a manager of a club (maybe somebody with whom he played and who is his mate) and mentions a player while winking, then the FA could argue that it was an agency activity and consequently a breach of the rules.

So, the agent has to contend with that and the financial demands of the ex-players who work for him as a scout. They know their price and their value, and as they quite often control the players, their demands can be fairly outrageous. They think nothing of taking up to ninety per cent from a deal, leaving the licensed agent who has fronted them with a mere ten per cent for his trouble and his risk. The argument is that he's done fuck all except put his name to the paper and the ten per cent is generous because he wouldn't have got anything at all were it not for his scout's ability to spot a young emerging talent and cosy up to the parents.

The cosying up can go quite a long way, as I know of one scout who got to a player by shagging his mother. The only problem there was that although the player did make the big time, the scout was married and had to decide if his marriage was more important than his investment in a player. I'm told he did hesitate, but eventually his wife made the decision for him by way of an ultimatum and he stayed with her while the player moved on to another agent – who didn't have his mum in his sights and could actually focus on his career.

Clubs get on their high moral horses about how much agents earn and allegedly take out of the game, but they're more than happy, when they want a player, to deal with an unlicensed individual and put the agent down on the paperwork even though they know he's just the middle man in the deal. Sometimes it's even more obvious than that, and clubs deal directly with the unlicensed bloke who controls the player and find a way to pay him by making him their scout and giving him a payment for helping to introduce some commercial deal. Football is all about consensual pragmatism. If a club wants a player they'll use any means to get him and won't be bothering to take up references on the person who can deliver him.

These 'unlicensed agents' come in all shapes, sizes and colours. Many of them are, as I say, former professional footballers who don't feel able to pass the agents' exam or simply can't be bothered to take it. Then there are those who have taken the exam and failed but don't see that as a real impediment to carrying on a 'shadow' business of a football agency and can, because they control a few players.

As I say, one or two of these unlicensed guys are really high-profile and even talk publicly about 'their' players. The problem faced by the FA is that these individuals aren't under their control or jurisdiction, because they've not signed up to the rules, so all the FA can do is punish clubs or players if the FA can prove they've actually worked through an unlicensed person. And proving any such thing is much easier said than done. If a player says he represented himself and the club confirms that they've only ever spoken to the player himself, or his dad, or a licensed agent, then there's fuck all the FA can do about it.

Innocents can get suckered in and are actively sought out by unscrupulous unlicensed individuals. One agent had recently got his licence, but as yet had no players at all and was holding down a regular job to earn enough to keep his family. He was approached by individuals who told him they were agents but needed to keep their names out of the transaction. They offered him a small share of a deal bringing in a player from abroad, and the newly qualified agent gratefully accepted. The 'agents' did everything: negotiated the whole deal and even picked up the player from the airport when he flew in from abroad. All the 'innocent' agent did was to sign off on everything. He got the shock of his life when the FA opened an inquiry and charged him with fronting because the so-called agents had no licences and, indeed, had even failed the exams. The FA threw the book at him, and the club claimed, quite properly, that they should not have taken the unlicensed guys at face value. Probably for the first time in living memory the real agent lost his licence before he'd even got himself a client, while the club was fined a six-figure sum. The two individuals to blame got off scot-free because they were outwith the jurisdiction of the FA, and it beggars belief that it's people like that who the FA will allow to become intermediaries when all that comes into play. More of that later.

Don't get me wrong. I'm with the FA on this one. You may not think so from what you've read so far, but we do at least try and pay some lip service to the regulations and operate in a fairly (well, comparatively fairly) open manner. We're also a bit buggered because we can only be paid through the FA after the club has paid them to pass the money on to us and once they've checked that everything is hunky dory and above board. These unlicensed guys are flying below the radar and sometimes their bombing raids can cause us real damage. We'd like to put an end to them, so what have FIFA and the FA done to help our cause? Well, they've said these guys can operate with impunity from 2015 – with apparently very few of the safeguards that have made our business so difficult to run for many years. Talk about the lunatics running the asylum. You honestly couldn't make this one up. It's as if the authorities have surrendered. Bitter, me? I don't think so . . .

It didn't take me too long to stumble upon 'Mr Fixit', who was not only unlicensed but seemed to control an inordinately high proportion of deals involving players coming into the country, largely because he seemed to own a slice of the said players. The FA were helpless to deal with him even though he was breaking all their third party ownership (TPO) rules, but clubs fell over themselves to find ways to pay him because of the quality of the players he could bring them. There was one deal due to complete on a transfer deadline day, and Mr Fixit knew of it and clearly had something on the player involved, even if he didn't totally own him. Everybody was sitting around in the buying club's offices when the phone rang. It was Mr Fixit telling them that unless he was paid half a million pounds the transfer wasn't going to go through. The buying club said they'd committed to as much as they would with what they were paying the selling club and the player himself. Efforts to persuade the player to sign anyway fell on deaf ears. After much bartering, all parties agreed to put something into Mr Fixit's pot. He got his half-million, and the deal went through without any of the relevant authorities knowing about the payment to Mr F. Talk about protection monies; talk about the mafia? Mr F could give lessons to all concerned. And he managed to stay above the law: both the law of whatever land in which he chose to do his business and the law of football.

Football is a honeypot and attracts all sorts of strange creatures around it trying to get a jarful of the amber nectar. (Or is that whisky? I rarely drink so I don't know.) It just all looks so easy to make money. Financial advisers, lawyers and accountants who have worked with agents look at the deals and, having seen just how much the agent has made, wonder why they should settle for paltry commission or fees based on time when they think they could do a more professional job of negotiating and concluding the deals themselves. It may mean biting off the hand that has fed them, will certainly mean the end of the relationship with the agent or agents in question but, hey, you know what? It's a small price to pay when they can walk off with the players once they've gained their trust – either by making their money work for them, saving them tax, or winning a legal action.

Then there are the player's 'mates'. They've grown up with him, played in the street with him, been in the same class at school, been teammates at various levels of football clubs before he moved on to bigger and better things, and just hung around to become part of his entourage. That entourage, those mates, have to be brought on board by the agent, whatever the cost. But, even if the agent mixes with them, gets pissed with them, pulls birds with them, even has threesomes or foursomes with them (as one agent regularly does), the fact remains that the player will usually trust them more than any Johnny-come-lately agent. I've been out on the town with some of my players, and trust me it isn't a pleasant experience. I'll come back to that even though I've tried to erase a few incidents from my memory.

Such players often refuse to sign with an agent, telling him that when he brings them a deal they might consider it but that he should work on the basis that when it comes to the paperwork he'll say that he's acted for the club. Apart from the fact that the player then pays no tax on any fees, it also means that he can expel the agent from his inner circle at any time. So the agent is constantly on trial, walking on eggshells, and forced to work with the entourage or its leader. And even if the player does finally sign a representation contract it might just as well be with his mate or mates given the influence they'll exert. The agent therefore has to work through two layers of approval – player and entourage – and any deal he negotiates is subject to scrutiny at both levels.

The players listen to their friends. Generally speaking, they can't be bothered with the trivial details of the deal, the small print. They just want the bottom line. I've been told by a player, 'If so and so [i.e. his mate] says it's OK then go ahead.' And the inference is that his mate has to be looked after financially, even though that's also a breach of the rules because it isn't something you're going to want to disclose.

That's how an agent finds himself cosying up to some tattooed thug who in a parallel universe would be serving time for armed robbery, drug dealing or worse. That hasn't happened, because he's found a better way of life, stroking the player's ego and generally doing whatever he tells him.

Players can be cruel, and even their agents aren't guaranteed to avoid that. They know the agent can't tell them to fuck off (well, they can, but it would be a brave one who would), so I've heard of tales where they get a mate to piss in the agent's expensive car (for a laugh, of course) or, in one case, put the poor agent in the boot of his own car and drive him around for a whole afternoon.

The player may dispense some beneficence. He'll buy his mates rounds of drinks or pay for their hotels (although if the agent is with him then he'll be expected to pick up the tab), give them freebies like boots, trainers and tracksuits from the kit deal his agent has negotiated, let them smash up his sponsored car (which his agent acquired for him), hand over the young women he's done with (which sometimes the agent is expected to acquire), but who has to sort out all that mess? Yes, you've guessed it: the agent who made it all possible and who on many occasions has created this monster into which the player has turned.

You might think that the player would look after his mates from the remunerative deals he has both on and off the pitch. Like fuck he will. He usually expects his agent to spread the cash around out of his fee, and although that can be substantial it quite often only equates to a week's salary of the player's own deal. The cost of a night on the town, the rounds of drinks at a club (often including total strangers) and the hotel rooms afterwards can make big inroads into the profit. Girls and drugs – no surprises there – can swallow them up altogether.

Now, don't get me wrong. Not every friend of every player is a total idiot. Some of them are really bright. They may even have gone to university or a college at least, and in a way they're the most dangerous to have around. In the same way that the professional advisers can see what the agent makes, so do the more intelligent members of his entourage. I've known these guys to take over the player's management and squeeze the agent out into oblivion, no matter the good work he may have done or how close he thinks he's come to them. They become the power brokers, sometimes legitimising themselves by bothering to get a licence, although more often not. Not because they're incapable, but at the end of the day a licence to do what they do is irrelevant. They may not have the bit of paper and the registration number that's issued by the FA, but they've got something much better than those. They have the player. And, in the words of Meatloaf, 'in the land of the pigs, the butcher is king'.

THE TOOLS OF THE TRADE

AFTER ALMOST TWO years of trying to build my business I was well into the psyche of players (at least those of them who actually had one). They have strong likes and even stronger dislikes. They like money, of course; that goes without saying. And generally they're young and fit-looking heterosexuals who like young and fit-looking (and amenable) women. They like Nando's, and Red Bull, and tattoos. They like expensive fast cars and the latest gadgets. They like loud music playing from the best stereo system. They like smart clothes, expensive footwear, jewellery and baseball caps. They read the tabloids but hate the journalists who write for them. If you put all that together then you get the picture, but with one notable piece missing. They love, absolutely fucking *love*, freebies. Even if it's something they have no use for whatsoever. Provided it's free, they want it.

Freebies can vary in accessibility and cost, but any agent who can't provide them might just as well give up the day job and go to the nearest Jobcentre, because football agency is most certainly not for him.

Starting with basics, the first question almost every potential client has asked me is, 'Can you get me boots?' If you're meeting a parent then they're programmed to ask the same question. I understand that in a way, because they're normally working-class, if working at all, and they've scrimped and saved to get little Johnny his boots since he was first old enough to stand upright and kick a ball. Now you've come along with your flash car and your smooth talk and your nice suit and the track record you've reeled off in front of them, so why shouldn't they expect you to assume this particular burden? I suppose it's also not unreasonable for the player himself to expect you to provide them because, after all, they're the tools of his trade and it's become something of a trade practice for the bloke most likely to make a barrow-load of money out of the player's career to provide them for him.

R used to reminisce fondly about the good old days of his agency work when the big boot companies like Nike, Umbro, Puma, Adidas and so on used to give a pair of boots to any Tom, Dick or Harry (must have been the good old days with names like that) who could kick a ball – and indeed to some who couldn't but whom the agent told them could. They worked on the basis that if you gave boots to a hundred youngsters then the odds were that two or three of them would reach the top echelons of the game which made the whole investment worthwhile. By the time I hooked up with R, and certainly by the time I branched out on my own, those days were sadly, at least for my pocket, long past.

So, many agents, me included, had to buy footwear for their clients. Now, boots don't come cheap, and even the youngest of players won't be fobbed off by the cheaper brands, even though they may do the job just as well. It's all about peer pressure, pride and ego, even when the kids are just in an academy – or even before. They all want top-of-the-range branded boots in the brightest of colours as worn by whoever may be their latest international idol, and they certainly won't settle for some foreign brand willing to spread samples around in an attempt to break into a saturated market.

When I first started out on my own, I did, just like everybody else, promise players anything (the Earth included) just to get them to sign up with me. You want boots? Sure, no problem. Any brand and as many as you want. Add that to holidays, cars, insurance, designer clothes, looking after their mums and dads, and you get the extent of what I had to do. If you miss a heartbeat in telling a player what he wants to hear, in selling yourself through your pitch, he'll spot it in a nanosecond. As you'll have gathered, I don't have the highest regard for footballers as academics, but they do have a built-in antenna for any lack of confidence or anything that might sound like bullshit.

Even if it is. It's all a bit like taking a lie-detector test and beating the equipment. However, once you have their signature on the dotted line then reality kicks in.

I once had a young player who seemed to have real potential. I managed to sign him in the face of fierce competition by persuading him (and of course his parents, not to mention their new partners as they were separated) that I could give him a much more personal service than any of the big agencies with their hundreds of clients all vying for attention. I was absolutely delighted to have signed him, even though I knew at this early stage in his career I wouldn't be making a fortune out of him. I just hoped to be able to impress him enough in the initial two years I had with him to re-sign with me just when his career was likely to become more lucrative for both of us.

The first problem I encountered with him was . . . boots. He asked for a pair of top-range Nike, and having tried and failed to get him an early sponsorship deal with the company, I bought him the boots with the discount on the price that most of the big companies offer to agents. He didn't even bother to say thank you – par for the course – but to add insult to injury he told me that he needed a second pair, this time moulded ones as he liked to carry both studs and moulded styles depending on the conditions.

Fair enough, I thought, sensible young man. Tools of the trade. The better he does on the pitch then the more likely I am to cash in when I do his next contract. And if it takes two pairs of the most expensive boots to make him a better player then who am I to argue or rock the ship for a halfpenny worth of tar. Whatever a halfpenny ever was. Long before my time. Bit like loyal one-club, one-agent footballers. I may have been set back over three hundred quid by buying these boots, but I'd convinced myself that I needed to look upon that expenditure as an investment.

But there are investments and investments, and less than a month later he was texting me again – cheaper than phoning me and also not giving me the chance to ask him for an explanation – telling me that some of his mates' agents had got them boots in the colour of their choice. And he would like orange, please. Well, actually there was no please. I just added that for dramatic effect.

What he was really saying was that if I didn't cough up, then there were agents out there, representing his teammates, who, given the opportunity, would perform hand-stands with bells on for him.

Anyway, four pairs of boots later (two studs, two moulded, one of each in bright orange), I was asked for another four pairs of boots and began to wonder if he was either into eating leather or was running a sideline on a local market stall. I'd always kept in touch with the lad's mother – a good ploy to always remember birthdays and so on – and in passing, having found an excuse to call her, I say, 'Your boy seems to be getting through a fair old number of boots.'

'Oh, yes,' she replies, 'he's always been heavy on shoes. Is there a problem?'

'Oh, no,' I say, gritting my teeth. 'Always willing to help. Your son is one of my favourites.'

They all were, as long as they made me money, but I wasn't going to be sharing that thought with her.

Fast-forward another month and a request for four more pairs. And he would like – for 'like' read 'demand' – some leisurewear thrown in. Because that was what all his mates were getting through their super agents. Now, this lad had done very little in his career to date. He'd got some schoolboy caps in the Victory Shield, been picked for an Under-17 tour but had never played, and the nearest he'd got to a first-team debut (and thus the renegotiated contract I'd built into his current deal and which would hopefully provide some payback for me) was a place on the bench for a League Cup tie when the manager chose to field eight reserves in his starting squad.

So, I'm starting to think he might or might not actually make it, and at this rate, in terms of footwear acquisition, I was likely to be about a grand out of pocket before the day he got released and ended up playing in the Football Conference. So, I seized the bull by the horns, or more accurately the player by the balls, and asked him if he really, really needed so many boots. And, you know what? He comes right out and tells me that some of them have been for his kid brother who takes the same size, although there the similarity in football skill comes to an abrupt halt.

I guess you're thinking, a whole chapter devoted to agents and players and their mutual relationship with footwear? Sounds like an extract from a book on foot fetishes. Well, as an old comedian my grandfather liked to quote actually said, 'You ain't heard nothing yet.'

VICARIOUS LIVING

YOU MAY BE wondering if there's something missing from my life and you'd be right. I have no real friends, no down time, no social life whatsoever. I mix only with footballers and their families, managers, coaches and just about anybody else who can make me any money. It's all about the deal and the pursuit of the next one.

I live in my car, and in fact I've just checked and seen that in the last twelve months I've driven over 50,000 miles. I work 24/7 and if 25/8 were on offer then I'd take that too. I don't see my parents, and they have to phone just to check I'm still alive. They know to try my mobile first because who uses a landline nowadays? My mobile bill last month was over £600 and that was without me even leaving the country. There are all sorts of deals for people like me on offer but who has time to sit down and consider them? My life is a series of questions I ask myself but don't even have a minute to answer and if I gave the questions a second thought then I wouldn't ask them anyway.

I even began to question my own sexuality. Was I so obsessed with footballers that I actually wanted to sleep with one? Another question. This time I answered with a resounding no. (I've only known a couple of openly gay agents during my time in the business.) To be honest, I've slept with the sister of one player and had an offer to sleep with the wife of another, but that would be pissing into the tent and I'm not that stupid. I even had the mother of one of my players come on to me when I arrived at their house for a meeting a bit early. And her one-year-old was asleep upstairs in his cot. I confess I was a bit worried about how to deal with that one. Having declined her offer, I was petrified she'd tell her husband that I'd tried to come on to her as some kind of revenge for the rebuff, but as it transpired she was all sunshine and light when hubbie got home, and I still act for the player. I just make sure I'm never left alone with her.

As I briefly mentioned earlier, nights on the town with players are a nightmare. You have to protect them from too many groups. Fans want to buy them a drink, ask them personal questions, become their new best friend. Opposition fans want to lure them into a fight. Girls want to make them the next notch on their footballers' bedpost. The paparazzi are always at the ready and gossip columnists cling to every word. But most of all you have to protect them from themselves.

To be honest, it would be easier herding mice than trying to control a bunch of footballers out for a good time. They're like kids on the day school breaks up. Even though, in their case, they have to return to school the next day or the day after if they're, at least, going out the night before a day off. I went out with one of my players who'd had a stinker the previous Saturday and who'd also had the mother-and-father of all rows with his missus just before he closed the door of his house behind him. He wasn't in the best of moods, that was for sure, and his first words as we got into the car (and I realised instantly that I wasn't just the minder for the evening but also the dedicated driver) were, 'Right, let's get some down us.'

I'd already arranged access to the footballers' venue of choice (there's one in every town and the photographers camp outside), so off we went with three of his mates, one of whom was a convicted drug dealer. Cocktails mixed with beers followed by some drinking games soon had my player ready to take on the world. I'd arranged a roped-off area, but he still had to get to the loo, and when he did, somebody told him he was crap and he thumped them. He thumped them again for good measure to the point that I wondered if he might have killed the guy. This led to my contact at the nightclub looking for me and dragging me over. They didn't want bad publicity any more than I wanted my client in jail, so we took the victim to the manager's office and cleaned him up, and while he was still a bit woozy I did a deal with him and got him to sign off on something I cobbled together there and then. It cost a few bob and a few free tickets (the player said afterwards that I'd been too generous), but it worked.

The player then carried on as if nothing had happened and managed to pull three different girls before the club closed. He shagged one in the same loo in which he'd just had a fight, one in the manager's office which he now seemed to regard as his own, and another on the back seat of my car while I stared straight ahead, blocked out the noise and just hoped they wouldn't do too much damage to my leatherwork.

He then wanted me to take him on to another place where he knew they did lock-ins, the drug-dealing mate offered me a line of coke, and I knew that somehow or other I had to get him home, which eventually I did only to be greeted by his still raging wife who had been calling him all night.

'It's all your fault,' she screamed at me. 'You just want to be seen out with him so he can help you get some more clients. When he sobers up I'm going to tell him he needs to dump you.'

And, guess what? She did exactly that. The player saw it as a way to appease his wife, and I was made the villain of the piece on both sides. You really can't make this stuff up. And believe me, I'm not.

As you can imagine, agents spend a fair amount of time dealing with the women in their clients' lives. Footballers tend to get married early and have children even earlier. Almost every wedding I've ever attended has had the couple's kid (and sometimes a kid who only belongs to one of them) as a pageboy or bridesmaid. The girlfriend of a footballer can see his potential as a meal ticket as soon as she realises he has a bit of talent, and even if he's never going to be the perfect father or husband, the credit cards, the nice house and the expensive car are more than compensation for nine months of pregnancy.

What they don't realise (and believe me, everything you hear about footballers' wives is true with bells on) is that while it may have been easy to pick up a player who has been on the lash in a nightclub it's a damn sight harder to keep him interested. Players like arm candy, and a pregnant wife or girlfriend rarely looks her best during or after the nine months of gestation. She may think she's been really clever trapping him into the commitment and even cleverer when she gets a second bun in the oven when he's grown a bit bored and started to waver, but that tactic, ultimately, only makes him feel more trapped. More to the point, it means that she's stuck at home more than ever, giving him the time to play away – in all senses of the word.

Players travelling to an away match and staying over in a hotel have the perfect alibi if they have a co-operative roommate who knows when to vacate his bed and let some groupie in, and then knows to say nothing after. To be honest, his teammates are unlikely to gossip as the odds are that the girl would've serviced them both and put another couple of notches on her footballer shag list.

Yet, when it comes to alibis and after illicit sex fallout, the poor old agent is first in line to be telling the fibs and shielding his player from the wrath of his wife. The alibis first because they'll, hopefully, defuse the situation. The first time I did this I had a twinge of guilt because the wife was so sweet. I'd met her at the same time as I'd first met the player because he'd brought her along to 'approve' me. They looked like the perfect couple. He was a decent prospect at a League One club and she was a trainee beautician. They'd been going out since school, and once I got him a move to a Premier League club they actually got married. For once, this couple did things the old-fashioned way, and he got her pregnant on their honeymoon.

Money, fame and opportunity do an awful lot to most footballers – most people, if it comes to that. Right after a pre-season tour he phoned me in an absolute panic. They'd been playing in the States, and he'd met a girl at a hotel bar, and what followed was a story as old as hotel bars and men on their own. It wouldn't have been so much of a problem had the girl been American and just fancied a quickie with a good-looking young guy with a nice physique. But she was from Leeds and she knew all about football. She also knew all about the media and she'd heard that a certain publicist did a nice line in placing kiss-and-tell stories about professional sportsmen. So there I was with Publicist T, lying through my teeth and telling him that on the night in question I'd been in the States and at the team hotel, the only drink my player had consumed was Diet Coke and that I'd been with him all night. I got the story backed up by another of my players on the team, and without any evidence of the liaison no paper would touch the story. The girl was dismissed as a fantasist, but I couldn't really feel any sympathy for her because she genuinely was trying to make a quick buck out of a meaningless shag.

That was an easy lie and not one likely to get me into trouble, but I've told worse than that. I had one player whose lovely wife was safely ensconced in the north while he plied his trade in the south. He went out to celebrate a win, and after over-celebrating somewhat, he woke up in a strange woman's flat where neither he nor she had a surfeit of clothing. Again, whatever the morals of the situation, nobody would've been hurt – had the girl not waited until my client had dressed and left, and then called the police to accuse him of rape, which led to his immediate arrest.

Now, as it happened, he hadn't raped her. He hadn't even had sex with her as a police swab eventually proved. And one of his teammates had been in the same room, albeit on the couch. I had to piece all this together while fielding frantic calls from the player's wife and trying to make sure she didn't become his ex-wife.

I had to think quickly. I couldn't say he was in hospital because she was the sort of loyal companion who'd be down in a shot. The best I could come up with was that he'd lost his voice. I went to the police station and managed to persuade them to give me his mobile phone after they'd checked all the messages and calls (none to or from the girl but quite a lot from the distraught wife). I began a text conversation with the wife pretending to be her husband. I must have been quite convincing because when the police released my client without charge the next day – and he'd miraculously recovered his voice – he told me that his wife had said she wished he lost his voice more often because he was so much more romantic when he was texting.

It didn't always end so happily. Another player was sexting a girl he'd only met the night before and sent her an explicit picture of his impressive private parts. She claimed to be so shocked that when she arose from her swoon her mobile automatically dialled a tabloid newspaper, who then called him, who then referred them to me. I decided it was time to use my brief acquaintance with the celebrity publicist to good use, and for the modest fee of ten grand he managed to tone the story down to one where the paper just reported he'd been sending drunken messages.

There is truly no justice in the world, because his wife blamed me for leading him astray and encouraging him to communicate with strange women. It seemed the player had told her that he and I had made a bet on the subject. As it turned out I was the only loser, having laid out the ten grand and then receiving a termination letter from the player which had clearly been drafted by his wife. Some you win and some you lose. You just have to ensure the wins outnumber the losses, a bit like a football manager.

So, as you'll gather, most of the women in my life are either with somebody else or are blackmailing my clients, and neither scenario forms the perfect basis for a meaningful, lifelong relationship. I know, I need to get a life. And I will. But not just yet.

THE BOOT BOYS

PLEASE DON'T GROAN, but after the sex and scandal of the last chapter I'm returning to football boots. There is a parallel universe somewhere in which money and barter will be obsolete and the only currency will be – yes, you guessed it – football boots. The banks will be run by the footwear manufacturers and its bankers will be the executives and employees who make the life-and-death decisions as to which players (and sometimes which agents) get the freebies – and of more importance, which agent gets the pick of the players over which these shoe-shop divinities exercise some control.

I seemed to be building a jigsaw of ever-increasing dimensions. Just when I thought I had everything in place, I kept discovering there were other puzzle solvers out there who were creating a bigger picture than mine and with substantially more pieces.

At that point in time, the piece I decided was missing was a 'tame' sports goods guy who'd not only push clients my way but would also supply them, and my other players, with an inexhaustible supply of the gear for free. Not really asking very much, was I? But seek and ye shall find is as good a motto as any for making a success of a football agency.

Let's make it quite clear that I'm not slagging off the whole of the sports goods manufacturing industry or suggesting everybody involved is corrupt. What I was planning could hardly be regarded as corruption anyway, at least not by the standards of my own industry. Most of the people at the sporting companies are decent honest folk with a genuine enthusiasm for not only their own company's wares, but also the developments and designs of their competitors. Everybody wants to develop the perfect, innovative boot, and just when you think there's nothing new under the sun a boot appears that tells you you're wrong.

But when a large company gives an executive the power to make gifts then it surely must be apparent that somebody is going to give them gifts in return to be sure they'll be the recipient. It's then that the temptation to break the corporate rules arises – and break the rules is precisely what the odd few do.

I could never understand why a whole clutch of young players at one club would go with one agent. Knowing some of the agents to whom these players migrated, I was sure that it wasn't because they were better at their job than me (or anyone else for that matter). There just had to be another reason. Was it the academy director, the youth team manager, the manager himself on the take? Maybe, but I worked out there was also another common denominator. Same club and same brand of boots.

This hadn't been an angle R had worked, so I had to figure it all out for myself – and this is how it works and how I made it work for me. The companies tended to put a couple of their guys in charge at each big club with one having a specific remit to look after the young players. The kids coming through are in their pockets because these are the men who supply them with boots and kit and so on from an early age, often well before they're even eight years old. Now, I know I've talked about kids as young as ten or eleven with agents sniffing around them, dare I say, grooming them. Yes, I dare, because grooming it is. Not for sexual favours of course but for another kind of control. Player representation.

That's not always the case for a kid with real potential, because somebody may well have got to him before the agent. That somebody may just be the guy from the sports manufacturing company who has got his trust and also that of his parents by spreading the gear around. He's given him boots, maybe a tracksuit, a sweatband, a T-shirt, sunglasses if the company makes them, perhaps even a watch. These companies have such a wide range of products nowadays that they can totally equip a young lad for the big wide world. I'm half expecting them to develop their own brand of condoms any day now. Maybe they do already and I just don't know. As with every free gift there's always a catch, and the catch here is that all the time the kit guy is whispering in the lad's ear, 'I know you're looking for an agent. You don't necessarily want to leave that sort of decision to your mum and dad. They're not football people like you and me, and they're not at the heart of the business like I am. I know who's good, who's bad, who's in and who's out, and more importantly who's right for you.'

That's the moment when they hit them with the name of the agent and the trick is to ensure that the agent is you. Or me, in this case. Yet, as you have probably gathered by now, nothing is for nothing in this dog-eat-dog world of ours. As I've said, there are many decent guys working their arses off for the big companies. But fortunately for us there are also a few who, as was put in a court case a while ago, 'like a bung'.

The bung (I really hate that word, but I suppose it's less sinister and sounds less criminal than a bribe) can take several forms. Either the agent simply pays the introducer from the boot company a lump sum for every player who signs with him (the sum varying according to the status of the player) or he puts him on his payroll permanently and gives him a retainer and/or a percentage of everything he makes from the player in question.

Yes, I know. Don't bother to tell me. It's a bribe and it's illegal, but so is driving at eighty miles an hour on the motorway and everybody does that. And so much of our business is illegal that you kind of get immune to thinking of it like that. This is a victimless crime all round, anyway, so there's little need for a sleepless night about it. The general rule in football agency is that if you stick to the rules you won't make any money. So, to get on in the business you have to bend or break them, simply roll the dice and take your chances.

Unlike in many other sports (the gentleman's game of cricket for example) I've never heard of any agents being prosecuted for bribery and corruption, while I have heard of a fair few making enough for an early retirement, so I'm thinking the risk of breaking the rules has to be worth it.

Lately a fair number of the experienced guys from the sports manufacturing industry have come across to the so-called 'dark side' and become licensed (or unlicensed in some cases) agents themselves. They've generally spent their whole working lives playing it by the book, earning a living wage but no more, and watched the agents for the players they service raking it in. So you can hardly blame them for waking up one morning, smelling the roses and realising that their contacts within the game are pure gold dust and can be sprinkled around to make pure gold for themselves.

I don't have a problem with that. There's nothing wrong with competition. If getting clients were like plucking apples off a tree it would be plain boring. What I do object to is unfair competition where the odds are stacked against you, and believe me there's a fair bit of that around.

So, to level the odds, I've got myself a real live boot guy. He didn't come cheap. These boys know their value and he's screwed me for half of everything I get from the players he introduces to me. But, as I've said before, half of something is better than a whole of nothing, so we'll see where it goes. I don't see it being a long-term relationship because tomorrow he'll want sixty per cent, the day after seventy and so on. And when he gets to ninety he'll think, let's push it to a hundred and strike out and I'll start my own business. I'm prepared for that. I've become very cynical in my few years at this game. It's the only way to survive. Optimists become complacent. Pessimists don't get off their arses because they think they're going to fail. It's a world for cynical realists. Which led me to the conclusion that if my guy left me it wouldn't be the end of the world because there would be another one waiting in line. There always is.

PLAYER AGENTS

AS IF THE business isn't tough enough already, FIFA and the smug fat bastards who run it are about to make it a whole lot tougher. Indeed, by the time you come to read this, they may have done just that. The Licensed Agent will be an extinct species and this will be a history book. Do I hear you say, good, you deserve it? Well, maybe so, but it's the only way I know how to make a living nowadays and a hell of a lot of the other agents plying their trade and trying to turn an honest buck are a lot nicer than me. Not hard, do I hear you say? Well, I promised myself that I'd be honest in this book so I surely get a few Brownie points for integrity.

I've talked about the raggle-taggle bunch of gypsies who operate unlicensed and unqualified. Well, in the perfect illustration of 'if you can't beat them join them', as I've mentioned before, FIFA has invited them into the football family and wants to legitimise them and call them 'intermediaries'. This lot will include all the various villains I've described in this book and a few more besides, not to mention the hundreds of wannabe agents who have never been able to pass the exam. It's a kind of reward for working under the radar for so long. That, in itself, wouldn't be so bad except that at the same time they want to delegitimise me and all the other agents and call us, er, 'intermediaries'.

That's right. Everything we've worked for now counts for nothing, and all those guys who have been putting two fingers up to the FA for years not only have an amnesty but an actual reward – the chance to go out there and compete against us on what is an allegedly level playing field. Only it won't be. Whatever our shortcomings, we do know what we're doing, not just for ourselves but our clients as well. These chancers think they can make quick and easy money at the expense of the players and the clubs. Oh, and at the expense of those of us who've been at it for years.

I don't have a crystal ball, but this is how I see it panning out. A current footballer, who's been tapping up your players during his own playing career with a view to persuading them to leave you and join another agency, can now retire from the game and seamlessly set up his own business alongside mine. I say 'his own business', but the truth is, as you'll have gathered by now, that there are quite a few footballers out there who have happily run their own agencies for years, even while playing.

You can imagine the conversations at the club and in the dressing rooms. The experienced pro (quite often a high-profile international) tells a young emerging talent that he'd like to look after him both on and off the pitch. You know, 'Stick with me, kid, and I'll see you all right.'

Managers tend to listen to their more experienced players who often, as their club captains, are their mouthpieces on the pitch. If the captain suggests to a manager that he's got a nugget in the reserves or even in the youth team and academy, then that kid will have a better chance of getting noticed. Of course he has still got to be a decent player to get on but he definitely has a better chance than another decent player with the same ability who doesn't have a senior pro batting for him.

Players know they're generally done in football at thirty-five unless they're a keeper. In fact, from thirty onwards it's generally a slippery slope, and in the descent they can see their salaries slip from twenty, thirty, forty, fifty grand a week right the way to a grand or even less. Once a player goes beneath the Championship then he's playing either because he's so hooked that he can't stop or (and this is far worse than any addiction) because he needs to carry on. He's had the money and for one reason or other he's blown it – a bad business decision, a dodgy tax-shelter investment (sometimes actually suggested by his agent in return for a not insubstantial commission), an expensive divorce or worst of all a serious gambling, drug or alcohol problem.

So, if you're on the outside looking in, you may not blame a player for seeking to feather his nest while he has the chance to get his hands on the material with which to line it. All he's doing is making plans for his life after football and if that afterlife is representing players and doing it totally for his own benefit, ridding himself of the agent he's used to front for him during his playing days, then who can blame him? Well, me and my fellow agents for one. We've no problem with the players who've passed the exam and done everything right, gaining their experience within a reputable agency on the job. It's these snakes who've slithered around nicking our clients to which we object.

Footballers who want to muscle into the agency game are in many ways our biggest threat. A really high-profile player, a household name and a so-called respected international specialised in trying to persuade players (whoever represented them) to leave their agents. He did this by bad-mouthing all agents, saying they were leeches taking money out of the game and in particular out of the pockets of the poor players. This didn't stop him then getting them to sign up to another agent he nominated just as soon as the player was free to sign (and sometimes even before that to get him to sign an undated contract to be dated as soon as his old one expired).

While he's waiting for the old contract to run down the player/agent guides the player through the troubled seas of the current agent's wrath. First of all, he tells him, don't return any calls or respond to any emails or texts. 'In fact, change your number – I'll arrange that for you – and don't give the new one to your agent. If a new deal comes along I'll advise you because I know what everybody at the club is earning. You can just say you acted for yourself and if you want to give me anything in cash out of the extra money I get you then that would be nice, but not obligatory. And if your agent threatens to sue you then I'll get someone to have a quiet word with him to tell him we'll make sure he loses all his other clients as well if he so much as calls a lawyer.'

The thing is that everybody knows this goes on. The tabloids are always sniffing around the story of a player secretly running (or at the very least, owning) his own agency. But as with so many wrongdoings, knowing is one thing and proving is another, and after the phone-hacking fiasco and the resultant pay-outs, the newspapers and their legal advisers are becoming increasingly cautious as to what they actually print. Even when they're certain it's true.

These wannabe agent-players are generally the brighter ones and know how to play their cards just right. There is the lead card of: 'All agents are thieves, and why pay one when you can get more money for yourself by working with the likes of me. I've been there. I've been ripped off. I can prevent it from happening to you.'

They're also not averse to playing the race card.

'Hey, I'm black, you're black. So come on, bro, why would you want to make your white agent even richer than the motherfucker already is? Let's keep it in the family. Right?' Right.

It's not just the players who are trying to be surrogate agents but the managers themselves. They can play one end against the middle as well. Tell the chairman that the player is worth more than he really is, put in an agent friend to do the deal, and Bob's your uncle. It works even better when a manager/agent wants to bring in a player from abroad. I've already explained to you how an agent can manipulate a transfer fee but how much better placed is a manager to do just that?

They bring the player in, recommend the financial package, get a friendly agent (either their English mate or his foreign partner) to do the deal and then take a walloping great slice of the commission from a totally inflated contract. Works every time.

I know of one case where a manager simply waltzed into a club with a player as his 'friend'. He sat quietly while the buying club made its offer and then told the player that he knew for a fact that there were players there on far more. He ended up getting the player double what had first been on offer and also ended up getting a very generous thank-you present from the player. I doubt the buying club or its manager were that grateful, but they still did fuck all about it.

That's one of the problems with being an agent who has never played the game. It's a them-and-us situation, and you're never going to be regarded as part of the football family which seems to be able to close ranks at the slightest hint of a threat from an outsider. They may seem to be deadly rivals when on opposite sides, but when it's one of their own against an agent they're suddenly all brothers in arms. It's a bit like the medical profession. I'm told on good authority that one of the hardest things to find is a doctor prepared to say that another doctor was negligent and give evidence to that effect.

This competition with agents can go even further up the ladder. There are directors, chief executives and even a chairman (or so I'm informed) at it as well. One of my players was arousing a fair amount of interest amongst other clubs. His manager told him that he was going nowhere, and although I did my best to persuade him to let him go he just wasn't having any of it. My player wasn't happy either with the club, or me for that matter. But then, suddenly, the chairman of his current club called him in and told him that he'd only allow the move to happen if he let him, the chairman, handle everything. Which he did, totally to his own advantage, and although the player got more money at the new club, there was no doubt that a fair amount which should've gone into his contract ended up in the chairman's pocket.

I did think about suing or going to the media, or even the FA, but I knew I'd get no sympathy, merely adverse publicity. It would cost me a fortune and I'd just be chasing my losses. And so, I had to be pragmatic and move on. Yet you never forget in this business. Jack Charlton used to talk about his 'little black book'. Well, I don't have the opportunity on the pitch to kick seven bells of shit out of those who have crossed me, but I sure as hell have made a mental note. What is it the Chinese say? If you sit by the banks of the river long enough then you'll see the bodies of your enemies float by. I was quite prepared to sit there – metaphorically speaking at least because I fucking hate fishing – until Doomsday.

What that chairman did to me was only one step away from the manager or the chairman putting in a close relation to set up an agency of which he owns a chunk. Or even if the relative has carved out a career for himself as a football agent, pushing players in his direction.

One very famous manager told a player that if he didn't drop his agent for a move that was in the offing he'd destroy his career and have him in the reserves for the rest of his time at the club. When the player cheekily asked him who he'd recommend he didn't hesitate putting a very close relation forward as somebody of whom he'd approve.

And so it goes on. Everybody wants a slice of the action. Everybody wants a piece of a player, a deal, and whatever else they've got – usually quite a lot in the case of a manager or a player – it's never quite enough. Money somehow or other breeds the pursuit of more money. It becomes another kind of addiction, another obsession. But then who am I to preach from the top of my high moral mountain? After all, am I really any better than those I look down on? Forgive me for saying that I truly think I am. And it's that thought that drives me on, that keeps me going when, as fast as I run, I don't seem ever to be able to move from the same spot.

CORNERED

THERE ARE LOTS of terms for illegal cash in our business: readies, sweeties, chocolate. Whatever you want to call it, there's an awful lot of it about and an awful lot of it stashed away. Whether it's kept in a security safe in a bank, a cardboard box under the stairs or one of the depositories that specialises in storing ill-gotten gains, it's still there and it's still illegal.

For a long while I couldn't figure out how it was generated but as I've mentioned before there are willing bag men amongst the agents (not to mention willing Swiss bankers) who are ready to facilitate its availability if not its creation.

I stumbled into a meeting once where a huge sum was about to be generated and I have to say, even though by that stage I thought I was unshockable, I was shocked.

I was acting – or thought I was acting – for a player moving between two medium-sized Premiership clubs. I'd spoken to the buying manager, and he'd told me he liked the player and that I should meet him for a chat. I thought it a bit odd at the time that he'd chosen a hotel room as a location, but what was even odder was that when I got there he was sitting down for a drink with the manager of the club that was selling the player and my old friend Mr Fixit.

They were all clearly old friends, reminiscing about this player and that, and I truly felt as if I'd arrived at a private party without an invitation and inappropriately dressed. They had a few drinks, tried, unsuccessfully, to ply me with a few as well, and although none of them were drunk they were loosening up while I remained stone cold sober and felt very uptight. And yes, I have to say it, a bit judgemental. I just felt better than them, superior, because whatever I might have done or been prepared to do, I'd never flaunted it, never broadcast it. Whatever I'd done, in or out of Vegas, had stayed in Vegas, and I liked it that way. Liked the fact that nobody had anything on me to give them the power to make me do anything I did not want to do.

Somewhere along the line they exchanged looks and left it to Mr Fixit to do the talking.

'Listen, there's a deal to be done here. It might not be the deal you thought you were going to do, but if you don't do it our way then I'm afraid there won't be a deal at all.'

Nothing like coming straight to the point, I thought, realising they'd summed me up and arrived at the conclusion that foreplay was a waste of time and they might as well just rip my knickers off and go for a full gang bang.

He took my silence for acquiescence and then continued. 'Right, so this is the deal. I've seen what you want for your boy. [I was always efficient and had sent a deal proposal ahead of the meeting.] You can fucking forget that. K here [he pointed to the buying manager] is going to give him [he named a figure a good twenty-five per cent below what I wanted]. You said you wanted five per cent from each side [I always tried it on, hoping to get five per cent between the two sides.] Well, you can fucking forget that too. In fact you can forget putting your name on the deal. We've spoken to your boy, and he's agreed to act for himself. We're going to give you [he named a figure which was about two per cent of the deal]. It'll be in cash, so you won't be that out of pocket. After that you say nothing. You don't comment on the transfer fee paid, you don't say you did the deal. You just say you and the player fell out, and you didn't want to stand in the way of his career. You cancel your rep contract and we all move on.'

'And that's it?' I said.

'That's it. Take it or leave it. Don't even think about trying to negotiate with us. You're playing with the big boys, and all you've brought to the party are your soft toys.'

I hesitated for a moment, tempted to make the grand gesture and walk out, and then thought maybe I should speak to my player first. I reached for my phone and saw just a flicker of emotion on Mr Fixit's face as, for a moment, he must have wondered if I'd recorded the conversation. No such luck. I'd not been expecting anything like this so I'd come unprepared.

'Go on,' he said, now anticipating my move. 'Call your lad.'

I did. It went to voicemail, so I tried again. All I got back was a text from the player asking me to leave him alone. I got the message.

Of course, I should've told them to get stuffed. But they were offering me a choice between fifty grand in readies and a long legal battle to get my money from the player for breach of contract. I made my choice. A bad one in hindsight because now I'd stooped to their level and I was one of them, whether I wanted to be or not.

It was only afterwards that I worked out just how they were going to generate the money for my payout, not to mention making far more money themselves. The buying club was going to be delighted, because the manager would show them what I'd wanted and what he'd managed to get the player to take while forcing me (and my hundred grand fee) out of the transaction. He was on some kind of bonus deal when he saved the club money. On the other hand, the agent for the selling club's manager would've carved out a commission deal for himself with him advising the club what was a fair figure and the buying club's manager endorsing that. All very cosy. And very remunerative for all concerned – except me, who'd had to take a cut in fees, and the poor player, who had got a crap deal and foolishly been persuaded to believe it was as good as he was going to get, and was the only way the transfer was going to happen.

It wasn't to be the last time I'd have problems with managers, but after this incident anything seemed possible. I'd tested my own boundaries and found I didn't really have any.

When I tried to move a player to another club, I received a call from another agent telling me this was 'his club' and he had to be involved in any transfers there so what was I offering. To be fair to him he did, at least, come up with a solution – namely that I carry on acting for the player, but that he would act for the club and we'd pool whatever we got, with him taking sixty per cent and me forty. That was generous after my Mr Fixit deal, which saw what I would've earned reduced by half.

It beggars belief that shrewd businessmen who buy clubs and bring in hand-picked managers then let them rape and pillage the club alongside their chosen agent. I guess it works, so long as the manager succeeds on the pitch and delivers trophies, but he can be very exposed once the results start going pear-shaped.

I've never been too sure how far up the tree this sort of corruption goes. I know there are one or two dodgy CEOs and I know at least one director who is right at the heart of the sort of scam I've described above. But who knows? If you buy a club, it's very hard to make a profit or take money out, so I suppose you could regard this as an inventive way of awarding oneself a bonus. Does it make it right? Is anything in football *right*?

THE MEDIA GAME

L IFE USED TO be so simple when it came to the media. The players would attend a press conference a few days before a match and then play, give a few interviews afterwards and that was it for the week. Not exactly stressful for the player or the agent, and if the agent was skilful he might even be able to manipulate a few bob out of a paper for an exclusive and charge his commission – twenty per cent of course.

How times have changed – and certainly not for the better. You have to satisfy not just the papers but also Sky and BT Sport and all the rolling news stations and of course the radio programmes and their phone-ins. There is a huge appetite for gossip and news about clubs, players and managers, and somehow or other the agent has to find a way to satisfy that. Every fucking day, if you represent a high-profile player or manager.

The problem is the unpredictability of your client and the all-seeing all-hearing eyes and ears of the press. I dread the danger hours at the end of the day when one of my players has either drunk too much and been thrown out of a nightclub or has been arrested for drink-driving or molesting a girl at said club. There are a hundred other scenarios that might happen and I keep a couple of lawyers' numbers handy. You'd be amazed at the number of times I need them.

There are some criminal lawyers who specialise in sorting out the problems of high-profile individuals, and footballers in particular. That doesn't make them bad people, but it does make them expensive people, and an agent is always torn between getting the money from his client or covering the cost himself. The player is almost always in a better financial position to pay, and it's usually his own fault that he's found himself up the creek without a paddle, but somehow or other he doesn't see it like that.

Forgetting the criminal or civil repercussions, it never hurts to have a couple of journos as mates. I was going to say 'in your pocket' but surprisingly, given the awful press the press gets from its own, they're a pretty incorruptible mob. I've never heard of an agent being able to silence a story with a bribe, although I have known of the sort of barter that the PR gurus indulge in.

'I've got a big transfer coming up and I'll give you the nod on that one if you take your foot off the accelerator on this one.'

The problem with that is if you think football is a village then Fleet Street and, indeed, the whole of the Fourth Estate is much worse. I know all about the phone-hacking stuff as I've had clients hacked. But somehow or other it's very hard to keep any secret from the media when it comes to football, and I've read about deals in which I've been involved in the paper before there was even a deal. The fact is that it isn't just agents and players to whom journalists speak: it's everybody from the kit man up at the club, and believe me, the kit man hears and knows everything.

Speaking of kit men I once negotiated a deal for a player which I thought was pretty good. The player then called me up to say it wasn't enough and he'd spoken to a few people about it who all thought I was suggesting a shit package. I asked him who he'd spoken to, and while he was at first reluctant to tell me, he finally admitted it had been the kit man. Oh well, when these new intermediary regulations come in, all the kit men can give up their day job and become intermediaries – as I'm sure they think they can do a better job than us lousy agents.

Back to the media. They also love sound bites from agents. The trouble is that the agents they pick to give them aren't always the ones the rest of us want to be judged by. They used to use the bloke with the long cigars a lot. Interesting guy, but one of a kind, and I've never met anybody else like him in the business. But he was entertaining, and the media loved him so that was the picture the public got of us. Recently they stuck a cowboy hat on another agent they interviewed and had him walking down a street market. What the fuck? Draw your own conclusions from how he fell into that one.

The thing is that when somebody sticks a mike under your nose you have to think in a nanosecond, and it isn't always possible to come out with what you really wanted to say. And you have to say something. The media rarely have direct access to a player unless it's at a club press conference, or they collar him going in or out of the training ground. Consequently, the second best route is through his agent. As I say, agents do have favoured journalists, and although that doesn't stop the bloodiest-minded and most vindictive of them writing what they want anyway, it does make them think twice before they burn their bridges irreparably with any given agent.

I've always been wary of the press but I do have a private rule that I'll give all and any of them one chance to show they're trustworthy by telling them something 'off the record' to see if it shows up in their columns. Of course, I've been let down. Every agent has. Journalists, particularly the younger ones, can't afford to play the long game so they'd rather go for the big story than the long-term relationship. That's their problem. Though on one occasion, it became mine.

I was trying to keep a story about my client's gambling and womanising out of the paper and said, 'off the record', that I'd look after the journo on any future transfer deals and give him a heads up. The bastard printed his story in full including my proposed deal. Neither the player (nor the player's mum, in particular) nor the player's current club were best pleased, and it eventually cost me the player, who wouldn't sign a new rep contract with me because he claimed I couldn't be trusted to keep my mouth shut with the press.

Some agents I know get hooked on fame and being a Z-list celebrity themselves. They love giving interviews and sound bites, love seeing their names in the papers just as much as their clients'. It's not a new phenomenon. The agents of George Best, Gazza and more recently Wayne Rooney became household names but, just as with the players themselves, the British press loves nothing more than to put a person up on a pedestal just to knock them down.

That's why I try to keep myself to myself. I don't want to be waking up in the morning and finding myself splashed all over the papers for something that some sleazebag of a journo has dug up about my personal life. Mind you, as you'll have gathered, they might have a hard job given that I have no personal life.

I've seen it happen to other agents though. Tax scandals, criminal proceedings, gaffes in public speaking, racist allegations, affairs . . . you name it, my compatriots have either done it or been accused of doing it.

So far, the worst I've experienced is when somebody wrote that I'd taken half a million quid out of a deal where, at its start, I didn't act for the player or either club. I did know the player, and he'd asked me for some informal advice, and we'd met for a drink from time to time, but on this occasion, although the clubs between them were alleged in a tabloid to have paid a million quid of agents' fees, none of that had found its way into my pocket. The player was amused, the FA less so and I had to satisfy them that the report was wrong. However, I decided to do nothing about it because I thought it might help my profile. Big mistake. When my accountant filed my tax return for the relevant year HMRC got interested and asked why I hadn't declared the half mill that the paper had said I'd received. It finally got sorted out, but not before I'd had to pay a hefty fee to my accountant and endure the lovely guys at the FA watching me like a hawk for a while to see what I got up to next below the radar.

It's all very well saying that anything you read in the paper is tomorrow's fish-and-chips wrapper, but you never know who reads the garbage. An agent acquaintance (I was going to say a friend but we can't afford that sort of luxury in this business) always used his media contacts to generate interest for any unhappy player. Unfortunately, for him and one of his clients, the player's current club used the articles to support their claim that the player had actually asked for a transfer, which meant that they were entitled to say he'd forfeited the balance of his signing-on fee (a small matter of two hundred grand). What had started as a favour to the player had become a serious liability. The player denied that he'd authorised or known about the articles, but nobody believed that. After some serious horse-trading the agent managed to get the club to agree to pay half, and also got the player a deal at a new club, which was so good that it meant he lost nothing. On that occasion the story had a happy ending but it's pretty unusual.

Another agent loved to play the system and act for the buying club when he was really always acting for the player. That sort of thing always sets off warning signals with the FA as well as the Revenue, neither of which are totally stupid and who realise that it's being done to avoid the player paying any tax on the agent's fees and also avoid paying any VAT. It doesn't sound the best when I put it that way, and I can see why the Revenue would be sore, although as with most 'avoidances' I really can't see why it should be any of the FA's business other than to stop an agent earning more than the bloke who is trying to stop him earning it!

This agent was taken by the smell of the greasepaint and the roar of the crowd and decided to play Billy Big Time by describing to all and sundry who'd listen that the player was 'his'. Now, there's a little man (it may be men, it may be women, it may even be a few of each) who sits in the department that HMRC have set up (I think in Birmingham), cuts out interesting little snippets from the papers about footballers (and other sportsmen and women and entertainers) and then follows the trail to see if they lead to any kind of tax evasion. Somebody saw the agent's comments, and when it came to the deal saw the agent had acted for the club. Bingo! For the Revenue that was it. They hit the player with a tax demand saying that the payment by the club to the agent who said he'd acted for it (the same agent who'd said in the media he acted for the player) was really a payment on behalf of the player and therefore a benefit in kind and therefore taxable. I'd love to have been a fly on the wall when the player got the demand and called the agent.

That's the problem with most of the guys running around in this business. They only think of today, not tomorrow. If a deal looks too good to miss then why miss it? If you can play the system and try and fool the taxman while inflating your own ego, then why not? The answer is very simple. Because tomorrow always comes a-knocking and very often has company in the shape of the taxman or the football authorities or even the police. Whenever I read something like that I always vowed to be more careful. I vowed, but then temptation gets put in my way, and hey, I'm only human. And I'm a football agent, and while some people may feel those two identities don't really fit too snugly together I beg to differ.

SWIMMING WITH SHARKS

I'VE NEVER BEEN one for gambling myself. I've always thought life to be a big enough risk on its own without stacking the odds even further against you. But, go tell that to footballers. Whereas an agent's time is precious, with every minute counting, footballers have all the time in the world to fill.

They will roll into training around nine in the morning, admire each other's expensive cars for a while, have some free breakfast provided by the club, run around for a bit, kick a few balls, have a free lunch and then bugger off. Some of the more progressive coaches are now organising double sessions so they actually have to stay for a while after lunch, but, generally speaking, unless there's a match in the evening then the rest of the day is theirs to waste as they will.

The options for their free time, their 'me' time, are standard. Sleep, golf, more sleep, shopping, a new tattoo, snooker (a bit passé now), a DVD, or . . . a bet. Or two, or three, or as many bets as they can make before the money runs out. I may be doing many of them a great wrong as I'm sure there are players who are happy to push a buggy, take the older kids to the park to play football (of course), or even go to Tesco with the missus. It's just that I've never met any.

I'm not the sort of agent who tries to interfere in my clients' lifestyle choices, so what they do in their spare time is entirely up to them. If they want to have an orgy or indulge in dogging, wife-swapping or a bit of S&M (and there are certainly some who do), well, good luck with that as long as they keep it to themselves and nobody takes photos. I've had to deal with blackmail attempts and investigative journalists, and neither situation is great fun. Only when their habits interfere with my lifestyle or my income do I start to get concerned. And a player who gets himself up shit creek with his gambling habits can be a real drain on his agent's wallet. And this is why.

As long as a player is making a fortune from a deal secured by his agent, then everything in the garden is rosy. When he loses that same fortune in one way or another, then the smell of rotting compost can totally overpower the sweet scent of the roses. The player may well have his back against the wall, will almost certainly not have told his free-spending wife that she needs to cut back on the pedicures and designer clothes, and will be looking to dig himself out of his situation. Generally this is done by the player seeking to get more money, one way or another, so that he can chase his losses because, like every compulsive, addicted gambler, he's convinced himself that his luck is just about to change. It isn't. But he won't believe that until he's run out of prospects from whom he can borrow.

There are plenty of loan sharks out there, many of whom have a connection to the sort of bookies who are happy to arrange preferential accounts for players with credit lines even beyond their astronomic means. Taking money from them is not a good idea. It is, in fact, a very bad one because they tend to get rather upset when the loans don't get repaid.

Another agent told me about a visit he received at his suburban home at two in the morning from a shark who suggested that if he wanted to have a live player to represent then he should consider paying the player's debt, as there wasn't a great demand in the industry for a footballer with broken legs and fractured kneecaps. The agent, wanting the visitors to leave, asked how much and was told it was sixty grand – but that the following week it would be sixty-five. The agent declined to pay, knowing his player was on fifty grand a week and, he thought, could well afford to pay the debt himself.

However, when he sat down with his client the next day to go through his finances, he discovered that the loan shark who had called on him was just one of several creditors chasing the player and, on top of that, there were half-a-dozen hire-purchase agreements for cars he'd acquired over the past few years at various stages of his career, not to mention a trophy house with negative equity. Agents often get involved in property as well, as most footballers like to buy off-plan new-builds. There is always a developer around to look to for commission along with lawyers prepared to throw in an introductory fee to get the conveyancing.

Footballers tend to stockpile cars in very much the same way as my nan used to hoard tins of baked beans. After she died we found over fifty of them in her pantry going back over a quarter of a century. Players will either get bored with the car they have or lust after bigger, better and more recent models than those their teammates are flashing about in the training-ground car park. They may acquire one for a girlfriend who then becomes an ex-girlfriend and departs in the seat of the very same car that has just been bought for her (that departure probably having been triggered by the player again lusting after a bigger and better and more recent model).

Another scenario is that the player has given a car to a mate or lent it to a teammate or even, in one famous instance, forgotten where he'd parked it. It's quite incomprehensible to the likes of me, who has driven the same car for three years or more, that expensive vehicles can simply vanish in transit, particularly when they belong to the finance company rather than the player himself. It follows that the players, like the bookmakers, are going to get a bit antsy when the asset they've bought disappears and the person they've lent the money to in order to buy it stops the repayments.

Anyway, this agent's player was trying unsuccessfully to service three major debts to cover his bookies, six finance agreements and a bank overdraft, plus pay off his maxed-out credit cards, keep a mortgage that was a hundred grand more than the house it was secured on, and in between all this – it was hard to believe he'd actually found the time – had fathered a child for which he was paying maintenance. All in all he was in total financial meltdown, and when his agent sat down with him to try to help him sort things out, the player came up with a remarkably simple solution.

'I tell you what, mate,' he told the agent. 'You've earned a fucking fortune out of me so why don't you sort it out.' Footballers aren't generally the brightest of individuals, but, as I've said before, when it comes to money they do seem to have the ability to cut through all the crap and get straight to the heart of the problem.

The agent was now faced with a major conundrum. He had, indeed, earned a fair old wedge from the deals he'd done for the player, but paying off his debts was going to mean giving most of it back with no guarantee there'd be more to come in the future. Eventually he agreed to sort things out on condition that the player signed a new representation contract with him, and he did in fact manage to recover most of his investment when the player moved clubs. But then the cycle started all over again. Gambling, losses, loans and this time around the agent decided to quit while he was ahead, particularly because the player's loss of form (doubtless caused by his head being at the race track while his legs were at the match) meant any new deal was unlikely to be as remunerative as the previous ones.

Gambling amongst footballers is pandemic. It often starts with card games on the match-day coach when players can lose amongst themselves what would be ridiculous sums of money to you and me. They chase losses even there, trying to impress teammates (they all lie about what they're earning anyway as nobody wants to be seen to be earning less than the next man, any more than he wants to have a cheaper car) and it spirals from there.

Although the current thinking among football authorities is to ban gambling in football altogether, until recently the restrictions only extended to games where the player had potentially some influence, or some inside information. Given that all players and agents know somebody at almost every club, that should be a very sweeping restriction, but it doesn't work that way in practice. Footballers are quite happy to shove their agents in the firing line when it comes to taking a bullet for putting themselves in the position where they stand to win money from a result they can influence in some way or other, or where they have inside information that can affect the result. An agent placing a bet is likely to attract less interest than a footballer, and most of them don't want to upset their clients by refusing a simple request like that.

Unusual betting patterns will get picked up by the larger betting companies such as Corals, Ladbrokes, Paddy Power and so on, but many of the gambling players have their own tame bookie who can be licensed, maybe just a guy who stands on the rails at the smaller race meetings, or unlicensed, the old-fashioned street bookie with his own unique methods of collection, as illustrated before. It's hard for players or their agents to fix matches because so many participants are required. It's much easier in cricket, and agents there haven't been slow in coming forward to assist. Yet it's not so hard to fix an element of a match, given that bets can be placed on almost anything: free kicks, yellow and red cards, goal times and so on. A dishonest player working in conjunction with an agent to whom he's feeding information can make a nice little fortune on the side.

I've had my own experiences here, and although I'm not easily scared I have to say they gave me a few sleepless nights. It all started off innocently enough. A couple of African guys contacted me and asked me if I wanted to help them in setting up some friendly matches. They seemed genuine, dropped the right names, and I reckoned it was at least worth a meeting with them. They came across and told me that they controlled the national teams of three different African countries and could get me exclusivity for their friendlies. They also said I could have free rein in the dressing rooms. As I quickly worked out, that meant access to half a dozen Premiership players so it had to be worth exploring further. Then came the catch. I had to go to one of the countries and meet the president of its national association, as he always wanted to know with whom he was dealing.

I started to feel a bit nervous. 'Does he want anything out of this?' I asked.

The two men looked offended. 'Of course not. He just wants to be sure that he's dealing with the right sort of people.'

So, I went ahead and booked a ticket and I did indeed meet the president who was charm itself as we sat by the pool at the five-star hotel he'd arranged as the venue.

'I do need something in writing,' I said.

Everybody nodded. *Of course, of course . . .*

I got back to England and had some paperwork drafted. And then things took a turn. My two new chums said they had an agreement for one of the countries to come over to London and play a friendly international here in an area where many of their countrymen lived. But they needed a company with a track record to sign off on the deal and they were fairly new at the game, so would I do it, please?

I took a look at the contract and fortunately got my lawyer to look at it too. He soon spotted something very odd. There was a clause where the promoter (me) had the right to appoint the officials for the match. As he wasn't slow in telling me, that was really not normal.

I went back to my buddies and asked the reason for the clause, and by then they obviously felt I was sufficiently involved to tell me that if we had our own officials we could control the score in the game, and if we could control that then certain friends of theirs in the Far East would be so happy that everybody – me, them and the president – would be royally rewarded.

I pointed out that this was in essence match fixing and that was a tad illegal. They looked at me blankly (well I guessed it was blankly as they rarely removed their designer sunglasses) and tried to persuade me that it couldn't really be match fixing because these were friendlies and nobody really cared about the result.

'Except these guys who plan to bet millions on it,' I pointed out. 'Listen, guys, thanks for thinking of me, but no thanks.'

And I was out of there. It was then that the threats started. To my body, my business, and when they got to my parents I decided it was time to go to the police.

The police listened and then asked me if I'd be prepared to go back into the ring but wired up, so they could nail them. It was now like something out of a TV thriller and I really was out of my comfort zone, so I refused. The police said they couldn't make me do it, but I sensed I wasn't making friends on the Force and there was to come a time when I knew that for sure.

Such scams aren't always successful. One agent was told by one of his players that his team was decimated by a virus but the manager had managed to keep the news under his hat. Knowing that his team was going to be under-strength for a weekend game, the player got his agent and his mates to place bets throughout the week on the opposition. Although the bets were spread out over any number of high-street betting shops, it got picked up when they laid them off with the big boys. Betting was suspended, and the weakened team duly lost by a hatful. The match wasn't fixed as such, so the bookies were in a quandary as to whether or not they paid out. The regulatory bodies weren't subject to such hesitation and began an investigation into the source of the leaked information and who had been placing the bets, ensuring ultimately that the big winners became big losers.

One player I knew was always in debt. He'd inherited the habit from his father, a small-time shopkeeper who, when in arrears to an impatient taxman, tried to charge wannabe agents for the privilege of representing his son. Some poor mug paid in good faith – always a mistake when it comes to footballers' fathers – only to find that there was an auction going on, and not only was he one of several bidders but the father regarded his deposit as non-refundable.

The player joined the agent who was 'chosen' by his father, but then as he himself ran up all sorts of debts arising from a disastrous gambling streak, he drifted from agent to agent, always spinning them a convincing yarn as to why he was changing. The only consistent factor was the chaos he caused along the way.

One of the lucky agents was convinced that whatever he lent the player he would recoup from the next deal. However, there were so many calls asking for just one more loan that eventually the agent ran out of patience – and nearly ran out of money. The player called again, asking for some money to put on a horse that was a racing certainty . . . that then lost. What he wanted to do was to back against the horse which was a hot favourite. Now, you might've thought that there would be alarm bells ringing for the agent, but not a bit of it. The agent got the name of the horse, told the player he'd get back to him and then promptly got a friend to place the bet the player had wanted to make, but this time for his own benefit.

The horse duly lost, and even before the agent could count his winnings the Jockey Club was on his case with an investigation into illegal betting using inside information that, in effect, the race was fixed. The agent ignored the Jockey Club, they warned him off in his absence, and what he didn't realise was that the effect of a ban by one sporting body meant that he automatically lost his licence with another, namely the FA.

The player moved on to yet another agent, caring not a jot for the fate of his erstwhile agent, and got another lucrative playing deal while the agent lost his business.

It just goes to show that it's not always the agents leading the players astray; it can often be quite the reverse. We're just a bunch of angelic choirboys, really.

SPECULATE TO ACCUMULATE

NOWADAYS, WHEN IT comes to getting clients on board, a slush fund not only helps but is a real necessity. There is so much competition to sign up players that, generally speaking, you need that little edge, and when it comes to players and their families that 'little edge' comes in the shape of a crisp fifty-pound note.

Inducements are more endemic when it comes to young players, particularly really young ones, but the older ones aren't slow to come forward when they hear the inviting rustle of folding paper. With them it's not need, it's greed.

After nearly four years of building up my business and my connections I was forced (OK, I wasn't really forced, I did it for the money not because a gun was being held to my head) into a deal with one of my more experienced clients where I had to give him back half of any fee (in cash, of course). Talk about half a loaf being better than none. Never truer than in my world. I learned from R that you always need to be on the lookout for deals with fellow agents, whether licensed or not, and it's often from the deals you do with the unlicensed guys that you're able to generate the cash to spread around. Sometimes I think I should just buy myself a pipe (musical variety) and skip through the woods scattering notes of the paper variety in front of talented young kids while tootling the other kind of notes. Yep, the Pied Piper of the Premier League. That's me.

You can share more with your player when he hasn't signed a representation contract with you, and you can represent the club in the deal when he makes his move. It's a high-risk strategy because the player can shaft you at the last minute either by bringing in somebody else (who might up the ante of the fifty per cent) or (and this is not unknown) going to the club direct, telling them you're no longer involved, and asking for all of what would've been your fee to be added to his contract. Really nice behaviour, but you come not to expect better.

Anyhow, if you do act for the club and it pays you your huge wedge, there can be advantages for everybody (er, except HMRC). The agent negotiates a fee with the club, which can be whatever he can get the club to agree to as he's not bound by the relatively small percentage of the player's guaranteed income (as would be the case if he had a standard rep contract with the player). As I mentioned earlier, the player pays no tax or VAT, and the club can pay back the VAT it pays on the agent's invoice.

Clubs are by no means innocent babes in the wood when it comes to payments to get hold of a decent young player. In fact, when it comes to anything, clubs are not innocent. They just pretend to be holier than thou when it suits them. They're quite prepared to get down and dirty when dirty is what it takes to acquire a player they want.

Some of the Premier League clubs can be absolutely ruthless when it comes to acquiring or poaching (the two often go hand in hand) the best youngsters, and often use an agent to get them exactly who they want. I went to see a club chairman (who should've known better) who told me he'd just seen a couple of agents who had guaranteed they'd get him three of the best under-14s in the country if he was prepared to pay them a hundred grand a player. He said he'd told them to get lost, but I got the feeling he'd just turned down the offer because he didn't trust them. So I offered him the same opportunity and he negotiated me down to fifty grand a player. He was one of the toughest negotiators in the business. What else could I have done? I had no connection whatsoever with these kids, and I suspect the agents who had offered them up didn't either. Now I had the chance to try and fit the two ends together.

I thought fifty grand a player was a decent budget and would leave me quids in, but that wasn't the case. The parents sensed blood and not knowing me from Adam didn't help. They wanted cash in hand and up front at that. These weren't cosy meetings in front of a hearth like I might have had when I was signing players. These were truly horrible, as dads and, in one case, a mum simply horse-traded their kids' future. The conversations went something along these lines.

'Listen, I know your son is at X Academy but I've got something better for him.'

'We've had lots of people saying the same thing and why are you different?'

'Because I genuinely act for the club who wants him and they want me to look after you to make it happen.'

'X Club wants to look after me too. What are you offering that's more attractive than what has already been put on the table in front of me?'

At least once they'd said that I knew I was in the game.

Eventually I managed to nick one of the kids I'd targeted, but it cost me nearly the whole of the fifty grand I'd been given as a budget, so for a very small reward I put my whole career on the line, which probably didn't make a lot of sense. Although it did prove that I could deliver, that I could be trusted and that I could be used again when the need arose. I just had to make sure that there was a need.

Just in case it all goes pear-shaped, clubs can hide behind agents and then, if anybody gets accused of tapping up minors, deny all knowledge and leave the agent out there, spinning on the end of a rope. This chairman I just mentioned did have a proposition for me though. I'd gained a bit of a reputation for getting things done and he wanted me to get him a fourteen-year-old from a much smaller club where he knew I had some contacts. It was going to be a high-risk exercise because I was fucked if I was found out and if the smaller club discovered it was me who had winkled out this little diamond from its mine then I was fucked with them as well. Not to mention the fact that I might get myself reported to the FA along with the club who were paying me. If that were to happen, no second guesses as to which of us would go down the heavier.

The target kid had a single mum, and they were both living on a council estate. So far, so good. They looked like easy pickings, but I know some of these mums are absurdly loyal to the club which gave their little Tommy his chance and they can also be very protective and genuinely believe that where he's at now is the best place for him. Silly them. I know the right place for him. It's where I'm going to earn the most money. Do I really believe that? Have I changed that much since I started out? You know, I'm not even sure that by this time in my career I can rely on myself to answer that question honestly. Time flies, and I'm worried I may not have fastened my seatbelt yet for take-off.

The little kid (actually not so little as he was already hitting six feet) had been with the club since he was eight years old and was now part of the academy while, of course, still being at school. Clubs have real problems with securing players at that age as they're a little too young to become EPPP (Elite Player Performance Programme) players and certainly not old enough to be offered a professional contract. Mind you, some of the clubs do get those signed and then leave them undated until the relevant time, the silence of the player and his parent or parents guaranteed by a huge payment, or the purchase of an even huger house, or a scouting job offer for the dad, or an administrative job offer for the mum. I could've made that sentence and those alternatives even longer as there are certainly more ways than one to skin that particular cat.

Any compensation payable to the unfortunate club which is about to lose its promising and emerging star is tiny compared to what a club will make available to the agent who is putting the theft (yep, let's be honest for once) together for them. The FA, the Premier League and the Football League (or at least the bigger clubs in that) have all bought into the new EPPP which is actually a charter to ensure that the big boys snaffle up all the talent in return for a few

BCP council

Westbourne Library

Alum Chine Road
Bournemouth BH4 8DX
Tel. 01202 761845

Borrowed items 18/11/2019 10:51

XXXXX8836

Item Title	Due Date
Grey wolves	30/11/2019
* Secret Agent : inside the world of the football agent	09/12/2019

---

* Indicates items borrowed today

Twitter @BCPLibraries
www.bcpcouncil.gov.uk

crumbs from the rich men's table for the smaller clubs. That suits me fine. More for me to play with, to ensure I deliver.

This kid was one of those 'talking players' I mentioned at the beginning of the book, and with half a dozen interested parties after him the mother had realised she had a valuable asset on her hands. She knew if she played it right she might never have to work again. I went to watch the kid a few times. Nobody thought anything about me being there, because I was in with the club.

I found an excuse to talk to the mother. She was pretty, and I spoke to her initially about everything but her son. Showed an interest in her and the rest of her family. Even learned a bit about the absentee dad – always useful in case he comes back when he scents a bit of money – and she started to trust me. Even asked my advice about some of the agents who were waiting to pounce. But then she made a big mistake by telling me the sort of sums that were being offered by other clubs either directly or through third parties. So now that I knew the price, I just had to work out a way to get into the bidding.

Patience was the name of the game, and, if I say so myself, I played it to perfection. Almost apologetically I told her that I'd heard a certain club was interested, that they'd outbid anybody else, that she'd be able to move to a nice detached home near their training ground, and that they had a reputation for bringing their young players through into the first team after some sensible loan arrangements. She fell into my lap like a perfectly ripe apple when she asked me if I could help the family to make it happen. Of course, I replied, and it won't cost you a penny. I'd be prepared to earn nothing because I trusted her and her son to do the right thing when he was sixteen and to sign with me. It was that easy. The lad left, the mum moved and the acquiring club paid me a huge finder's fee dressed up as a scouting contract because they couldn't be seen to be paying anything to get a kid that age.

And the real plus was that the kid's original club never knew that I'd been involved. I even told them I'd tried to persuade the lad to stay when I found out what was going on. Brownie points all round. Dib, dib and all that. Did I find it hard to look in a mirror after that little deal? Did I fuck. I was too busy working out how to spend the money I'd just earned – if and when I ever found the time to get off the treadmill and have some time to myself.

In fact, deciding what to do with the money didn't take long because now I had the dough to get players like the one I'd just delivered. It's money that oils the wheels, money that makes the world of football go round, and by now I wasn't just on the gravy train. I was practically driving it.

INVESTMENTS

PLAYERS LIKE TO spend money on themselves. They like to make money and think they're being clever in the process, even if it is their agent who is doing the thinking for them. They're super-suspicious when they first meet an agent but once they get to know him, once he's done a good deal for them (and it only takes one) then they tend to trust him. Until they find out otherwise.

Now, please don't confuse trust with loyalty. I've already made it clear that commodity is rare when it comes to player–agent relationships. But while the relationship exists, and as it develops, then there is some trust – at least until something or someone better comes along.

That means there are all sorts of service options for the agent to provide either directly or indirectly. Depending on the honesty of the agent, or those he's dealing with, they can benefit both parties or just the agent. Generally speaking, they won't benefit the player alone. Altruism is not a trait that most of us have deeply ingrained in our souls. If we had it when we started out, we tend to lose it rather swiftly.

I quickly realised that if you control a player's money then you have a better than average chance of controlling him, particularly if you appoint somebody to handle it who appears to do well with it. The challenge is to stay in the loop. You don't want your player dealing directly with the Independent Financial Adviser because he might then eventually rely more upon him than upon you. And the IFA may get some fancy ideas as to how he can also be an agent and just nick all the players you've sent him. It happens.

What the player doesn't need to know about are the commissions you get by putting the business the way of the IFA. They can be quite tasty, although the commissions are in inverse proportion to the risk of the investment. Consequently, you do have an incentive to persuade the IFA to go upmarket when it comes to risk. Sometimes that works out for the player. Sometimes not.

When it doesn't, you still have a Plan B. Players often don't understand the sort of reports and statements that investment companies issue. I must admit I don't necessarily understand them myself most of the time. What you have going for you is that nobody on that side of the business, whether it be the large insurance company, the fund managers or the IFA ever want to admit that they're not only failing to beat the market but are actually losing money for their clients. So, in those statements and reports, the bottom line can become a bit blurry, and you can blur it further by saying that it's a long-term investment and that historically the fund has proven to have done well over five-year periods. So the player has to be patient and look to a five-year growth and income pattern with blips, particularly at the start. Best not to mention that everybody has had a bite out of the investment at the start by way of fees and commissions which the IFA has had to disclose to his client. Only you are there when he tells the client and it isn't difficult to ensure that the player has no idea what the IFA is earning and what he's sharing with you. Yes, the IFA will put it all in writing, but will the player read it? What do you think? It isn't the *Sun* and it doesn't have any pictures so it's highly unlikely.

By the time any bad investment has proved to be irretrievably bad, either you or the player has moved on, and while he may moan a bit to whoever is acting for him then the chances of him taking any action are pretty slim. Now, don't get me wrong. Unlike some agents I'm not totally reckless. I've already told you I work really hard to get a player to sign with me so I'm not looking to lose him down the road because he's lost money thanks to some duff advice from somebody I introduced him to. However, even with a relatively conservative investment strategy it's not a bad little earner and if the investments do well (as most of mine have done so far) then it's a nice little earner. There are IFAs and IFAs, and what you want is not somebody so dodgy that they invest in wind farms in Patagonia, but somebody who understands that you have put a decent client their way and that you need to be rewarded for that.

Then there are cars. As we know, footballers have a weakness for cars. The bigger, the better. The more expensive, the better. Provided you can convince them that your man is competitive and that the car will come with every extra of which you can possibly conceive, then the likelihood is that you're on to a very remunerative and, as I've explained before, more than regular income stream. There are many agents from whom you wouldn't buy a second-hand car, and there are quite a few car dealers from whom you wouldn't want to buy any car at all.

One agent in particular caught a real cold when he teamed up with a guy who claimed he could supply cars at real bargain prices. For a while players bought into the idea, and when he told them they were saving several thousand pounds on each car, why would they not believe him? In fact it transpired that they weren't actually being sold the models they thought they were buying and even if they'd been buying the real thing without some of the accessories that normally came with the cars they were substantially overpaying. The car dealer was doing well and so was the agent on his split of the profit, but they pushed their luck too far. The dealer started taking deposits for cars he didn't have and couldn't deliver, and eventually he did a runner to the Middle East, leaving the agent to fend off not only his own angry clients (soon to be angry ex-clients) but players who he didn't even represent who had also been conned.

Then there's jewellery and watches. Footballers and Rolexes go together like love and marriage. Or perhaps not, when it comes to footballers' wives. However, it remains an incontrovertible truth that footballers do like expensive watches. Not just one, tons of them. I mean, just how many watches can you wear for fuck's sake? I know of one player with a couple of dozen watches, each of which had cost upwards of five grand, but he only wore one because that was, as he said, 'the one I like'. You may wonder why he bought the others. I'm about to tell you. Because just as with investments, just as with cars, there are loads of agents out there who have a thing going with jewellers. Now, I don't mean the sort of thing going that leads to an engagement ring. I mean . . . well, by now I'm thinking that you know exactly what I mean. You have a ready and willing, not to mention gullible, buyer, so get your friendly neighbourhood jeweller to sell him whatever he (and you) can at inflated prices and cream off as much as you can by way of a commission from the jeweller.

As you can imagine, like so much I've related in this book, it just doesn't end happily. One player bought and bought. A nice player, this one, just buying for his wife, and not a girlfriend or a mistress or even a hooker. No, these were birthday and Christmas and anniversary presents, all selected with love with the help of his agent who was carefully noting the prices to see how much he was going to get out of it at the end of the day. The answer was a lot, because rather than negotiating the prices down he was, in fact, fixing them with the jeweller beforehand and then seeming to get him to give large discounts to prove what a good agent and friend he really was.

This all worked well for a long while, and indeed the jeweller was recommended to loads of other players to whom he sold jewellery and watches. Sometimes their own agent got involved and also asked for a kickback (nobody ever wants to be left out in the world of agents where there's money to be earned), and sometimes he just sold directly to players, not even bothering to tell the original agent in case he asked for commission on those indirect sales as well. Where it didn't go so well was when the nice responsible player decided, after a spate of break-ins to other players' homes, that he really should get all his wife's expensive jewellery insured. The insurance company asked for valuations, and as luck would have it – or bad luck as it transpired – the dodgy jeweller was away on holiday (well, by now he could afford a few of those a year) and couldn't supply the valuations himself. The nice player wandered into an equally nice local high-street jeweller to get the whole lot valued, only to find what he'd thought to be a hundred grand's worth of expensive necklaces, rings, bracelets and watches was only worth about thirty.

His first port of call was his agent who, to be fair, hadn't realised the extent of the jeweller's dishonesty, although to be equally fair hadn't delved too deeply into the valuations placed on the purchases either. The conversation between agent and jeweller on said jeweller's return from holiday was fruity to say the least, and the whole thing ended up as a court case. The jeweller made an offer to settle, and the footballer, not wanting to look totally stupid in the public eye, actually accepted it. Yet, with the instant jungle tom-tom of football gossip it didn't take long for the jeweller to become a pariah who didn't dare even set foot near a footballer for the preservation of his own legs. Even as their agent I never lose sight of the fact that if these guys didn't have an exceptional talent in their feet they'd probably be serving time at Her Majesty's pleasure, and even if they were not going to seek revenge then they'd know somebody who could do a pretty good job on their behalf. There are some agents who can look after themselves in a scrap, but a footballer wronged is a footballer wronged, and I've known at least one agent end up in casualty when he refused to return something a player thought was properly due.

Property investment is another popular winner on the agent's money-making charts and, believe me, this can go *really* wrong. Getting players to invest in UK-based buy-to-let schemes can be remunerative for all parties concerned. Except when the player, at the agent's instigation, through an estate agent or property adviser introduced by the agent, has bought a property (or a dozen, which is more likely) and found that they aren't that easy to let. And when they're let, the letting agent takes a commission, and when things go wrong at the property there are more hidden charges, and then suddenly the property market has flatlined and a deal that looked to be better than his pension, that was actually going to be his pension, is in fact a total dud.

If that's happening in England then the disaster as far as the player (and the agent if he's an innocent party) is concerned is sort of controllable. Lawyers can do wonderful things, at a price, and at the end of the day properties are truly worth more at the end of a five-year cycle than they were when they were bought.

However, if the property is overseas, in some country whose name you only ever come across when its only contestant at the Olympics is in the spoon-bending events and has to carry the flag into the arena on his own, then there are almost guaranteed to be problems.

The brochures for these foreign property investments always look wonderful. I get so many of them sent to me that I could tear off the covers and open my own travel agency with them. However, when an agent and a developer are working hand in hand, and the agent loses all perspective and caution for his client because of what he's about to make, then there's likely to be trouble in Paradise with a capital T to add to the capital P. One agent told everybody that he had the best deal in the world in the Middle East but could only share it with a select number of his clients. He omitted to tell them that he was in fact the selling agent for this development (no self-regarding agent is ever going to risk his own money, particularly on some properties thousands of miles away in a country ruled by a cabal who could nationalise all foreign assets in a heartbeat).

The money poured in, a big hole was dug (it was an oil-rich country so they were good at digging holes), although sadly, as things turned out, they were nowhere near as good at building tower blocks of luxury apartments. They actually did not have the money to do it and had been hoping to sell properties off the plans, but as only this agent's players were contracted to buy anything (some twenty apartments out of a hundred) that scheme, like the apartments themselves, was never going to get off the ground. The company went into liquidation, the players saw not a penny back of their investment and the nearest they ever came to seeing the apartments were the lovely pictures on the front of the gorgeous brochure.

Needless to say, the agent lost all his players, having lost a fair old chunk of their money. For the Middle East read the Caribbean, odd tax havens, Central America, remote islands and, every time with the encouragement of the agent, the players fall for it. And most times, because they don't want their teammates to know just how dumb they've been, they just take it on the chin and move on.

I did a better deal for my clients and, you won't be surprised to learn by now, for me too. I found a lovely development in Portugal and told my players it was so good that I was buying there myself. It looked great and the prices were fair. Again, as you may have noticed I become a bit of a salesman when I believe in something. And sometimes when I don't believe in something as well.

The players flocked to the scheme. I was going to say like lambs to the slaughter, but I really wasn't selling them a pig in a poke. Amazingly, players do like to be around fellow players and go where their contemporaries have gone before. You visit one footballer's house and it's very much like another. One buys and fits his house out, and then another visits, likes what he sees and copies it all. Imagination and footballers do not go hand in hand off the pitch. Players like to spend holidays together. They speak the same language, relax in the same way and their wives generally come from the same background.

My development had a super golf course nearby, a spa, tennis courts, an Olympic-sized swimming pool and an even bigger cocktail bar. My lads – and even more so, their wives – were delighted with their purchases, particularly in comparison to the disastrous investments some of their fellow professionals had made. I was delighted too. You see, I'd told a little white lie. I hadn't really bought a unit myself although I had acquired one, so that was kind of close. The developers had given me my property for nothing in return for all the introductions. Nobody got hurt and nobody lost out. My conscience was totally clean, at least the small part that remained intact.

There is a kind of moral lesson to be learned here. Honestly. There is a common theme to all the above examples of agents' greed linked to third-party dishonesty and player naivety. The theme is that whether it's property, cars, investments or obscenely expensive watches, although an agent may make money in the short term in the long run he'll always lose the client, not to mention risking a law suit or two – or even jail.

So me, I'm going to keep playing the long game. I know by now when to stick and when to twist, when to bet and when to burn, when to bluff and when to hold. This whole business is one massive never-ending card game and if you sit at the table long enough then maybe, just maybe, you're going to get so lucky that you'll beat the house or even break the bank. Unless, of course, the house breaks you first.

SOCIAL MEDIA

YOUNG PEOPLE LOVE Twitter, and Facebook and Whatsapp and Facetime and Snapchat. Or rather they loved it because, even as I talk, they're finding new ways to communicate instantly which makes all of those totally yesterday's news. I say instant communication, but what seems to be demanded now is communication before you even know you want to, or need to, communicate. Some form of telepathic social media can only be a mere thought away.

Most footballers use social media, which can be an asset and a liability for an agent. It's a plus because it opens all sorts of doors for actually getting to players. According to all the rules and regulations, you can't approach (or tap up) a player who is contracted to another licensed agent; I mean the poor sod of an agent who has probably done everything right. He's legitimately targeted the player, worked hard to get him to agree that he can be represented, he's finally got him to put pen to paper and commit for the next two years, and he's put the representation contract in an envelope to the FA with a goofy love-struck grin on his face so that they can register it. From then on he can hold himself up as the exclusive representative of the player for all his playing and (usually) his commercial contracts. The FA may take a lifetime to formally register and send it back, but that's a sideshow. He's in business once the envelope goes through the slot of the pillar box.

Yet, the minute his player-client ventures out into the wild and wacky world of social media his exclusivity is at risk and, in reality, his contract gives him little or no protection from wily predators. I know because I've tried it myself.

I found a player I liked who seemed to be switched on; he had accounts with Twitter, Facebook and LinkedIn. I started to follow him on Twitter. To be honest, his posts were as boring as shit. Running commentary during a match, telling his followers how glad he was that his team had won, a hard workout at the gym, exchanges about reality television programmes: pretty much nothing to get your teeth into, until he started mentioning a band or two. Now, I like music. If I had to do anything else but be a football agent I wouldn't have minded managing a band or two. I used to play drums when I was at school and I still find that having music on both in the car and when I'm working helps me to relax *and* concentrate.

Anyway, I responded to his music tweet, and we had a bit of an exchange about the virtues of this band. At that stage I didn't even mention I was an agent. I waited a short while and then asked to be his Facebook friend, and he accepted. So now I could see his more personal posts. I noted he had a fiancée and a small child (footballers do tend to do the whole engagement–marriage–child sequence in reverse) and I could also see the sort of holidays he liked, where he liked to eat, the films he saw (all pretty predictable) and even his favourite tattoo parlour.

On reflection, it all sounds a bit like stalking, and I suppose it is in a way. You, the stalker-agent are looking for some kind of consummation of the relationship while avoiding being the creepy follower who becomes a bunny-boiler. When I saw he was looking for a ticket to one of the big summer music festivals I told him I could arrange it, and you know what? He was really pleased. So I assumed that his agent had either not got the contacts or was so complacent that he couldn't be bothered. A personal handover of the tickets – which could oh so easily have been posted – was worth the trip, even though the lad didn't exactly live on my doorstep.

I got the tickets, which cost me an arm and a leg despite pulling in some favours from a friend, duly met the lad for a coffee, did the handover and we got on really well. It kind of came out in conversation that I was a football agent (I tried to steer away from the subject, I really did, I swear it), but then it also came out that he wasn't too happy with his agent. That agency represented over a hundred players, and he reckoned he was way down on their list although he felt (and I encouraged this thought, I admit it) that he ought to be way up it. Which was how he came to ask me to have a look at his representation contract, which was how I came to show it to my lawyer who found a couple of issues with it. Again, I didn't ask, but when the player asked if I could help him get out of it I sprang for the legal fees and, although the agent didn't want to roll over, I got the feeling that he wasn't looking for a public fight either.

There's always a way, and when I suggested to the player that he offer the agent a third of his commission on the next deal if he agreed to tear up the contract, and when I – by now the player's new best mate – offered to indemnify him against anything he had to pay, I'd got the whole plan over the line. The player signed for me as soon as he could, I did his next deal, told him what to pay his old agent and true to my word I coughed up with the loot. Job done, and thank you, social media.

However, it's not so great when your player goes off on one on Twitter or the like. For some reason people don't like being slagged off or threatened in the public arena. For such a brutal business as the football industry it does contain some delicate flowers. It never ceases to astonish me how a player who is an absolute beast on the pitch can be upset by comments aimed at him on social media. Or how quickly they can threaten to turn to the law to maximise profit from any alleged damage.

I've seen all sorts of comments, some of which have involved my intervention. I've had to bully players into apologising for the most inane things: questioning another player's commitment, his manhood, his ability, his integrity; suggesting that he may be putting his own interest before that of his teammates; and calling him by all sorts of fancy and/or derogatory names, some of which are funnier than others.

Sometimes they get sorted out between the protagonists themselves but sometimes they can get so heated that I have to call the other player's agent or lawyer and broker a deal to avoid a major lawsuit. It's then that the non-social media can get busy and criticise the player's agent as well as the player. I've seen the names of agents in the columns of journalists who should know better blaming them for their client's behaviour. You've earned a fortune from a player, so in their somewhat perverted and conveniently sensational view you can be held responsible for everything they do.

As I've found out, people looking into the industry from the outside assume that you're a lot closer to your clients than you really are. Sometimes that's a perception you've deliberately created to boost your own reputation or to warn off competitors with the message that there's such a bond of steel and undying loyalty between you and your player that they'd be wasting their time even thinking of making an approach. As you'll have gathered by now, in reality that's a pretty delusional notion.

The fact of the matter is that players will do exactly what they want to do, no matter how much time you spend with them. They really don't think ahead and rarely think of the consequences of their actions, and it's a brave, not to mention foolhardy, agent, who claims to control his players. Quite literally I've come off the phone to a player having told him not to engage in the likes of Twitter when the next exchange starts off. Basically, to get on as an agent you have to learn how to fight fires, and however often you warn your clients about smoking in dry woodland they're still just as likely to toss away a cigarette butt without a second thought.

Unfortunately, that holds good for everything, not just for social media. I was in the middle of a delicate contract negotiation for a player and made the mistake of telling him why his manager didn't think he was as good as he thought he was, which was why we weren't getting the deal we wanted. I told him this before telling him that it was in confidence and to keep it to himself. That was a really stupid thing to do when it came to a footballer, and like all the other mistakes I've made as I work my way up the ladder, it wasn't one I was going to repeat. Ever.

Anyway, I told him to leave it to me, and his interpretation of that was to rampage into the manager's office without any warning and call him a cunt. The manager promptly reciprocated and told him the offer was withdrawn and that if he thought he was worth what he thought he was worth he could fuck off and get it elsewhere.

It was a real challenge to piece that one back together, particularly as I knew I wouldn't get a better deal elsewhere, but I did it eventually. Not that the player was grateful. They never are. My players, and I suspect everybody else's, just assume I'll sort out their media fuck-ups, and if I don't it will reflect badly on me and not on them.

They may well be right. I've had managers and chairmen cut off diplomatic relations with me because they've not been able to distinguish between what I say and the crap that so often comes out of my players' mouths. I used to dread waking up to the morning sports columns. What was Charlie Sale or Martin Samuel going to say about my players or me? Who had let their guard down in public or in a bar or nightclub? Not any longer. They and their like are no longer my concern. What I truly dread is a social media storm that has blown up overnight to the point that my player is trending, or worse still that I'm trending.

Players rejoice in the number of their followers. Normally they're not in their millions unless they've got something interesting or controversial to say like Joey Barton. But even a few hundred can present serious problems if you upset just one of them. He retweets, and somebody who has even more followers retweets again, and all of a sudden a player is aggrieved about the kind of trivial issues I mentioned before.

Social media moves so much faster and yet seems to leave a longer impression than traditional news media. Once your client has called another player 'hopeless' or worse, and that's got to the eyes of a good few thousand followers of people you'll never meet or even know, then the genie is pretty much out of the bottle. It can get really nasty when the players meet up on the pitch and try to sort matters out behind the backs of the officials. I can think of several recent bookings which had their roots in social media.

It's just another headache for agents, and the only positive when it goes wrong for one of your players out there in cyberspace is that you can be pretty sure he's a player worth representing. However, clubs aren't stupid, and although they all have clauses in their playing contracts ensuring responsible use of social media and commitments not to say anything that brings the club into disrepute, I'm starting to get them to insist on specific clauses, in cases where my client is well known, for making controversial public utterances.

Just when you think you have a nice secure pipeline of income, having negotiated a four-year contract with your fees paid every year (and rising when the player's salary rises), it only needs one moment of madness for the club to impose a penalty on your player (and you need to foot the bill for any appeal because it's always your responsibility when it comes to paying out), or even worse they terminate the contract and bang goes your money. Yes, there's probably another deal to be done out there, but this time you're negotiating for slightly damaged goods, and buying clubs are not slow to make some mileage out of that and push the salary (and consequently your fee) down.

The public like lippy players. Clubs less so. But try telling your player to button up and he'll soon be looking for somebody to represent him who is more prone to admiration than criticism. Damned if you do and fucked if you don't. It's bad enough trying to keep a player when things are in your control. It's just impossible when they're not.

COMMERCIAL EXPLOITATION

A S I'VE JUST noted, the public like a player who speaks his mind. If a player is truly great then he doesn't need to be controversial to be marketable and, indeed, the bigger companies tend to steer away from anybody they think may implode in public. We've seen in other sports such as athletics or golf how a little thing like a very public extramarital affair can reduce the value of the sportsperson in the branding department. And a very large thing like a positive drug test or the manslaughter of a loved one (or even an unloved one) can reduce the brand value to less than zero. And the sponsor can ask for its money back.

Branding. That's what it's all about now. Brand Beckham set the benchmark. Brands Best and Gazza started off fine until both superstars became so unpredictable and so unreliable as to become unmarketable. As an agent you have to understand that the great British public likes nothing more than a sporting hero until it comes to knocking down that very same idol they've worshipped.

Every agent is looking for a Becks, of course, but we may not find him again in my lifetime so we have to work with what we've got. Just because you represent an England international doesn't necessarily mean that you have control of a licence to print money. Indeed, being part of Team England isn't always helpful when the agent is going out to maximise the commercial aspects of a player's career.

The player can be so associated with the brands linked to England that other companies hesitate as to whether or not he'll be able to maximise their brands sufficiently to justify what people like me want for their services. Mind you, all the companies love a bit of what they call 'ambush marketing', so you have to demonstrate that your player is up for it.

The sort of thing I'm thinking of is wearing boots that aren't made by the shirt sponsor, coming off the pitch pulling off (and waving around) shin pads made by another rival, turning up in all sorts of magazines and TV programmes wearing the player's personalised products. Sometimes it's the agent who gets the flak when it's a pretty blatant breach of FA regulations relating to international obligations, but who is going to drop a star player?

The problem is always getting the player to comply with the mega commercial contract you've negotiated for him. It doesn't help when a player who has a sponsorship with an aftershave or deodorant says at a launch that he never uses them because he's allergic. It doesn't help if, despite your plonking a branded cap on his head for an interview and a photo shoot, he wears totally different head gear because one of his mates has set up a company designing and selling baseball caps and has asked him to wear one as a favour.

It happens. You wouldn't believe what can and does happen when you have a player for whom big companies are prepared to pay big bucks to have him endorse their wares. Not everybody is a Gary Lineker whose campaign for Walkers crisps seems to be never-ending, mainly because he has the brains to know which side his bread is buttered on.

It's not easy getting sponsorship or broadcasting deals for players nowadays, but I like to try, not only because I can charge twenty per cent of what they get, but also because it gets me out there among the movers and shakers. When you've negotiated a deal for one of your players to be a pundit at a televised game then you can push on with that when it comes to bigger matches or even international tournaments. You get to know who to speak to and the broadcasters get to know you as somebody who delivers. So when they come looking for a 'talking head' on something that affects agents you may well become their first port of call. That's always good for business. Players are instantly recognisable. Less so, most agents.

I've been pleasantly surprised by the number of players who say that they've seen me on the telly or heard me on the radio and who've liked what I've said. You can even play that to your advantage a bit by praising a player in an interview, even if he isn't yours, and saying that he's the sort of player who could and should be playing at a higher level. You make plans to ensure your paths cross and hope he remembers – and if he doesn't then you remind him of what you said. When I started out I thought it was a big advantage to keep under the radar, to avoid publicity like the plague. But after four years and with a stable of about fifty decent clients, I admit that I rather like the exposure. Maybe it appeals to my ego, and if that should concern me then I don't let it concern me for too long.

It's all about probing the soft underbelly of the relationship between the player and his current agent. Once you do that you can find it can be very soft indeed.

It doesn't hurt to do a few favours for the regular TV broadcasters themselves. They're always looking for a few quid to supplement their incomes and they can also be in a position to recommend your services as an agent. It's occurred to me to try and get one or more of them on my payroll as unofficial ambassadors, and I've heard whispers that other agents have tried it on too. But for the moment I'm leaving it on the 'I'll scratch your back if you scratch mine' basis. You never know where any particular road might lead, and that's one of the things I love about my job – the unpredictability.

I went into a TV studio for a show and found myself in the green room talking to a player I'd always fancied representing. He'd been with the same agent for donkey's years, and I doubt many people thought they had a chance of prising him away. We got on well, we went on air, and I did a fair job of buttering him up. Afterwards we went for a drink and he asked me what he thought I could do for him that his current agent couldn't.

Now, this agent had done a decent job for years. I knew I wasn't going to reinvent the wheel with the lad but on the other hand I was thirty years or so younger than his current bloke so I decided to play the youth-and-energy cards against the experience-and-complacency ones. It transpired that the agent had trusted him so much that he'd never had a contract with him that covered commercial matters, although he'd had to have one in place for his club transfers. I suggested he give me a chance to see what I could get for him and that meanwhile perhaps I could review what he did have in place. It was crap for his status in the game and showed me that the agent had relaxed. He'd made fortunes out of some deals and he could've ensured that the commercial stuff was the icing on the cake both for himself and the player. Getting great deals at a club that wants the player to play for them isn't rocket science but creating a brand for a player really is.

I blagged him a bit and told him we were bringing in a new brand manager to work on our high-profile players. I'm not quite sure how high the profile of many of my players was at that stage, and certainly the brand manager was a figment of my somewhat overactive imagination, but he bought into it all. I found him a boot deal that was about fifty per cent better than the one he had. I've got a note in my diary for when his rep contract runs out and I've got my fingers firmly crossed. Mind you, he's shown a distinct lack of loyalty to the guy who's been with him for years, so who's to say that he wouldn't do exactly the same to me. I've got accustomed to lowering my expectations. It helps to soften the blow.

Commercial deals don't come along every day and certainly not for every player. So when you get one you're not too pleased if the player screws up. And you won't be surprised to learn that they do and generally when they do then they do it big time.

Just not turning up is as good as it gets when it comes to bad. You can always make an excuse. Family emergency, traffic, car broke down, cat got stuck up a tree, kid swallowed a spoon. A sponsor may believe that once, but after that you've run out of road.

Bad, really bad, can take several forms. The sponsor has spent a fortune on renting a specific location and your player finds something better to do. Or you cover for him only to find he's all over Twitter about where he actually is. That's really bad.

Disastrously bad is when a player is discovered shagging one of the models for the shoot at the back of the set, and to avoid her embarrassment she claims she wasn't a willing partner. Go ask any sponsor what they feel a sexual assault when filming their ad will do for the family target audience. On the other hand, don't bother.

I know agents who have had their players turn up drunk for a sponsorship event, dressed in their competitor's clothing, slag off the product within earshot of a mike or a mobile phone and even on one memorable occasion, and this qualifies as disaster beyond disaster, have the shoot reduced to a brawl when another player involved appears and who turns out to have been shagging the player's wife.

You may wonder why you haven't heard about some of this, why it rarely makes the papers, even in the more sensational tabloids who are not averse to flashing the cash around to get stories just like that. The fact is that the sponsor generally flashes its cash around first and quietly puts the situation back in its box while at the same time either terminating what could've been a highly remunerative deal or simply not renewing.

So what happens to the payments to the players under that contract? The affronted or disappointed company wants anything it's paid back. That of course includes our twenty per cents. I confess that on the one occasion it happened to me I just made the player pay it all back and kept my commission. He was earning so much money he didn't even notice, and anyway my conscience was clear because I'd delivered on the contract after all.

You should never steal from your clients just because they won't miss whatever you take. Trust me – and most of my players do – other agents don't have such a principled approach to life as me. If they've got access to a client's money and they've convinced themselves he won't miss it then why not just pocket it? Why not? Well, because it's wrong, but that doesn't seem to trouble some of my contemporaries.

I like to take the moral high ground sometimes. You can't do it all the time in this business so you have to grab every opportunity you can.

Sometimes, an agent can get really lucky and create a brand for a player, or the player effectively creates a brand for himself. Gazza was like that in the nineties before he imploded and had a lawyer and an accountant handling his affairs. I read once that after the 1990 World Cup semi-final when he famously cried that his entourage felt like they were handling the Beatles so great was the commercial interest. Nowadays I think it would be easier to market a beetle than poor Gazza which reflects how quickly things change in our business.

Brand Beckham was totally more reliable and more professionally marketed with a whole team of expertise behind him. To a lesser extent Brand Rooney (less good-looking and more unpredictable) was handled in the same way. The trick for the agent, if he gets that lucky, is to bring in the right people before his client realises that his agent just can't cope and brings in people himself who put the agent's own position at risk.

R would've laughed if I'd mentioned PR and marketing to him when it came to players. 'Just let them kick the fucking ball and you do the rest,' he once said to me.

Only now, that's not enough. The world has moved on. There are still dinosaurs amongst us agents, but I don't intend to be one of them and become extinct. Football, like everything else, is constantly developing, and you have to move along with it. If your player is talented – maybe even hugely talented at that – it goes along well. If he's also good-looking with a great personality then you're almost home and dry. You just need to know how to exploit it and somewhere along the way you may need to give up a bit of that twenty per cent you're charging him for commercial matters.

I know one agent who took all that and then sent his client an invoice every month for all the other costs he'd incurred: public relations, marketing, website design, even a stylist. Players are notorious for only looking at how much is in their bank account, not necessarily what comes off before it gets there, but this one did, and he went crazy when he realised, having taken some independent advice, that with all the bits and pieces on top he was giving away about forty per cent of what he earned. When he did a search of the company that had been set up to market his image he also found that his agent had put himself and a few others on the payroll, not to mention taking twenty per cent of the whole company. So he took his twenty per cent commission off the top and then actually owned twenty per cent of the remaining eighty per cent, which meant that, if my arithmetic is correct, he was getting thirty-six per cent of every commercial deal. There was some heated legal correspondence and the agent hastily left the arena.

I've figured out that it doesn't do to be too greedy. If you're lucky enough to get a golden goose then why kill it? And if you try, then the likelihood is that it may kill you.

TRAVEL AGENT

I'VE FOCUSED ON representing players and clubs, but there's another way. There's always another way, and as long as there is, agents are going to try and make money out of it.

FIFA used to issue special licences to agents to enable them to arrange matches. They might have considered a licence to fix matches as well, but I doubt those who would want to do that would be seeking consent (I've told you of that experience and how I actually survived it). No, this is when you bring over a foreign team to play an English side pre-season or during a break. Or arrange matches between two foreign countries on English soil when both countries have enough of their nationals here to give you hope of a decent crowd.

Sometimes it goes further. An agent puts together a whole pre-season tour abroad for a club and arranges everything: flights, transportation, hotels and the opposition. A word of advice. Don't. I got involved when I was with R and it's the biggest nightmare you can imagine.

Let's look at the tour first. R was never going to sign up for something unless he was fairly sure he was going to make something worthwhile out of it so he'd always try and cover all the bases. He'd get a kickback from the travel agents for arranging the flights. He'd ensure that he also got something from the hotels. He'd make deals with local restaurants in return for him ensuring the travelling party were going to eat there. If it was the Far East he'd have tailors going in to measure up the players for suits and clothes that would be ready for them before they departed. Local jewellers would arrive with bargains galore. Then he'd have 'arrangements' with the clubs who were going to be the opposition.

Cash from gate receipts, a share of any television deal, merchandising, even takings from the drinks and food at the stadium. He had it all down to a fine art . . . but it could still go wrong.

The agent who takes a football team abroad needs the experience and guile of a tour guide on an Under-20s holiday to Magaluf. I arranged a trip to Spain and lost, yes, *lost* two of the players and one of the club's directors, only to find they were down at a local police station having 'allegedly' failed to pay the three girls with whom they were having an educational night out on the town. They hadn't realised that the girls had a deal going with the local police who were not best pleased that their cut of the night's takings was under threat. The only upside to all of it was that the director was never going to risk crossing me in the future and I got both the players to sign with me rather than risk me tell their wives. As if I would.

It has to be said that the players are the least of the agent's problems on such a tour. The directors act as if they're on a stag weekend (or week, as the case may be) and as they've usually left their wives at home they're not as easy to control as the players, who have to answer to a gimlet-eyed manager who does hourly inspections of their rooms at night and fixes them with a stare that can shatter crystal at 500 metres.

The players also become totally indiscreet, particularly when they're out on the lash. I had a player at a club and decided to combine a holiday with seeing him play in a pre-season friendly (that's how sad I've become). I was sitting in the hotel bar when a group of four men came in, already fairly well refreshed, who began to order cocktails like there was no tomorrow. Not unsurprisingly they were soon joined by four girls young enough to be their daughters, or nieces, but from the way these middle-aged guys were all over them it did not need a genius to work out that the only relations that might come into the situation would be sexual ones.

The men's voices rose in direct proportion to the alcohol consumed (although my guess was that anything else was going to have a hard time rising that night), and I was able to discover that the manager of their club was walking a tightrope and that he was only in the job anyway because the owner had something on him which had enabled the club to get him cheap for the job.

I also learned the names of a couple of players they wanted at the club and a couple they wanted out. I wasn't slow to contact all four. Not too tricky when two of them were, of course, in the same hotel, but a bit more of a challenge when the other two weren't even on the same continent.

When I told the two who were about to be shown the door that they were unloved and unwanted by the club and pointed out that their own agent should've known this, I had a couple of potential clients who, as luck would have it, were both coming to the end of their current representation contracts. They both signed with me, recommended by my existing player at the club, and as far as I was concerned it was a good evening's work for the price of a couple of drinks.

It transpired to be a somewhat less positive evening for the club officials. A journalist had also been listening, he'd summoned a photographer, and they all woke up on Sunday morning to see themselves and their young female friends plastered over a tabloid. So did their wives, and I suspect that cost them a lot more than their not inconsiderable bar tab.

R always sussed out the local talent before he embarked on any tour. If he controlled the girls indirectly then at least he could be fairly safe there would be no accusations of sexual assault or any souvenirs from the trip in the shape of STDs for the players. But if the girls were prepared to go for four overweight and balding officials (albeit, I suspect, with a bit of a financial inducement) then there was no holding them back when it came to virile, fit young men who looked like Greek gods, except for the tattoos.

Although he didn't hold with it himself, R also told me of an agent who always had a local drug dealer on hand whenever he had a tour abroad. Although players are routinely tested, there's far less chance of being subjected to a drug test in a friendly in a foreign country. This agent had all the bases covered because he also used to pay whoever was doing the tests, if there were to be any, to ensure that he knew the result beforehand.

There are a few druggie agents out there to my knowledge, mainly the younger ones. They tend to be the guys who drive themselves insane to get to matches, to be on the phone to players, to arrange a dozen meetings a day (or night) to ensure that some of them come to fruition.

However, in respect to pre-season friendlies, generally speaking, it's money rather than drugs that's always a problem for the agents. I know of an agent who, naively, had signed off on the contract for an Eastern European club, and when the club went missing when it came to paying the visiting English club, then the agent received a letter from the English club's lawyer demanding payment as he'd been the signatory to the contract.

It's not much easier when the agent brings the foreign team over. Normally he has to get them to agree to bring their first team, including such international stars as they might have. The problem is that there's a very strong possibility that the said stars will have been on international duty somewhere in the world when their domestic season has ended and will have buggered off on a late holiday, missing the pre-season matches. That does not please the English clubs. It's hard enough to get their fans to pay for meaningless friendlies when there's now so much top-class football on TV for free. When the star attractions go walkabout then it becomes even harder.

If a club is making a loss on a match, then they'll look for somebody to blame, and it's usually the poor old agent who finds himself in the firing line. The bombardment can get much worse when the visiting club wants cash up front, irrespective of what the contract may say, and the home club refuses to pay anything until it satisfies itself that the opposition the agent has lined up is both genuine and credible and not a bunch of academy kids.

The risk for the agent is not just financial. One European club was effectively mafia-owned and made it quite clear to the agent what, not just might, but what would happen if they were not paid up front. The agent's pleas to the English club fell on deaf ears and he was forced to borrow some money from individuals who proved to be every bit as unpleasant as those who had threatened him.

The numbers in the visiting party are also up for debate. The club brings its players and its manager, which is fair enough. Players share rooms, so a squad of, say eighteen, will only need nine rooms with a couple more for the coaching staff. However, a visit to England is quite often appealing to directors and their wives and various hangers-on passing themselves off as security and medical staff, which is yet another challenge to the agent to get close to making any pre-season or international break tours anything like profitable.

As R said when he'd completed what he swore was going to be his last operational tour – in the commercial rather than the military sense – 'There are easier ways to make a quid or two. I'm done.'

An agent has just so much time to develop his business, and although there's always a chance that you might pick up a contact or a player or two when you bring in a foreign club, the only certain thing that you'll pick up is a headache and believe me, any agent has more than enough of those.

FOREIGN ADVENTURES

THEY DO SAY that travel broadens the mind, and I've found that to be the case, only not in a good way. Don't get me wrong. I'm not racist or xenophobic, like so many people in football. What? I hear you say. If there is xenophobia in football then how come there are so many foreigners playing here? Well, signing them and paying them doesn't mean you have to like them, and I know for a fact that most agents (apart from the money from foreign deals) would prefer to represent English players, and most managers (apart from the fact that most of them aren't as good as the foreign imports) would prefer to have home-grown talent – players who know what it means to wear the shirt and who, when they kiss the badge, don't merely do it because it pleases the fans.

Sometimes you just have to make your players travel to satisfy their financial needs. Actually 'needs' isn't quite the right word. In the real world one hundred grand a year would be enough to satisfy anyone's most basic needs. However, what you quickly learn as an agent is that your client's perceived needs are based upon what his contemporaries are getting. That's why every effort by the leagues to impose some kind of informal cap on salaries by an unwritten and tacit agreement between their clubs has failed miserably. Player power always wins in the end, and player power means agent power, which is why the clubs and the authorities hate us so much.

I've never really understood it myself. Does Hollywood hate Tom Cruise's agent because he demands trillions for his client to make a movie? Was Brian Epstein reviled because he tried to do his best for the Beatles? The answer is a resounding no, which is why I'm always asking, why us? Anyway, we do our best to make our clients happy and if you can't get the guy a deal here that does just that, then you look abroad.

Now, not every player is good enough to play in the top foreign leagues like La Liga in Spain, Serie A in Italy or Germany's Bundesliga. What I have learned is that, for example in Spain, apart from the top clubs like Real Madrid or Barcelona, Spanish players can earn more playing in the Championship here than they can back home. So, to move a player into a smaller club in Europe or a lower division isn't going to set the pulses racing or the bank balance soaring.

No, the places to earn the money are in the likes of China, Russia, Turkey, and any of the Middle East countries like Dubai or Qatar. Even some of the big Greek clubs pay serious money. Or do they? This is the problem that faces the agent. It's all very well doing the deal and getting your client a huge net salary in a country where the quantity of the pay cheque far outweighs the quality of the football. However, having a contract, having an agreement for the club to pay you, the agent, a six-figure sum, is no guarantee that you're ever going to bank those sums.

I once took a player to an Asian club because they offered five times the best I could get for the player here. The only snag was that the player wanted to see for himself what he was letting himself in for before he signed. The club agreed to pay for his flight out there, and I let him go on his own as this particular city wasn't on my bucket list.

In fact, as it transpired, a bucket was a sort of luxury there. The minute he arrived, the player found himself deprived of his passport (allegedly for immigration and security reasons) and was then taken to stay, not in the five-star hotel which had been promised, but an Eastern bloc-type high-rise where the television reception was non-existent, his phone didn't work and the plumbing was so basic that a bucket would've been well and truly welcome.

The club's facilities were not much better. He was asked to train on a pitch that was so uneven, cracked and bereft of grass that he feared for his personal safety. He should've been more concerned about the security of his belongings; on the first day, his expensive watch and a few hundred dollars that he'd been advised to take as a preference to the local currency just disappeared.

He called me and told me that he wanted out and wanted out that day. Not so easy. The club said they'd brought him over in good faith, liked what they'd seen from his brief training session and wanted to sign him. They had his passport and they were going to keep it until he did sign. Discussions ensued. I felt more like a hostage negotiator than a football agent, as it was quite obvious that the player was being held to ransom.

Eventually, it was agreed that the airfares and 'accommodation expenses' would be reimbursed and that a 'compensation' fee would be paid. I had to fork it out – very noble I felt as I gritted my teeth. I'm sure some agents would've just left their client there until he came up with the dosh himself. It wasn't an entirely altruistic gesture. I already had another club lined up for the player that would reimburse me and more so.

You learn from experience. I've sent players off to exotic places for what seemed like really good deals, for them and for me. One lad turned up in the Middle East and was delighted. A plush suite in a luxury hotel, a private car to collect him and take him to training every day, all his food paid for and the fact that the hotel was dry was no problem when he was invited to regular 'tea' parties at the compounds in which many other ex-pats were living.

The problems started on the second month when his salary didn't hit his bank account. He tried to find someone to talk to at the club, but everybody who had been so friendly and helpful on his arrival was now unavailable. So he called me. I'd done the deal through a local agent with whom I was to share my fee. That also had not yet been paid, or if it had then my local partner hadn't bothered to tell me about it. He made some sympathetic noises, but then made it clear that this was by no means an unusual occurrence as far as this club was concerned and they'd sort it out in the end. I asked him when and although I couldn't see him I could feel the shrug all the way down the telephone line. This wasn't good.

The player and I agreed to give it another month, but there was still no money forthcoming. My local guy wasn't taking my calls, and I felt I had to get tough so I found myself a local lawyer who was recommended to my own English lawyer and who, we were told, unlike most of his compatriots was incorruptible. He may well have been but he was also bloody expensive and insisted I transferred ten thousand dollars to him before he'd even look at it. This whole deal, my first in the area, was not going well. Instead of making money I was well out of pocket because the travel agent with whom I'd arranged the flights (first class, at the club's insistence) now told me they'd also not been paid and were having to look to me as their regular client.

We got the money to the lawyer, the lawyer threatened the club, and when the player got back to his hotel he found that his room had been emptied and all of his belongings had been thrown into his suitcases which were waiting for him at reception.

We had two choices: hang around and hope that things would improve; or terminate the contract because of the non-payment and get out of Dodge. We decided to take the latter course. Even then, the officials at the airport detained him long enough to ensure he missed his plane, and we then had to begin the long and what at times seemed endless action through FIFA against the club. We won in the end and, very reluctantly, when they were subjected to a transfer embargo, they paid up. A nightmare for me and my player.

What I did after that when I took a player abroad to non-EU countries was to try to insist that the club deposited the whole value of the contract in a bank account, including my commission. I tried that on in China too, and they were most offended. It was as if I'd insulted their national integrity. When I asked in Russia I was threatened. When I suggested it in Greece (and yes, I know Greece is in the EU) they laughed.

The thing to do is to avoid the temptation of the quick and what seems to be the easy buck. I try to tell myself that. But it's hard. If I don't find a club for a player then there will be a dozen other agents whispering in his ear to tell him that they can. That's the pressure. That's why, eventually, you have to pack away your caution with your conscience and go for it. Those are the rules of the game. You either play by them or you fold. Me, I decided to draw another card and take the risk of going bust. I wouldn't have done that when I'd first started out, but I was a different person with four years in the industry under my belt. Not better, just different, and there were times when I woke up in the middle of the night and simply could not get back to sleep as I wrestled with that fact. Previously, I'd slept like a log, gone right off as soon as my head hit the pillow. Those days were gone, and, as I counted pounds rather than sheep, I wondered if perhaps, just perhaps, I might have got it all wrong. But agents can't work with doubts. They can't work with greys. Black and white certainties are what it is all about: certainty in your own ability, certainty that whatever you were doing was absolutely right. There is no other way.

CHAIRMAN K

YOU NEVER KNOW just how bent club officials are until you test them out. You can hear all the rumours about this or that manager, CEO and chairman, but nobody is going to broadcast the truth to the world at large. There is always the suspicion these days that you may have done a deal with a newspaper or a television programme and been recorded.

There are clues that a prudent agent can follow. I once took a player to a club, and the chairman seemed really interested, telling me they'd been following the player for a while, hadn't known who represented him and had even spoken to the player directly. Quite innocently, of course.

I raised my eyebrows. The chairman couldn't see that because we were on the phone. My player hadn't mentioned the conversation, and that in itself was a cause for concern. I was guessing they'd slagged me off and said it would be simpler if I wasn't involved in the deal at all. So, my call to the club had been timely to say the least.

The chairman said he'd get back to me but he didn't. In fact Agent L called me and told me frankly that if I wanted to do a deal with this particular club then I'd have to do it through him because he represented them exclusively. I pointed out that the chairman hadn't mentioned that, to which he suggested that I try and call the chairman again, although on second thoughts not to bother, because he wouldn't be taking my calls. I needed to face up to the reality. If I wanted the club to take my player then I needed to tell L what he wanted and not to bother about what I wanted because that was going to come down to what he was prepared to give me. And I could fucking well forget about five per cent because there simply wasn't going to be that amount left in the deal after everybody else was kept happy.

I thought about what to do next. I could try and find my player another club, although I knew he had his heart set on this one and I had little doubt that he'd already been told by L (who I assumed had been the one to have spoken with him) that this was a done deal and if it didn't happen then I'd be the one who had fucked it up.

I could get on to the FA and tell them. But tell them what? I knew that both the chairman and L would deny everything, and anyway this wouldn't get my player his move and would certainly mean the end of our relationship. So, I decided to go along with it. I took the few grand I could from the deal, which amounted to about two and a half per cent, and as soon as my rep contract with the player expired he promptly signed with L along with the other half a dozen players he already had at the club.

I didn't like any of it, and my reaction when I don't like something that has been done to me is to see how I can get myself into a position where I can do it to others. I know that isn't the sensible thing to do, but by now I'd kind of gone past sensible. That's what this industry does to you. It moves so fast it sweeps you up in a tidal rush and you just get carried away. You've no time to stop and think about repercussions – only the money you're making at that particular moment.

There was one club where I'd done a few deals (both in and out), and I got on well with the chairman who was a bit of a Jack the Lad and had sold out his business in an industry where cash was king. I reckoned he wouldn't be averse to doing a deal with me. I wasn't wrong. We'll call him Chairman K.

The FA have a bee in their bonnet about third-party ownership. What that basically means is that they don't want to have anybody other than the club to which the player is contracted having any control over the player or his sale. They seem to think that owning a part of a player means you have influence and that influence can affect the outcome of . . . well, practically anything, I guess.

This all blew up over the Carlos Tevez deal and ended with Sheffield United claiming damages against West Ham who had got the advantage of Tevez, even though it was revealed that certain individuals were benefiting from an interest in his transfer fee. That has reduced a very complicated issue to a few lines, but all I really need to make clear is that an agent can be paid for introducing a player to a club. He can be paid by the club and the player if he acted for the player. He can be paid a higher fee if the club stays up, but what he can't receive is any share of anything the club gets paid for the player in the future.

I need to explain that one too. If a club sells a player for, say, a hundred grand to another club (usually a bigger club), then to ensure they get an upside if the players kicks on (excuse the pun) with his career, they seek, and often get, a sell-on. Which means that if the buying club sells him for a million and they have a ten per cent sell-on clause, they'll get another ninety grand when he's sold, based on the buying club's profit.

The FA won't register any kind of agreement with an agent that contains a clause like that, but as with most things in football there are more ways than one to get to where you want to be – or to circumvent the rules in this case. Although all payments to agents in relation to player transactions have to go through the FA, that doesn't apply to retainer or bonus payments, and unless the FA comes in to go through the club's books (which will only happen if the club is in trouble or under suspicion) or unless it asked to look at my accounts (again unlikely as I strive to keep below the radar), I reckoned this might be a good way to earn some extra money in the middle to long term.

So, the approach I made to Chairman K was simple: I'd find him players from whom I reckoned he could make money when he developed them and sold them on. K and I got on well. He was a big, bluff guy from up north, always in braces and long-sleeved shirts whatever the weather. He seemed to be permanently cold and even at the height of summer had the central heating stoked up, maybe to ensure that visitors were glad to get away.

I wasn't asking for a fortune but I did reckon that if they sold a player for a hundred grand and then earned another ninety grand because I'd negotiated the sale for them, then it wasn't unreasonable to pay me twenty per cent of the whole shooting match. I started at twenty, knowing they'd offer ten and with a view to settling at fifteen. As you can imagine, I love bartering. I'm a nightmare when I visit markets abroad and I've left stallholders on the brink of suicide because of the prices I've got them down to. I just can't help myself. My mother is exactly the same. If it wasn't for the fact that she hates football she would've made a great football agent.

K and I agreed that he'd produce some documentation by way of a consultancy agreement to cover what I was going to get, and it seemed a perfect arrangement. Everybody would gain, and quite frankly neither of us thought it was any of the FA's business that we'd be making a buck or two.

As far as I was concerned, it also led to another interesting discussion where I offered the chairman what was, essentially, a kickback: whereby the club paid me a fee for any deals I did either for players I was bringing in, players I was taking out or even contracts I was renegotiating. I admit I hesitated here. This was really crossing the line as far I was concerned. I'd bent the rules before – we all did – but this was smashing them into smithereens, and I was worried that I might get seriously hurt by a sliver.

K was a minority shareholder, so he didn't really control the club and was grateful for anything extra he could make on the side. Just my sort of guy. A pragmatist.

A helpful one too, because now that he was effectively on my payroll he was also trying to push players my way. I've known managers do that but here I had a real live chairman, the man who held the purse strings, the man who made the final decision on contracts and who was able to tell players that either he didn't like their agent, or that their agent was no good, or, best of all, that I was the agent who did the most lucrative deals for his clients.

I actually had to rein him in, so enthusiastic did he become, because players might have grown suspicious and thought that we were hand in glove. As if. Yet, even with him proceeding with caution and even with me being choosy about which players I wanted to represent (I mean, if you don't have some standards then you have no respect), we still had a nice thing going. Yes, quite a nice little thing indeed.

It got to the stage where I was fast becoming the gatekeeper for this particular club. Other agents would come to me if they had a player they wanted to place there, and I was always happy to oblige for an entry fee which was, in this case, a slice of the action. OK, I had to share it with Chairman K but as I've said so many times, a little is better than nothing and a lot of littles add up to quite a lot.

As you can imagine, I wasn't earning a lot of friends along the way. K and I had another chat and decided that it might be wiser if I wasn't paid directly by the club. The idea was for him to cream off enough from the club by inventive invoicing to pay into the account of another company, which would ostensibly be providing a whole raft of marketing, public relations and IT services to the club, and then that company would pay a service company of mine. In that way, if the FA ever got suspicious after a complaint by another agent they'd have the devil's own job to prove anything.

I know what you're thinking. This was, in essence, a total fraud. The second company was one huge slush fund, a kind of money-laundering exercise, but K and I didn't think of it like that at the time. Truth to tell, we didn't really think about anything other than the amount of money we were both making.

That's the problem when it all comes so easy. You get complacent, you get careless, and looking back I admit I got more than a little up myself. Whereas I'd always had time for agents even younger than myself, to meet them for a coffee and give them some free advice, now I just ignored their emails and didn't return their calls. Time was money, and money was everything.

FOREIGN TRAVAILS

I MAY HAVE painted a Hogarthian picture of some of my fellow agents in this country but they can't hold a candle to the guys I now encounter in some of the more volatile countries in the world.

I heard about a Russian agent who went to meet his player in a hotel only to be met by a hail of bullets instead, because he'd refused to share his business with the local mafia. Everything there depends on who you know, who you have paid off, and your ability to keep in with not just the ruling party but also the billionaires who make the machinery go round by greasing the wheels.

Russian agents and, indeed, Russian players are laws unto themselves, largely because they're often armed. They're not individuals you want to cross, either singly or as a group. Things are what they say they are there, and facts become facts simply because they're voiced. It's all about 'protectzia': protection. I'm guessing this attitude is, in part, due to their Communist upbringing and in part because they're a tough, miserable bunch of bastards.

Tax liability is a concept unknown to the normal Russian player, hence their agents, when they ask guys like me to help them place a player, are always talking 'net' when it comes to salaries. As the figures they want are pretty high to start off with and are virtually doubled when they add the tax on, they become a pretty hard sell.

I once tried to move a black player to a club in Russia and was shocked by the racism, which they regarded as quite normal. They told me it would be unkind for me to sell him there because he'd be subjected to monkey noises for the entire match. I acted for an Israeli player in Europe, and he had the crowd making gas-chamber hissing noises and waving the Palestinian flag. Once you get exposed to the fans then the players actually seem quite nice.

Dealing in Turkey is an experience as well. I got quite excited when a South American agent assured me he 'owned' a player and gave me an exclusive mandate for a few countries, including Turkey. I got Turkey because I'd talked up (well, lied about actually) the strength of my connections there. I did actually know somebody who had done a fair amount of work in Turkey and so I decided to cut a deal with them to help me place the player.

It took a little over twenty-four hours for my guy to call me back and tell me that so far he'd come across half a dozen other agents who also claimed to have the exclusive right to market this particular player.

Not that getting a player into Turkey is such a big deal. The odds are that whatever attractive package you may get him and whatever chunky fee you may negotiate for yourself, that's just the beginning and by no means the end. Because so many clubs simply don't pay.

Well, eventually they might pay the player, but that will be for purely selfish reasons, usually to avoid some kind of universal embargo being put in place to stop them buying players. There's no such penalty when it comes to not paying agents. We're not what are called 'Football Creditors'. We have no leverage whatsoever to encourage clubs to pay our fees. When it comes to the UK we can't even sue a club in a court, which is what any other creditor can do when they've been owed money for months (or even years) for a job well done. All we can do is bring an action under an FA system called Rule K, whereby we have to start off a claim, pay a fee, choose an arbitrator, pay a fee, receive directions, pay more fees, and then if we're lucky finally get a hearing and a judgment. But that is useless anyway, as we have to take it to the High Court to turn it into a proper judgment and then, and only then, can we try to get the player or the club to pay us.

By then clubs usually will cough up, as they don't want to be wound up, but with players it can take so long that they may not even be playing in this country by then, which leaves you even more out of pocket and trying to track them down in the wilds of Uzbekistan and the like.

When you're working abroad then it's even more difficult. You can bring a complaint to FIFA, but given their track record you might only have a chance if you can find someone to bribe. Otherwise you end up in a tangled Kafkaesque process where you pay an awful lot of money and indulge in endless correspondence in a form of broken English that leaves you wondering if they even want to understand what your claim is all about.

You can't even do what you can do here when a claim is absolutely clear-cut, that is, go for a summary judgment or bankruptcy or a winding up. However spurious the defence of a foreign club or player or agent, he'll be allowed to buy time with it, and I can just imagine how many agents must give up on the process because they've run out of patience or, more likely, money.

Even when you have some kind of enforceable judgment you still have to enforce it. I've recently gone all the way with a player who owed me money. I did it reluctantly, for all the good reasons I've explained before, but I just couldn't let this one go because the two fingers he was sticking up in my face were so belligerent and cocky that I felt he needed to be taught a lesson.

I had got this player a contract worth five grand a week. The club, unusually in this instance, hadn't paid my fees, but I'd got them to give him a signing-on fee of fifteen grand a year which, after tax, netted down to what I'd agreed he'd pay me. He'd just banked it and then spent it, because when I came to try and enforce my judgment he was able to show the court that after all the bare essentials of life he needed to pay – a mortgage, support for his estranged wife and kids, the cost of his new live-in partner and her kid, trade essentials like travel, a car and equipment – all he could offer me was a hundred pounds a week, because he was no longer on the same contract I'd secured for him and had moved to a smaller club with less money (a deal I'd been denied doing even though he was still, just about, under contract to me).

I could've brought another action against him for the fees on that one, but he'd just worn me down and I couldn't be bothered. My lawyer helped me to get an attachment of earnings order where his club deducted what he owed me monthly and paid me direct, but it was going to be a long hard path and I'd wasted six months of my life that I was never going to see again.

I know I've drifted off the subject of working abroad but I suppose I want to show that there are times when this business isn't all it's cracked up to be – and it certainly isn't when you get sucked into deals in the Middle East.

Like everybody else in football, we agents read about the Qatar World Cup bid and the FIFA corruption, but all I did was shrug my shoulders and think, what's new? Every deal I've ever known of in the Middle East has been rotten from the ground up.

The first problem is that you can never get to the clubs direct like you can here. There's always some middleman or middlemen who'll assure you that if you want to bring your player over they can make it happen, albeit at a price. In other countries your contacts are prepared to bide their time for their share of the deals, but in the Middle East there are times when it's made clear that you have to make an up-front payment.

Even if you do that, there is no guarantee that you've paid the right man or that he can actually do what he says he can. The fact that he may be a sheik himself means absolutely nothing. It's a bit better if he's a member of the relevant royal family, but even that isn't necessarily the biz as the families are so huge and extended. There's no point in talking to the coaches either, because they tend to take what they're given, and if the owner of the club has a child who supports a particular club or idolises an individual player then they may be the ones responsible for any signings.

I've managed to complete one deal out there without even visiting, and if I'd needed to go, then I would've done so reluctantly. I know of one agent who was detained so long at immigration over his entry papers (he'd obviously not paid off the right people) that he missed the deal completely. They let the player who accompanied him through and did the terms directly. He had signed without any provision for agent's fees before the agent had been put on a plane back to England with a warning that if he decided to visit again he might not be so lucky.

The player got his first month's wages but not the second, and then had the gall to call the agent who had gone with him to seek help in getting paid.

I could go on forever about the countries where deals are to be done without any guarantee of payment: Greece, all the old components of the Soviet Union, South America, some parts of Eastern Europe and even countries like Italy, where every club seems to be walking a financial tightrope and agents are the first to suffer when it comes to making the economics work.

The fact of the matter is that we're the whipping boys when it comes to getting paid for what we do. People may say we get paid too much but not to be paid anything at all just isn't right. Maybe that's why we get tempted to cross the line into criminal behaviour. Can you really blame us?

SWITCHES, SHADOWS AND SCHEISTERS

THERE ARE SOME agents who are frightened to death by the FA. But then there are also some agents who are scared of their own shadows. They tend to be the same agents. The regulations for agents are a bit like regulations about paying tax. Everybody would avoid them if they could. If you're rich and pay for proper advice they call it tax avoidance. If you just don't pay then it's tax evasion.

R told me about the good old days before licensing. He reckoned that there were only about a dozen agents and players who would actually ask to be represented rather than having to be virtually bribed. One player who eventually became a regular England international actually invited him to his house for tea and had his wife bake a vast array of cakes as if he were an honoured guest.

'Can't see that ever happening again,' he'd said wistfully, shaking his head.

Too right, I thought. Now you'd be lucky to get past the driveway, and even then you'd be stumbling over all the other agents queuing up to get in.

Fathers would phone to see if R would look after little Johnny, and all this would be done on a handshake with R even sometimes charging the player rather than the club.

Then word got out, and individuals flocked to become agents in the same way as they rushed to California to find gold or Kimberley in South Africa to seek diamonds. Some were good, some were professional, but few had any idea of what was expected of them and simply learned on the job.

The FA watched the whole drama unfold and then, it would appear, decided that as everybody representing the players was earning barrow-loads more money than they were they had to try to put a stop to it. So they decided in their wisdom – not a word commonly heard or used when the FA is mentioned – to regulate. This wasn't a Magna Carta or Declaration of Independence moment. This was them saying that anybody who had experience was now regarded as a Licensed Agent, but that anybody who wanted to get into the industry afterwards had to pass an exam. And I've already pointed out what a farce that is.

Then, when all the agents had worked out how to work around the regulations, the FA spent a fortune bringing in a whole raft of even more complicated and challenging regulations. It was a hard battle, R explained, but by then all the leading agents had formed their own association and clubbed together to buy expensive legal advice, which saw the FA back down and try again, this time with a bit of consultation. 'They treated us like schoolkids, only when we turned on the teachers, they ran away.'

To those of us trying to operate now it doesn't seem that they ran away because, after 2007, it became a bit of a challenge to evade them. But I reckon we've not done too badly. At first they said we couldn't act for both parties, so all the tax burden of the fees fell on the player. The agents just went into the clubs and told them they needed to pay more, so whatever extra they gave the player netted down to pay the fees. That was when the big clubs, who it hit the hardest and who'd been the biggest opponents of duality (acting for both sides), backed down, and it was reinstated.

Then they banned what they called 'switching'. This meant acting for a club when they bought a player and then changing sides and acting for the player when he moved on. The FA said that there had to be a clear two-transfer-window gap before we could do that.

I once asked somebody from the FA who'd turned up at an agents' meeting what the reasoning behind that was, and he wouldn't tell me, so I told him I reckoned it was just to make life more difficult for us, and he wouldn't comment on that either.

Then they banned 'shadowing'. By now they were making the words up as they went along, and I reckoned a ban on 'breathing' was just around the corner. Anyway, what they meant by 'shadowing' was that you acted for a club when a player joined. Then, when they sold him, you acted for another club. However, they reckoned that all the time the agent was really acting for the player.

That may not have been the best for HMRC. No players are registered for VAT, so they wouldn't have been able to claim back the VAT they paid to their agents on top of the fees if the agent had been acting for them. Clubs of course can reclaim back the VAT. I know this is getting a bit dull, but I just want to illustrate what a bunch of spoilsports the FA really can be.

These restrictions were so easy to get around it was laughable. I just made deals with some acquaintances whom I kind of trusted (well, as much as you can trust other sharks when you swim in shark-infested waters) so that when I couldn't act – because it would've been a breach of the switching or the shadowing (or the breathing) regulations – I'd put one of these friendly sharks in to front it and then give him a small percentage of the fees for the favour. And then he'd return the favour when the boot was on the other foot. It was and still is a cartel, and after five years I'm at the heart of it all and one of the real players. Or at least I like to think so.

The FA knock off a few small-fry agents just for appearance's sake, but the big boys are generally too clever for them and remain beyond their reach. If they had any real brains they'd be out there with us agents making a bob or two, rather than being pen-pushing footballing civil servants trying to apply rules that simply aren't worth the candle.

By the time I appeared on the scene there had to be an agreement with the player, and it had to be in a form that the FA approved and it couldn't be for more than two years and it couldn't be automatically renewable. There were lots of things it couldn't be, but the one thing it most certainly could be was crap.

Most of us have worked out ways to get round it all, of course. I'd get my players to sign two contracts, date one and lodge it with the

FA. Then, when it was coming to the end I'd date the second and lodge that. I was so canny I even got the player to use different pens to sign the contracts, so they looked different.

I try to hedge my bets and generally have the sort of relationship with my players that enables me to do so. I get a player to sign and not lodge or date the contract (they're supposed to be sent to the FA within five days of signing). Then, when a transaction looms, I can see if I can act for a club who would pay more than the commission percentage I have in the representation contract with the player. If so, I'll switch and just keep the contract for the future.

As I've said, for some that could be a risky strategy if the player turned rogue and signed with somebody else, but it doesn't seem to happen to me. Either my players love me to bits, warts and all, or else it may be that by now I know a secret about each and every one of them that keeps them close to my bosom. I never really found out which it is.

The FA have also decided to play bankers. All for transparency, they say, but given the time they take to pass monies on to us from the clubs, I reckon they were all taking holidays in Barbados on the interest. One brave agent took them on and challenged their right to hold deposits, and although it didn't enamour him to the powers that be, and although he was probably right, they just kept right on doing it.

A favourite trick is to launch an investigation into any transaction that seems to them to be dodgy – haven't they realised that most of them are dodgy? – and delay payment until they're satisfied all is well. One poor bastard was totally reliant on money from a deal and nearly went to the wall when a substantial sum he was due got locked into the FA's bank account because they didn't like the smell of a transaction.

They play all sorts of games, like claiming that the money that arrives from a club can't be identified as it's part of a bulk payment, so they've had to send it back. I had a deal where I'd done the player a favour and charged him less than the commission rate in my contract, and they even queried that. They must have thought I'd taken the balance in cash. I hadn't on that occasion, but there were other times when I felt I'd done a really good job for the player (which wasn't reflected in a five per cent commission that I was getting, and that spread over the three years of the contract) and asked him for a bit more on the side – and he was happy to pay it.

R did it as a matter of course, and then stashed the cash away for his holidays and such like. Did I mention that R had a penchant for young, pretty women? The cash also helped to buy the jewellery they'd wear by the side of the pool, jewellery more often than not a hell of a lot chunkier than the bikinis they wore.

So much for the FA as a governing body. Nobody had elected them to govern us. Nobody ever asked us what we thought or felt about it. Nobody at the top, or the middle – or even the bottom, if it came to it – gave a flying fuck. So why should we care that we make fools of them? That was how I thought about it then, and it was to contribute to my downfall. I seriously underestimated them and overestimated myself.

EXPANSION

YOU CAN SEE by now I'm a bit of a loner. OK, I'm not the sort you read about in the papers who buys half a dozen AK-45s and goes on a shooting spree, I'm just somebody who prefers his own company and finds it hard to trust anybody else. Mainly because I've seen so many people let down by others.

I've decided that a full-blown partnership is simply not for me. I've seen too many of them go horribly wrong. One agent went to use his debit card and found it rejected, even though he knew he had several hundred thousand pounds in the account having just been paid for a profitable deal. He went back to the office he shared with his partner only to find that his partner had removed his personal effects along with everything else of value they had in the office.

When he called his partner and heard the ringtone that tells you for sure that the recipient of the call is abroad, then he knew he had a problem. And it got worse. The partner had assumed responsibility for all the administration and the finance, while the other guy had been the rainmaker when it came to getting in clients and doing the deals. In the partner's desk – he hadn't bothered to remove that as, like all the other office equipment, it was leased – he found a huge pile of bills, lawyers' letters and correspondence from various debt collectors, some quite clearly more reputable than others. Everything he'd worked for during the five years of being together with somebody he'd thought to be a friend had been destroyed.

He called the police. But given that the erstwhile partner was sunning himself on a beach after marrying a very attractive local girl and given that the partner was a full signatory on all the accounts and had unrestricted use of all the company cards, there wasn't a lot of interest shown in the agent's plight. He instructed lawyers but was in such a financial mire he found it difficult to fund their efforts; something that the errant partner had obviously worked out for himself before he'd embarked upon his asset-stripping spree.

Just when it seemed that things couldn't get any worse, the naughty partner's players started to complain that they'd not heard from him and then initiated an orchestrated series of letters (obviously drafted by a lawyer or a sharp rival agent) saying that they were giving notice to terminate their contracts.

The standard representation contract provides for a period of notice to be given to remedy any breach, but given that the agent was several thousand miles away and, as the hapless guy left behind thought, unlikely to be contacting the players very soon, there appeared to be little or no chance of any remedy in the immediate future.

The agent tried his best to persuade the players to re-sign with him but, although he thought it a bit odd at the time (he knew some of them quite well), not a single one agreed to do so. It was only some time later that he discovered that they'd, virtually to a man, signed for a rival agent. Eventually he figured out that his former partner had orchestrated the whole thing and done a deal with the new agent, so that he continued to benefit from the players' deals to the exclusion of the man he'd left behind.

Just when he thought it could get no worse, the pipeline income upon which he'd been relying to bail himself out and build himself up again, suddenly dried up. Every agreement that triggered off that income from deals his partner had done contained a clause that if the agent ceased to hold a valid licence then all bets were off. The partner who had fled had decided that not only did he no longer need a licence when he could use equally unscrupulous individuals to front for him, but that by advising the FA that he was surrendering it he also had the advantage of removing himself from their disciplinary process, as he was no longer a participant and subject to their rules and regulations. In any event the monies were to be paid to him personally as the FA (and FIFA) simply don't recognise companies (unless in FIFA's case they're offshore for stashing away their ill-gotten gains), only individuals.

Talk about being fucked every which way but loose.

You can see why taking on a partner did not seem a very attractive option to me, particularly when I was doing so well all by myself. Having somebody work for me though was becoming more of a necessity than an option because I was signing up so many players that I simply couldn't get to watch them all on the regular basis that had been my practice. One player I signed told me he'd dumped his former agent because he never came to watch him play and that had always stuck in my mind as a warning.

I was a reluctant employer though, I must say. Apart from the drag of setting up a PAYE system and having employment contracts, I'd seen what employees could do and what some employers do to them. There was one poor guy who had mystifyingly been persuaded to take a second-hand car in return for commission that was properly due to him. Nothing appeared on the books, so our old friends at HMRC were the losers again on the grand stage of football agents. That was the employee's choice, of course, but things went awry when he left. The employer demanded his car back, alternatively requesting payment for it and virtually accusing the guy of theft. The employed agent's problem was a lack of paperwork, not to mention a lack of money to fight off any claim. I gather that particular dispute did have a happy ending with David beating Goliath, but it was just another example of how things can go wrong when you try to operate outside your own private bubble.

Another warning was given to me every time I looked in the mirror. I knew what I'd done to R and I wasn't proud of it. What I also knew was that I didn't want it done to me. So many agents had told me (not realising the irony) of how they'd trained up a young agent and given him every opportunity, only to find that the minute he found himself with a potential star player on his hands he headed off for greener pastures, even if he didn't, like me, set up his own business.

It's so dog-eat-dog that the idea of inviting a hungry dog into your kennel isn't an attractive one. Apart from that I'm not sure I want to get much bigger as an agency when one of my selling points is that I'm not like the big agencies. I know what goes on out there with agents scrapping over the driest of bones. A player signs for one of the agents at an agency. Everybody knows that. Maybe he's gone with a younger guy at the bottom of the food chain. Then the player starts to do it on the pitch, and the big hitters at the agency get interested. They don't hesitate to try and steal the player away from the lad who brought him in and then not only try to claim the credit but try to do the kid out of his slice of the action.

There's pressure on them to deliver big deals, but they've already won their seat at the table. The poor sod who watched him play on freezing-cold winter afternoons up north, who invested time, effort and money on persuading him to sign, is now left to start all over again because the pressure is back on him to perform. And if he doesn't repeat the miracle, if this time around the players don't kick on, then he'll get a kick up the arse while being shown the door. The bigger the company, the more ruthless they can be. Maybe you've come to the conclusion that I'm not the nicest of individuals either, and there are times when I'd have to agree with you, but I still don't think I would, or could, do something like that. Mind you, there are quite a few things that I didn't think I'd do when I set out on this career path, so who knows? At my age there's still a fair old way to go until I get to the end of the road – unless I burn out before then.

I've noticed lately that a few of the old-time agents, men I admired when I was first thinking about this business, are giving up on player representation. They've moved on to media consultancies, entertainment, even other sports. Nothing compares to the stress of the rat race of this particular profession. It's becoming a bit like football itself – a young man's game.

I'd had my eye on one young up-and-coming agent, J, for a while. I'd seen him when I'd been watching one or two of my young kids playing and I quite liked his style. He got on well with the parents, the mothers in particular, although that could be a double-edged sword . . . You can flirt with them a bit because they like that, but you don't want to offend them by turning down their advances and you certainly don't want to sleep with them unless you don't want to represent their offspring. Yet another example of the delicate balance that faces us.

I noticed him chatting up the mum of one of my players and decided that if I could persuade him that he couldn't beat me, then he might well want to join me. And that's what transpired. I had my first paid employee. Like a lot of the younger agents J had played a bit himself. He had the brain to realise fairly early on that he wasn't ever going to be good enough to earn the sort of money that could persuade him not to bother with a degree and a career. He'd seen how the agents had hit on the fourteen-year-olds who had trained with him and, as he put it, some of them were so desperate just to get numbers on their books rather than quality they even hit on him.

He knew how the kids thought, knew what their parents wanted from them, and how, for so many working-class parents, the talented footballing child represented a meal ticket for life. He'd worked as an intern in a large agency during his university holidays so he knew how they operated, and he'd shown enough foresight to gather a handy collection of phone numbers and contacts while he'd been there.

He also had the talent for being invisible at times, so he knew which of the agents at the large agency had players who could be targeted, and once he'd identified the weak links he was ruthless in trying to close a deal. Because he'd never had a contract he had no restrictive covenant stopping him from poaching clients.

It always amazes me how lax agents are with their paperwork. Maybe they're so busy running after the next big deal they don't have time to attend to the little details, but those oversights can cost them more than they make from the big deals themselves.

Even when they do have a proper contract, so many agents are too mean to use a proper employment lawyer or cobble something together themselves from stuff they've seen or been subject to. That's a formula for disaster, and it's not a trap into which I'm ever going to fall. I told you, I have a good lawyer, and anything I spend with him is money well spent. It's an investment as far as I'm concerned, and having approached J and his having taken to the idea of joining forces with me, I was going to ensure that his agreement was as watertight as it could be.

The challenge with contracts in our industry is that I'm told you can't actually stop the guy working in it after he's left you. Yes, you can put something in it to stop him approaching your clients or nicking your staff, but the fact is that as long as he's out there working then everything is at risk. I thought very carefully about it before I put pen to paper with him, but then I thought, 'Fuck it. No pain, no gain.' I wanted to move forward, I needed to move forward. I feel frustrated when I sense I'm standing still. Call it what you want. Greed. Ambition. To be honest, there are times when this whole thing goes beyond the money. I want to act for the best there is. I want to find the best young talent and water them and see them grow. Now, for better or worse, I had somebody to help me achieve that. But if I'd known how it was going to pan out, believe me, I would've stayed exactly as I was.

RUNNING TO STAND STILL

I'VE NEVER REALLY wanted to have a whole bunch of footballers as my best friends. I mean, footballers themselves don't necessarily have their teammates as their best friends and tend to stick to their old mates. But some kind of personal touch is not only necessary but makes a welcome change for players whose previous agents would just pop up out of their boxes when a deal was in the offing – for which they appeared to have some kind of sixth sense.

Players like to have tickets for major events. If there's a big boxing match on, then you can be sure the ringside seats will be filled by footballers and their mates. Tickets for those don't come cheap, but I've managed to set up an arrangement with a promoter whereby we exchange tickets – big matches for big fights.

It's the same with music festivals. I sometimes wonder if I'm running a football agency or a ticket agency, but it's just one of those things that has to be done. The other thing that has to be done is to keep up with your rivals when it comes to doling out gifts or providing services.

One agent waits until the end of the season and then, depending on the achievements of his players, buys them presents. If a player has been an essential part of the title-winning side they might even get a car; a promotion justifies a Rolex; and international caps get a player the best and latest electronic gizmo.

Although it's difficult to get players together at the end of the season, when they leave as swiftly as swallows in the winter for warmer climes, another agency always rents a luxury boat for their end-of-term party and fills it with fine food, finer champagne and hand-picked lovelies to make the voyage a memorable one.

There are a lot of other 'presents'. A day at the races with 'free' bets afforded to your player-guests. That can be expensive, as I found out at Cheltenham one year. Tickets for Wimbledon, grands prix and even FA Cup finals: you'd be surprised how difficult players find getting tickets for themselves, particularly when they generally can't be arsed to ask and certainly aren't prepared to pay. It's much easier, not to mention cheaper, to get their agent to do their shopping for them.

I've just started taking over a whole nightclub for one night. I've called in a few favours, got a few B-list celebrities along from the TV reality programmes they all seem to watch, and hired, at no little expense, a band whose music gets played in a fair number of dressing rooms around the country. Not that there's any great consistency about that sort of music as one (usually self-elected) player tends to be in charge. So, you can get hip-hop at one club, indie at another, blaring rock at a third and rap at a fourth. The band I chose were all big football fans, and the players, for the most part, liked them too. When they all sat around at the end of the set like lifelong mates, girls draped around them in various stages of intimacy, then I reckoned I'd got myself quite a few Brownie points with all my players who had come, and made the ones who hadn't feel as if they'd genuinely missed something.

But it's not just at celebratory times that an agent has to be there for his players. One of mine has just broken up with his wife. She came home unexpectedly and found him in bed with the kids' nanny. Nanny and player were promptly dismissed. Nanny went back to Poland, but player was faced with the choice of a hotel or my spare bedroom and chose the latter.

I could've put up with his drinking and whining, and even the womanising, but when his wife found out where he was and decided to use my little home for the re-run of the *Gunfight at the O.K. Corral*, I came close to throwing him out myself. She arrived shortly after midnight, pretty well tanked up herself. Trust me, hell hath no fury like a wronged footballer's wife. She leaned on the front-doorbell until my neighbours screamed complaints, and when I decided that the choice lay between calling the police and creating an ugly newspaper story, or letting her in, I made the wrong choice and opened the door.

She went for him like a wild animal, nails extended and, strong athlete though he was, she managed to draw first blood. I couldn't let him beat the living daylights out of her, so I tried to hold him back while I reasoned with her. She just took that as an invitation to go for his eyes, and rather than have a player blinded on my premises, I let him go. He flattened her with a perfect (or as he said later in court 'defensive') right hook.

I promised myself never again to get so involved in a matrimonial issue. Now, I introduce the player to a good divorce lawyer (with whom I also have an arrangement for an introductory commission and a share of his fees) and then restrict myself to saying yes and no during interminable phone calls from the player where he uses me as a sounding board for everything that has gone wrong with his life.

Yes, I've stood by players at funerals sobbing their hearts out for their mums or dads. Say what you will of professional footballers, I've never known one of them abandon his parents, however awful they've been to him as a child. And some of them have had pretty rotten upbringings. Yet, there's this sentimental streak in most players when it comes to their parents that makes them forget all that and go the extra mile. Which means that you, the agent, have to travel that road with them too.

I've even had to spend Christmas Day with one player's family because he'd broken up with his girlfriend in the run-up to the holiday and didn't want to turn up at his parents' on his own because he was too scared to tell them that they wouldn't be seeing their grandchildren that year.

So, you do your best. You spend to earn. You accept that most of what you do is taken for granted by players, because it's what they expect – largely because they're a selfish bunch of tossers, but also because it's what others will do for them if you don't. You're on this treadmill now and you can't get off, even though every so often somebody comes along to empty your wallet. You stay running to keep up with yourself because you hope that another deal will arrive to refill your wallet. But I'm beginning to realise that you can't run forever.

THE GOOD GUYS

GIVEN THAT I'VE frequently called players a bunch of tossers, and given my experiences throughout my career so far, you may be surprised when I say that there are some really good guys amongst them.

It often works out in football that like attracts like. Good managers get good players because they know how to inspire loyalty. Players may have a great ability on the pitch but that doesn't necessarily make them nice people. But when you get the combination of a talented player who is also a really warm-hearted and loyal person then you really have struck pay dirt.

I've not being doing this long enough to have represented players from cradle to grave (well, not literally but certainly from their first to their last playing contracts), but I do have a few players who are on to their third contracts with me so I must be doing something right.

The dream player involves you in everything he does. He confides in you, seeks your advice and, most important of all, actually takes it. I've got this little group of players now who do just that. When another agent phones them they call me at once, having told the invasive agent that they're with me, they're happy with me and that if he has anything for them then he needs to speak to me.

Sometimes, they go the extra mile. I had one player who got called by a club for which he had always wanted to play. I knew it because I'd tried to put him in there and been rebuffed. Then, suddenly, the club calls him direct and say they've agreed terms with his current club and can he get there as soon as possible for a medical.

There are some players – quite a few actually – who would've done just that and been pelting down the motorway to put pen to paper before you could say David Beckham. This lad hadn't done that. He'd fought my corner and told them he was with me.

'That's a problem,' the manager had told him. 'You see, we've had some bad experiences with your man and we won't deal with him.'

This was totally untrue. In fact the only experience they'd had with me was when I called them (politely) about my player and they told me (impolitely) that he wasn't for them.

'So, who's going to negotiate my deal?' my player asked.

'Don't worry about that. We've an agent we deal with all the time. He's very good and he'll fight for you to get every last penny. And best of all is that we'll say he acted for us, so it won't cost you any tax and what we pay him won't come out of your deal. Now, when can you get here? We've got some other irons in the fire and if we can't get this signed off today then we need to move on to other targets. But you're number one on our list so we'd really like to get this done, if we can.'

Even though my player knew it was going to cost him the move of his career he had the guts to call me and relay it to me word for word.

I was in a quandary. He'd been good as gold, and I knew an angry call from me to the club and another call to report them to the FA would put the kybosh on the whole deal. So I gritted my teeth, told him to do what they'd asked and let him know what the deal should be worth for him. Which was fortunate, because when he got there and was introduced to the sleazebag who the club had introduced he was told, 'I've got you a great deal. You just need to sign off and do your medical.'

'Er, can we go through it first?' my player asked.

'Are you not trusting me, son?' the agent replied aggressively, and with some reluctance set out the terms which were about half of what I knew he could get and were not much better than what he was on.

My player got in his car and drove home, and then even came with me to my lawyer to give a statement so that I could have a letter before action written to the manager and the club for defamation.

Ultimately, it all worked out well and the player and I were rewarded. The club's chairman called me when the legal letter landed on his desk and apologised (doubtless because he didn't want a scandal), and then invited us back to negotiate a proper deal. The manager was less than happy, and I was really worried about how my player would be treated at the club, but as it transpired what came around, went around. With his card well and truly marked, and some dire results at the start of the season the manager got his marching orders. I went on to develop a great relationship with the club and even helped to recruit his replacement. And my player got the move of his dreams.

Other long-standing players of mine go out of their way to talent-scout for me. They tip me off about youngsters at their clubs and put in a good word. They don't want anything back in return, and it's their way of saying thank you for the great deals I've achieved for them. As I say, what goes around, comes around.

I've got one particular player who regularly phones up for a chat, and when I ask him what he wants (in a nice way, of course) he just says that he hasn't heard from me for a while and just wanted to check that I was OK. In fact, all my players hear from me every week. If I don't call or make contact through Facebook, then I text. It gives a small agency like mine an edge over the bigger boys who have 600-plus clients and can't possibly preserve the personal touch.

I'm not one for showing a lot of emotion (or even feeling it, if truth be told), but when one of my players asked me to be the godchild for his son I did feel a few tears welling up. Mind you, when I went to the christening and the little bugger weed all over me I felt a different kind of dampness.

There's always a warm glow when a player calls me and tells me he wants to speak to me in confidence. It isn't always good news. He might have broken up with his girlfriend or left his wife (or she's left him), or there might be a child who's ill or a parent diagnosed with a terminal illness, but the fact is, it's me that he trusts with the secret and it makes me want to try even harder for him.

Of course you can't like all your clients, and so many footballers just aren't likeable. Yet, it makes it much easier to act for somebody if you're really fond of them, although that in itself brings another kind of problem. The fear of failure, of letting the person down who has placed his blind trust in you. You've always found him a club, so he assumes you always will. However, there are episodes in all players' careers when they simply run out of road, and try as you may there are no clubs for them. Or at least no club that will pay him the sort of money you feel he deserves. Honestly, it doesn't bother me when I let somebody down at the end of the day who has just taken, taken, taken from me, but when it's somebody who's given his all to stick with me, then I'll move heaven and earth to stick by him.

I've used all my contacts and powers of persuasion to get a player I like into a club even when, in my heart of hearts, I fear they may be punching above their weight. It's not often that my heart rules my head, and I'm well aware of the dangers of lying to a club about a player's ability or fitness, but sometimes I just feel the need to go that extra mile even if I may end up with egg on my face.

Once, I had a player in desperate straits. His marriage had broken down, he was drinking too much and although he'd had enough skill in the past to earn himself (and me) some decent money, there wasn't a club in the country who would touch him despite all my efforts. So, I found him something abroad through a local agent, waived my fee just to make it happen and paid for his fare out there myself so that he could have a trial. It must have happened on one of his better days (it was a Muslim country and he couldn't drink) and he was offered what was a really lucrative contract given his age and physical condition.

A week later, a DHL package arrived at my door. Somehow or other he'd managed to get hold of a Rolex watch in Duty Free and then get it out of the country for me. He'd even had it engraved: 'To the best agent in the world'.

Gestures like that make this stressful industry bearable. For a while . . .

LEGAL EAGLES

THE PROBLEM WITH lawyers is that they're fine when they act as lawyers, but not so great when they think they can do anything better than anybody else – including being an agent. For a long time they were exempt from registering with the FA. They could act for players because they could treat them as clients and they felt that it wasn't for another regulatory body to regulate them when they already had the Law Society and then the Solicitors Regulatory Authority (SRA) regulating them to high heaven. However, so many unlicensed agents were using a lawyer to front for them on transactions, paying them an hourly rate and keeping the bulk of the fee for themselves, that the FA finally managed to persuade the SRA to allow them to be brought into the tent. This they did by creating a new class of agents called Registered Lawyers. All the lawyer had to do was register with the FA, and that was that as far as his right to represent footballers in contractual transactions was concerned.

I understood what the FA were trying to do. Until then, lawyers could put two fingers up to them as they weren't participants, so they had no need to co-operate on any investigation. The FA could turn spiteful from time to time and report a non-co-operative lawyer to his own regulatory body, but unless there was a clear breach of his professional code they never got terribly excited about things that had the FA jumping up and down with frustration.

I was never quite sure how lawyers put through the monies they received and paid out through their books. I understood that there were all sorts of rules about not sharing professional fees with others who were not lawyers, but I'm sure they found a way around it. Where there's money then there's both the will and a way when it comes to lawyers.

I've been to see players who are 'interviewing' a few agents. That's quite often the way it works nowadays, particularly if there's a greedy parent involved. They might say it's to see who they feel is the best qualified to represent their kid but more often it's to see who offers them the most. I saw one young player and his parents recently. I knew they'd already seen one of the big agencies, a local guy who had been watching the boy since he was tiny, and a registered lawyer who seemed to be running his agency in parallel to his law practice rather than through it.

It was all so well rehearsed. We had a chat, the dad said nothing but still managed to consume three pints, and then the mum said she had to go, leaving me and the dad to our 'men's talk'. I knew what was coming. Within minutes he told me the big agency had already offered to help them financially as well as offering him a job, but I was taken aback when he told me the 'reputable lawyer' had offered them a house near the club to which he'd virtually guaranteed them a move, as well as half the fee he'd be earning.

I did some quick mental calculations, went through the motions as to why they'd be better off coming with me – knowing I was wasting my breath – and then called it a day. I just couldn't understand why a lawyer would risk losing his professional status for what would, at the end of the day, be scant reward after he'd given so much away. So much for the integrity of that profession.

I know of one lawyer who continued to specialise in fronting transactions for unlicensed individuals who could not sign off on deals themselves, even after he'd become accountable to the FA. It was really simple. The individual did all the work, recruited the player, spoke to clubs who were happy to talk to him (despite it being a blatant breach of the regulations), actually went in with the player to discuss and negotiate the terms, and then, when all was done, finally and belatedly brought in the lawyer to 'check' the contract and sign off on it. He charged a basic ten per cent, so I suppose he was acting as an agent for all the flotsam and jetsam who still managed to thrive in football.

Lawyers sell themselves to players as a cut above the rest of us. They claim to be professional – like none of the rest of us – and say that a football contract is a complicated document that needs a legal brain to make sense of it. Players' families in particular seem to fall for this line, especially when the lawyer persuades them that a club won't raise the same objections when a player says he has a legal adviser to when he says he has an agent.

I'm not sure it matters a toss to the club. They'd rather have the player without any representation at all so they can rip him off. One lawyer was really taken down a peg or two when he rolled up at a club with his player only to be told by the secretary that the manager had a thing about young players having any advisers at all and that he would see the player on his own, although the lawyer was welcome to wait in the car park and give advice if and when the player sought it.

There ensued a bizarre series of events with the player shuttling to and fro between the manager's office and the car park, bringing offers from the club and then returning with a counter-proposal from the lawyer. When they finally got to the point where the terms were agreed, the lawyer asked about his fees and the player brought back a message from the manager saying that he (the player) was his (the lawyer's) client and he could fucking well pay him. End of.

I've had clubs refuse to speak to me as well, but nothing quite like that. The fact of the matter is that when a player signs with an agent, and the agent registers the contract with the FA, then the club is obliged to speak to the agent. However, I've yet to meet an agent brave enough to complain to the FA about a club refusing to do so. They know it would get the player into trouble with the club and the club would make sure that the player knew his problems had been triggered off by the agent's complaint. Which would mean that the relationship between the player and the agent wasn't likely to be one for life.

Don't get me wrong. As I've said, I've got a good lawyer myself. But I don't let him loose on my clients. I'm not saying he'd try to nick them away from me but I've seen it done so why tempt fate? Personally, I try to use them for what they're good at, like getting my clients off speeding offences. I even took the rap for one myself when the player was on nine points. The photo we requested didn't show definitively who was at the wheel but it did reveal two blokes in the front seats. There are times when you just have to go the extra mile for your clients, although I was a bit shocked when the Huhnes went to jail for precisely what I'd done. I won't be repeating the favour, that's for sure.

Divorces, drunken punch-ups in bars or the street, paternity claims, plain ordinary conveyancing, tax planning, wills: it's all good stuff and I don't mind paying for it. Somehow or other my players never quite get around to writing out the cheques, but as long as the fees I get for their transfers more than compensate me then I'm not one to complain. I try to make a merit out of it all, but, generally speaking, they just take it for granted. I suspect they take me for granted too. If something happens to me then there will be another agent close behind to mop up my clients. And even if nothing does happen, the likelihood is that eventually they'll get bored. What I don't want though is a lawyer stepping in who knows all my business and is able to tell them exactly where I've gone wrong.

I know of one player who got a bit suspicious of some of the investments his agent wanted him to make. He thought the agent might have a vested interest in a couple of the businesses or was getting too high a kickback. So he went behind the agent's back and consulted the lawyer to whom he'd been introduced by that very agent.

You might have thought that the lawyer would feel conflicted or, even if he didn't, would've felt obliged to mention it to the agent who'd regularly sent him work. Not a bit of it. He was in like Flynn. Muddying the water, only too keen to show exactly what the agent had done wrong. To be fair, the agent had pulled a fast one in some respects, but it still didn't seem right to me. Anyway, the end result was that the player dumped the agent and used the lawyer from then on, who in turn used him as his calling card to develop a very nice sports law practice with an agency tucked neatly into it. So much for professional standards.

Just made me even more careful. Trust nobody except yourself and even then keep looking in the mirror.

HUBRIS

O NE OF THE great benefits of having J on the payroll was that I could use him to help deliver the bespoke service I promised every player I signed. I encouraged J to get out there with the younger lads and make them feel as if he was one of them.

I gave him a budget. I prefer to call it a budget rather than a slush fund, but if it means keeping the players happy, in every sense of the word, then I'm good with that.

J's much more of a techie than me and he set up a database which detailed every piece of information we could possibly want on the players: family birthdays, wedding anniversaries if they were married, clothing sizes for freebies, personal likes and dislikes for presents; even a rating as to how much we might make out of them so that I could estimate how much to spend to keep them happy. I've always understood the need to balance investments against reward.

I took J to meetings with me, and he learned at my knee just as I had with R. As fate would have it, one day we ended up at the same Midlands club where I'd received my slight from the CEO. And fuck me, if he didn't do it again to J.

'Can you get your lad to pour us a coffee?' he said, pointing to the pot on a side-table. 'And I'll have a couple of biscuits as well.'

Not even a please. I stopped J in his tracks before we considered a 'thank you'. 'He's here to learn how to be a football agent, not to be a tea-lady,' I said sharply.

J poised in mid-air, having risen from his seat to do as the CEO asked. I nodded to him to sit down, and he did, knowing on which side his bread was buttered.

The CEO wasn't going to admit defeat. He just lifted the phone to his secretary who was seated outside and asked her in to serve the drinks. I was seriously tempted to tell her not to bother and that the CEO would be doing it for himself, but I resisted. I didn't want to screw up the deal we were negotiating.

J thanked me when we went out, said he'd learned a lot and was grateful to me for sticking up for him, but somehow I didn't get the feeling that he was as grateful as I'd been to R in the same situation.

Gradually I realised I should've stayed on my own. J proved to be good at getting players, but he had his own methods, some more orthodox than others and a few of them not just outside the FA regulations but beyond anything they could conceivably have envisaged.

Within months of J joining he had the signature of some really good players on undated representation contracts. The reason they were undated was because the players who had signed already had contracts with other agents, but J knew when they expired and was ready to shoot the contract off to the FA to register it for the very next day.

Some of the agents were so taken by surprise they didn't even know they'd lost the player until he stopped taking their calls and they read about a new deal in the papers. Of course I got the blame for all this, and with a few agents I knew I even went to the length of offering them a bit of the next deal to appease them. I kept telling them the kid was just enthusiastic but I could see that he was as driven as I'd been when I first started out. Just how driven he was I didn't realise until it was too late.

My relationship with Chairman K was still useful, as his club had recently got itself into Europe. This meant that they had a fair amount of money to spend, which in turn meant that they were the first port of call for some of the players I was acquiring through my little helper. That was another mistake. I should've kept him out of it, because when we did a deal at the club I had to tell J his commission was going to be based on the net figure after I'd paid off K.

I thought he'd accepted it and could see that the relationship was going to be good for us all, but I guess I underestimated his ambition, which had clearly taken on the heights of a Shakespearean tragedy. The only problem here was that I was going to be playing the title role, and we all know what happened to Hamlet.

It all came to a head when K's club indicated that they wanted to sign one of the players J had brought in. There were other clubs interested too, but I wasn't about to kill the golden goose so I actually encouraged the player to sign where I wanted him to play rather than at a club where he might have earned more money and certainly where the commission wouldn't have been tainted by a kickback.

I could tell J wasn't happy but I thought he'd get over it. I told him I was so pleased with him that I was upping his basic salary and increasing his commission by five per cent. Surely he'd be pleased and grateful given that he hadn't had to come to me to ask for anything? How wrong can you be . . .

It started with a letter from the player's lawyer – not the tame one who I used – putting me on notice that he was terminating my representation contract because I'd breached all my obligations of acting in good faith. Oh, and by the way he'd also be coming after me for damages because I hadn't told him about the better deal on offer.

I didn't even have time to think about how he could've known about the better deal before I got a letter from J telling me that he was resigning with immediate effect because he 'didn't like my business practices'.

I was disappointed but consoled myself thinking what a little shit he was and how I was just grateful that all the players were signed to me, and how his departure wouldn't have that much impact. I was confident that I could get all the players he'd recruited to stay with me, even when their contracts ran out, by schmoozing them and convincing them that I was the one with the ability to do the deals while J had just been a boy doing my bidding.

All that optimism evaporated with the next post. I got a letter from the FA instructing me that they were launching an investigation into the transfer to K's club and, as a participant, I was invited to come in and sit down with their nice regulatory people to assist with the inquiry.

I reckoned that the second company and the club's separate bank account were not going to be easy to discover, so I still wasn't too concerned. However, this complacency was a huge mistake. By the time I got to the FA for my interview, my lawyer, whom I thought it wise to involve now, had received a huge bundle of papers, which included a statement from my erstwhile assistant (now a totally ungrateful little cunt rather than merely a little shit) telling them what he knew about my relationship with K and his club, and how I'd carved up the player on the transfer.

I could've bluffed that one – they had no proof, and I could've just said that J was trying to destroy my business so that he could steal it himself – but they had a silver bullet.

They'd done what the Americans call a plea bargain with K. In return for his blowing the whistle on his entire under-the-radar operation (which to my surprise extended to a couple of other agents I knew and a few unlicensed guys as well) they'd said they would take his co-operation into consideration.

What could I do? I've always liked a fight, but this wasn't one I was going to win. My lawyer told me that all I'd do by pleading not guilty would be to piss them off even more than they already were. Come the day of the hearing, I put on my best suit and tie, sat alongside my lawyer and the eye-wateringly expensive barrister we'd engaged to lodge a plea in mitigation, and felt like a murderer from days gone by waiting for the judge to put on his black cap and sentence me to hang.

They read out what they were doing to everybody else first – just to extend the agony. The club was fined a hundred grand and had twenty points deducted, of which ten were suspended to acknowledge their assistance. My old partner in crime had already resigned as chairman and director, and had even got rid of his shares to show that the club, at least, was starting afresh. One of the agents received a twenty-grand fine and a year's suspension of his licence; the other got ten grand and a year as well, but with six months suspended.

So that just left me. By that time I realised I wasn't going to get a Good Conduct Medal despite the impassioned plea made by my counsel, which had painted a picture of me that I hardly recognised. In fact, I decided I'd really quite like to become the person he'd described if I ever got the chance. But at that moment it didn't seem very likely.

They threw the book at me. Said that I'd concocted the whole thing and brought good people down, that K had been in the industry with a totally blameless record until he'd met me, that the whole accounting structure had been my idea, that a player had found himself funnelled into a club (which was now likely to be relegated because of the points deduction) just to satisfy my relentless financial greed, and that they had to set an example. The sacrifice on the altar of high moral standards – OK, they didn't quite use those words, but that was how I saw it – was going to be yours truly.

I was hit with a five-year ban from any involvement in football whatsoever, a fine of £150,000 and an order to pay costs which, with the fees of my own legal team, were likely to be in the region of about another £50,000. All in all, a really great result for me.

It wasn't as if this was going to be the best-kept secret in football either. They issued a press statement, posted it on their website, and even posted the whole hearing word for word for all to read. Overnight, it seemed to me, I'd become a pariah in the sport I loved.

So that was it. All my contracts with my players were terminated. So were all my deals with clubs, including a ton of pipeline income they would've had to pay over the next couple of years. I reckoned that the cost to me in actual terms was about two million. And that didn't take into account the money I would've earned over the next five years. It was, basically, a case of what goes around comes around. R had taken me on as his apprentice and I'd fucked him to set up on my own; I'd taken J on and he'd now done the same, but with more devastating effect.

A few people called me to say how sorry they were. Only a few, to be honest, but when you'd been as ruthless as I'd been in building up a business, even those few were a miracle. R was one of them, and I really appreciated the gesture. I'd acted badly towards him when he'd given me the chance in the first place, and he'd no reason to feel any regret for my demise within the business.

He asked me to meet him for a drink which I gratefully accepted. My lawyers had gone back to their offices and chambers to gird their loins and don their gowns for the next case. To them it was just business. To me it was my life; R understood that.

I got calls from some of my players to say that they, at least, appreciated all I'd done for them, and one of them even asked if I needed any financial help. That really touched me, as I'd put them all in the same box when I'd been in business.

When I arrived at the bar, R had already ordered me a large whisky. He'd remembered that I didn't drink a lot but I did have a weakness when it came to expensive Scotch, and as it slid smoothly and numbingly over my palate I knew it was probably the most expensive the bar had to offer.

'It's not the end,' he said. 'If you play it properly then the game is never over.'

EPILOGUE

THE GAME IS never over. R's words never left me and R never abandoned me as he was quite entitled to do. We agreed that he and I would go back to where we started off. I'd find him the deals and he'd front for me. It was a risky strategy, because it only needed one player or club to tip off the FA that I was back in the game and they'd be down on me like a ton of bricks. Though what they could do to me that was any worse, I wasn't quite sure. It was really R who was taking all the risks.

I think he'd become just a little devil-may-care, because we all knew by then that FIFA had decided that all licences had to be handed in in April 2015. The irony wasn't lost on me. Hundreds of good guys who had obeyed the rules, played it by the book, and missed out on all the opportunities that I'd seized upon were now in exactly the same position as me. Licenceless. (If there's such a word and my spellcheck seems to be telling me there isn't.)

FIFA had finally thrown in the towel. They couldn't cope, they couldn't administer and they'd kind of lost the will to regulate. I mean, there's obviously a lot more to be earned by taking backhanders to dole out the largesse of World Cups and sell the tickets for the tournament on the black market, than there is in drafting and supervising incomprehensible, vindictive and, as it transpired, meaningless regulations for agents. Perhaps the AFA (the agents' trade union) should have had a whip-round to pay FIFA off like everybody else seems to do, but they didn't, so goodbye it is to the licensing system.

As I've related, they've come up with something to replace it called intermediaries. No qualifications whatsoever are required, other than to prove you're not dead. It may well be that even somebody like me who's been banned can rise from the dead and register as an intermediary, but I've not been able to test that yet. I'm thinking that if a serial killer out on parole can register, then why not me? But with the vagaries of the FA one never knows.

However, that's April and this is now, and there's a whole two transfer windows stretching ahead for R and me to make hay. He's struck a hard deal: all I get from everything I generate is twenty per cent, but as you'll have gathered by now, anything you get is better than the zero you have, so I didn't even try to negotiate on that.

R raised an eyebrow when I just accepted what he offered. 'I hope you haven't lost your old skills,' he said.

'Watch me,' I replied.

And I hadn't. The players were as good as gold, and I had to eat my words about their loyalty to me. I knew I'd done well for them, and they didn't seem to hold it against me that the FA had found me guilty regarding the player who had gone to Chairman K's club. He was known as a moaner in the game anyway, and the deal he'd got had hardly put him on the poverty line.

We were doing fine, R and me. He was still the best in the business, and after a week or two I kept asking myself why I'd left him in the first place. I answered myself by saying that I was younger then, more impatient and that I'd just not understood the game. The fact of the matter was that it wasn't football itself that was the game. It was being involved. What I did, what R did, what all the people I'd met along the way did off the pitch, that was our game. Not the beautiful one that the likes of Brazil and Spain play, but a brutal one, an unforgiving one, where losers tend not to get a second chance. Maybe in some way I had lost, but I couldn't admit defeat to myself. That was why I'd needed to get back into the game, where the regulators think they lay down the rules but where, in reality, there's only one rule: to make as much money as you can in the shortest time possible.

Did I still believe that? Was I still so arrogant as to make that my mantra? I really didn't know and right now I'm doubting whether I'll be given the time to find out.

At five a.m. this morning there was a knock at my door. I looked out the window and my stomach fell with the heaving sensation I used to get on seaside rollercoasters. It was the police, and they weren't the friendly neighbourhood type. They explained, politely, that they had a warrant for my arrest and a search warrant permitting them to remove my computer and any other papers or equipment they deemed necessary. Deep down inside I'd felt this might be coming. The Bribery Act had caught up with me. And that was what I was charged under, for all the payments I'd made for favours.

It was like my whole life flashing in front of me, as they say in the movies. Managers I'd accommodated, sports manufacturers, players' relations and last but by no means least, my old friend Chairman K.

Somehow, none of it had seemed wrong at the time. If what I'd done was criminal, then where were the victims lining up to accuse me? Where were those who had been defrauded or lost money? Already, in my mind, I was preparing my defence just as I was contemplating how to explain it all to my parents when my face was plastered across tomorrow's papers.

I just wanted to be rich – not famous and certainly not infamous. I wanted what they never had. Was that such a crime?

R's come through again and bailed me out, even though there was a chance he'd now be in trouble if the FA saw anything on my computers they didn't like. I'd tried to be careful in my dealings with him, but had I been careful enough? Time alone will tell.

I still think I can get out of this. I have to. The basic essential of any good agent is optimism and I've always had it in spades. I'm still alive, and as far as I'm aware there isn't a death penalty in the UK for the offences of which I've been accused. I'll work through this and find the solution. There's always one.

In the meantime, with all the time I now have on my hands, maybe I'll write a book. And tell it like it is. If anybody will believe it.

ADAM
TRANCE
SOUTHWARD

THOMAS & MERCER

Published by Thomas & Mercer, Seattle

www.apub.com

Amazon, the Amazon logo, and Thomas & Mercer are trademarks of Amazon.com, Inc., or its affiliates.

ISBN-13: 9781542093651 (hardcover)
ISBN-10: 1542093651 (hardcover)
ISBN-13: 9781503958661 (paperback)
ISBN-10: 1503958663 (paperback)

Cover design by kid-ethic

Printed in the United States of America

To Kerry, Isla and Daisy, with love.

CHAPTER ONE

The professor kneeled with care to avoid the blood, which was already pooling on the cheap classroom lino, and placed his hand on the woman's shoulder, wincing at the warm sticky fluid. He looked into her eyes and she blinked. She tried to speak, gasping as her throat bubbled with blood. Her lips parted but the words never came. The sight of her life slipping away caused the professor's stomach to cramp, and he tensed with pain. Tears blurred his vision, but he was powerless to save her.

Who was she? He recognised her face, but couldn't place the name. She had pale, lined skin and red lips. Her hair was short and dark with specks of grey; a floral scarf was tied loosely around her neck. A colleague, perhaps. Or one of his students? So many people passed through his faculty on a daily basis, he couldn't remember everyone.

He glanced at his watch. He was late. His wife had tickets that evening to a performance at London's South Bank. It was starting at seven o'clock. Elgar's Symphony No. 2 was his favourite piece and he hummed it now, hitting the notes with satisfaction, as is only possible to do when music plays in your head. The music stopped with a sharp pain through his right eye.

The woman moved, her right leg twitching, but it was wet, bloody. He watched her movements slow as her breathing quickened into shorter, shallower gasps. She was bleeding from several wounds to her chest, and her eyes were glazed. She was still alive.

'I'm sorry,' he whispered, and with his right hand he grasped the knife, pulling it clear. With a deep breath and all the effort he could muster, he forced it into her chest again.

It was a kitchen knife, serrated but blunt, and he pulled it out with a shaking hand. He couldn't remember where the knife had come from, but it looked old. He frowned as the blood dripped from the plastic handle on to his wrist and under his watch strap.

The professor touched the woman's cheek, leaving a smear, ruining her make-up, but she was dead now so it didn't matter. Besides, the panic was coming in waves and he was forced to stand, head up, gulping air into his lungs, trying to push the bile back into his throat.

The classroom was large, dark but for the illumination provided by the streetlights outside the northern window. The tables had been arranged in a loose U-shape for seminars, but it was a mess, tables and chairs strewn at various angles. It would take a while to put right.

A few feet away from the woman lay an elderly gentleman, face down between the tables. The table legs had marked the floor – black lines where the man had lashed out, desperate to escape. The gentleman was the professor's assistant head of faculty and a brilliant scientist. They had worked together for twenty years. He was dressed, as always, in a formal suit, with a black tie and polished brogues. His grey side parting was still in place, although his glasses lay shattered, one of the arms snapped and resting on his cheek. He was already dead. The professor had stabbed him four times in the back. He was supposed to be the only one, but the woman had turned up and interrupted him. What choice did he have?

The professor stared at the broken glasses for several seconds before the nausea became unbearable. He turned his head to fight it, looking away from the two prone bodies, hyperventilating as his confusion spiralled. Glancing at the wall, a picture of Jung stared back at him. He'd hung the poster himself, along with the others. It was above the shelf of neatly stacked first-year texts, still in their place.

The poster of Jung blurred as fresh tears welled in the professor's eyes. He groaned as his chest tightened.

He looked over to the classroom doorway, desperate for help, but the dark figure in the corridor shook his head, just as he had done earlier, and muttered something under his breath, before stepping forwards into the light.

The figure emerging from the shadows was slight, but plump, dressed in a sloppy suit with scuffed shoes. His head was polished bald and his glasses were perched on the end of his nose. His eyes were fixed, his stare holding the professor's mind in an unyielding grip.

The figure remained in the corridor and whispered a few words, reeled off quickly. The whisper hissed across the space between them like a breath of wind, and although the professor couldn't make out the words, the fog cleared in his head, the confusion channelling into purpose. The nausea was still there, and the bile rose in the professor's throat once again. His legs filled with static as the suggestions were planted into his consciousness. He knew what he must do, and the realisation filled him with terror.

The wave of panic caused his head to spin. He staggered, grabbing the nearest table. It screeched on the floor and he nearly fell, but stood his ground.

'Why?' said the professor, his voice rasping. 'Please?'

But the man shook his head, whispering again, making the instruction clear.

The professor pleaded, begging, but was met with a sharp pain in his temples. Each time he cried out the pain increased. He asked for mercy, but it was no use, and he lowered his eyes in resignation. There was nothing he could do. He had no control.

The man backed away into the darkness, becoming a shadow once more, standing in wait.

The words jostled in the professor's mind, seeking their place, settling in the cracks, happy they'd found their target. The professor fought but the suggestions planted themselves firmly in the bedrock of his consciousness so that they became part of him, and their power was absolute. They told him what to do, and he did it.

He had no choice.

The professor found the knife went into his own neck more easily, and although he could feel the tugging in his throat, the pain was distant, dull and unimportant. He was aware of the blood pouring from his arteries, but it registered as a detached sensation, the metallic smell alerting his nostrils, but triggering nothing else.

Within a few seconds he was too weak to stand, and his legs folded. He slumped, first to his knees, then his side. All the while his eyes were fixed on the figure in the doorway. The man who smiled, and spoke again to him, even as his hearing began to fail.

The last thing the professor saw before closing his eyes was the man pull up a chair. He sat, looking exhausted, holding his head. His right foot tapped on the floor.

The professor made out one last whisper from the man in the doorway. It was in a foreign tongue, and at first he didn't understand it, but then the recognition came. *Te iert.* I forgive you. The language was familiar, and it brought a rush of memories, long suppressed, to the front of his mind. He knew now why the man had come, and he knew what was happening. He also knew it was too late to stop him.

CHAPTER TWO

Dr Alex Madison woke at 6 a.m., aching and groggy. The alarm clock had failed to go off – because he'd forgotten to set it. He pushed himself up and yawned, flexing his neck muscles, trying to ease the stiffness out of his back.

He felt washed out, tired and gloomy. Too much red wine and not enough quality sleep. Alex slid open the bedside drawer and reached for his pills. He stared at the packet, willing himself to put them back as he did every morning. Just one, he thought, to settle him into the day. He popped it out of the foil and swallowed it dry.

Jane lay next to him on her front, naked, sheets around her knees. Her blonde bob covered the side of her face, almost perfectly sculpted into place. Alex stared, willing himself to feel aroused, willing himself to manage more than six months of a relationship before getting to this point. He watched the back of her head, wondering what went on in it, wondering if he cared.

Jane arched her back and rolled over. 'You were home late,' she said, wiggling her hips. 'Fancy staying in bed for a bit?'

'I can't,' Alex said with a frown. 'Sorry. Work.'

Jane huffed, blowing a strand of hair out of her face.

Alex saw the flash of hurt in her eyes. 'I would love to, honestly,' he said, 'but I can't today. New referral. Maybe in a few weeks things will calm down.'

It was only half a lie. He didn't want to stay in bed, but he did have a new work assignment. That said, he could have taken the opportunity to finally break things off and ask Jane to leave. He owed her that much.

As it was, Jane sighed and rolled back over, closing her eyes.

Alex watched her, tracing the lines of her legs, over her buttocks and the small of her back. Her breathing was shallow, the tension clear in her shoulders. She was upset, angry, probably both. They'd performed this routine for weeks now, as Alex steadily demolished their relationship. She still tried. He'd pretty much given up.

He reached out, placing his hand on her back. Her soft skin tensed, then relaxed. She didn't move. He paused, staring at her, mentally checking off the things he should say, before withdrawing his hand. He stood and the bed rocked slightly.

'See you later,' he said, backing out of the bedroom, grabbing his robe from the hook on the door.

After a quick shower, Alex slipped on his suit, grabbed his phone and wallet and headed downstairs to make coffee. Another two missed calls from Grace. He checked his watch. He had time to call before breakfast.

'Alex,' Grace answered, her voice conveying the usual disappointment in him.

'You called,' said Alex, stirring three heaped sugars into his coffee.

'I call a lot,' said Grace, 'because our daughter is a busy girl and needs at least some input from her dad. You don't often answer.'

This was true, although Alex loved Katie and tried to be available. However, Grace frequently called late or at the crack of dawn. He suspected she knew he wouldn't be able to pick up, giving her the higher ground from which to judge him. He deserved it, every bit, but it didn't mean he liked it.

'I can't answer if I'm asleep and my phone's switched off,' said Alex, picking up several stray grains of sugar from the worktop and dropping them carefully into the sink.

'Do you ever switch your phone off?' said Grace. 'That other woman managed to get hold of you night and day when we were married. Or have you forgotten?'

Alex hadn't forgotten, and was seldom able to suppress the waves of guilt when Grace brought it up. He had his excuses, albeit poor ones, but Grace had enough examples for the rest of their natural lives.

'How can I help?' said Alex. 'What do you need? Can I speak to Katie?'

'You could have done,' said Grace, 'if you'd called back two days ago when I first called you. She's gone to the New Forest, camping. A place near Lyndhurst. I told you about this.'

She was right. She had told him.

'I don't remember you telling me,' said Alex, annoyed he'd missed her. 'Does she have her phone?'

'No mobiles except in emergencies. It's a back-to-nature forest school. They can't very well keep the kids' attention if they're all on Instagram. Mobiles stay in the tents.'

'Sounds dangerous,' said Alex, thinking that it sounded wonderful and exactly the sort of thing children her age should be doing.

'Apparently people camped before mobile phones and the Internet,' said Grace. 'The teachers will call if anything happens. It's safe, OK?'

'OK,' said Alex. 'So—'

'I was calling about a couple of things.' Grace sounded reluctant. The hostility was gone and Alex knew this was about money. He paid Grace child support, over and above the court order, but as a single mum there were always expenses. Alex wished she didn't feel guilty about asking.

'First thing, the trip was expensive,' said Grace. 'Nothing I can't handle, but I wondered if you'd like to contribute – you know, so we can say both her mum and her dad made it possible?'

Grace's tone was cutting, but he deserved it. Alex had always promised himself never to screw up his family. He'd hated men who broke up happy families. The kids never deserved it. Katie didn't deserve it.

'Grace,' he said, 'tell me how much a reasonable contribution would be and I'll transfer it right now. You know it's not a problem.'

'Easy, Alex,' said Grace, the hostility edging back in. 'Money only gets you so far.'

Alex swallowed. What a crappy start to the morning.

'But three hundred should cover it,' said Grace. 'I had to pay for everything on the credit card.'

Alex wrote 'Grace – £500' on a notepad. 'It'll be with you today.'

'The second thing,' said Grace, 'is when she gets back she wants to come and stay with you.'

Alex's frown disappeared and he smiled. 'With me?'

'Just for a few days,' said Grace. 'I said it was OK.'

Alex took a deep breath and the knot in his stomach relaxed. After the rather messy separation, they'd agreed Grace's home was best for Katie. She had been eight years old and needed stability more than anything else. Alex took her out for midweek dinners and she stayed with him sometimes at the weekend, but it was difficult to make time around his busy work schedule and her burgeoning social life. She was now twelve and her days off from school were filled with piano lessons, gymnastics, parties and friends. Now that Katie had a phone, they sent each other texts and jokes, and had catch-up calls a couple of times a week. He knew he had been a disappointment as a husband, but he wanted to be a good father.

Alex thought of Jane, still upstairs. He realised he didn't want Jane here when Katie came to stay. Jane was so different to Grace – what would that suggest to Katie? Having a woman in his bed suggested some kind of permanence or commitment he didn't want Katie to believe in. Not now, and not with Jane. He wanted Katie's visit to feel safe and secure and, above all, normal. Jane couldn't be part of it.

'That would be wonderful,' he said. 'Thank you, Grace.' He meant it. His heart melted at the thought of Katie. He tried to swallow the guilt away but it tugged at the back of his throat. When it came to family, he was a disaster.

Grace was silent for a few moments. 'It's time she did,' she said. 'I can't forgive a lot of the things you did, but neither can I keep you and Katie apart. I don't want to.'

'When?' said Alex.

'Not for two weeks,' said Grace. 'She's away for a week and a half, then she'll need a couple of days to recover and clean the mud from her ears and fingernails.'

Alex smiled. Two weeks. His new case might be over by then, one way or the other, and he could take a few days off. His private psychology patients could be rescheduled, and he was already making plans in his head: the science and natural history museums, the theatre, the zoo. Had she been on the Eye? Katie had spent all her life in London. When Alex and Grace split, Grace had kept the family house in Ealing, and Alex had moved north into Harrow. Perhaps it would be good to take her out of the city, to the country or maybe the beach. They could head to the south coast and hit Brighton.

'Sounds perfect,' said Alex. 'I can't wait.'

Silence at the other end, followed by Grace clearing her throat. 'And you're OK, Alex?' she said. 'I heard you'd taken a case. Back with the police?'

Alex frowned. Gossip got around fast.

'You don't need to do it,' said Grace. 'You don't need to make up for anything. Your practice is fine.'

'Fine?'

'Try and ignore your father,' said Grace. 'I know he's on your back. You've nothing to prove.'

Although Alex tried to ignore his father on principle, he struggled to brush him off entirely. Influential in the medical world and advisor to various boards, Alex's father was a prominent research psychologist and let Alex know it whenever he could. In the last month, Alex had received three rather cold phone calls from his father, suggesting he take a break from therapy and do something useful with his education.

'Private practice suits you,' said Grace.

Alex clenched his jaw. 'Suits me?'

'You know what I mean. Christ!'

'I'm being asked to consult, Grace. I'm rather a well-respected psychologist in my field, you know.'

'I know. That's not what I meant.'

There was a pause, an awkward silence as Alex tried to wind down his frustration. It wouldn't help.

'It wasn't your fault, Alex. The case. Nobody blames you.'

Alex bit his tongue. Those words had been repeated to him so many times they'd become meaningless. They might be true, but they didn't work. The guilt remained.

'I'll transfer the money,' he said. 'Speak to you soon, Grace.'

He heard Grace sigh, but she knew better than to push it.

'Take care, Alex,' she said, hanging up.

Alex put the phone down, cursing himself for reacting so petulantly. Grace did understand his work. She was one of the few who ever had. The fact that it was his work that had contributed to his marriage breakdown was not lost on Grace. She was fair, but firm. His last case for the police had ended in tragedy, but his behaviour at the time had been a choice. He knew better, and he wished he could go back and change things.

He closed his eyes and smiled. He missed her voice. He missed a lot about her, but he never told her. It was too late for that.

CHAPTER THREE

Alex shivered as he stopped the car at the first security checkpoint. He cranked the heating up. The red-and-white barrier stayed down as a guard walked over, a thickset man with a tattoo of a snake devouring its own tail on the left side of his neck.

The prison entrance loomed, and Alex felt numb. He had been disconnected from this world for so long, yet it still felt familiar: the dirty orange brick walls of HMP Whitemoor hiding a lifetime of secrets and grime. The gatehouse was hostile, stacked with barriers and warnings. It granted entry to a different realm of human experience.

Alex opened the window and put on his practised doctor's smile – insincere at this time in the morning, but useful for masking the growling discomfort in his gut. The cold air smelled damp and tingled in his nostrils.

'Staff?' said the guard, not returning the smile.

'Kind of. Dr Alex Madison. I have an appointment.'

Alex held out his ID and the guard took it, sniffing as he scanned his clipboard. He flicked over to the next page and raised his eyebrows. 'Not on my list,' he said, lowering the clipboard, handing Alex's ID card back through the open window.

Alex's neck burned. He swallowed, then raised his eyebrows, forcing another smile. The guard continued to stare. Alex was aware he was physically unimpressive compared to the guard, probably half his size and weight, his groomed hair and stubble not currying any favours.

'Can you check again, please?' said Alex. 'Dr Bradley is expecting me at nine.' He glanced at his watch. It was eight fifty-three.

The guard huffed, turning and ambling back to the guardroom. Alex could see him speaking into a phone. *Patience*, he said to himself. *Agitation will not help this situation.* He glanced at the rear-view mirror, sweeping a few stray hairs back into place, judging his receding hairline with a frown. He watched the cars queue behind him. *Sorry*, he mouthed in the mirror, anxious that his first impression was spoiling by the second.

The guard made him wait another full minute before strolling back over. 'Tell your boss to submit his paperwork on time.'

'He's not my boss . . .' said Alex, but the guard didn't wait for a reply, turning to give the nod towards the guardroom. The barrier lifted. Alex nodded in turn and mumbled an apology, not bothering to ask where to go after he got through the main gate, although he had no idea. He smiled his thanks and drove into the prison grounds.

Alex followed the signs to the staff parking lot and pulled into the one empty space. He wondered if he was entitled to his own. He doubted it. Not for the short time he'd be here.

The parking lot was tucked around the side of the main entrance. Unpleasant smells from a kitchen wafted over as he exited the car, billowing from vents set high up on the wall. Crisp packets and tissues drifted across the tarmac towards him from a cluster of black-wheeled bins. A stray cat yawned on top of a stack of old tyres against the wall, its yellow eyes lazily following Alex as he walked away.

Following the directions emailed to him by Dr Bradley, and after enduring several more stop-and-check routines, Alex entered the D Wing staff entrance.

If the outside was impressive and daunting, the inside was barren and decrepit. A public-sector building with less character than a warehouse, it reeked of underinvestment and lack of care. The floor was pocked and marked, the skirting boards held on with duct tape, while lazy carpentry held together the more substantial structures.

Several warning signs on the wall clarified the rules about contraband, forbidden items and electrical devices. A guard offered him one of two battered plastic chairs in the corridor while he waited to be escorted to his office. He was reminded to get his security photo and biometrics taken today otherwise he'd be delayed at the gate again tomorrow. He needed an HMP Whitemoor-approved prison ID to be granted access. At this news he offered another fake smile.

He stared at the stained cream wall for a couple of minutes, trying not to inhale the faint smell of bleach, before the inner doors buzzed and swung open.

'Dr Madison.' A woman raced up to Alex and grabbed his hand, shaking it hard. She was tall, with tanned skin and dark hair. Her hands were soft and her eyes beautiful.

Alex cleared his throat. 'Sorry,' he said, 'trouble at the gate.'

'They stop people getting out as well,' she said cheerfully. 'Don't worry, you get used to it. I'm Sophie.'

'Alex.'

'I'm your assistant,' she said with a smile, pulling her hand away.

'An assistant? I don't—'

'I know,' said Sophie, 'but I'm a trainee in need of a supervisor, so you're it, if only short term. Is that going to be a problem?'

Alex paused, assessing his new companion. She talked fast, with what he assumed was a light German accent. Attractive and outwardly confident, Alex warmed to her immediately, although beneath her physical charm he saw something deeper – a flicker of nervousness in her eyes that she couldn't quite hide.

'No problem,' he said, not wanting to debate the finer points of his contract in the corridor with an assistant he wasn't supposed to have. 'Shall we—'

'Of course,' said Sophie. 'Follow me. I'll take you to your office, you can get settled, maybe grab some coffee, and then I'll take you through a few details – if that's OK?'

'Dr Bradley's expecting me.' He checked his watch again. Four minutes past nine.

'Robert? He's not here,' said Sophie, skewing her mouth. 'He got called away. It happens a lot: he covers three prisons. Didn't you know? I guess not. You'll meet him soon enough, maybe tomorrow. I expect he wants to talk to you before you start your work.'

Alex frowned. This wasn't what he'd expected. This was his first criminal case in three years. Dr Bradley knew it and knew why. But this time the referral had come from on high: a senior official at the CPS wanted Alex on this case and had provided enough information to pique Alex's interest. A bizarre multiple murder followed by the death of a clinician – none other than the psychologist tasked with assessing the murder suspect. That sort of case didn't come along very often, if ever. Despite his reservations about taking on another criminal case so soon, might this just prove to be a chance for Alex to rescue his career – and himself?

Whatever Grace had said about private practice suiting him, she knew he wasn't satisfied with it. His heart and soul lay in forensics. He might have nothing to prove to the police, but he did to himself.

Today, however, he'd wanted a professional introduction with the psychologist in charge, to go over the finer details of the case and the suspect he was tasked with assessing. He was not expecting a rushed intro from a young post-doc over a cup of coffee.

The staff admin area of D Wing felt like an NHS hospital, a location with which Alex was familiar from his own clinical training. Overcrowded desks tucked away in badly designed office cubicles, the smell of bleach from the corridor replaced with the smell of biscuits and coffee. It was a far cry from his current office, which housed hand-stitched leather couches and solid hardwood furniture, his reproduction Regency writing desk in pride of place.

There weren't many desks in Sophie's unit. Dangerous and Severe Personality Disorders was a small department, dealing with ninety inmates who were kept separate from the other four hundred and thirty in the main prison population. Among those ninety were twenty or so in segregation, or solitary confinement. Among those twenty was the one inmate he'd been asked to assess.

'This is DSPD.' Sophie indicated a set of desks surrounded by partitions. 'Forensics over here and all other disciplines through there.' She pointed at five empty desks. One of them had a dead plant on it.

Alex nodded, wondering if the prisoners' cells were better or worse than this.

'Your desk is here.' She pointed to the cleanest one of three. 'I'm next to you and the third is used by Robert – I mean Dr Bradley – when he's here.'

'No offices?' said Alex, surprised the three doctors were expected to share a cramped cubicle. He tried not to look at the dirty cup marks marring the desktop.

'We did have,' said Sophie, 'or at least my old manager did. They're being used for storage at the moment. They said they'd clear and reno-vate them. We moved out here and I guess they forgot.' She put her hand to her mouth, smudging her lipstick. 'Is the desk OK? I could clean it again if you—'

'The desk is fine,' said Alex, aware that Sophie was trying hard to make him welcome. He should try a bit harder. He dropped his bag on a tatty swivel chair and sat on the edge of the desk, facing her. She chewed at one of her fingernails. He studied her hands and saw that all her nails were short and ragged.

There was an awkward silence. Alex glanced at a radio on a nearby filing cabinet. Soft jazz floated out of the speaker. Sophie leaned over and switched the radio off.

'If it's just me I have it on,' she said, 'for company.'

Alex smiled.

'A bit different from Harley Street?' said Sophie, pointing at the desk.

Alex was surprised. 'You researched me?'

'A little,' said Sophie. 'When Robert gave me your name I googled you. You've been in the tabloid limelight – lucky you.' She raised her eyebrows in amusement.

'Lucky me,' he said, hoping she'd only read the good tabloid reports, not the bad. He frowned.

'Sorry, I don't mean to pry,' said Sophie, her smile disappearing as she saw his expression. 'I'm interested in your practice, how you apply your procedures in the private sector.'

'Don't apologise.' Alex shook his head, annoyed at himself. His current practice was quite well publicised. He pulled out the chair and sat. 'It's fine. What would you like to know?'

Sophie remained standing. 'You've done this before?' she said. 'Forensic assessments for the CPS? Robert mentioned that you used to, but don't any more.'

'I used to, yes,' he said, pausing. Would she know why he'd stayed away for so long? 'Not for a while though. If I'm honest, most days I sit in my practice and listen to people with small amounts of anxiety and large amounts of money.'

'Clinical? CBT? Stuff like that?'

'A lot of that. I'm a clinical psychologist by profession and by branding. If you ever work in the private sector you'll realise branding is as important as your training, perhaps more so.'

Sophie tilted her head. 'So that's how you started working with celebrities?'

Alex smiled, the tension easing away. She'd obviously read the gossip online.

'I don't work exclusively with celebrities. A couple of years ago I made a name for myself by treating a footballer with performance anxiety,' he said. 'Word spread and before I knew it I was the go-to man for several big clubs. I got calls day and night from managers and agents. It was a . . . very successful period for me. I set up my practice and it's still going on the same basis.'

'Psychologist to the stars,' said Sophie.

Alex wasn't sure whether Sophie was making fun of him or not. Her expression remained serious, but she smiled.

'That's what *Women's Own* magazine labelled me,' he said. He didn't admit to Sophie he'd given the magazine that strapline in a telephone interview. He was still unsure if it had been a good idea – it had earned him a certain amount of scorn in professional circles, but had been good publicity at a time when he was convinced he'd never go back to forensics. Building up his business had been top priority, at the expense of almost everything else.

And he was being truthful. Alex's clinical background, combined with several years of specialising in forensic psychology for the CPS, had given him a wide range of experience to call upon. Generalised anxiety disorder, phobias, depression, addictions – Alex had treated them all and earned quite a name for himself as a result. He'd let the magazine run with it.

What they didn't say was that no form of psychological intervention was foolproof, and things didn't always go as planned. Alex had already learned that the hard way, to disastrous effect. Shutting himself away in private practice had been the easy option.

'I'm afraid private work isn't all that glamorous,' he said. 'Exposure therapy, behavioural activation, some regression and hypnotherapy.'

'Hypnosis?' Sophie's smile had faded. Something was bothering her. 'For controlling people?'

'Not controlling,' said Alex. 'No, that's not what it's for.' He was puzzled at her query. 'But in the right hands it's effective. And lucrative.'

Sophie stepped forwards and glanced at his hands, then back to his eyes. Her smile didn't return. She was odd, but despite the direct questions, Alex liked her more by the minute. Having an assistant might not be too bad after all.

'Enough about me,' he said, aware that he was staring at her again. He averted his eyes and glanced around. 'Tell me about this place, Sophie. You like working in DSPD?'

Sophie's expression changed and her smile returned. 'You bet. Dangerous and Severe Personality Disorders rule!' She waved her hand at various books and folders on her desk, all branded with the title DSPD in bold type. 'I'm lucky to have a placement here. Well, lucky might not be the word, but I'll learn a lot. It'll be good for my career.'

Alex nodded and stayed silent. Sophie's smile remained on her lips but not in her eyes. Something troubled her about her career. Alex waited for her to continue.

'Our unit is one of only four in the UK,' she said. 'Most of our inmates have committed extremely violent or sexual crimes. Some are sectioned already, but several are still awaiting assessment.'

Alex frowned. 'What do you think about a DSPD diagnosis?'

'Well, it's not a clinical diagnosis, obviously, but rather a catch-all for those prisoners whose personality and behaviour is dangerous to society – to say the least, in certain cases.'

Alex smiled. '"Not a diagnosis" is the best description I could give it too, given there is no evidence for either the disorder or the treatment.'

'But in practice it's just an extreme version of antisocial personality disorder,' countered Sophie. 'That's a real diagnosis.' She shuffled her feet, her boots scratching on the floor.

'True,' said Alex. 'So are you telling me all ninety of your patients in DSPD have antisocial personality disorder? That's rather neat.'

'Erm, I guess not. Although a lot of them haven't finished their assessments yet – it's possible some don't belong here.'

Alex nodded. Sophie was honest, if a tad wired. But she knew what she was talking about, which would be useful for him. Alex had studied HMP Whitemoor's management of DSPD. He doubted it would give him much insight into the suspect, but he knew that establishing the culture in a place like this was important. DSPD could be used to lock violent offenders away indefinitely, delaying proper assessment and treatment and reducing the chances of moving them back into the general prison population, or a lower security prison. At least Sophie understood that DSPD was more of a political mechanism than a clinical one.

He jumped as his phone vibrated, causing his keys to jingle.

'Excuse me,' he said to Sophie and pulled the phone out to check the screen. It was Jane. He watched it vibrate for a few seconds before answering.

'Hi,' he said, standing and turning away. Sophie busied herself at her desk, switching on her ageing Dell laptop.

'Just checking you got there OK,' said Jane. Her tone was interested, if a little cold. 'What's it like inside the prison? Is Dr Bradley nice? I wanted to see if we were OK. After this morning. You know . . .'

'I'm fine,' said Alex, annoyed she'd called during office hours. What did that say about him? She was just trying to show she cared.

Sophie's computer beeped and she whispered an apology.

'Look, I've gotta go,' said Alex. 'I'm in the middle of something.'

'Oh, OK,' said Jane, sounding disappointed. 'Perhaps we can talk later? I feel a bit, you know—'

'I've got to go, Jane,' said Alex, pausing for a second before hanging up. He turned to Sophie and smiled.

'Wife?' said Sophie.

'Girlfriend,' said Alex. 'I have an ex-wife, but we don't see each other so much.'

Sophie laughed. 'Sounds complicated.'

'It is,' said Alex, deciding he'd rather not start another line of questioning. 'Can you show me the segregation wing and the cells? If I can't speak to Dr Bradley, I may as well get familiar with the place.'

'Sure,' said Sophie, standing and throwing her bag on the chair. 'I'll need to alert our guard detail. We need an escort and you'll have to leave your phone here.'

'Not a problem,' said Alex, placing it on the desk. 'Lead the way.'

Sophie kept glancing at Alex as they descended the stairs to the guard station. He noticed it and wondered what was bothering her.

'Will you be assessing him?' she said, after several steps.

'Him?'

'Him. Thirteen. Victor Lazar.'

Alex slowed and turned to her. 'Mr Lazar is why I'm here. Thirteen?'

Sophie's eyes narrowed. 'It's what he called himself when he arrived. Thirteen. So that's a yes?'

Alex was surprised at her reaction. 'What do you know about him?'

Sophie bit her lip. 'Not much,' she said. 'His case is sensitive. Robert has access to the full case file. I don't.' She shrugged and walked faster.

Alex hadn't seen the full case file yet either. He'd had a summary history emailed to him by the CPS but was told the full information would be available once he was on site.

As well as the unusual circumstances surrounding Victor Lazar's arrest, there was the headline mystery, which was that Victor's previous psychologist had committed suicide while treating him. Dr Henry Farrell, an experienced clinician close to retirement, had interviewed Victor alone in his cell for an hour. He'd left the cell complaining of a headache and driven home to call his wife, who was out of town. He'd made various nonsense statements over the phone, which his wife couldn't accurately recollect, then jumped out of a third-floor window, landing on the concrete driveway. He was pronounced dead by paramedics at the scene.

Alex could no doubt suggest several theories why a sane and intelligent man would take his own life, but the association with Victor was bizarre and curious. Victor appeared to be special – a potentially untreatable psychopath if the initial report was anything to go by. But that didn't explain Dr Farrell's behaviour. Connected or not, Alex intended to find out.

Alex didn't push it, but Sophie's demeanour had changed at the mention of Victor Lazar. She now looked sullen, a drastic contrast from her enthusiastic greeting of twenty minutes earlier. Alex wondered if her mood swings were typical. He guessed he'd find out soon enough.

'He's not your only patient,' said Alex, steering the conversation away for the time being.

Sophie's expression changed as if he'd flicked a switch. The nervousness faded and her shoulders straightened. 'Indeed,' she said. 'There are several interesting new inmates here. One of them doesn't speak any English, which makes everything a little difficult, but there are four others presenting with fascinating histories. They'll be here a long while if Robert's initial assessments are anything to go by. But I might have better luck with you helping me.' She smiled again.

'I'm not here for any other patients, I'm afraid,' he said. 'I hope that's not the expectation.'

'Probably not.' Sophie smiled. 'But I thought it worth asking.'

Alex returned the smile and kept glancing at Sophie as they walked, struggling to keep his eyes off her as they trudged along the stale, green-painted corridors towards segregation. There was something a little furtive in the way she talked and carried herself. And she seemed far more mature than a post-doc on a training contract.

'Here we are,' she said, pressing a buzzer next to a metal door. It opened with a clang and a young guard appeared.

'Hey, Sophie,' he said. He looked a good deal friendlier than the guard at the gate, smiling at Sophie as if she was the highlight of his day. Alex didn't doubt it was the case.

The guard gave Alex a quick up-and-down appraisal and his smile hardened. Alex's wristwatch probably cost more than the guard earned in a month. He made a mental note to dress it down a little.

'New friend, Sophie?'

'New colleague. Simon, meet Alex – I mean Dr Madison. Dr Madison is with us as a consultant.'

The two men shook hands, Simon puffing his chest out and trying to squeeze the life out of Alex's hand.

Alex smiled and said nothing.

'Your partner not here?' Sophie said, looking past Simon through the open door into the guardroom.

'Damian? No, he's sick today. Been a bit unreliable lately. I just can't get the staff.'

'Oh, OK. Well, I want to show Alex around the segregation wing,' said Sophie. 'Let him get a feel for the place.'

'Not a problem,' said Simon, letting go of Alex, 'although it *feels* like most other prison wings – full of scum. Sophie, I keep telling you, you're too nice to spend time with these monsters.'

Alex smiled at the jibe. It seemed to be the standard attitude towards medical staff in prison settings. Doctors were soft, wanting to care for and treat murderers and rapists. The guards, on the other hand, were tough, ready for action, protecting against the enemy. Alex knew to expect it and didn't let it get to him. He wouldn't be here long enough to worry about it. Getting the guard onside would be the better strategy.

'Well, you may be right,' he said, nodding. 'These are dangerous people. I expect most of them belong here. Thanks for letting us through, by the way.'

Simon's face softened. He'd scored an ally. 'Told you,' he said to Sophie. 'Your boss agrees with me.'

Sophie raised her eyebrows at Alex.

'I'm not Sophie's boss. I'm only here for a few weeks. I'd still like to take a look around though,' said Alex, 'if that's OK with you?'

'Sure,' said Simon, puffing his chest up again. He pulled the guard-room door shut and locked it with a heavy-looking key from the collection on his belt. 'Follow me. It's a small unit. Keep close and ignore the shouts. We've got six illegals here awaiting deportation, and they're not leaving without a fight.'

'*Inmates*, Simon,' Sophie corrected him. 'And they're on remand.'

'Whatever,' said Simon, buzzing them through the next door and into the wing. 'This is it,' he said, 'segregation. Temporary accommodation for the most part. Inmates find themselves here for breaking the rules – adjudications – anything from a fight to a murder. I know you medics frown at the idea of keeping prisoners in here for extended periods but sometimes we have no choice. A solitary cell away from any other human being is the only safe way to keep them.'

Alex was faced with a long grey corridor with brown doors set every three or so metres into the walls. The floor was damaged with black scuffs and grooves – the marks of trolleys and beds wheeled back and forth, sometimes with signs of a struggle. The smell of bleach was fainter here, mixed with stale body odour. The only natural light was filtered through a row of high, dirty windows. Fluorescent bulbs took over and cast a bright orange hue across everything, causing Alex to squint. At the end of the hallway a single door faced him. It was painted a dull red, chipped near the bottom and dirty around the viewing hatch.

'That's where Thirteen is,' said Sophie. 'Victor Lazar. The end cell.'

Alex nodded, noting that Sophie was biting her lip again. She appeared reluctant to continue.

'May I?' he said to the guard, indicating the corridor.

'Thirteen?' said Simon. 'Sure. You don't need my permission at this point. Feel free to check through any hatch you like. Try not to upset anybody though; we don't have enough staff today for too many sedations.'

'Sedation?' Standard practice, but Alex couldn't help frowning. Tranquillisers in lieu of treatment was a standard response to underfunding and a lack of qualified staff.

'Lorazepam, or whatever you guys cook up,' said Simon. 'Sedation is standard if they won't calm down. Normally sends them off to sleep for eight hours or so. We do it a lot.'

Alex raised his eyebrows but said nothing. He wasn't really interested in any of the inmates except Victor, and he felt drawn to the end cell. While he wouldn't be attempting an assessment yet, there was no harm in checking out what his patient looked like.

He found himself creeping towards Victor Lazar's cell, treading lightly on the concrete, as if making a noise would awaken the beasts lurking behind the locked doors.

A metallic clang startled him. He recoiled and wheeled around to the right. Two thumps, followed by a howl of laughter. It wasn't Lazar's cell. Another inmate coming to life, despite Alex's careful footwork.

'Fuck?' said the voice, the inflection muffled by the thick door. It howled again, repeating the obscenity over and over. 'Is that why you're here?' The voice grew fainter and Alex guessed the inmate was retreating further back into the cell.

'I'll fuck you,' said the voice, high pitched, tapering to a wail. 'I will.' The voice cracked again into laughter, then abruptly ceased.

Alex shuddered, his hand straying to his jacket pocket, feeling for the small packet of Xanax anti-anxiety pills he always carried. They were there, tucked away for when he needed them. He shook himself off and continued walking, stopping short before the door of the end cell. The one that held Victor Lazar. He leaned in to listen.

'They can't bite you through the door,' called Simon. Alex glanced back and saw the guard grinning. Sophie didn't seem to share his amusement, and stood to one side, her expression unimpressed.

Alex unlocked the viewing hatch, letting it drop down in front of him. A thick pane of reinforced glass with a thin gap underneath for a food tray separated him from the dimly lit cell.

The smell of body odour seeped through the gap, pungent and bitter. Alex tried not to screw his nose up as he surveyed the small room. Twelve foot square, the once white walls were covered with years of graffiti, swastikas and gang tags etched deep into the plaster. A metal grille on the ceiling covered the single yellowed bulb, its light diminished by grime and dust. One wall housed a combined toilet and sink unit, the metal dull and scratched and encrusted with limescale. The other wall held the single metal bunk with a thin mattress and two sheets, folded at one end.

On this bunk sat a man, stiff, upright, staring at the opposite wall. Alex was surprised at how slight he was. Plump, but small, with narrow shoulders, his bald head reflecting the harsh light. Metal-rimmed glasses sat perched on the end of his nose.

The inmate, Victor Lazar, turned his head towards the door. Alex resisted the urge to recoil and managed to force a smile.

'Who are you?' said Victor, his voice muffled by the distance and the glass. Alex detected a foreign accent, eastern European.

'Good morning, Mr Lazar,' said Alex. 'Just doing my rounds. I'm new, working with the medical team here.'

Victor smiled, causing a small shiver to creep down Alex's back.

'A new doctor,' said Victor. His eyes narrowed and he frowned. 'How nice.' He opened his mouth and muttered something Alex couldn't make out, then said, 'You're young.'

Alex's unease deepened as Victor's grin widened. The man turned away and muttered under his breath. He looked agitated, his head shaking. He paused every few moments to clasp his hands together, cracking his knuckles.

Alex instinctively began to diagnose, ticking off visible symptoms and positing what conditions might cause this behaviour. Victor appeared to be repeating himself, which could indicate a condition known as logorrhoea or a form of aphasia, both of which could be linked to schizophrenia. It was difficult, not to mention inappropriate, to do any sort of assessment through a glass hatch, but it was a curse of his profession. He couldn't resist analysing people from the second he met them.

Victor stopped his muttering. 'Pardon me. I must have drifted off there for a moment. Are you sure you're my doctor?'

Alex was intrigued by Victor's behaviour but decided he wasn't prepared to interview the man without first meeting Dr Bradley to get a proper background. 'One of them, yes.'

'Will you come in?'

'No, thank you, Mr Lazar,' said Alex. 'Maybe later in the week. I have to go now, but it was good to meet you.'

Victor fixed his smile. 'You haven't met me, Doctor.' He spat out the last word. 'Not if you stay the other side of that door.'

Alex tensed. He should have expected a certain amount of hostility, but it caught him off guard. Now wasn't the right time to tackle it. 'We'll meet soon,' he said, with more confidence than he felt. 'Properly. I promise.'

Victor laughed, a soft hiss escaping his mouth. He dragged it out for several seconds before standing, then stretched, arching his lower back and rolling his shoulders. Approaching the door, he leaned forwards until his face was up against the hatch. Barely inches apart, Alex could almost feel the man's breath as it fogged the glass.

'Be careful with promises, Doctor,' whispered Victor. The man gazed into Alex's eyes, his face a mask. Alex could read nothing in the stare, and it increased his unease. He swallowed awkwardly and found himself nodding.

Victor muttered something further under his breath but then stopped. He tilted his head to one side. 'Goodbye, Doctor.'

Before Alex could respond, Victor broke eye contact and turned away, shuffling back to his bunk. He lowered himself to the edge, sitting as before, staring fixedly at the opposite wall.

Alex watched Victor for a few moments longer before lifting the hatch back into place. As it locked Alex realised he'd been holding his breath. He let it out slowly and paused to regain his composure before heading back to Sophie and Simon. Sophie looked tense, her fists clenched by her sides.

Simon smirked. 'Crazies, the lot of them,' he said, shrugging, and grabbed his radio as it spluttered static into the corridor.

'You're joking,' he said into the mouthpiece, staring at Alex. 'OK, be right there.'

'Sorry, folks,' he said. 'There's trouble in B Wing. I need to head back.'

'What, now?' said Sophie. 'I thought they were all in lockdown today.'

'It's a protest,' said Simon. 'They've changed the menu again and it's being used as an excuse to kick off. Started peaceful but the first punch has just been thrown. Shouldn't be a big deal, but I've gotta go.'

'No problem,' said Alex, following Simon out of segregation, glad to put a few locked doors between himself and his new patient. The experience had made him anxious and he found himself hurrying out.

As they left, he watched Sophie. She was staring towards the end cell, her eyes narrowed and her jaw clenched. She was scared, but there was something else too. Silent and deep in thought, she paused for a moment before catching his eye briefly, then turned away to lead him briskly back towards the office.

CHAPTER FOUR

Two women, mother and daughter, face down on the carpet of their home. A crime scene photo, the blood overexposed and the skin washed out. Dr Alex Madison, consulting psychologist. *It wasn't your fault*, they had told him.

But it was his failure. His last case for the CPS.

The dream was subtly different this time. The bodies were in a corridor, cold and dark, with a single metal door at the end. As he approached the door he could smell decay and fear, but something stopped him going any further. The door was a cell, and although he couldn't see who was in it, he could hear a voice, calling to him. He couldn't make out what it was saying.

Alex stared at his bedroom ceiling for a few moments before taking his pulse. He felt sluggish and he realised he'd woken before his alarm. It was only five fifteen. His shoulders ached and his neck was stiff again. There was a dull pain in his right wrist, as if he'd pulled a muscle. He hoped he wasn't coming down with something.

He crept out of bed, leaving Jane asleep, showering and leaving the house early before she woke. Last night Jane had started asking questions about his failed marriage, his relationship with Grace, the bond they still shared as parents to Katie. Then she'd started asking about his parents. Perhaps she thought it would make him open up. Alex found it did the opposite. He couldn't bring himself to talk about his past, particularly his father, and he'd snapped at her, more harshly than he'd meant to.

Jane was likeable. She had her own life and her own collection of friends. He considered her career to be superficial, but if he was honest he'd like to earn what she did in the two or three days a week she actually did any work. Her family connections gave her a collection of wealthy property clients who had a penchant for buying up chunks of London. Jane was an agent happy to oblige, and had no discernible morals about the gentrification of her home city. When she wasn't earning a ludicrous commission on property, she spent her time networking. Alex often pointed out how long it had taken him to study to earn what he did. She always smiled, looking rather smug, but never arrogant. She let him claim the superior intellect.

But lately, her interest had started to feel probing, her attention possessive. He wouldn't let her in, not where it counted. He kept her distant. Last night he'd fallen into a guilty sleep, promising himself that he'd end it before he damaged them both even further.

He checked his phone before getting in the car. There was another missed call from Grace. She'd called late last night. He must have been asleep. What had he forgotten this time? He'd paid for the trip, transferred the money. It was too early to call back now. He'd try to remember to call at lunch. He must remember.

He glanced at the photo of Katie on the screen of his phone. She was laughing into the camera, her hair blown half across her face by a sudden breeze and right into her ice cream cone. Alex smiled as he looked at her pink cheeks and lightly freckled nose. It had been the school holiday, work was quiet, and his allocated time with his daughter had landed on what turned out to be the hottest day of the year. A perfect day. They hadn't had one like it in a while.

He still couldn't pinpoint exactly when it had all gone wrong. Blaming his work was a cop-out and he knew it. His marriage had been in trouble long before that disastrous case. But he took the blame anyway. His family suffered. Katie suffered.

He slid the phone into his pocket and stared at his reflection in the car window. Forgiveness had to be earned, he thought, and doing something useful was part of it. He would make this a good day.

The second trip into HMP Whitemoor was better than the first. Alex listened to the radio on the drive in – warnings from community groups about police cuts. What was the police commissioner doing about it? He flicked through the channels to Classic FM and cruised towards the entrance on a wave of Chopin. He recognised the piece. Opus 27, No. 2. Chopin had always drifted out of his father's study when Alex was a child, filling the house with his evocative melodies. Alex wondered why his life couldn't be as ordered and perfect as the Nocturnes.

The guard gave him the same stare and suggested he get a security badge. Alex produced a smile and promised he would, before heading into the office.

'I'm glad you came back for a second day.'

Alex turned as he approached the desks to see an overweight man, balding, with large gold-rimmed glasses. His white shirt was grey and too tight.

'I couldn't stay away,' said Alex, holding his hand out. 'Nice to meet you, Dr Bradley.'

Dr Bradley took it and gave a limp handshake before wiping his hand on his trousers and opening his briefcase. 'Your reputation precedes you, Dr Madison. The CPS said you could help, so I'm glad you're here. And call me Robert, please. Sorry I missed you yesterday – they've got me running around.'

He shrugged as if it was a bad thing, but kept smiling, the fat bunching in his jowls, giving the impression he was chewing on something.

'It's OK,' said Alex, glancing around the office. 'Sophie was good enough to show me the place. Is she—?'

'Sophie?' said Robert.

'Sophie.' Alex was puzzled. 'She said she was my assistant. Dark hair, tall . . .'

'Oh, right,' said Robert. 'Sophie. Yes, absolutely. Sorry. We get a constant stream of trainees and I can't always remember their names.'

'She sits there,' said Alex, pointing at her desk, not impressed with Robert's lack of attention towards his own staff.

'Yes, I know who she is.' Robert's face flashed with annoyance. 'She comes in late some days,' he said. 'Study time. She should be here around eleven.'

'Can I ask you something?'

'Sure.'

'Has she worked in a prison before?'

Robert glanced up, shrugging. 'Like I said, these post-docs go through here quicker than shoplifters. She has an interesting background if I remember, but you should probably ask her.'

'OK,' said Alex. 'She seems friendly, personable.'

'You two hit it off?'

'Er, yes. Sure.'

'Good,' said Robert, eyeing him up and down approvingly. 'Good work.'

Alex frowned. 'I have a girlfriend,' he said. 'Look . . . I'm only here for a few days – a couple of weeks at the most. Should we—'

'Oh. Shame,' said Robert, reading through his morning post, not looking up.

Alex wondered which bit was a shame.

'Any kids?' said Robert.

'One – a daughter. Katie.' Alex sat at his desk, unnerved at Robert's personal questions. He stared at the antiquated PC in front of him and wondered if he should turn it on. He had his MacBook Air in his bag, but wasn't sure he'd need that either.

'A daughter!' said Robert, looking up. 'I wanted a daughter. I've got three sons – brilliant, wonderful children.' He looked wistful, his eyes clouding over. 'I don't see much of them now, since Maggie and I split up. But still . . . brilliant boys.'

Alex stared at the keyboard, deciding he and Robert would not be hitting it off. The man was too abrasive, too loose with his thinking and too open with his personal problems.

'How many days a week are you based here?' said Alex, wondering how he could schedule his assessment work to include minimum time with this man.

'Two.'

'Oh.' Alex felt better already.

'Sometimes three. But now you're here to help the CPS with this particular case, probably fewer.'

Good to hear, thought Alex. Whatever the doctor's professional qualifications, which on paper were impressive, he was not the sort of person Alex wanted to befriend. He decided to change the mood.

'Shall we talk about him,' he said. 'Victor Lazar?'

Robert raised his head again and stared at Alex for a few moments. His smile was gone. He folded his mail with care and put it to one side, smudging one of the envelopes as he did so. He slid his briefcase off the desk and winced as he lowered it to the floor. He suddenly looked ten years older.

'We shall,' he said, glancing at his watch, eyes darting to and fro. 'Let's do it before anyone else gets in.'

CHAPTER FIVE

'Let me start by saying what this isn't,' said Robert, leaning back in his chair, shirt buttons straining at their threads. 'I don't believe in paranormal nonsense,' he said, as if that statement itself wasn't absurd coming from a forensic psychologist. He closed his eyes and gulped, the skin on his neck straining with the effort.

Alex waited, puzzled at the remark, notepad and pen poised, deciding it was more fitting than his MacBook in the current environment.

'I'm not sure how much the CPS told you—'

'A summary,' said Alex.

'OK. Well. From the beginning then.' Robert gulped again and cleared his throat. 'Victor came to us thirteen days ago on remand. Did they tell you he's a Romanian national?'

Alex shook his head.

'Well, his legal status is unclear, but he's in the hands of the CPS now. He was arrested at the scene of three murders at the University of Southampton. The bodies were found in a classroom in the psychology faculty building. All three were brutally cut and stabbed with a kitchen knife. The forensic assessment, backed by a single witness statement, was that one man, a Professor Florin – Head of Psychology – killed the other two in a frenzied attack, before committing suicide with the same knife.'

Alex raised his eyebrows. The press hadn't got hold of the details and the summary he'd been sent had skipped over it. Murder–suicides were rare, the causes either very simple or very complicated. He assumed this wasn't the former, or he wouldn't be here.

'Indeed.' Robert nodded and continued. 'Our man, Victor Lazar, was found sitting outside the classroom. The police report says he appeared dazed and they assumed he was in shock, because he clammed up. There was no blood on his skin or clothes and the murder weapon was clean of his prints. He remained quiet throughout processing, giving us the minimum. The CPS has left him with us.'

'Why?' said Alex, puzzled at the vagueness of Victor's legal status. 'Surely he's a witness, not a suspect?'

'He was present at the scene and offered no explanation.' Robert shrugged. 'That's enough for the CPS while we do our assessment and the police try to build a case.'

'He's been charged with murder?'

'Yes,' said Robert, 'and apparently immigration is having a hard time getting any useful information out of the Romanians. Personally, I think if it weren't for his immigration status, he'd be out by now. But anyway.' Robert rummaged through a folder on his desk. 'His arrest report is strange. I've not had the time to assess it properly. The police certainly couldn't, and they're being next to useless on the matter.'

'Why?'

'There's no evidence,' said Robert. 'Nothing they can use.' He pulled out a sheaf of papers. 'Here it is.'

'What am I looking at?' said Alex, as Robert passed him the top sheet.

'Witness statement. A student at the university. He was handing in a paper when he saw the events unfold. It's the bit at the bottom that caught our attention. Plus the disturbing events since he arrived at our prison. The CPS wants a full psychological evaluation before they proceed – that's why you're here.'

Alex skimmed through the fragmented report, probably gathered in stages from a witness in shock at having seen three people die in such a gruesome manner. There was a lot of jumping around in the order of events, which suggested the witness was being truthful – false accounts were typically ordered and rehearsed.

Alex read from the statement: 'I could hear him screaming, "Please don't make me do it. Please don't make me do it."'

He frowned at Robert. 'Who did the witness hear?'

'Professor Florin. The professor shouted it several times before stabbing himself in the throat.'

Alex raised his eyebrows and placed the paper on the desk. 'Well, that is interesting.'

'Indeed,' said Robert.

'And your initial thoughts?'

'The witness misheard. Or he heard someone else shouting. Or Professor Florin was hearing voices.'

Alex shrugged. 'So?'

'The professor was staring at our man Victor while he was shouting. Read the rest of it. It's pretty clear. Hard to fabricate, and why would he?'

Alex studied the rest of the report, chewing the inside of his lip, his thoughts racing with the intrigue. Professor Florin, according to the witness, had stabbed the other two victims multiple times with a kitchen knife, pausing on occasion to scream for mercy. He'd staggered and held his head, as if under the influence of drink or drugs. Then he had stared through the doorway at Mr Lazar, pleaded for ten seconds or so, and finally cut his own throat.

The arresting officer's statement said that when police had arrived on scene Victor looked sick, remaining silent, still sitting outside the classroom containing the three mutilated bodies, blood thick on the floor. The bodies were lacerated, with slash and stab wounds to the neck, heart and lungs. The police report supported the witness as far as it went, for the professor's dead body was found still holding the knife, his throat cut ear to ear.

Victor had offered no information at his arrest or at any time since. He had a brief session with a solicitor and a doctor before being transported to HMP Whitemoor.

'His solicitor?'

'A guy called Burrows,' said Robert. 'Fresh-faced and obviously drew the short straw. I get the feeling he's terrified of Victor.'

'Does he want to be present when I assess Victor?'

'No. He's happy for us to talk to Victor, as long as it remains clinical – in other words, no police. He wants the psych evaluation before he does anything else. I got the feeling he's not in a rush.'

Alex slowed his breathing and tried to concentrate. 'I'll need to speak to the witness,' he said, 'the guy that saw all this at the university.'

'We've tried,' said Robert, 'but the police say they got everything they needed, and the witness has clammed up. Probably mild PTSD. He's being medicated and refuses to talk about it.'

'Not even to us?'

'Especially us. They said it's too risky.'

'What's that supposed to mean?'

Robert shrugged. 'The witness was a psychology PhD student. They said, and I quote, "That was some violently disturbing shit."'

'And we trust his statement?'

Robert held his palms out. 'I was hoping it might make more sense to you. I've never seen anything like it.'

'Neither have I,' said Alex truthfully, 'and I'm not about to make a snap judgement based on a witness statement. However . . . there is the other matter.'

'Dr Farrell's death,' said Robert.

Alex nodded, writing the name with a question mark next to it, noting his hand shaking with adrenaline. It had been such a long time since he'd discussed a suspected murderer. He felt the surge of professional pride that was lacking in his private practice. Taking a deep breath, he examined Robert. His face was red, flustered. Perhaps the case had hit him in the same way as with Sophie. Alex rested his pen on the paper. Robert's chest was heaving and his face was pasty.

'Do you need a minute?' he said.

Robert sucked in slowly and blinked. 'No, I'm fine.' He didn't look fine. Even an amateur could have diagnosed him as being very far from fine. His forehead was beaded with sweat and he clasped his hands together convulsively.

'You're scared of him,' said Alex. 'Mr Lazar.'

Robert's eyes widened and he slapped his palms on the desk, startling Alex. 'You're damn right I'm scared of him,' he said. 'Dr Farrell was a friend of mine.'

Alex nodded. He suspected he wasn't going to get an objective assessment from Robert, who already seemed convinced Victor Lazar was responsible for his friend's death.

'What do you want from me, Dr Bradley?' Alex figured he should change tack. 'What do you expect me to do?'

Robert frowned and cleared his throat. 'Sorry for the outburst,' he said. 'I'm just a bit . . . you know.'

'Understandable,' said Alex.

'We need help,' said Robert. 'You've worked in clinical and forensics. We need to know what we're dealing with . . . You need to . . .' Robert shook his head and pinched the bridge of his nose.

'What?'

Robert stood slowly, easing his overweight frame out of the chair. He indicated for Alex to follow him. 'Come with me. It's easier to show rather than tell you.'

Alex shrugged but followed Robert out of the office and along the tatty walkway between sections. They walked through dull corridors and offices coming to life with managers, medics and guards all starting their shifts. Phones were ringing and printers humming as the prison administration woke up for the day. No one looked at Robert or Alex as they passed. The atmosphere was cold and uninviting. They passed along another corridor and through two locked gates before Robert stopped outside a door with 'D Wing Surveillance' written on the outside in peeling gold letters. He thumped on the door.

'Mr Lazar is a scary man to be around,' said Robert as they waited. 'Dr Farrell realised too late. You never asked why Victor is in segregation. I'm going to show you why.'

The surveillance room was impressive. Twenty wall-mounted monitors with a sixty-inch screen at the centre. The archaic nature of the prison seemed to be transformed by the technology on display in this room. The video feeds were controlled by three desktop PCs and a dedicated console control. The guard who'd let them in smiled at Robert.

'Can we have the room?' said Robert. 'I need to show Dr Madison the footage of Mr Lazar.'

'Oh,' said the guard, his smile disappearing. Worry creased his forehead. 'I don't need to stay, do I?'

'Of course not,' said Robert. 'I'll call you when we're done.'

The guard's relief was palpable as he exited the room and closed the door.

'Have a seat,' said Robert, taking one of the keyboards and navigating through the archive software. He browsed by date and picked out specific days, dragging them into a folder, ready to be played.

'They'll show you later how we catalogue surveillance. We store key footage with the case records in our own system – for example, if we need it for court, a parole hearing or suchlike. But the raw footage is all stored centrally. If we want to see it we have to come here.'

'Fine,' said Alex, now seated, hoping most of his contact would be face-to-face rather than via video.

'I have to complete the security checks,' continued Robert. 'Everything is logged, for our safety and theirs. You watch a video, you need a reason. Simple as that.' After a few more clicks, Robert pointed at the central screen. 'On arrival, Victor was housed in the general population of D Wing,' he said. 'Standard drill: two to a cell, facilities for exercise, leisure and personal time. For the first twenty-four hours he kept to himself, talking to nobody.'

A low-resolution image appeared on the screen. The video played and Alex saw twenty or so inmates walking back and forth in green prison-issue towels.

'This footage was recorded on Victor's second night,' said Robert. 'The camera covers the entrance to the shower room on the first floor – where Victor's cell was. We don't video inside the shower room, but the sinks and toilet cubicles are visible.'

Alex nodded, watching as a tall black man approached one of the sinks. He had a towel wrapped around his lower half. His upper half was muscular, with a series of tattoos across the back of his shoulders.

Robert hit pause. 'The man there is Tyrone Jeffries, Victor's cell-mate. He was nine years into a twelve-year stint for supplying Class A. A nasty piece of work. Outwardly well behaved, but off camera he was running the wing. The guards never managed to pin anything on him, but they think he was responsible for a number of revenge beatings in here.'

Robert glanced over at Alex and caught his eye. 'This man is hard as nails, and was going to be out in a couple of years.'

He pressed play. A few seconds later another man approached the sink next to Tyrone.

'There's Victor,' said Robert.

Victor appeared. Out of the cell he appeared even shorter, tiny in comparison with Tyrone. He adjusted his glasses, turning to the wall so neither his nor Tyrone's faces were visible to camera.

A few more seconds passed before Victor moved, quickly, putting his right hand on to Tyrone's left shoulder. He leaned in and appeared to be talking, straining his neck, his mouth a few inches from the tall man's ear.

Tyrone didn't move, but both hands dropped to his sides. They stood there for another twenty seconds, Victor talking, Tyrone listening.

With another quick movement, Victor stepped away, taking his hand off Tyrone. He stood still for a moment before walking off, out of the camera's field of view.

Tyrone remained where he was, motionless, both hands hanging by his side. The clock ticked. Thirty seconds, then two minutes. Alex turned to Robert.

'How long—'

'Twenty-four minutes,' said Robert, pressing fast forward. As the video played, Alex watched the stationary figure while dozens of other inmates darted around, back and forth. A few other inmates appeared to take interest, pausing briefly next to Tyrone before moving on. One of them waved his hand in front of the man's face, before backing away.

'He appears catatonic. Static and unresponsive. Then this,' said Robert, pressing play.

Tyrone moved. He lifted both hands and pressed his palms against the wall. He started to sway towards and away from the tiled surface, his head coming within a few centimetres of the wall each time. He did this several times, Alex counted five, before he jerked his head as far back as it could go then rammed it into the wall with such force he staggered, holding himself against the sink.

Alex sat up straight, astonished.

Tyrone pulled his head back and did it again, headbutting the wall with such force that the tiles cracked and splintered. Two other prisoners appeared, standing off to one side. They were waving their arms, shouting, but didn't go any closer.

Again, the huge muscular man smashed his head face first into the wall. Dark patches of blood appeared on the wall and dripped to the floor. Several other inmates joined the first two, some standing to watch, others trying to get Tyrone's attention, going close enough to talk. Nobody touched him.

'Notice how the other inmates stay away,' said Robert. 'They're puzzled, but Tyrone is a big lad with a reputation. They don't want to get involved.'

'Where are the guards?' said Alex, inching forwards in his chair, squinting at the low-resolution images, trying to study the event, watching again as the man drove his face into the wall.

Time and time again, the big man smashed his face against the broken wall. After four more attempts, his legs gave way and he collapsed at the base of the sink, rolling on to his back. The sight of his face made Alex turn away. Not normally squeamish, this was enough to make him gag.

Tyrone's facial features were hidden by the bloody mass of tissue and skin that had burst across the broken tiles. His nose was flat, shattered, and several of his teeth were hanging out. The blood was pumping with some force from his forehead, creating a growing pool around him. He convulsed several times before falling still, the circle of inmates closing in.

Robert paused the video and cleared his throat. 'The guards arrived thirty seconds later. Tyrone died four hours after that. Epidural haemorrhage. Fatal build-up of blood and pressure in his skull.'

Alex swallowed several times and looked away from the screen, trying to process what he'd seen. A man dashing his own brains out against a wall. Ten minutes ago Alex would have sworn such a thing wasn't possible.

'There was nothing else wrong with him?' he said, trying to apply some logic, trying to push away the images of blood and gore from his head. 'Nothing underlying?'

41

'Nothing,' said Robert, his hands back on the keyboard, bringing up another video. 'Tyrone was physically and mentally as healthy as they come. He wasn't on any uppers or hallucinogens – hospital blood tests ruled out any drug use. He sold plenty, but never used.'

'Alcohol? Homebrew?'

'No.'

'Personal issues. A visit gone bad. Girlfriend? Boyfriend? Somebody cheated on him?' Alex was grasping and he knew it.

'No, nothing. The one change to Tyrone's routine in the last few months was his new cellmate, Victor, who happened to be in the medical centre at the time, complaining of a headache. He went there straight after his visit to the bathroom. The CCTV verifies it.'

Alex rubbed his temples, his composure weakening as he struggled to offer a reasonable explanation. He closed his eyes, but all he could see was the man's nose spread across his face.

'I don't see how this has anything to do with Victor,' he said after several moments.

Robert frowned.

'All they did was talk,' Alex continued. 'You don't even know what he said.'

'I agree,' said Robert. 'Which is why he was left on an open block. But that's video one of two. Try this for size.' He pressed play and the screen displayed another scene. This time the camera was on the wing, facing a row of cell doors. They were all open and inmates strolled between them.

'Leisure time,' said Robert. 'Three hours before lock-up. Victor's cell is the third from the left. He was moved up a floor after Tyrone's death.'

Alex saw Victor appear on screen in profile. He walked with a weariness – slumped, bad posture. He didn't look like a killer.

'The cell he's entering isn't his?' said Alex, as Victor disappeared behind one of the battered blue doors.

'No,' said Robert. 'The cell belongs to Graham Dunstall, a rapist serving fifteen years, and Ben Chargate, GBH, serving seven. Ben wasn't there at the time. He was in visitation seeing his girlfriend. Graham was a nasty human being. Victor obviously thought so too.'

'Graham and Victor are alone?' said Alex.

'Yes,' said Robert. 'For the next nine minutes.' Robert fast-forwarded and watched the timer. The video flashed with other inmates scuttling back and forth. He hit play as Victor and the other man appeared outside the cell. Victor glanced across the wing. Alex couldn't be sure but it looked as if Victor was staring directly into the camera.

'Do the inmates know where all the cameras are?' said Alex.

'Most of them,' said Robert. 'We're not allowed to hide surveillance devices, strictly speaking.' He shrugged as if he didn't quite agree. 'The one we're looking through is obvious. Big and white, mounted on the wall.'

'So Victor knows we're watching him.'

'It would appear so.'

Victor continued to stare for a few seconds, before shifting his gaze back towards Dunstall. He uttered something, his lips mouthing the words slowly.

'What's he saying?' said Alex.

Robert shook his head. 'I couldn't make it out. Give? Forgive?'

Alex peered at the grainy image. 'Did anybody else hear them?'

'If they did they wouldn't say.'

Victor turned. Staggering slightly, he grabbed the handrail. Pushing himself up, he shuffled back to his own cell, nudging the door closed. It remained open a few inches.

'Inmates can't close their doors,' said Robert. 'They have stoppers preventing it during leisure time. It's supposed to discourage secretive congregations, barricading during riots et cetera.'

Alex nodded, watching the other inmate, Graham Dunstall. His eyes were open, his expression blank. His right hand drifted to his pocket. He pulled out a thin object.

'What's that?' said Alex, squinting, struggling with the low-res image.

'A shiv,' said Robert. 'A toothbrush shaft with a razor blade stuck on the end. Quite common.'

Alex nodded, aware that prisoners managed to make stabbing weapons out of almost anything. He'd read one case of a papier mâché shiv being used to stab an inmate through the throat. He had a sinking feeling that he knew what to expect next.

'Seven minutes this time,' said Robert. 'In a trance – catatonic, perhaps. He didn't move, speak or gesture for seven minutes, then this.'

The prisoner lifted the hand containing the shiv to his face. His expression changed. It broke, he clenched his teeth and his eyes widened.

'He's scared,' said Alex. 'Hiding it, but the signs are there.'

'That's what I thought,' said Robert. 'But his fear isn't enough to stop him doing it.'

Alex was about to ask what, when the man took the shiv and cut his own throat from ear to ear. It was deep; the skin parted easily and opened up. Blood rushed out of the cut arteries, spurting outwards and coating his shirt.

He gasped two or three times before dropping to his knees, head banging against the railing on his way down. He didn't move after that, as several pints of blood emptied themselves on to the floor, through the cracks, raining on the floor below. Victor's cell door remained closed as several inmates rushed over. One tried to move the man, putting his hands over the gushing throat, but it was obvious to Alex any treatment would be in vain. The man was dead the second he cut both arteries.

Robert paused the video, leaving a fuzzy image of the dead man wobbling on the monitor. 'Seen enough?'

CHAPTER SIX

'When can I speak to him?'

Robert shook his head and sniffed, pouring a teaspoon of sugar into his coffee, spilling half on to the desk. He swept it on to the floor.

They were back in the office and Alex's mind was at work, the images of both men burned into his eyes. He was sure he'd see them tonight in his dreams: washed-out images of men in their moment of death. Painful deaths.

'Nobody has been in Victor's cell for six days,' said Robert. 'The guards push his food through the hatch. The mandatory medicals are performed through the door.'

'I heard,' said Alex, sipping his own coffee, fresh from Robert's cafetière. The man could do one thing right, after all. 'That's off protocol, isn't it? He hasn't been sectioned. He's on remand.'

Robert sniffed and shrugged.

'You have no qualms about that?'

'It's legal,' said Robert. 'He's withdrawn. Looks in pain but won't accept any meds. The governor has seen the footage. She's not willing to risk any more contact at this time, whatever the cause. Victor stays where he is, unless he starts talking.'

Alex wondered if he had any say in the matter. As a consultant on the case, he had a duty of care to Victor, but he had no explanation for what he'd seen. No simple diagnosis or deduction. He'd been expecting an overblown and overhyped account of Victor Lazar and had intended to follow this up like an expert, with careful patient time, diagnosis and treatment, to put to bed any rumours or fear. Instil some reason into this situation and come out on top. This was an opportunity to reassert himself in forensic psychology and start a new professional chapter in his life. To show the CPS he was the right choice.

But what he'd just seen was incredible. He considered and discarded several possibilities: suggestion theory, manipulation, hypnosis techniques. None of them even came close to explaining what he'd just witnessed. This was beyond him.

Or was it? Was anybody else qualified to work on this case? Robert certainly wasn't. Alex could name a handful of ex-colleagues who'd jump at the chance to interview Victor Lazar, but none were more qualified than Alex himself. Besides, the CPS had called him. They were giving him the chance. He should grab it with both hands.

'And he's not talking? Have you assessed him yourself?'

'No. No, I haven't,' said Robert, looking uncomfortable.

'Why isn't he sedated? I mean, that would be an obvious precaution. Do you think it would help?'

'We're not allowed unless he's presenting an immediate danger to himself or us,' said Robert. 'That was one of the few things the solicitor did say. If we sedate without a full psych assessment we'll leave ourselves wide open – too risky.'

Alex nodded. 'You know I have to see him,' he said. 'I can't be here unless I do.'

Robert smiled. He took a long draught of coffee.

'Yes,' he said. 'I half expected you to drop the case after seeing those videos, but I hoped you'd insist on staying. Believe me, I think we should bury the man in a hole and never let him out, but . . . I'm baffled.'

'And you're sure that Victor had something to do with these deaths?'

Robert stared at him. 'You're not?'

Alex leaned back in his chair. He wasn't sure what to make of Robert. He seemed terrified of his patient and certain that Victor had caused the gruesome deaths of his fellow inmates. But although the videos seemed to indicate that Victor was somehow involved, there was no easy explanation as to how or why. Robert seemed to have lost sight of that fact.

But he had just lost a colleague and friend, Alex reminded himself, and was bound to be feeling anxious. Robert had worked closely with Henry Farrell, yet the man's suicide had taken him completely by surprise. It was understandable that he would be searching for quick closure.

'So,' Alex prompted gently, 'do you have any theories as to how he did it?'

'Direct suggestion? Conversational hypnosis?' said Robert. 'We've all studied it as undergrads. I put in some time at Guildford on the subject.'

Alex shook his head. 'Even if we pretend for a second that Victor is a master hypnotist, hypnotising people into committing crimes or violent acts just doesn't happen. It's impossible to break a person's value judgements. The person being hypnotised knows it's wrong and stops it.'

'I agree,' said Robert. 'I have refreshed myself in the latest literature. What you say holds true. I wish we had more history.'

'Do we have any?'

'Nothing of value,' said Robert.

'And he won't tell you?'

Robert shrugged. 'I haven't asked. He might tell you.'

'Drugs?'

'Nope,' said Robert, shrugging. 'But you know as well as I do there are several mind-altering drugs which cause violent behaviour.'

'I do,' said Alex, 'but nothing can cause what I've just seen.'

Robert chewed his cheek and studied his coffee mug, twirling it in his hands. 'Look. I won't tell you what to do.'

Alex cocked an eyebrow.

'But take this as a strong recommendation: tread carefully with Victor. Do your initial assessment, but if you don't think you can do anything, tell the CPS as much and get the hell out. You have other patients, other people who can be helped. Go back to your safe world and leave this man alone.'

Alex nodded, mulling it over. He thanked Robert for his candour and stayed with his thoughts, his mind shaken but whirring, wondering what his next conversation with Victor would reveal.

CHAPTER SEVEN

'Do you want me to join you?' Robert's reluctance was written all over his face. They'd taken some air and reconvened at Robert's desk half an hour later.

Alex's head was clearer, if not entirely composed. However, he didn't think it necessary to include Robert in the interview. He preferred to build relationships with patients on his own. 'Thanks, but no.'

Robert nodded, looking relieved, but stood anyway. 'At least let me walk you. The guards will tell you the procedure for calling them if anything happens, but I'd rather be nearby, just in case.'

Alex shrugged. 'I'll be careful. I'll play it by ear.'

'You know to use a pseudonym?'

Alex paused. 'No, I never have before.'

'Ah,' said Robert. 'New security regulations on this category – he's an illegal with no history. We don't risk exposing personal details at this stage.'

Alex blinked. This was alien to him. The whole purpose of his approach was establishing trust. 'I can't—'

'You can, and you will,' said Robert, 'or you don't go in there. Look . . .' He gave an apologetic smile. '. . . nobody likes it, but it's for your safety. What's your wife's maiden name?'

'Ex-wife?' said Alex. 'Carter.'

'Then you're Dr Alex Carter for today. Only if he asks. OK?'

A few minutes later the metal door to the segregation ward clanged shut behind him. It made Alex jump and he took his pulse, breathing evenly to slow it. He was accompanied by Robert, but Alex would enter Victor's cell alone. That was how he needed to play it. He didn't say it, but he wanted Victor to see him as an outsider to the prison system. Somebody he could open up to.

Alex walked towards cell fifteen, the final cell in the corridor. Robert stopped short, twenty or so feet away.

Alex stood outside the door and looked up at the ceiling camera. It flashed a red light at him for a few moments until the buzzer sounded, then there was a click as the door unlocked. He paused, taking a deep breath.

'Mr Lazar, it's Dr . . . Carter,' he said, stumbling over the name, but regaining his composure quickly. 'I'd like to come in and speak to you.'

The door swung open, creaking as the hinges strained with the weight. Alex was hit again by the smell of body odour. The waft through the hatch on his first visit had been unpleasant, but this was revolting. Still, he tried not to react as he stepped inside the cell.

Victor Lazar sat, as before, on the thin mattress. His sheets were messy and draped at the end of the bunk. Victor was slouched this time, staring at the opposite wall with a vacant expression. He scratched his bald head and adjusted his glasses.

'Dr Carter,' he said, his voice soft and calm, his accent crisp, 'come in.'

Alex shuffled into the cell and leaned against the wall. The door swung shut behind him and the buzzer sounded, muffled from the inside. He didn't reply immediately, using silence as a positioning strategy. It was important to get the upper hand and keep professional control over the conversation. He suppressed a wave of claustrophobia, screwing his nose up against the rancid air. He stood tall and puffed his chest out, shoulders back, trying to imagine the chemical changes in his brain that would result from a change in posture.

Victor cleared his throat and examined Alex, his eyes magnified by the thick glasses as he peered through them. He was short-sighted and angled his head to meet Alex's eyes.

'You must excuse my manners, Dr Carter,' he said, in his thick accent, casting his hand around the room. 'I can't offer you much in the way of refreshments.'

He pulled a wide grin, which unnerved Alex. Alex knew how to present a fake smile, but at least his were friendly. Victor's was menacing.

'Perhaps it would be better if you sat? You might be more comfortable.'

Alex shook his head. 'I'd rather stand, Victor. May I call you Victor?'

Victor looked surprised for a brief moment before his smile returned. 'You can call me what you want, Doctor. But for the sake of conversation, yes, my first name will be fine. Please sit.'

Alex watched Victor's body. He sat still and straight, the slouch gone, giving away nothing. His face was a mask and his eyes were obscured by the glasses.

'I'll be OK standing,' said Alex.

'Very well,' said Victor, leaning back, lying out full length on his bunk, hands behind his head, staring at the ceiling. It would make it more difficult for Alex to read his body language, and Victor acted as if he knew it.

'I'd like to talk to you, Victor,' said Alex, 'about why you're being held on remand.'

'Why?' said Victor. 'Ah yes. First things first. What is your particular method, Dr Carter?'

'I don't follow,' said Alex, starting to feel out of his comfort zone. Alex had become used to timid, often frightened patients who viewed his white coat as a symbol of infallibility and the cure to their many problems. They wanted his input and were paying for it. They never questioned Alex or his methods. He was frustrated at his own naivety in thinking this man would behave the same way.

'I've been subject to quite a few assessments over the years, Dr Carter. Is this a quick assessment for bipolar or schizophrenia? If so, I can save you the time. I have neither, nor do I have any other normal mental health disorder.'

Alex cocked an eyebrow. 'That's interesting, and I believe you, but will you indulge me anyway?'

'It depends.'

'On what?'

'On your real reason for being here.'

Alex nodded. 'My reason is to assess your mental health. I'm a psychologist. You still have rights when you're in here. You have not been convicted—'

'Liar,' said Victor.

Alex paused. 'You don't believe me?'

Victor lifted his head off the pillow to peer again at Alex.

'Carter. What's your first name?'

Alex paused. 'Alex.'

'Alex. You're here for one thing, or possibly many things, depending on what you've been told.'

'I . . .' Alex paused again. 'I'm interested in your—'

Victor laughed, the noise echoing around the confined space. 'You're interested? Oh, I know, Alex. I'm the most interesting thing in this prison. Even more interesting than your pretty young student. What's her name?'

Alex opened his mouth and closed it again. He let out half a breath.

'Pretty, isn't she?' said Victor. 'Surely she's a more interesting subject to assess? It's on your mind, isn't it?'

Victor gave a cackle and the back of Alex's neck tingled. He shivered. Victor was misdirecting and distracting. Alex knew this, yet he couldn't help the anxiety rising and his past behaviour flashing into his memory. The affair and the breakdown of his marriage. He thought of the way he'd been looking at Sophie when they met. His heart thumped and his fingertips prickled.

'You should calm down,' said Victor. 'Sure you won't sit?'

'I'll stand,' whispered Alex, aware that Victor already had complete control of the conversation. He was being made to look an amateur.

'Do you have any children?' said Victor, taking a different tack. 'Of course you do. You look like a father.'

Alex kept his face still. Answering personal questions was always a challenge in his profession. The standard approach was to decline to answer because it wasn't relevant. In this case, in front of a murder suspect, Alex felt a flash of fear, but put it to one side. He understood now why the pseudonym was important. He knew so little about this man. He wasn't about to give him a passport into his own life.

Alex focused on his breathing, pulling his thoughts together, deciding his traditional assessment method was out of the window. This would be a case of forcing the interview where he wanted it to go, and ignoring Victor's misdirection.

'I'd like to talk about the University of Southampton, Victor.'

Victor turned away. 'Those people died terrible deaths,' he said, his voice wavering, rising in pitch. Alex remained silent. 'But it was a long time ago, Dr Carter.' Victor tilted his head, raising his eyebrows.

Alex paused. What did Victor mean?

'I'd like to understand what happened on the day they died, Victor,' said Alex, focusing on the present. 'What were you doing there?'

Victor pulled himself up, twisting to face Alex, folding his legs. He frowned. His grin was gone and he stared right through Alex.

'I told you, it was a long time ago,' said Victor. 'It's a shame, because it's not the victim's fault. It's never the victim's fault. You'd agree with that, wouldn't you? In your profession?'

Alex was careful with his reply. Victor was intelligent, but flitted between thoughts. Symptomatic of dementia, perhaps? Alex wasn't sure.

'The people who were killed are not to blame. Are you to blame, Victor?'

'Blame.' Victor's voice was dry and low. He sat bolt upright, sliding off the bunk to stand in front of Alex. Alex flinched. Victor's small frame appeared threatening and alien in the confined cell.

'What do you know about blame, Dr Carter?' Victor's stare was piercing, his foul breath wafting over Alex's face.

Alex paused, taking small breaths. His anxiety bubbled, his heart rate thumping in his throat as he counted slowly. *Take control,* he said to himself. *Don't let the conversation run on the patient's terms.*

'Perhaps you'd like to tell me what you think,' Alex said, trying with difficulty to hold Victor's stare.

Victor's mouth stretched almost imperceptibly into a smile.

'What I think,' he hissed, nodding. 'Yes, interesting.'

'I'm not a prosecutor,' Alex ventured further, 'I'm a doctor. I can help you.'

Victor didn't react as Alex expected. 'Doctor,' said Victor, spitting the word. Alex felt droplets of moisture hit his face. He instinctively reached up to wipe his cheek with his hand.

'Doctor,' said Victor, softer this time, but with malice. He turned the word over in his mouth, saying it again. 'And you want to listen to me?' He smiled. Alex forced himself to swallow. He was losing this one. He needed to change tack.

Victor parted his lips, baring his teeth. He began to mutter, whispers under his breath. Alex couldn't make out the words and found himself leaning in. Not English – Romanian, perhaps, the words rhythmic and structured.

Alex felt muzzy, his eyes struggling to focus. He shook his head as a loud buzzer sounded. A click came from the door lock. Victor's mouth remained open. His tongue darted out like a snake and he licked his lips.

A muffled voice crackled over the public-address system in the corridor, asking all cells to be vacated by staff and closed for lockdown. Victor snorted, his face twisting into a grin as he backed away.

Alex blinked a few times, his head clearing. Puzzled, he pulled the heavy door open. He glanced back at Victor, who hissed a final few words before sitting on the bunk, staring at the wall with a calm, almost vacant expression.

'Sorry for the interruption, Mr Lazar.'

Victor didn't move. His lips remained clamped shut.

'We'll continue this later,' Alex added, leaving the cell and pulling the door to behind him. He heard a click as the lock re-engaged.

Robert stood in the corridor where Alex had left him. He was cupping one ear towards the public-address system, straining to make out the message. When he saw Alex he beckoned him over.

'What's going on?' said Alex, hurrying towards Robert, ignoring the shouts from the other cells. He felt a deep shiver down his back.

Robert shrugged. 'It happens a lot,' he said. 'Staff shortages. They can't monitor every block at once. There's probably a scuffle somewhere. You're out until the guards return to their posts. Sorry.'

Alex wanted to protest but saw no value in doing so. He needed to get back into the public-sector swing of things and swallow it like a professional. He followed Robert out of the block and back towards the office complex, his anxiety fading with every step, but feeling disappointed with himself. He'd failed to control his conversation with Victor from the first second and he hadn't had time to put it right.

There was still no sign of Sophie, but as Alex grabbed his bag and phone from the desk, he reassured himself that today hadn't been a total loss. Victor Lazar had proved to be as intriguing in the flesh as on paper. True, Victor deserved better than Alex had given, but Alex could put that right. Before he spoke to Victor again he'd get properly prepared – a better workup of Victor's history, his background and influences. Victor was being treated as an enigma by Robert and the prison, which was great for academic papers but useless for diagnosis and treatment. Alex needed basic childhood and parental information. He needed education and employment details, a traditional background sweep, before moving on to the more peculiar aspects of Mr Lazar's behaviour. Alex didn't relish the thought of reviewing the prison CCTV footage again, but he owed it to Victor.

He was starting from scratch with a new patient and a high-profile criminal case. Against the background hum of his ever-present anxiety, Alex felt a small thrill as he left the office. He recognised it as professional excitement, and realised, with a small smile, how long it had been missing in his work.

CHAPTER EIGHT

Alex heaved the next textbook on to his lap. Stanley Milgram's *Obedience to Authority: An Experimental View* was a thick tome and, like the previous three, which lay on the coffee table bookmarked for later reference, told him nothing he didn't already know. He eyed the stack of back-issue copies of the *International Journal of Clinical and Experimental Hypnosis* he'd picked out of storage. He doubted they'd offer any answers either.

Alex topped up his glass, watching the red liquid cling to the crystal as he swirled it around. He corked the bottle – a 2005 Rioja – and placed it carefully on the table to avoid marking the waxed rosewood finish. He was back in his city office, feeling comfortably recovered from his prison experience and reflecting on how wonderful benzodiazepines were – even better when mixed with alcohol. His particular prescription – 1 mg Xanax – had the beneficial property of being almost impossible to overdose on. The more you took, the higher you got, but a dangerous dose was difficult to achieve. That's why so many people abused them.

His habit had started early. As a child, Alex would help his mum collect her prescription, wondering at the transformative effect the medication had on her. Her OCD and panic disorder disappeared into the background for hours, sometimes days. She credited her little magic pills, and Alex believed her. With his own anxieties developing fast and without the maturity or the support to explore them, he tried the magic himself. One evening he waited until his mum was asleep – his dad was working, always – and popped a couple of pills into his mouth. His nervous symptoms stopped within the hour. Stomach ache, dizziness and sore throat all melted away. His constant worry, that gnawing feeling that tugged at his gut and throat night and day, reduced. He faded into a warm fuzzy reality, relaxed and ready to tackle the world.

He tried it again the next day, and the day after that. His mum never questioned the rate at which her pills disappeared and her GP didn't seem to either. He kept taking them and his life was easier. He coped. That was all that mattered.

It was only a temporary thing, he told himself, but by the time he became aware of the benzodiazepine's addictive properties it was too late. School, college and university took their toll as he battled exams by day and cared for his mum by night. Alex finished his PhD with a regular benzo habit and a plan to stop it when the time was right.

That was fifteen years ago. The time was never right. Career, marriage, child, divorce. At what point did life get easy enough to kick such a habit? Perhaps when he retired.

Certainly not now.

Alex gazed up at a framed piece above the fireplace. It was a bright blue abstract canvas by one of Jane's friends. Alex hadn't been sure about it at first. Now, on reflection, he hated it. He would take it down the second he split up with Jane. Thinking about it dulled his mood, and he brought his gaze back down to the wine glass.

Alex hadn't remained long at Whitemoor after his short interview with Victor. Robert had offered very little in terms of a case history and Alex decided to leave with a promise to be back. He needed thinking time, away from the bustle of the prison. Somewhere familiar and comfortable. A safe place from where he could examine the events of the last twenty-four hours.

His phone vibrated. A text from Jane:

I forgive your moods if you forgive my persistence? Make it up
to me with dinner tomorrow night?

He dropped the phone on the table, feeling even worse about how he'd
been treating her.

Alex didn't tell Jane anything about his work – it was confidential
and he told himself that he couldn't risk her letting anything slip to her
friends. But Jane hadn't given him any reason to distrust her, and he
knew that the problem was him, not her. He'd convinced himself that
their relationship was temporary, that there was no need to involve her.
No need to open himself up, to form a meaningful connection.

After the breakdown of his marriage to Grace, the pain of being
distanced from his daughter's life, the guilt and shame of knowing it
was all his own fault, he had shut down. He'd always been emotionally
distant, but now he was a closed book. His issues and their roots were
easy to identify – a straightforward case for an experienced psychologist
such as himself. So why couldn't he change? Why couldn't he be better?

He might have permanently damaged Katie's childhood by messing
up his marriage, but making sure she felt loved and supported by both
parents, despite their separate living arrangements, was of the utmost
importance. Katie knew that her dad loved her – but did she feel that
she could rely on him? Alex sighed and rubbed his temples. She was
growing up so fast – he felt the time slipping through his fingers. He
wanted to be a better father to her than his own had been to him. He'd
lost count at an early age of the number of times his father had let him
down, emotionally and practically, never being there when it mattered.

He was thirty-nine and divorced. The woman who'd divorced him
thought he was a loser, but he still loved her. The woman he was with
attracted him in all the wrong ways, but he was too much of a wimp to
tell her. To blank both of those women out, he thought about his new
assistant, Sophie, a woman he barely knew but who was already playing
on his mind, a strange desire he could do without. He was drinking

more than he wanted to. He wasn't in a mood, he was just preoccupied. He frowned as the wine glass clunked on to the coaster, annoyed at the constant distraction of his failures. He needed to focus on Victor.

He stared at the books, trying to concentrate. Whatever his learned colleague Robert thought Victor could do, it was undocumented in the world of psychology. It wasn't possible, according to the literature, for Victor to compel people to do the things they did. Even in clinical study conditions, manipulation and suggestive techniques took time and trust from both sides. Victor had only been with the deceased for a matter of seconds in a busy prison environment. The CCTV footage was baffling, but it didn't constitute evidence. There could be many other explanations for what had occurred at the prison. None, admittedly, sprang to mind, but it would be a ludicrous and incompetent leap of faith to suggest mind control.

Victor's manner was more than a little unsettling, but Alex also knew that he was rusty, out of practice. It had been a long time since his last case and he needed to factor that in. He wondered how many more excuses he could make for his lack of insight. To help, he poured himself another large glass of wine and swore at the ceiling.

Tossing the books aside, Alex grabbed the paper copy of Victor's file. He frowned as he flicked through the brief case notes and timeline, annoyed it was so thin, so lacking in information.

Alex drained his glass, picturing the vivid images he'd seen on video and comparing them with the crime-scene photographs from Victor's file. The similarities were striking. Death by violent means, using a sharp object or blunt trauma, or both. Victor hadn't been in the room when any of them were killed, but appeared to have influenced the outcome from afar.

Sighing, he tried to pour more wine, found the bottle to be empty and thumped it back on the table, wincing as the glass hit the wood. Instead, he flicked through a few pages of his notepad, looking at the numbers. He'd made a few calls in the car on the way over but had got voicemail on every one. He picked the first name again and dialled. The call was answered on the third ring. On his request he was directed to a detective chief inspector in Hampshire Homicide. A man called Laird.

'Yes?' The voice was polite but impatient. Probably used to eighty per cent of his phone calls being a waste of time.

Alex introduced himself and jumped straight into the reason for his call. He presented his argument in a professional manner, but was soon interrupted by the detective.

'Forgive me, Dr Madison, if I sound a little sceptical,' said the DCI. Alex could hear a keyboard tapping in the background. 'I'm looking you up. It says here you provide private therapy services?'

Alex bit his lip. 'I'm a clinical psychologist. On this matter I am operating as a forensic consultant to the CPS, out of HMP Whitemoor.'

'I see,' said the detective, sounding unconvinced. 'And you want me to re-interview everyone who's had contact with this . . .' The detective paused. 'Victor Laz—'

'Lazar. I gave you the case reference.'

Alex heard the detective sniff and hammer at his keyboard several times. 'Yes, I see. This case was handed over to the CPS. We're not working on it at the moment, pending . . . Ah yes, a psych evaluation. That's you, is it?'

'That's me, and the other members of the team here, yes.'

'And you've completed your evaluation?'

Alex clenched his fist. 'No. I thought it would be prudent to—'

'Prudent, yes,' said DCI Laird. 'Prudent is good, but we're not twiddling our thumbs here. I've got several cases in front of me with plenty of evidence, and I don't even have time for those.'

There was silence on the phone, followed by more tapping.

'Look,' said the detective. 'I'll be honest with you. I can't do anything with your request.'

'But—'

'We don't have the resources to interview God knows how many people – thirty or more – just because you want us to.'

'I see.' Alex stared out of the window. Heavy clouds chased each other across the grey sky.

'That's a polite way of saying bugger off and come back when you have something concrete, Dr Madison. Perhaps new evidence or an admission of guilt. That would be great.'

Alex nodded to himself, resigned. Of course the police wouldn't do anything. He'd given them nothing they didn't already know.

'It was good of you to consider us in the course of your evaluation,' said the detective in a softer tone. 'Good luck with your assessment. Please call back if you have something I can work with.'

The detective hung up, leaving Alex rather pissed off and feeling very much put in his place. Years ago, he would have dominated the conversation with the inspector, negotiating his position and having significant influence on the proceedings. Three years of private practice had lost him his edge and he needed to regain it. He grabbed his coat. His next conversation would do nothing to improve his mood, but he knew he must do it anyway.

CHAPTER NINE

'Alex.'

His father opened the door and stood with his legs wide, hands on hips. He regarded Alex for a moment, eyeing his expensive suit with contempt and making an obvious glance at the Porsche. His father considered Alex's penchant for fast cars infantile and wasteful, so Alex made a point of always arriving in the Porsche, or his other favourite – a classic Alfa Spider, kept in his garage under cover.

'Your mother's in bed. Sleeping. You should have called.'

Alex was disappointed, but it was often the case. He glanced up at his childhood home, a large 1920s townhouse. It evoked the usual complicated mixture of emotions. He stared at his father's Volkswagen Passat, parked on the immaculate block-paved driveway. Neat borders held pruned rosebushes, ready to emerge in the coming weeks as spring dragged them out of their winter slumber.

The door had been painted green since his last visit. Not by his father – he'd never touch DIY – but his mum often had sudden ideas and wouldn't be satisfied until the urge was met, whatever it might be. She would have arranged it all – his father wasn't home enough to notice what colour the door was, or present enough to care.

'I was passing,' said Alex. 'I wanted to ask you something.'

His father nodded and stood aside. Alex entered the hall but stopped. He didn't feel like he belonged here. He was a guest and the formality was stifling.

They went through to his father's study – somewhere he was forbidden to enter as a child. God forbid he should be allowed to encroach upon his father's personal space and share quality time with him. His father sat in a recliner by the window. Alex scanned the floor-to-ceiling bookshelves, overflowing with textbooks and journals, several of them with his father's name on the spine. He remained standing. He didn't plan on staying long enough to get comfortable.

'So?' A lack of emotion in his father's voice. Alex expected nothing more. 'You're taking the case then?'

Straight to business. Typical of his father. No pleasantries. No *How are you?* or *How is Katie?* or even *How's your career going?*

'Did you tell them to call me?' said Alex. 'The CPS?'

His father shrugged. 'I thought it would be good for you,' he said. 'Call it one final attempt to stop you wasting your talent.'

'How's Mum?' Alex wasn't going to let this conversation run on his father's terms, like it usually did.

'Catherine is the same as always. She won't accept my help or anyone else's. Don't pretend to care. You haven't visited for three months.'

Alex bit his tongue. If he didn't have to put up with his father, perhaps he would visit this place more often. He found it hard to meet his father's eye, instead focusing on the rows of dusty periodicals.

'Why me?' he said.

'The prosecutor is an old chum of mine. He asked my opinion, naturally.'

Naturally, thought Alex.

'And I thought it would be good for you. Get you out of the tabloids. Stop you dwelling on the past.'

Alex ignored the jibe. 'Do you know about the case? Victor Lazar?'

'Not my thing.'

'Why do you think I can help?' said Alex.

'Because you're a clinician? Because I paid tens of thousands of pounds for you to get the best education in the field? Because treating footballers and celebrity chefs is getting too stressful for you?'

There was no humour in his father's voice, the sarcasm edged with distaste. Alex's father had helped him get police work in the first place, his wide contacts ensuring Alex got treated with respect and was given serious work. Alex always wondered how much of it was to boost his father's reputation, rather than his own. Since Alex had taken up private practice, his father could barely contain his disgust. In his view Alex was throwing it all away for an easy life. He didn't understand why Alex felt so guilty for his mistakes. He knew about Alex's failed case and simply encouraged him to shrug it off with professional arrogance. *Get back in the saddle*, he'd said. *Forget it.*

'Can you offer me anything useful?' said Alex, wondering why he'd come. What did he expect from this man? This stranger who happened to be his father.

His father huffed. 'You can't do this yourself?'

'I can. But I wondered, through professional courtesy, what information you might have to assist me.' Alex spoke through his teeth.

'Have you spoken to the prosecutor?'

'Not yet.'

'Then start there.'

Alex listened to a few moments of silence. 'Is that it?'

'That's it. Look, I'm busy, Alex—'

'Fine. I'll leave you to whatever it is you do.'

'Work, you mean?'

'If you say so.' Alex was being petulant now, but he wasn't quite at the stage of forgiving his father. A childhood of endless repetition, watching his mum suffer through fruitless trips to the GP, cycles of drugs and behavioural therapy. All of it ending in failure. She never wanted help. What she wanted was a husband who wasn't quite so self-centred and work-obsessed. One who would help raise their son and be there once in a while to read him a story at bedtime. Her OCD progressed throughout Alex's teens until she was housebound and dependent on carers.

'You have no idea, Alex. You're just like your mum.'

'Happy to be that way,' said Alex. He turned and faced his father now, conscious of the lie. He was well aware his own anxiety was a product of his upbringing, his mum's OCD rubbing off on him. How could it not? Caring for your own mum from six years old was bound to leave its mark. But he would defend her to the death against an insult from his father.

Alex squeezed his fists together, angry at himself. He never expected anything useful from his visits. Why did he expect it now? His father wasn't interested in helping.

His father closed his eyes briefly. Alex could see the struggle in his face, but offered him no help.

'It doesn't have to be like this, Alex.'

Alex bit his lip for a moment. 'You made it like this.'

'I gave you the chance to understand it.'

'Living takes more than an expensive education, Father.'

His father frowned and Alex lost sympathy. His father, of all people, should understand that the damage done at an early age will resonate forever, however normal the adult might appear.

'I'm pleased you've taken the case,' his father concluded, nodding to himself.

Alex huffed, turning away again. His eyes were drawn to a stack of dusty brown texts at the far end of the bookcase, near the door. He recognised many of the titles, having them on his own bookshelves.

The crests of several universities jumped out at him, but most were from King's College Cambridge, which was his father's establishment and place of employment for most of his career. The words on some of the spines were so old and faded as to be almost unreadable. The titles were wide and varied: *Clinical and Forensic Assessment of Psychopathic Manipulation*; *Stabilizing Bipolar Manic Episodes Through Hypnotic Imagery*; *Unconscious Agendas in Deep Regression Therapy*.

Alex hadn't realised his father was so well read in clinical disciplines. He was a research psychologist, not practising. It wasn't like Rupert to be modest about anything. Alex was surprised, and a little peeved.

'It's time I woke Catherine for her dinner,' said his father, appearing behind Alex.

Alex nodded, looking at his father. 'I've never seen these,' he said, waving towards the shelves.

'Nothing useful, I'm afraid,' said his father, a faint, cold smile on his lips. 'A gift from a visiting professor.'

Alex looked at his father's face and saw the familiar impatience he'd grown to hate over the years. He'd wasted his time coming here and was glad to leave the cold and unwelcoming man behind.

Alex turned the Porsche around and spared his father one last glance before he roared off. Rupert stood at the doorway, his face a mask. He reached over and plucked a couple of leaves from a climbing rose before discarding them. He didn't wave before heading back inside and slamming the door behind him.

CHAPTER TEN

'Mr Lewisham? It's Dr Alex Madison. Thank you for taking my call.'

'Ah, Dr Madison. Morning. The CPS is pleased to have you on board. You come highly recommended.'

'I'm not sure I can help,' said Alex.

'Your father spoke highly of your talents.'

Alex paused, deciding not to tell the prosecutor that most of his father's motives were self-serving. 'My father and I have a professional understanding,' he said. 'He thought I should look at the case, perform my assessment. No guarantees.'

'Dr Madison, I have five dead bodies including the suicides at Whitemoor, and I need to provide an explanation to the families and a case for the CPS. I'm not asking for guarantees. As it stands, this case will be dead within months and Victor Lazar will be deported. If he's responsible I need to know.'

'Which is why I agreed to take the case,' said Alex. 'I've met Victor.'

'And?'

'And the man is intriguing,' said Alex, 'unnerving – terrifying even. Everything Dr Bradley said he was, but I need more background. Mr Lazar made references to his past, but nothing specific. Our first conversation was cut rather shorter than I planned. I was hoping to be better prepared before I next see him.'

He heard the prosecutor take a deep breath. Deciding how to proceed.

'To be effective, I must—'

'Yes, you must,' said Lewisham. 'But that does seem to be a problem for us. Victor's history is incomplete. He appeared in the UK a few months ago and was arrested at our scene of carnage. Before his arrival in the UK he was in Romania. He is a Romanian national.'

'And what did he do in Romania?' said Alex.

'We don't know,' said Lewisham, 'but the Romanians are being obstructive. He cannot be returned there at this time, and he cannot be released.'

Alex suspected the police and legal teams would have gone to considerable effort to trace Victor's background. But there had to be something.

'Can you at least give me a contact? A medical lead? It's what I do. I'm trying to establish motive and the source of Victor's behaviour. I'll struggle without more information.'

Lewisham sighed. 'I can put you in contact with Dr Aron Petri at the University of Bucharest. The police have already spoken to him. Other than the Romanian immigration office, he was the only official who would acknowledge Victor Lazar's existence during our research. My impression was that the Romanians are embarrassed by the man and happy to leave him imprisoned here indefinitely. I don't know how responsive Dr Petri will be – we had to request the initial information through quite sensitive channels. It's all very political. I'll ask my secretary to send you his details.'

'Thanks,' said Alex, doodling a series of question marks on the paper. 'Any reason why this information wasn't in the case file?' Alex knew he was pushing it, questioning the CPS's motives for withholding information. But if you don't ask, you don't get.

'We gave the prison service what we thought they needed,' said Lewisham. 'None of this is secret, Dr Madison, but it all takes time and work. Now, if that will be all, I'll leave you to it.'

Alex made a coffee while he waited for the details to be emailed through. It was still early and he decided to contact the Romanian doctor right away. He remained at his office, thinking that the privacy of his study might be better than the open desks at Whitemoor.

At first he thought he'd been given the wrong number and cursed. The series of beeps at the other end sounded like a disconnected line, but they stopped and a brief hiss was replaced with a male voice.

'*Bună dimineața.*'

'Ah,' said Alex, looking at some notes he'd scrawled on his pad. '*Bună dimineața. Vorbiți engleză?*' There was a pause and Alex hoped he'd got the phrase correct.

'Yes, I speak English,' said the man.

Just as well, thought Alex, *or it would have been a short call*. He cleared his throat. 'My name is Dr Alex Madison. I'm a clinical psychologist consulting for the British prison service. I'm trying to get hold of Dr Aron Petri. I understand he teaches at the psychology department there in Bucharest?'

'You've found him,' said the voice, sounding suspicious. 'I'm Dr Petri. I head the faculty of psychology here.'

'Great,' said Alex, 'and apologies for my appalling lack of Romanian. I've never had much of a need to—'

'What can I do for you?' said Dr Petri.

Alex paused. The line crackled. 'Your name was given to me by the British Crown Prosecution Service.' He waited before continuing, hoping for some recognition or outpouring of useful information. There was nothing but silence. 'It concerns the case of Victor Lazar, a

Romanian national who is imprisoned here at HMP Whitemoor.' Still silence. 'Are you there?'

'I'm here.' The suspicion remained.

'So you know who I'm talking about?'

There was a tapping at the other end, as if a pencil or a fingernail was being repeatedly struck on a table.

'Look, Dr Madison. When your authorities first contacted us about this man they were rude and demanding. They made various requests and managed to get our immigration department to support them. I made some enquiries and I told immigration and your prosecutor what I found at the time. That was several days ago and as far as I'm concerned my involvement is unnecessary. If the man is a criminal I'm sure he'll pay for his crimes in your prisons. I'm not sure what else you want from me or my country.'

'I'm sorry if the prosecutor was rude,' said Alex. 'It's unacceptable. I didn't call to make demands or insult you. I'm rather desperate for your help.' Starting with an apology was an old trick, but it worked on everyone. 'Mr Lazar will be deported,' Alex continued, 'if we can't connect him to our case and prove his guilt. He'll be heading back to Romania.'

'What are you trying to prove?' said Dr Petri, his voice softening. 'What did he do?'

'Something I was hoping you'd help me understand,' said Alex. 'I can't give you the full details—'

'Which is what your CPS said.'

'OK, OK,' said Alex. 'I can give you some details. Some I can't because it's an ongoing criminal investigation. You can appreciate that, Doctor. I'm bound by patient confidentiality.'

'You're his doctor now?' said Dr Petri. 'What is his diagnosis? What is his treatment plan?'

'I can't, er—'

'Of course you can't,' said Dr Petri.

'He was arrested at a murder–suicide, Dr Petri,' said Alex, unsure if legally he should be sharing this information but aware he needed to give Petri something. 'He may be an innocent bystander but he's not acting like one.' Alex struggled with what to tell the man. He wasn't comfortable telling this foreign doctor the gruesome details over the phone.

There was an audible sigh on the other end of the phone, and the tapping stopped.

'Look,' said Dr Petri, 'I don't want to repay rudeness with rudeness. It's not my way or the Romanian way. I don't want to hear about his crimes, so I will tell you what I know, then you'll leave me alone. OK?'

'I'll be grateful for anything,' said Alex.

'I have some information about this Victor Lazar. He's not well known to the state, but his childhood is recorded in our faculty research programmes. Some of this I told to your CPS. Some emerged later and to be honest I didn't bother passing it on.'

Alex's ears pricked up. Information the CPS didn't have. 'What did he have to do with the university?' he asked. 'I assumed you were only involved because you once treated him for something.'

'I never treated Victor Lazar for anything,' said Dr Petri. 'I've never met him either. But he was sponsored by this university for a time. My involvement, as requested by immigration, was to search back through the faculty records.'

'Sponsored?' Alex scribbled on his notepad. 'I don't understand.'

'You know he was an orphan?'

'I didn't know that.'

'OK. Well, he entered the Romanian social system at three years old. This is going back some time – pre-revolution. Back then the care system in my country was underfunded and poor by any standards. We've been judged by the international community for it and most of the criticism was justified, although I suspect we were no worse than other similar countries . . . But still, care homes were of varying quality and most required financial sponsorship of some kind.'

'So your university sponsored the children's home where he lived?'

'It's not as simple as that, but yes.'

Alex double-underlined the university's name on his notepad. 'Why?'

'I beg your pardon?'

'Why were you sponsoring it? What did the university get out of it? I'm assuming it wasn't a charitable arrangement.'

Another sigh. 'I have already told the authorities what I was able to discover on this matter,' said Dr Petri.

'Which was?'

'The university was running a research programme in childhood trauma management, behavioural therapies and suchlike. Although I can't find any specific records involving Victor, it's quite possible he was involved in the research. The dates fit.'

Alex took a moment to digest this. On the face of it, it might sound innocent and reasonable. Unless you happened to work in the medical profession and knew what it meant.

'The university was buying test subjects from the children's home for research. Orphans,' he said, as bluntly as he could, before clenching his mouth shut. He didn't want to risk alienating Dr Petri.

'I can't comment on that,' said Dr Petri, 'because I don't know. If I'm honest, it wouldn't surprise me if that went on under the old regime. The ethical controls weren't in place then – and don't pretend it was any different across much of Eastern Europe.'

'Can you give me more details on what they were doing?' asked Alex.

'I'm afraid not,' said Dr Petri. 'All I could find is a list of children and trial names, and the name Comănești Orphanage. Whatever other information was recorded is gone.'

'Names?' said Alex. 'Perhaps—'

'Forget it,' said Dr Petri. 'Our immigration department already refused you the names. These are Romanian citizens and we're not prepared to give you their details unless they're suspected of a crime.'

Alex bit his lip. If he could find somebody else who was alive and involved in those trials, he might find some answers about Victor. He scratched his forehead and took a couple of deep breaths.

'There is one name I can give you,' said Dr Petri, as if sensing Alex's unease. 'This emerged recently from our archiving department. It got lost in my original request and I was sent it just a couple of days ago.'

'A child?'

'No, an adult. One of the faculty. He was involved in the research programme. He's a British citizen now, which is why we don't object to giving you his name. Let's see . . .'

Alex heard the rustling of papers and a filing cabinet being opened and closed.

'Here it is,' said Dr Petri. 'Professor Nicolae Dumitru. A child psychologist. He worked in Bucharest from 1967 to 1990 and was with the university for seven years. He stayed after the revolution but left Romania in 1996.'

Alex scribbled the details down and froze. Dr Petri obviously hadn't been given the names of the people killed at Southampton. Alex rummaged through his own papers, holding the phone between his cheek and shoulder.

'Do you have any contact details?' said Alex, cursing as his folder dropped to the floor.

'No. That's all I have. You'll have to find him yourself, I'm afraid,' said Dr Petri.

'OK,' said Alex, swearing under his breath as he spread the case notes out on the carpet.

'Look,' said Dr Petri, 'if anything else turns up, I'll send it to you. At least in our profession we can extend professional courtesy, even if our legal colleagues cannot.'

'Much appreciated. Thank you, Dr Petri.'

'Now I must go. I have a lecture. *La revedere*, Dr Madison. Goodbye.'

The line went dead and Alex dropped his phone on the table. He hadn't paid much attention to the names of the Southampton victims, but he riffled through the papers until he found what he was looking for.

The Assistant Head of Faculty at the University of Southampton, stabbed four times in the back. Dead at the scene. Professor Nicolae Dumitru.

CHAPTER ELEVEN

Comănești Orphanage
Bacău County, Romania, 1986

Victor was nine years old when he watched Laura die in the courtyard of Comănești Orphanage. The stairwell window was grubby and he'd wiped it with his sleeve, so he could see the blood trickle into the gaps between the stones, painting a trail across the ground, pooling around her small body.

She was eight. A year younger. His best friend. And she was dead.

One of the orderlies appeared with a trolley. He'd been waiting to one side until it was over. The man grabbed Laura's body by her coat and lifted her up, dumping her on to the wheeled base.

Victor held back the tears. He swallowed the hurt and the anger. It would do him no good. Not now.

The orderly paused and rummaged in his trouser pocket, pulling out a cigarette. He lit the harsh tobacco and drew on it heavily, blowing the smoke upwards into the cold air. As he raised his head he glanced at the building and saw Victor at the window. Their eyes met and they stared at each other, both squinting in the morning sun. Victor was frightened – he shouldn't have been watching – but he didn't move. He muttered a few words and tried to make his voice carry through the window to the man below. It didn't work. Victor's small voice drifted away, and besides, the orderlies were trained. His words would have no effect on the giant below.

Victor swallowed hard as the man took another long drag on his cigarette. Blowing smoke from his nose, the man raised his free hand and pointed it at Victor, wiggling his forefinger to warn him off.

Victor heeded the warning and nodded, backing away from the window, breaking eye contact. He crept back into the corridor, shivering as his bare feet touched the concrete, heading for his dormitory.

The smell of bleach was strong in the corridor, but as he approached the dorm, the smell of urine was stronger. Victor was dry most nights, but many of the younger children weren't. They had their sheets changed only once a week, so it was bound to smell. You got used to it, and besides, Victor didn't know any better. His parents had disappeared long ago and this was all he knew. He was a *decreţel* – a child of the state, born after the edict against birth control – and he belonged to this place.

Victor arrived to find the dormitory empty. The twenty metal beds all stood cold and grey, the dirty sheets hanging limp. It was forever damp, black mould growing in every corner of every room.

He was pleased, despite what he'd witnessed. You learned to take perks quick in this place, and bury your grief even quicker. With the dorm empty, he might grab a few minutes to himself. He raced over to his own bunk and reached under the thin mattress, retrieving several sheets of paper and a small stub of pencil. Sitting cross-legged on the bunk, he began to write, marking each word with care on the crumpled paper.

Writing of this sort was forbidden. He knew this. Literacy was allowed, but the recording of events was not. The orphanage's business was its own, and nobody else's. The fewer records kept of this place the better, as far as they were concerned.

He'd been caught before, beaten and humiliated. Sometimes they withheld food or water, or refused to let him use the toilet. The supervisors had many means of punishment. He still had a bruise on the back of his neck from the last account he'd written. He'd almost blacked out, and he had no wish to receive another beating.

His dormitory supervisor knew how to break the will of children. She'd been practising for years. She held his chin up, keeping his eyes on hers as she hit him. She was strict on eye contact, particularly when she was angry. Clinical and methodical, she kept his face clean, for the most part. The rest of his body took the brunt, flinching under the blows.

But he needed to write his stories. He couldn't keep it all in his head.

He had barely ten minutes before the alarm sounded. He folded the paper in half around the pencil and slid the bundle under his mattress. It wasn't a great hiding place, but it was the only one he had.

CHAPTER TWELVE

Alex tried Sophie's extension, Robert's and the main switchboard, which put him through to Robert again. No answer.

He considered phoning the police. There was a link, and possible motive, however speculative. But it wasn't enough, and the more Alex thought about it the more he wanted to find out for himself, before opening the floodgate of police interviews, which, given Victor's current behaviour, were unlikely to reveal anything useful.

This was something only he knew and he could use it to his advantage. It could be just what he needed to restart his assessment with Victor – talking about the orphanage might push Victor into opening up. If Victor had been subject to some kind of abuse in his childhood it could explain any number of psychological conditions. Alex felt slightly uncomfortable about keeping it from the police, but in his experience it was sometimes best to drip feed information so they didn't go in cack-handed and ruin everything.

As he gathered his bag and papers, he decided not to tell Robert or Sophie either, at least until after his next session with Victor. His stomach lurched a little at the thought of going back into Victor's cell, but he didn't have a choice. Victor had unnerved him but nothing more. Alex knew the onus was on him now, to gain Victor's trust and persuade the man to open up.

Alex found Robert at his desk in the prison, resting his usual mug of coffee on his belly while browsing a thin sheaf of papers. A stain grew on Robert's shirt where the coffee had dripped.

'Alex,' said Robert, glancing up. He placed his cup on the desk and arched his back, stretching.

'I'd like to see Victor again,' said Alex, dropping his bag on the desk, removing his phone and wallet and popping them in his front pocket. He took off his jacket and looked around for a coat rack before placing it carefully on the back of the chair, smoothing out the shoulders.

Robert nodded. 'You've had some thoughts?'

'Some,' said Alex, 'but to be honest I'd just like to start again. I didn't have time to introduce myself properly.'

Robert raised his eyebrows, waiting for Alex to continue. Alex tapped the desk but said nothing.

'Well . . . OK,' said Robert. 'I think we have a full rota of staff today, for once.' He smiled, although he looked strained around the eyes.

'Shall I head down now?' said Alex.

'You don't want a coffee first?' Robert looked at his own cup, half-full, seemingly annoyed at the thought of leaving it.

'I'd rather get started,' said Alex.

Robert sighed. 'Very well,' he said, hoisting himself out of the chair, which creaked in relief. 'Same rules apply. Don't give him your name and keep other personal details to a minimum.'

'Sure thing,' said Alex.

They bumped into Sophie in the stairwell. She was out of her normal work clothes, dressed in tight jeans and a black top. She smiled warmly at them both but hesitated when Robert announced they were headed down to segregation. She asked what Alex's plans were for Victor. Was he going to recommend continued segregation? Would he look to sedate and move him to the medical block? Her questions were rapid and unplanned. Alex was a little taken aback at her interrogation.

'I don't know yet,' was all he could offer, suggesting she came with them. Sophie thought for a few seconds before agreeing. Alex noticed her hands fidgeting as they walked. This wasn't the first time she'd grown anxious at the mention of Victor. Perhaps she behaved like this around all of her patients. It was endearing, provided it didn't interfere with her work. It showed empathy, a quality not always present in his profession.

'Are you OK?' he said.

Sophie paused. 'I'm fine,' she said, her eyes saying the opposite. Alex nodded and smiled. Their eyes remained locked for a few seconds before she looked away. He wanted to stop, to talk to Sophie and find out more about her, what was on her mind. Perhaps later.

The slamming of metal doors and the shriek of the buzzers had less of a startling effect today. Alex was easing back into this world and the background din of the prison faded as he focused on what he had to do.

Victor had been mistreated as a child. Of that, Alex was certain. He'd need more background on the orphanage, but he had enough to get started. Abused? Possibly, although what kind of abuse? Victims of abuse responded very differently when presented with their histories, and there was no right way to do this. Alex would be constrained by the fact that Victor was in custody. There might not be time for a full programme of therapy, but Alex hoped he could elicit something significant from Victor. At the very least, Alex might quash the more fantastic suggestions about his patient.

They reached the wing and once again Robert waited just inside the main gate, slouching on to a chair meant for the guards. Their guard escort looked peeved and headed back to the next gate, repeating the usual instructions about how to enter and exit the prisoners' cells.

Sophie stood to one side, keeping distance between herself and Robert. She crossed her arms, shuffling her left foot. Alex watched but she kept her eyes down. She looked vulnerable and agitated, just as she had done the last time they'd come down here. Alex felt drawn to her but pushed the thought to one side. *Be a professional,* he told himself as he headed towards Victor's cell.

CHAPTER THIRTEEN

Alex ignored the smell as the cell door swung open. He controlled his facial expression and pulled his shoulders back as he stood in the doorway. 'Mr Lazar,' he said, 'Victor, may I come in?'

Victor sat as before, upright and rigid, staring at the opposite wall. The light from the ceiling reflected off his head and the rim of his glasses. He remained motionless for several seconds before turning to Alex.

'Dr Carter,' he said, 'Alex, you may.'

Alex stepped into the cell and eased the door closed. The buzzer sounded and the lock clicked. Alex felt his heart jump but he remained in control, if awkwardly sandwiched between the toilet and the door. The cell was even smaller than he remembered.

'I want to apologise,' said Alex. 'My first visit was cut short. I don't feel we had an opportunity to introduce ourselves properly.'

Victor took a long breath, his nostrils whistling. He let out a small snort. 'Apology accepted. Won't you sit?'

'Thank you, but I'll stand. I spend a lot of time sitting.'

'As do I,' said Victor, pulling the same menacing smile as before.

Alex swallowed, with a slight shudder. Taking a breath and leaning against the wall, he adjusted his feet, thankful he'd left his expensive jacket in the office. On the way down he'd thought about how to start this conversation – with the murder–suicide at Southampton or the suicides in the prison. That's where the police would start, naturally, and it's where Alex would have started, had he not spoken to Dr Petri.

'I'd like to talk about Comăneşti,' said Alex. He paused, holding his breath, waiting for Victor's reaction.

Victor closed his eyes. His neck stiffened and his head jerked a couple of times. His breathing quickened. Alex was about to continue when Victor spoke.

'Sit down, Doctor. It would be polite, no?' Victor's eyes remained closed, but his hands grasped the edge of the bed.

Alex waited, judging how far to go. He'd started in the right place. 'I'll stand, thank you,' he said. 'Does that place have significance for you? Comăneşti?'

Victor would know Alex had been researching. Perhaps he'd be surprised at what Alex had found, but Alex didn't want to reveal the extent of what he knew, or didn't know.

Victor cleared his throat and his breathing slowed. 'What would you class as significant, Doctor?'

Victor had composed himself, already responding with questions. He'd regained control faster than Alex had thought he would. There was a strong mental wall inside the man, possibly built over many years. It would need breaking down. It would take time.

'Part of my job is research,' said Alex. 'I discovered some disturbing information about Comăneşti. The orphanage.'

Victor opened his eyes but continued to face the wall. He didn't repeat his question. His left hand twitched.

'In the eighties,' said Alex, keeping it deliberately vague. 'It was not a well-regulated system.'

Victor sneered. He moved, turning to Alex, his hands unclenching. 'You don't think?'

Alex paused. What did that comment suggest? He decided to proceed. 'I think many children were mistreated. The information I received suggests unethical practices may have occurred.' Alex frowned, unhappy at his choice of words. He'd made it sound too official, too clinical. He was better than this. Why not just come out and say it?

Victor beat him to it. 'Unethical practices,' he said. He laughed, a short snap, full of hate. His eyes burned through Alex.

'I think . . .' Alex faltered. Victor had an ability to throw him off kilter. 'I think you were mistreated in Comăneşti, Victor. I think the orphanage did things to you, to the other—'

'Stop!' Victor shouted. He stood and closed the distance between them in a heartbeat. His movement was so rapid that Alex cowered into the wall.

Victor stared at Alex, eyes darting. He bared his teeth, muttering something under his breath. His face contorted, his lips curling, the muscles in his cheeks twitching. Deep furrows appeared in his forehead and his eyes glazed over. Victor looked deep in concentration.

'Sit, Alex.' Victor's voice was stern and abrupt. His words sounded loud and crisp in Alex's ears, as though he was wearing headphones, all other sound blanked out.

Alex felt his muscles weaken. His joints trembled and a shiver ran down his spine. Within a second he felt his legs collapse, as if his knees had been hit from behind. He slid down the wall, unable to stop.

Alex watched the cell fade away, the colours weaken as if a fog had descended. He felt sluggish and confused. He tried to reach out but his arms wouldn't move. They hung at his side, limp and useless. He ended in an awkward squat, held up by the side of the toilet unit and the wall. Victor smiled, his lips parted slightly, muttering something under his breath. Alex tried to talk but nothing came out. His mouth wouldn't open and his lips wouldn't move.

He was paralysed on the floor of Victor's cell.

CHAPTER FOURTEEN

Victor walked down the rear stairs of the orphanage towards the class-rooms, joined by others, thirty or so of them, some friends, some strangers, all headed for a day of education in its various forms. Denis and Maria both looked sleepy, no doubt wakened in the night for punishment.

At the bottom of the stairs his number was called and he stopped. 'Child thirteen.' The call came again. His heart thumped and he shivered, his stomach lurching. He hadn't expected to be called today. They always had a break between sessions.

The doctor caught his eye from across the corridor and beckoned him over. He ticked Victor off his list and pushed him through a door into the medical room. It was small, grey-walled and without windows. The floor tiles were broken and Victor could see black mould on the walls, and in the corners. He screwed his nose up and shivered. There were three other doctors in the room, easily identifiable by their white coats. A small tatty chair stood in the centre of the room, the kind that leaned back when they wanted to examine you. It was empty, and he was asked to sit.

His ears thumped with the beat of his heart as he fought the shakes. He wasn't ready. He wasn't any better at it than Laura, and she'd lost. The boy who'd won was two years older than Victor. It wouldn't be fair to pitch them against each other. Not until he'd had a chance to practise a little more.

He opened his mouth to protest but the doctor waved him into silence. They weren't violent, the doctors, but they recorded those who complied and those who didn't. They left it to the orphanage supervisors to deal with the latter. Victor held his tongue and his eyes were drawn to another doctor, who waited with a large syringe in his hand. He plunged the blunt, used needle into Victor's arm. It tore his skin, but he remained silent.

They injected him with the drug, whatever it was, and let it seep into his bloodstream and into his brain. While it worked, the doctors talked. They were optimistic, it seemed. Results were improving, and the next batch was very promising. They talked about Victor but not to him, referring to him by his number and his batch. His ability, no doubt, was strong, and getting stronger. After the drug took effect he would be subjected to the next round of conditioning. Victor knew from experience what this meant, and he shivered again.

Frightening, confusing and alien images were shown repeatedly in four-hour sessions. Those children who refused were strapped to the chairs, eyes prised open with whatever came to hand, most often thick tape holding the eyelids in place. The images flashed and waned, embedding their message, whatever it might be. Victor didn't know, and while he cried at the content, he assumed it was necessary. Desensitisation. A word whispered by the staff, misunderstood by the children. Is that what the images were for? To desensitise him? Then why did he feel so wretched? Why did he gasp with sorrow at night, listening to the cries of the other children?

Linguistics followed. The children spoke Romanian, but they were taught many other phrases from different languages. It wasn't conversational and made little sense to the youngest, but certain words and phrases were hammered into Victor and the others. He wrote them, spoke them and dreamed about them until he could recite the words on demand, in a whisper.

And then the games began. Language, posture and tone. Passive, aggressive, neutral and silent. Micro-expressions, facial contortions, misdirection and a hundred other ingredients to create a storm of signals a silent orchestra played solely for one listener: the target. The sole purpose: to take control.

It hadn't been like this in the beginning. The tasks had never been fun, but they hadn't always ended like they did these days. Now, he knew he wouldn't be allowed to stop until he'd completed it. He'd be given a target: sometimes a homeless person from the streets of Comăneşti, or occasionally a convict. The worst was when it was another child at the home. Then he'd be given his instructions.

For each and every task there was a winner and a loser.

More often than not, the loser died.

In the following weeks, Victor adjusted to the new drug and performed his tasks. His beatings became less frequent as his ability improved. The doctors were pleased with him, which meant the supervisors were under extra pressure not to damage him, at least not so it showed.

But inside Victor's head, the hatred grew alongside his talent. Victor knew he couldn't leave – nobody ever escaped the orphanage. It was a small town and the police brought back every single child who ever tried to leave. Stories of what the police did to the children before they returned were whispered throughout the dormitories, but no child ever complained. Their eyes dulled further and their souls festered.

But Victor dreamed of one day seeing the doctors in the testing ground. Forcing them to make the choices. Forcing them, in a battle of wills, to kill or be killed.

Forcing them to die, just as Laura had. She hadn't been ready; they'd put her forward too soon.

But even as Victor became one of the trained, one of the *păpuşari*, a 'puppet master', his supervisors remained in control. They were protected with drugs that blocked the abilities unleashed during the training, when frenzied attacks raised screams that echoed across the courtyard, through the skin of the orphanage and out into the rock of the mountains.

The supervisors were untouchable, or so it seemed to Victor.

And so Victor's outlet was his stories. He told Laura's story in the minutes after he'd seen his young friend slit her own throat, scribbling his feelings into the paper. He described her opponent, untouched but having had another mental scar added to the growing notches inside, before being congratulated and rewarded with a hot supper and a hot shower instead of the usual cold bucket.

Victor made mention of every death, but the most detailed stories were his own. These were stories of his own trials, of what he was told to do and how he did it. How he carved his own words out and made them stick, how he whispered his instructions and passed them across the void, to grab his opponent's body and bend it to his will.

These stories, Victor believed, must one day be told.

CHAPTER FIFTEEN

Victor crouched in front of Alex, their faces inches apart. 'You're an interesting one, Dr Alex Carter.'

Alex could feel Victor's breath on his cheek. It smelled rotten and sour. It swirled around the air, mixing with the mist, seeping into his mind. The fear rose from his gut, growing as his chest tightened.

'Why are you here?' Victor studied Alex's face. 'Did they send you?' Victor slanted his face, left and right, his eyes searching and probing Alex's. He looked surprised. 'Oh. You really don't know? Interesting. Well, you'll no doubt discover it in time, but be under no illusion: there is nothing you can do. You might think you have certain expertise, but you are nothing compared to me, so stay out of my way. You can't stop this.'

'Stop what?' whispered Alex, finding his jaw had relaxed. He was starting to hyperventilate. He needed his pills, but was unable to move. The tension spread across his chest and shoulders, causing him to clench his jaw.

Victor crouched again, coming close enough for Alex to see his eyes. They frightened him.

'They cursed us,' Victor whispered. He tilted his head, his eyes drilling through Alex.

'Who?' said Alex, breathing through the panic.

Victor snapped his head back and laughed.

'You're probably a fine doctor, Dr Carter, but you should go back to what you're good at.'

'I—' Alex began.

'You are the same. You came in here expecting to manipulate me and get what you needed.' Victor closed his eyes. He breathed over Alex's face. Alex could do nothing but shiver. 'But I forgive you,' Victor whispered. 'It's not your fault. It's theirs. They made the wrong choices, Alex. But don't worry, I will show them what they created.'

Victor leaned back and stood. He sat back on the bunk and closed his eyes. He touched his right hand to his temple and winced, clenching his teeth. Alex saw the muscles in his jaw lock up. He waited several seconds.

'It's nice you came, Dr Carter, even if you don't know why you're here. It was a pleasure to see you again. It allows me to make my one and final warning. Stay away from me and my business. Get out of my cell and leave this place. Go home, Dr Carter.'

Alex's shoulders slumped as Victor's control disappeared. He raised his hands to his face and looked at them. He wiggled his fingers and they moved freely. His legs felt weak but back within his control. He stumbled to his feet and backed towards the door, banging it with his fist. The buzzer sounded and the lock clicked open. He pulled the door and fell out of the cell, without looking at Victor or offering any parting farewell.

Robert and Sophie were still where he had left them, near the entrance to the corridor. Robert looked up in concern as Alex stumbled towards them. He doubled over, drawing in several large breaths. Sophie ran to hold him.

'Alex, are you OK?' said Robert, pulling himself up off the chair. 'What happened?'

Alex straightened his collar and forced a smile, shrugging off Sophie's arm. 'I'm fine. I'm fine,' he said, counting slowly, breath in, breath out. He had to control this.

'You don't look fine,' said Sophie, glancing at Victor's cell door.

'Really,' said Alex, walking back along the corridor, smiling at them both. 'It was the smell and confined space. I'd forgotten how claustrophobic it can be.'

Robert and Sophie glanced at each other. Robert shrugged, but Sophie narrowed her eyes.

Alex put his hands up and did his best to fake it, but he was aware that two trained psychologists might be able to see through to his near state of panic. He might not have fooled them, but there was no way he was going to admit to what just happened. As they left the segregation wing, Alex made his excuses and dived into the staff toilet. For several moments he leaned against the wall, focusing on his breathing. His hand scrabbled around his trouser pocket until he found what he was looking for. His pills. He swallowed the two Xanax dry.

CHAPTER SIXTEEN

The double doors slammed against their shutters. Alex lurched into the parking lot, shivering against the cold. He'd avoided Robert and Sophie, leaving them in the office. Against their protests he'd headed towards the nearest exit, making his excuses through the security checkpoints.

He found his car and sank into the leather seat, feeling the Xanax flood through him.

The radio came on and he silenced it, reducing the speakers to a low hiss. He heard his heart punching his chest, surging with adrenaline, gradually relaxing, minute by minute, as the drug took hold.

All of Alex's training and experience screamed that what had just happened was impossible. To say that Victor had the most powerful suggestive ability he'd ever observed would be an understatement. Victor had held Alex's mind in a clenched fist and left him entirely powerless.

Dr Alex Madison, a reputable clinical psychologist, veteran of several high-profile cases for the CPS, had been revealed as an amateur in front of his patient. Victor Lazar, a Romanian murder suspect, had rendered him impotent in less than five minutes.

The Xanax worked fast. Alex regained control with each breath. He counted to ten and began to think.

What had just happened? It was unlike anything he'd ever encountered before. Perhaps he'd had a panic attack, brought on by Victor's intimidating manner and the claustrophobic cell? But no, he knew that wasn't right. Victor had exerted some sort of control over him. Could it have been hypnotism? But Alex had been hypnotised before – it was essential to any training in the field. The experience of being in a hypnotic trance shouldn't feel unusual or unnatural. On the contrary, it felt like countless other moments in your life where you zone out – in the car, in the shower, or on a country walk, when the birds and the breeze conspire in perfect harmony to take your mind out of the present moment and into a dream. In every case it was possible to jump out of the dream, if you wanted to.

But not this time. Victor had thrown Alex down the rabbit hole, and it had affected him so acutely he could think of nothing else. Victor had plunged Alex so deep he was unable to stop it. He wouldn't even have described it as trance-like. He'd felt foggy, as though the air was thick, but he'd been conscious of what was happening. And that was the terrifying thing. One of the golden rules of hypnotism is that you cannot be hypnotised against your will: it only works if you agree to let it happen.

Victor's method didn't abide by those rules. This wasn't hypnotism, suggestion or any other standard form of manipulation.

This was something else.

And it meant Victor was guilty. The realisation crept over him with a shiver down his spine. The Southampton murders, the inmates and Dr Farrell: each one coerced into taking their own lives. Could it be possible?

Alex attempted to replay every minute, as far as he could remember. He and Victor had talked for, what, maybe three minutes before Alex lost control? He wished he'd recorded the conversation. He couldn't remember any of Victor's exact words, what it was that had made Alex so susceptible. Was he aware of the whole technique, or simply the moment of being put under? He was unsure and a twinge of anxiety gnawed at his stomach.

The orphanage had been the trigger. Alex had expected a reaction, but not this.

Victor had asked him, 'Did they send you?' What did he mean? Nobody had sent him. What game was Victor playing?

'Even if you don't know why you're here.' Victor Lazar's words echoed in his ears. The ramblings of a struggling mind? Possible, and probable, yet there was more to it. Something Alex was missing.

He took a few long breaths. His heart rate was settling. What would it mean for him if he told Robert what had happened? He'd be taken off the case, for sure. Something so serious would compromise his position, as well as cast doubt on his ability and professionalism. His credibility would be tarnished forever. He could ask Robert to keep it quiet but it wouldn't happen. Robert would be forced to report it and Victor Lazar would be sedated and isolated until they found another expert. If the press got hold of it, his private practice would be finished too. His career could be in tatters.

No. Despite the nagging feeling tugging at his gut, pushing through the Xanax and the adrenaline and the high blood pressure, Alex knew he must keep this to himself. He needed to counter, react and come back fighting. Victor had taken the upper hand, but Alex wasn't done.

He took a deep breath and started the car. He wanted to go back and get his bag and coat, but he couldn't, he had to go home. He needed to get his anxiety down and make a plan.

He must face Victor again. His only problem was he had no idea how to go about it.

CHAPTER SEVENTEEN

January 1990 and the revolution reached Comăneşti. The government soldiers came for Victor and the other children in the middle of the night. Too many to count, their footsteps thumped on the hard concrete as they marched through the entrance gate into the orphanage. Victor woke along with the rest, and they ventured out of their beds, into the corridors of the dark building, to see who had disturbed them.

The soldiers wore camouflage clothing with thick boots and black scarves covering their mouths. Each had a rifle either slung over his shoulder or in his hands. They all, without exception, wore large, thick headphones, covering their ears. Victor knew why.

In the corridor outside Victor's dormitory five of the soldiers stood guard, while others raced around ransacking the offices and the storerooms.

Victor was among the brave children who stared at the soldiers, rather than running. He watched in wonder as his dormitory supervisor was dragged out of her room, frisked, then kicked in the back of the legs, on to her knees. A doctor was brought to join her, and they were both blindfolded. The doctor's hands were tied with rope.

One of the soldiers kept his eyes on the children. He fingered his weapon, raising the barrel towards Victor. His hands were shaking and the barrel jumped. Another soldier shouted an order, resting his hand on the barrel until it was lowered. The giver of orders smiled and raised his hands. He wanted to talk to them.

The children were told to stay calm and welcome their comrade soldiers. The military, they were told, had decided to close the orphanage because it was a wicked place, created by a wicked government, and now the government had fallen, the children would be transferred to a better facility. A nice home with wooden floors and heating. Many of the children smiled at this news. Victor, as one of the oldest, kept his emotions in check. He was wary of the soldiers, even though they handcuffed the supervisors and led them away, their howls of protest echoing through the halls.

The children were given a matter of minutes to gather their belongings. The soldiers didn't know the children owned few, if any, possessions. Some had shoes; some had had items stolen over the years. All had identification papers, but those were in the office. Victor knew what he must retrieve from under his mattress and he raced back into his dormitory.

He found four more soldiers in the dorm, ripping the bunks apart and tossing the bedding on the floor. His own mattress was in a heap and he howled with anguish, jumping over and under the scattered sheets, searching for his writing.

The soldiers looked on in amusement and teased him, but Victor knew better than to confront them. He wasn't good enough to take them all on, and they had weapons. Even if he could tackle one of them, the others would step in and he'd be shot. After a last, frantic look around he left the room having failed to find his precious stories. Stepping out into the corridor, he spied a wad of papers shoved behind the door. He checked the soldiers weren't looking then picked the papers up, hoping it was his stories, swept there by mistake.

It wasn't. It was some sort of staffing list. The doctors and their assistants. Lists of people and information. Victor was disappointed, but shoved the bundle down his trousers. He might be able to reuse the paper for something.

He managed to hold back the tears as he was led out of the building, towards the courtyard.

Two army trucks reversed through the main gate and stopped. The trucks were dark green with canvas tops and huge tyres. The children were lined up behind one and the supervisors and doctors behind the other. The children watched in silence as the orphanage staff were herded into the truck by a handful of soldiers. Any who protested were beaten hard with the butt of a rifle. One doctor collapsed, unconscious, and he was lifted into the truck.

'Don't worry,' said one of the soldiers to the children. 'They are wicked. Don't concern yourselves.'

But Victor was concerned. *They must know about us,* Victor thought, *or at least suspect.* He watched the eyes of the soldiers and knew what he saw. They were jittery, scared, and had the look of those about to commit an awful act. He'd seen the look many times before, in his friends and in the doctors.

The smiling soldier appeared and asked the children to jump into the other truck. *We have a long drive,* he said, *but we'll give you food, drink and blankets, yes?* Victor stood back while the younger children jumped on, some trying to hug the soldiers as they passed. A couple of soldiers tentatively hugged back, but received orders to return to the building. A bonfire was being lit in the corner of the courtyard and all of the bedding and files were being thrown on to it.

Victor looked on in agony. His stories would be in there, burning. Never to be read.

He was the last to climb on, and he sat on the edge of the bench as the truck revved its foul-smelling engine and lurched off into the night.

Several children screamed. Some with excitement, some with fear. Victor agreed with the latter. He didn't believe for one second they were going anywhere nice. He knew this was the end.

CHAPTER EIGHTEEN

Nearly three decades later, the screams had faded, but they hadn't disappeared. As Victor woke in his cell, the morning sounds seeping through the walls, the memories stung and he could taste the cold air he'd gulped back that night, many years ago.

His path was blurred, and as daylight hid his visions of the past, his urges reared their vicious heads, taunting him into action.

His search was nearly complete. He'd kept the papers he'd found on the floor of his dormitory – the personnel records of the staff working at the orphanage. Years of surviving and hiding had finally led him here to England, and yet his sickness was increasing. Every time he used his ability now, to push, influence or to hurt, he fell violently ill. The headaches had always been there, since he was young, but now the nausea came in waves and his head throbbed, ready to explode. And his ability departed – suppressed, unusable, dormant – until he'd recovered.

His imprisonment was a distraction, if inevitable, after his actions at the university. The stampede in his head had turned into a catastrophic migraine-like pain, which throbbed until his vision narrowed at the edges. He was so weak he could barely move, let alone resist. They'd taken him and they'd placed him here. Days had passed. How many? It was still a blur.

The men who'd taunted him in his cell, they had to learn and they had to die. They tried to control him, reminding him of his time at

Comăneşti, when he'd had no choice but to submit to the will of those physically stronger than him. Not any more. He'd lost his temper with the first, and was disgusted at the second, who had bragged about what he'd done – the lives he had ruined. Victor listened intently before giving both their freedom from this prison. Perhaps not the freedom they would have chosen for themselves, but he forgave them as they died.

But they'd set him back even further. Those two acts had caused a violent sickness which lasted days. He'd vomited for three hours after the second prisoner had died.

It worried him, and so did the arrival of this new doctor, the rude psychologist who'd stuck his head in and attempted his pathetic assessment. He looked oddly familiar, but Victor couldn't place him. Perhaps he was imagining things, but something nagged at his gut. His gut was often right, and he sensed his hand was being forced. Victor was done with being forced, and he knew how to handle people who tried. If a new doctor appeared, he'd been told to come, which was bad news. It wouldn't be a coincidence, and for Victor it meant only one thing.

He sat up on the bed. It creaked. The cell stank. It had stunk from day one, but today he noticed it for the first time. It was poor, unhealthy, and it wouldn't help him concentrate. He had so much to do.

He was feeling better now, and he made up his mind as he sat on the toilet. The guards were pliable. He'd already tested several and found them susceptible with little effort. He would do what was necessary. The list was in his head. The ones he'd managed to find. Who they were and where they lived.

They didn't know he was coming. They should never have left him alive.

CHAPTER NINETEEN

The carpet had been a light blue, before the blood. Now it was magenta, a growing patch of bright colour surrounding the bodies. Mother and daughter, face down. His failure, his doing, but all he could see was the carpet.

The image screamed at him, repeating, insistent, until Alex woke. The screaming pulsed, vibrated, and transformed into a distant ringing. It stopped for a few seconds then began again. The ringing washed the dream from Alex's mind until it faded away, back into the box, ready for next time.

Alex shuffled on to his elbows. Jane had gone. He had a vague recollection of her saying she'd be out early in the morning.

His mobile rang again. He picked it up from the bedside table. It was Robert.

He stared at it for a few seconds then put it down. He reached into the drawer for a Xanax and crunched the small pill between his teeth. Better. Or at least he would be in a few minutes.

'Robert,' he said, answering at the next ring, 'I—'

'You need to come in,' said Robert.

'I will,' said Alex hearing the stressed tone of Robert's voice, wondering how much Robert had deduced about his meeting with Victor. Had Victor talked?

'You need to get here now,' said Robert, his voice sounding hoarse.

'I'll be in soon,' said Alex. 'Why the urgency?'

'It's Lazar,' said Robert. Alex could hear him breathing heavily on the other end. 'He's gone.'

Alex sat up straighter, controlling the rush of adrenaline. He thought carefully before responding.

'Gone where?'

'Gone. Escaped,' said Robert. 'He walked out the bloody front door. I think we need to talk, don't you?'

Two hours later, Alex sat at a tatty desk with Robert and Sophie, grasping a cup of the inevitable coffee. The news of Victor's escape was sinking in, and he was trying to suppress his anxiety and the feeling that he was to blame. He stared at a brown envelope that Robert had passed him on the way in. It held his new photo ID. Probably too late, he reflected. He doubted he'd be here much longer.

He couldn't have known Victor's intentions. Victor had warned him to stay away, but he didn't indicate any plans for escape. Alex tried to convince himself that admitting what had happened in Victor's cell wouldn't help matters. All it would do was confirm Victor's inexplicable ability, and it would seal Alex's fate, removing him from the case, which wouldn't help anyone.

The office was a flurry of activity, guards shouting at each other and into their phones as the damage was assessed.

Sophie stared at him. Their eyes met for a second, both of them pulling a brief, strained smile, before hers darted away. She was agitated, troubled, although she still managed to look stunning, her hair tied back in a ponytail, a few wisps escaping on to her face. Alex dragged his eyes from her towards Robert, judging himself for being so shallow. It wasn't just physical though. Sophie's behaviour stirred something in him, an interest he couldn't quite put his finger on. He tried to shut it out. Now was not the time.

'The guard duty received orders last night to move Victor out of segregation into the main block,' said Robert.

'Why?' said Alex.

'The governor is keeping her thoughts to herself.'

'But she ordered it?' Alex frowned, and bit the inside of his mouth.

'Apparently,' said Robert. His face was red, flustered. 'Victor asked to meet her. Nobody thought to check with me.'

'Why aren't the police here?' said Alex, raising his voice over the cacophony of guards, who were having their own significant argument about protocol violations at the other end of the office.

'They were,' said Robert. 'They left.' He glared at Alex. 'They'll be back. They want a full workup at our end, but they're following their own procedures now Victor's on the outside.' He eyed Alex with dissatisfaction and Alex swallowed hard, aware he was not proving very helpful so far.

'CCTV?' said Alex. 'How did he just walk out?'

Robert huffed, his shirt straining at the buttons. 'What happened between you two in his cell?'

Alex inhaled deeply, consciously slowing his heart rate. He fixed his eyes on Robert, not looking away. 'Nothing happened. He didn't offer much, and like I said, I found the cell too claustrophobic, so I left.'

Robert held his stare for a few seconds. 'He's been here less than three weeks. You turn up and he's gone within days.'

Alex blustered. 'What the hell are you getting at?'

'He didn't talk about getting out? To you? You didn't make any promises?'

'No,' said Alex. 'I would have mentioned it, obviously.'

'His emotional state? You left him calm?'

Alex shook his head. 'Nothing I was concerned about.'

Robert huffed, but his face dropped. He breathed out a couple of times and took his pulse, holding his wrist for fifteen seconds.

'My GP says I need to watch it,' he said. 'Look, I have a hundred calls to make. Sophie can show you what CCTV footage we do have, but there's nothing of note. The police already have copies. Victor didn't hurt anyone this time. He simply walked through the doors, which had all been unlocked, until he was in the visitation hall. He waited for five minutes or so before a guard let him out through the visitors' entrance. It was over an hour before his absence was noticed and we followed protocol from there.'

Alex raised his eyebrows, wanting Robert to say it. Not wanting to voice it himself. 'And the guards let him go?'

'None of the guards remember seeing him,' said Robert. 'Nothing at all. It's as if Victor was a ghost, or all the guards were blind. We've restricted the CCTV at the police's request, but even the guards seen talking to Victor can't remember doing so. Hence the shouting and general confusion in the office.'

Robert eased his frame out of the chair, grabbing his mobile phone and shuffling off. Alex had no doubt the man was up to his neck in it, and Alex needed to ensure he wasn't buried alongside him.

Sophie stood. Alex followed her. They were out of earshot before she spoke again.

'He didn't hurt anyone,' she said, in a low voice. They slowed and stopped outside the surveillance room.

Alex was close enough to smell Sophie's perfume. It was subtle, but strange, like everything else about her. He found himself taking a deep breath.

'He just sauntered out,' continued Sophie, knocking at the heavy door. She seemed angry.

Alex forced himself back to reality as the door swung open. Sophie asked the surveillance guard to display footage of the escape. They sat and watched from various angles as Victor strolled through D block,

C block, into A and visitation. He was stopped at one particular gate and spent forty-three seconds talking to the guard before the gate was unlocked for him.

'Do you know these guards?' said Alex.

'Most of them,' said Sophie, scanning back and forth through what little footage they had. 'That's Damian there – Simon's pal.'

'He's in a few of these shots. Does he remember anything?'

'I haven't seen him,' said Sophie. 'It's all gone a bit formal here. We seem to be getting the cold shoulder.'

'Was your friend Simon on duty?'

'No. He was off.'

Alex nodded, but didn't know what to say.

Sophie leaned back and huffed. 'What a mess,' she whispered.

'Sorry?'

'You were sceptical when you first arrived,' said Sophie. 'Not so much now.'

Alex nodded, but resisted the urge to tell her why. He didn't know Sophie well enough yet to trust her. She might run straight to Robert and his time here would be over. Besides, her behaviour still concerned him. There was something distinctly odd about the way Sophie reacted to Victor's escape. She seemed annoyed, but more than that. Alex couldn't put his finger on it.

'But if he was able to do this all along,' said Alex, pointing at the last grainy image of Victor's back, 'and let's say that he was, then why did he come here at all? Why didn't he just leave the scene of the crime in Southampton? He could have walked away and avoided spending any time in prison.'

Sophie shrugged, examining the nails on her right hand before chewing at one of them.

'I don't know,' she said. 'He was sick at first – after his arrest. They put it down to shock.'

She looked up again and Alex found himself staring. Her eyes were dark and full of sorrow – until she smiled. She held his gaze for a few seconds before glancing at his mouth. Alex felt his stomach flutter.

'Fancy a drink?' she said.

'I, er, sure,' he said. Professional or personal, he wasn't sure. He struggled to compose himself. 'Tonight?'

Sophie's eyes widened. 'I meant another coffee,' she said, 'back in the office.' She shook her head and smiled, before walking off.

Alex followed, his cheeks flushed with embarrassment, kicking himself for not reading the situation better. He'd shown he was as human as the next man. He hoped she wouldn't hold it against him.

It didn't seem to bother Sophie, although her demeanour changed again as they headed to the main security block. After a few forced pleasantries with Simon, Sophie withdrew, biting her nails. She touched Alex softly on the arm. She looked frustrated, but covered it with a smile. She turned away and they headed back to the office.

CHAPTER TWENTY

The army trucks drove for a little under two hours before it started snowing, huge white flakes swirling around the canvas top and into the children's faces, many of whom pulled blankets over their heads. Victor remained where he'd started, staring out at the road and the receding tyre marks. The trucks were forced to slow as the road became covered in slush and ice, and their headlights struggled to penetrate the blizzard conditions. There were shouts from the cabin as the truck slid and swerved around corners, but they didn't stop.

Victor was almost asleep when the truck suddenly jolted and veered off to the side. He reached out too late and his hand grabbed snowflakes as he tumbled from the back of the truck. He spun around twice in the air before landing in a thick blanket of snow which knocked the wind out of him. Otherwise uninjured, he gasped and spat, turning himself over to see what had happened.

Fifty feet away he could see the brake lights of the truck as it skidded to a halt, having come off the road in a tight corner by a huge suspension bridge. Victor had landed near the edge of the road, and he peered over to see a sheer cliff face. He was lucky he hadn't been thrown further.

Doors slammed and the soldiers shouted. A few children cried out – perhaps others had fallen – and there were a few minutes of activity around the truck. He stayed where he was, creeping behind a thick bush when two soldiers with flashlights walked back along the road, casting their torches to and fro, calling out for the missing. They didn't stray far from the truck, and after a few more shouted orders, the soldiers headed back and climbed into the cabin. The truck's engine roared to life once more and Victor watched it disappear across the bridge.

After a few cold moments, a voice permeated the air. It was crystal clear through the driving snow and wind.

'Thirteen.'

A child. Victor recognised him. He turned to see a boy staring through him, his right hand splayed, held out towards Victor. It was Luca, child nine, the boy who'd killed Laura. Victor knew him, and saw the threat immediately, closing his mind. He was swift and practised. There was no way in.

'Thirteen, you should have stayed on the truck.' The other boy assumed his superiority, which would work in Victor's favour. He would leave cracks that could be exploited, chiselled, jammed open and used to his advantage.

Victor smiled. He needed a little time, and a little distraction.

'They're all going to die, I think,' said Victor, indicating the empty road where the truck had left them. 'The soldiers were taking us somewhere. To kill us.'

The other boy frowned, perhaps annoyed at Victor's attempt.

'That's why you should have stayed on it,' said the boy. He shook his head and whispered, muttering to Victor, exploring his weaknesses.

But he was too late. Victor was closed and wouldn't be pliable to any form of attack. Victor whispered his own instructions and did what he knew he must do. He formed the words with care in his head, moulding the sequence together as he'd been taught. His eyes were fixed but his face was moving, morphing; expressions came and went as he teased his target and spoke his instructions. He adjusted his stance, bringing more power to bear. Feet forward, shoulders tilted, one dropped. He flicked one foot out, then back in. It added to the distraction, widened the cracks through which his words would enter. And enter they did.

He saw it working. He whispered more gentle suggestions before raising his voice. He was in. Luca had, for all intents and purposes, lost.

And he knew it.

'Walk towards the bridge, Nine,' said Victor, watching the flicker on the boy's face grow with fear and panic. The boy's eyes widened as he realised, too late, that it was over. In his haste to take Victor he'd neglected to protect himself. Victor had him and was sending him under.

He pleaded as he backed towards the bridge and the sheer drop. His mind was taken and his body wasn't his any more. He would have been in this situation many times during training. But he'd never lost.

'You don't need to do this, Thirteen. Please. We can survive together.'

Victor strengthened his grasp. He kept his grip tight and bound Luca to him. He shook his head and voiced his command. 'Turn towards the bridge, Nine. Walk to the edge.'

Luca jerked, his feet shuffling. He groaned: a small, childlike whimper. Victor saw the tears appear on the boy's cheeks.

'At the edge, jump outwards over the cliff. You will fall to the bottom. It is your fate.'

Luca's face drained and his eyes glazed over. He was wholly under now, and Victor could see the struggle leaving his mind. The boy walked, dragging his feet to where the bridge met the cliff. He shuffled around the protective barrier to the edge. His feet slipped on the snow and loose stones.

'Stop.' Victor forced another command and the boy halted, inches from the cliff edge, swaying in the wind.

'You killed Laura,' Victor said, then with strengthened resolve, 'it wasn't your fault. Or mine. But I can't forget.'

Victor edged towards the boy. Luca pleaded, but it was too late. Victor had made his decision. As he gave his final push, he wanted to close his eyes, to hide the pain, but he didn't. This was what life had become for him, and this is what he must deal with.

Luca wouldn't die because of Victor. He'd die because of what they'd done to them both – the doctors, the orderlies. The men and women in white coats who treated them like animals.

Luca's screams echoed across the mountains as his small body slipped and scraped down the side of the cliff. The wails cut off after a few seconds. Victor didn't lean over to watch. He took no pleasure in killing the boy, but he knew only one of them was walking away tonight. He'd fought, just as he'd fought so many times before.

Victor pulled his jumper around him and looked in all directions. The lights of a village shone in the near distance. He'd head there. He knew he couldn't stay long, but he also knew he had nowhere else to go. He'd persuade somebody to take him in, feed him and hide him. They'd give him all their money and clothing and arrange for him to go somewhere else, somewhere more permanent.

He trudged along the road, feet numb in the snow. Luca's screams stayed with him for hours.

He wondered if they'd ever go away.

CHAPTER
TWENTY-ONE

The next three hours were a blur. Alex was brought up to speed on the procedures involved after an escape. The police had Alex on a list of essential interviewees, but they deferred it while they spent their efforts outside the prison. The best chance of tracking Victor was in the first twenty-four hours. As soon as the trail went cold it would become much more difficult, involving a lengthy and costly investigation. They'd established a perimeter within the first precious hours and directed a search, but given the circumstances and the drip-feeding of only essential information out to the general force, their chances weren't good. The consensus was that the immediate window for recapture had passed.

Robert, Sophie and Alex were seen as the ones closest to the case, and therefore would make good scapegoats. No wonder Robert was so stressed. Alex had no intention of taking the blame for this, but he struggled to piece together in his own head what he would tell the police when his turn came.

'That was DCI Hartley,' said Sophie, placing her phone on the desk. 'We're not needed today. They'll speak to us tomorrow.'

'Have they found him?'

'No, although they're unlikely to keep us informed of their every move. There seems to be some issue with the press.'

'How so?'

'The DCI has withheld photos and information on advice from the CPS. Apparently the press don't like that.'

'Poor things,' said Alex, wondering whether press involvement was good or bad. He'd used them for his own benefit in private practice, but wasn't sure the same principles applied here. Should the general public be on the lookout for Victor? He shivered at the thought of innocent people coming into contact with such an unpredictable force.

Sophie shrugged but her jaw was clenched. She examined the nails on her left hand. She made to bite one but chewed her lip instead.

'I need to get out of here,' she said. 'I have some reading to catch up on.'

Alex was worried for her. 'Don't you think you should stay here?'

'Why?' Their eyes met. Sophie's were deep and unreadable. 'Victor doesn't know me,' she said. 'Why would he want to hurt me? I expect he's long gone.'

Alex hoped she was right, but he couldn't shift the anxiety in his gut. It lingered while he watched her gather her possessions. She paused at the door, hesitated for a few seconds before looking back.

'Or we could have that drink. If we're both at a loose end?'

Alex, knowing a bad idea when he saw one, agreed without a moment's hesitation. If nothing else, they could discuss their statements to the police and ensure that whatever blame was flying around didn't stick to them.

They settled for a bar a few minutes from the prison, arriving separately – Alex in his Porsche, Sophie in a thirteen-year-old VW Golf GTI. They met at the door of a shabby-looking pub that had been serving prison employees for many decades.

The pub was quiet. It wasn't shift change so the usual guards weren't there. Alex and Sophie slid into a cubicle near the back. He ordered the house Merlot; she ordered a vodka and Coke.

'So, what are you thinking?' said Sophie.

Alex swallowed the vinegary wine and grimaced. His limited time with Victor hadn't revealed much, but Alex knew motive, or at least part of it. A tentative link between the Southampton murders and Victor's roots in Romania had been established, which couldn't remain a secret. He'd have to fill the police in tomorrow. Alex had wanted to keep it to himself until his next interview with Victor, which obviously wouldn't happen now.

But it didn't explain what Victor planned next. Would there be more attacks, or had it finished? Was the act in Southampton the extent of Victor's rampage? If so, the escape was his disappearing act. That might be it – Victor would be gone forever.

It was a reasonable conclusion, but probably inaccurate. If Victor was a psychopath, the chain of events might make perfect sense to him. Although Victor had demonstrated rational conversation and anger in their first meeting, and no signs of being disinhibited, it could have been an act. Alex had seen it before in his hospital training. Psychopaths found it quite easy to act normal and fool the people around them, which is what made them so difficult to diagnose. The thought made him shudder, because it meant the Southampton murders were the first, but wouldn't be the last. There would be others, not necessarily planned, but equally violent. Victor's unique psychological talent made the prospect even more terrifying. Again Alex thought back to his own loss of control at Victor's hands. He shivered at the thought of such a man being loose in London.

'You have to speak out loud for me to hear you,' said Sophie. She leaned across the table and her perfume wafted over him again.

Alex took a deep breath, realising he was in the zone. A trance of sorts. The mental place where his excitement and train of thought hurtled along too fast to get off. He rarely experienced such a feeling these days with his private clients. Not since the case that had almost ruined him.

He told Sophie word for word his conversation with Dr Petri at the University of Bucharest.

'So I think Victor is seeking revenge,' he said, 'but I also think he has psychopathy. I think the Southampton murders were the first. There'll be others.'

Sophie's expression was unreadable. He saw her jaw clench and her shoulders stiffen.

'I can't explain his stay at Whitemoor.' Alex took another gulp of wine, puzzled at her reaction. 'But his ability won't be infallible.'

'Which could have led to his capture.' Sophie's expression didn't change. 'I'm more interested in what he does next.'

'That's up to the police. I'm not sure they're listening.' Alex was aware of the police's thoughts on him; his private practice reputation wasn't doing him any favours here. Despite the CPS asking for his involvement, he knew he'd need more than conjecture.

'You'll give them motive. They can't ignore that,' said Sophie.

'It's only motive if the Romanians back the story.' Alex thought back to Dr Petri. 'I'm not convinced they will. If Victor was abused in a Romanian orphanage they won't want it aired in a public murder enquiry.'

'And the police can't force them?'

'Doubt it.'

They stared at each other for a few moments. The door swung open and two young lads made their way to the bar. Eighties rock played softly in the background.

'So.' Alex sipped at his wine. 'How long is your placement at Whitemoor?'

Sophie stared down at her own drink. She seemed to tense up. Alex wondered what in her past caused her anxiety, if that's what it was. She was clearly capable and intelligent, but the prison triggered something in her.

'Not sure,' she said, downing the rest of her vodka and Coke. 'Right, I think we should get going.'

Alex took the hint as Sophie stood abruptly and grabbed her coat. He shouldn't have expected anything more – they barely knew each other, after all. He found himself concerned though, and couldn't help his natural tendency to probe, even if his motives were straying away from strictly professional ones.

They left, agreeing to be as open as possible with the police the next day, although Alex retained his own little secret about his meeting with Victor and what had happened.

He walked Sophie to her car. She opened the door and paused. Alex thought he could detect the sweet smell of marijuana wafting from the interior, which was a mess, filled with fast-food wrappers. A pair of tatty men's trainers and jeans adorned the back seat. A rucksack with a sleeping bag strapped to it sat in the footwell. Sophie caught his eye and looked embarrassed.

'It needs a clean,' she said. 'My friends borrow it a lot.'

'My car's the same,' lied Alex, tapping the roof, wondering who her friends were, and if there was a special someone.

They both stood, silent and awkward, as though at the end of a first date, neither party quite sure what they were expected to do. Alex stepped forwards until their faces were less than a foot apart. Sophie met his gaze and the nerves hit him. He opened his mouth and closed it again. Sophie smiled then looked away. Alex's gaze fell towards the ground. Sophie's boots were badly scuffed. She shuffled her feet.

'It's nice to have you here, Alex,' she said. 'I'm glad it was you.'

Alex looked up. 'Me?'

'You're good at this,' she said. 'I like your style.'

Alex was breathless. He opened his mouth to speak but Sophie backed away.

'See you tomorrow?' she said.

'Sure,' he whispered.

Sophie climbed into her car and drove off without another word. Alex could see her staring at him in the rear-view mirror.

She was getting to him. Part of him felt like a teenager, falling for a woman who remained utterly mysterious, giving him just enough to keep him interested. Another part chided him for being so unprofessional. Whatever the case, they were stuck with each other, at least until they found Victor.

CHAPTER TWENTY-TWO

The wind howled down from the mountains. Victor didn't notice the shadows following him in the snow. After leaving the cliff face, a girl and boy followed him, keeping their distance, keeping their voices to whispers and their footsteps clean and light. They stopped when Victor stopped, and continued only when Victor started walking again.

They followed him to the village and paused. The shadows had seen what Victor had done to Luca, and they feared for their own safety, for neither of them was as strong as Victor. Talented, yes, but not as practised. They knew they'd need to find their own way.

One of them, the eldest, a girl named Natalia, watched the boy they knew as Thirteen walking towards an old farmhouse. She shook the hardened snow off her nightgown, rubbing her shoulder. It ached where she'd fallen from the truck, although her companion seemed unharmed. She resisted the urge to call out, to challenge Thirteen and tell him who she was. She'd bitten her tongue at the sight of Luca tumbling off the precipice. Now, she stared at Thirteen's back with fear, subconsciously whispering her chant, preparing her words in natural defence.

She wanted an ally, but she knew better. Her own ability was weaker. She could persuade and coerce, but she never excelled. She was never a master, and her tutors knew it. The boy she was with, well, they called him Freak for a reason. His ability had never developed in the proper way, the desired way. He couldn't control people, not in the traditional sense, but neither could he be controlled. Freak caused white noise, interfering with other's abilities but providing no useful talent of his own. Attempts by the children to plant suggestions in Freak's head sometimes ended in bizarre and grotesque ways, damaging their minds beyond repair. Like hitting a mental tornado, Freak was shunned and misunderstood. He was an outcast, useless and forbidden from practising. He wouldn't have been long for this world, had they remained at the orphanage. He leaned against her now, and touched her hand.

'We should go,' he whispered, wincing. Freak had never been pitched against Thirteen, but Natalia knew the prospect scared him.

She nodded. One day, maybe, she would introduce herself to Thirteen, but not now. This day she had to survive, and as she looked at the young boy next to her, she shivered with anticipation.

She took the boy's hand, turned her back on Thirteen and left the village behind her. She wondered if she'd ever see him again.

Part of her hoped not.

CHAPTER TWENTY-THREE

Twenty-four hours since Victor's escape. Alex hovered between his kitchen and home office. He tried to call Sophie but got her voicemail. His text messages went unanswered. He called Robert, who said Sophie was probably doing one of her usual 'disappearing acts', which unnerved Alex a little. It suggested that Sophie was even more complicated than he'd first thought. He'd keep trying.

His attraction to Sophie troubled him. He found it hard to bury, and if he was honest, he didn't entirely want to. Her behaviour was professional, and her anxiety in certain situations showed she was human. There was definitely something else though. She often looked puzzled, inwardly battling. Her eyes pleaded for help, but darted away whenever he approached. She distracted him with flirtation, laughing it off.

If he were sensible he'd leave her be, but her face was increasingly present when he closed his eyes. Alex knew this was a hopelessly inappropriate time and situation to be attracted to someone, but what could he do, other than ask for her to be removed from the office? He dismissed the idea immediately.

'Penny for your thoughts?' said Jane, striding into the kitchen while texting. Her heels made Alex wince as they stamped across his hardwood flooring. She glanced at him and wiggled her eyebrows. He returned a weak grin.

Last night he'd fallen asleep thinking of Sophie. The dreams had come fast and vivid, the fantasy strange yet fascinating. They'd embraced but Sophie had resisted, looking at Alex with pain and sorrow in her eyes. He felt himself sinking into them, unable to climb out of the darkness.

Jane had woken him in the early hours and told him he was snoring. He'd ignored her and drifted back into a cold and dreamless sleep.

'I'm tired,' he said. 'Work is . . . busy.'

'Oh, OK,' said Jane, not taking her eyes off her phone as it buzzed with messages.

'I heard something at the agency yesterday,' she said. 'A murderer on the loose in London.' She looked up from her phone, nodding, eyes wide. 'What do you think of that?' She stared at Alex for a few seconds before her phone vibrated again. Alex watched her eyes shine as her attention was diverted. 'Oops, sorry,' she said. 'It's Diane.'

Alex moved over to the fridge, muttering under his breath, deciding he needed more coffee, wondering what the press were running with today. He hadn't checked the news since yesterday.

'I'm sorry?' said Jane. She stopped texting.

'I haven't seen the news,' said Alex.

Jane stopped and looked aghast. 'Wait a minute. I think he escaped from the prison you're working at. Do you know him?'

Alex shook his head and opened the fridge door, shielding himself from Jane so she couldn't see his face. A moment's silence passed as he pretended to rummage for something to eat.

'Well, why would you?' said Jane, laughing. 'Murderers need more than CBT.' She giggled in a way Alex had once found attractive. Why did he now find it irritating? He let her rant on, zoning out as she talked about her friends. One had a new job in the City, banking or something. The other did nothing except drink.

'She could do with talking to somebody,' said Jane.

Alex paused. 'What?'

'Helen,' said Jane. 'She works fourteen-hour days for Goldman Sachs and has panic attacks every Sunday morning in the shower.'

Alex zoned back in. 'She should.' He thought about it some more. This was something he could help with – should help with. 'Talk to someone, I mean. I'll give you a number to pass on.'

'Thanks,' said Jane, giving him an appreciative smile.

'Although leaving her job would probably solve the problem.' A great bit of advice, Alex thought, coming from a man struggling to manage his own.

Jane nodded, turning back to her phone. She laughed, reciting one of her messages.

Alex busied himself grinding more coffee than he needed. As he switched the coffee machine on he was vaguely aware she'd stopped talking again.

'Is that OK then?' said Jane.

'Sorry, what?'

'What I just said.'

'I didn't hear you,' said Alex.

Jane huffed. 'On the twenty-first. Staying with Peter and Cara for the week at their cottage in Petersfield. OK?'

Alex faded back in and looked at the fridge door. There was a cute kitten calendar hanging on a magnet. The twenty-first. Two weeks' time.

'Oh,' he said. 'No, I can't. I've got Katie coming to stay. I forgot to tell you. Sorry.'

Jane's face dropped. 'Coming to stay here?'

Alex bristled. 'Coming to stay with me, her father, in my house. Yes.'

Jane's expression didn't change. 'And when were you going to run this by me?'

Alex clenched his jaw. 'I didn't think that necessary. She's my daughter, Jane. She is part of me. I thought you understood that?'

He ignored the little voice in his head that said Jane had a point. He'd forgotten to keep her in the loop. It was disrespectful and he knew it, but he still struggled with her reaction. She'd led a privileged upbringing – Daddy's little girl, surrounded by money. Her looks attracted both male and female admirers and she rarely came second to anything. Perhaps she couldn't grasp the concept of anyone else being more important than her. In a way he didn't blame her, but it was an unattractive trait. But it was his weakness. He was to blame. Why not end it?

Jane put her palms down on the worktop.

'I'm not asking you to give up your daughter,' she said. 'But you don't include me in any of your plans. You just turn around and inform me—'

'I don't need your permission to spend time with my own child!'

'That's not what I said and you know it.'

'Then what's with the reaction?'

'The reaction?' said Jane, pouting. 'Don't start analysing me now, Doctor. My reaction is normal. You and your ex-family are the weird ones.' She paused, probably realising she'd gone too far. Insulting his family was a no-go area. She knew that.

He turned away from her as she approached him.

'I didn't mean—'

'I don't care if you meant it,' he said.

She huffed again and managed to force a couple of tears. She sniffed loudly to make her point. 'Put yourself in my shoes,' she said, 'just for a second. You spend all your time working or thinking about working. I don't know what goes on in that head of yours. Days can go by without us even talking. Of course Katie is lovely. I didn't mean . . .'

Alex didn't care whether she meant it or not. He didn't have the time or inclination to continue this conversation at the moment. He wanted time to think about Victor Lazar and whether he could rescue his career from the apparent precipice it teetered on.

'Go and see your friends, OK?' he said. 'We'll talk later.'

With another small sniff, Jane turned and left, the door slamming behind her. Her Maserati roared into life, spitting gravel as she drove off.

CHAPTER TWENTY-FOUR

There were three police cars in the prison parking lot when Alex arrived, one of them unmarked, but obvious by the police jacket slung over the passenger seat. All were empty, the officers presumably inside.

He entered the office to see a group of uniformed police occupying the empty desks on the far side. They were with Simon – the guard he'd met a few days earlier. Robert was over to the left, talking to a tall, thin woman in a grey trouser suit and black coat. She had mousy hair tied back tightly from her face and her arms were crossed. She looked distinctly unimpressed with whatever Robert was telling her.

Alex found Sophie hunched over her desk, reading her way through a stack of typed papers. She shuffled and pushed them away as he approached.

'I take it the police want to talk to us today,' he said, glancing at Sophie's small frame. Her face was paler today and her hair was tucked casually behind her ears.

'I think so,' said Sophie. She was fidgeting, fingernails scraping against palms.

'What are you reading?' he said. 'Anything good?'

Sophie's face reddened. 'Just a case study.'

Alex moved closer and peered over. As he did so, Sophie grabbed the papers.

'One of yours, OK?' she said. 'It's one of your published papers from 2007 – *Controversies and Issues in Forensic Psychology.* I wanted to . . . you know . . . explore a little more about your subject.'

Alex was flattered, his own face flushing. *Finding out about the subject or about me?* he wondered.

'Well, I don't know how useful that paper is,' he said with genuine modesty – a rare thing for him to offer. 'I think my most recent work has been with patients who would never give me permission to publish as a case study.'

'No, of course,' said Sophie. 'All those celebs. There'd be scandal.' She graced him with one of her beautiful smiles.

The moment was broken with a noise from further along the corridor. Sophie's eyes darted away as more uniformed prison officers and police entered.

Robert glanced over and gestured for Alex to join him. 'Detective,' said Robert, as Alex approached, 'this is Dr Alex Madison.'

The detective extended her hand and gave a thin smile. 'DCI Hartley,' she said.

'Pleasure,' said Alex, trying to portray calm and control.

Hartley released Alex's hand and suggested they find somewhere to talk.

'I thought you'd want to talk to me yesterday,' said Alex.

'Sorry,' said Hartley, though not looking it. 'Something came up. I had a few minutes with Dr Bradley. He brought me up to speed.'

Hartley wove her way between the partitions towards a group of empty desks. She pulled out a chair, indicating Alex and Robert should do the same. Alex noted the impatience in the detective's body language. He wondered what exactly Robert had brought her up to speed on.

Hartley pulled out her notepad and flicked through a couple of pages, before closing it again and resting it on the desk.

'So we're clear, I'm the SRO on Victor Lazar's escape. I'm not leading the Southampton murder case.'

'OK.' Alex nodded, glancing at Robert. SRO stood for senior responsible officer, which meant Hartley had the freedom to do whatever she wanted on this case. She'd also made it clear what she wasn't interested in.

'You've spoken to Victor Lazar,' said Hartley. A statement, not a question. Alex glanced at Robert.

'That's correct,' said Alex, conscious he was being assessed. 'I've spoken to him on three occasions. Once through the door, twice in his cell. I was in the preliminary stages of my assessment.'

'Do you know Damian Reed?' continued Hartley. Police officers at Hartley's level undertook a little forensic psychology training themselves. Hartley was studying Alex's body language as he responded. What did she want?

'No,' said Alex.

'What about Simon Thomson?'

'The guard? I met him this week. In the corridor. He showed me the segregation wing.'

'So Mr Thomson took you to see Victor Lazar this week?'

'No,' said Alex. 'He showed me the seg wing. Look, can we start from the beginning? I only arrived this week, as requested by the CPS. There are some things you should know.'

He raised his eyebrows at Robert, hoping he would jump in.

'That's correct,' said Robert, sounding anxious.

DCI Hartley huffed and scratched the back of her neck. 'What?' she said, looking distracted.

'Dr Bradley's told you about Victor Lazar?' said Alex. He could tell the inspector was agitated about something. 'I contacted one of your colleagues about him.'

'Yes, I know,' said Hartley. 'DCI Laird at Hampshire. He told me.'

'And you don't think it's worth doing what I asked? Re-interviewing those people from his case, given the circumstances?'

'No, I don't, because it's got nothing to do with his escape. We don't know how Victor Lazar managed to walk out of here, but we'll find out. It may be simpler than you think.'

'Meaning?'

'Damian Reed.'

Robert frowned, wiping sweat from his forehead. He loosened his collar.

'And he is?' said Alex.

'Damian Reed is a guard employed by this prison,' said Hartley. 'He has been here for the last seven years. An unexceptional employee, he's been behaving erratically for the last week or so, according to Simon Thomson, his friend and line manager. He hasn't been heard from since Victor Lazar escaped.'

'OK. So?' said Alex. Hartley appeared to be missing the point.

'Damian was assigned to both D Wing and segregation. He spoke to Victor every day since his arrival. And now he's gone. We dispatched a squad car yesterday to Damian Reed's house. It was empty. I managed to persuade the magistrate to give us a warrant and we conducted a room-by-room search. Mr Reed wasn't on his sick bed. He wasn't there at all. All his stuff – clothes and food – remains. But he's gone. The officers searched for any clues as to his whereabouts before waking the neighbours. Nobody had seen Damian, but apparently he was a quiet, withdrawn person, so that wasn't out of the ordinary.'

Hartley scratched her chin, fixing a questioning stare at Alex. Alex felt uncomfortable, a deep worry settling again in his gut.

'In short, Dr Madison, we're connecting Mr Reed with this escape. He left the prison at the same time as Victor and his whereabouts are unknown. He's divorced, lives alone and his friends are mostly prison employees – some we've questioned and some are being traced. Nobody knows where he is.'

Alex glanced at Robert. 'You think Damian is an accomplice?' he said. 'But you've seen the CCTV footage of Victor from within the prison?'

'I've seen it.'

'And Robert has discussed Victor's time here with you? In detail?'

'He has.'

'And you accept the tentative diagnosis that Victor is a probable psychopath with motive and means? Yet the governor moved him into the general wing.'

Alex narrowed his eyes. He considered his own scepticism of Victor's ability only a few days before and accepted her scepticism was warranted. Neither he nor Robert had been able to offer any reasonable explanation based upon established psychological theories. His assessment had barely started and there seemed little chance of progress now. But still, he hated it when the police played catch-up. They were wasting time.

'With all due respect, it doesn't explain anything,' said Hartley. 'Suicides aren't uncommon in places like this. It's not my place to judge the governor's running of her prison.' She lifted her head for effect, looking with mild disgust at her surroundings.

'But these weren't normal suicides, Detective. And our theories are quite rational. Victor wields an unnatural ability to influence people. It could explain how he managed to walk right out of this prison. Just look at his history, for Christ's sake.'

'Or, he had an accomplice who arranged it.'

'Perhaps. Or perhaps the accomplice was unwilling. The CCTV from the escape—'

'Mr Reed was out of camera shot for most of it,' said Hartley. 'He was on shift, then he disappeared. It doesn't take much to connect his disappearance with Victor.'

'No. This was Victor's doing, Detective,' said Alex, neglecting to mention that what Victor could do had never been observed in the history of psychological research. 'His ability is rare, but not supernatural.'

'So you say,' said Hartley. She raised her eyebrows. 'So what is it?'

Alex paused. 'I don't know,' he conceded, 'but what I've seen so far suggests Victor wields a manipulative ability to render people under his control within a matter of seconds using high suggestibility. Whatever it is, it would explain the horrific events surrounding Victor's time here, including his escape.'

Hartley pulled a face. 'Hypnosis?'

Alex shook his head. 'Not like I've ever seen. The mechanism and action here are unique. The subject's response is different. Psychologically, this is far more complex.'

'OK.' Hartley frowned, her brow creased in thought. She examined Alex. 'A manipulator. Suppose I believe you. The victim is still conscious?'

'I . . .' Alex considered his own experience in Victor's cell. 'Yes. Conscious and resisting – or trying to. That's what sets it apart. This is new.'

'New?'

'Undocumented.'

'Then I suggest—'

'Research is what I'm doing,' said Alex. 'I need more time and a fuller background on the man. I can't yet be certain that this is what he does to his alleged victims. I can't say whether this Damian Reed could have been susceptible.'

'No?' said Hartley, taking a styrofoam coffee cup off the table. She took a sip and screwed up her face. Producing a pack of sweetener from her pocket, she popped three tablets in before swirling the drink around with her index finger.

'We're talking about psychological control,' said Alex. 'Deep trance. This is uncharted territory.'

Alex let that hang. He spoke in a confident tone but was aware his own uncertainties were breaking through. He'd been as truthful as he could – he didn't understand the mechanism of Victor's ability, and he hadn't been able to break his own trance at Victor's hands. Admitting that was not the right thing to do, but Hartley needed to know she was dealing with an extraordinary individual, even if Alex couldn't prove it.

Hartley leaned back in her chair. She raised her hands in a conciliatory fashion. 'OK. Look, I didn't mean to be quite so blunt. But what you're describing is fanciful. You can appreciate why I can't work with it.' Hartley paused and cleared her throat, flicking through her notepad. 'As I understand it, the CPS is still struggling with motive for the Southampton case. That isn't the way you see it?'

'No,' said Alex, aware of Robert's surprised look.

Alex explained his conversation with the prosecutor and subsequent call to Dr Petri. He gave the name of Professor Dumitru, spelling it out as Hartley took notes. Robert remained quiet as Hartley scribbled in her pad. She paused.

'You've had this information for over twenty-four hours?'

'Yes,' said Alex. 'I had planned to use it over the course of my sessions with Victor.'

Hartley narrowed her eyes as she scribbled further. 'You didn't think motive was rather urgent to my colleagues in Southampton?'

'I did, I just . . .' Alex struggled to formulate an excuse for having kept it to himself. 'I didn't think.'

Hartley raised her eyebrows and put her pen on top of the pad, lining it up with the edge. She tapped it a few times with her finger. 'Anything else?'

Alex paused. He saw the frustration in Hartley's face. She was no doubt under pressure and his omission wouldn't have helped things.

'Be careful, Detective,' he said. 'I'm sorry I can't give you more, but Victor Lazar is a very dangerous man. Approach with caution and with numbers. You don't want to find yourself alone with this man.'

Hartley gave him the long stare before standing and grabbing her notebook in one swift movement. 'OK. Thank you, Doctor. Please don't stray too far. I might want to talk to you both again. Thank you for your time.'

Alex breathed a sigh of relief as Hartley and Robert left, but worried they were no closer to understanding Victor or what he'd do next. If Victor was out there seeking revenge, the police were a long way from catching him, and Alex was powerless to do anything about it.

He decided to head home, checking his phone on the way out. Another missed call from Jane and one from Grace.

Grace's name triggered the usual wave of guilt, and he promised himself he'd call her later. Jane was another matter. He couldn't think of Jane without Sophie popping into his head. Sophie was attractive in all the right places, body and mind. She was new and interesting in a way Jane should be but wasn't. Sophie had a flawed beauty . . . He thought back to what Victor had said to him in the cell and shivered. Was he that obvious?

How did Victor know that? Alex was a relationship car crash, he knew that much. Grace knew it when they were together. If Jane didn't know it yet, she would soon. Was Sophie his next bit of fancy? Is that all Alex could do? Lure the next one with his professional arrogance, then toss them aside and move on? No wonder Grace was done with him. She was far too bright to put up with such a man. Why did he have to be that person? His fingers reached for his pills and he swallowed one dry, cursing the necessity.

Alex forced his thoughts back to Victor. He was worried, and there was a sense of urgency, a nagging doubt he couldn't quite put his finger on. He thought back to the last few days. He could picture Robert and Sophie, both at their desks. He remembered Robert's tired, haggard face, his creased shirt and scuffed shoes. He saw Sophie's fidgeting, the way she sometimes shook her head as if warding off unwelcome thoughts. He remembered two of the guards on the way to the office. One was picking dirt off his trouser leg. The other was rubbing his eyes.

A prison nurse had sat across from them, writing her notes. She'd reached down to rub her calf, which had a large bruise on it. Her shoes were scuffed too. Another nurse walked over and said something, then walked away, laughing. She had a limp.

He noticed everybody, their quirks and appearances. Each gave away something about themselves, but nothing significant. Not the things Alex was looking for.

CHAPTER TWENTY-FIVE

The first few months of freedom were terrifying for Victor. With the orphanage behind him, he struggled through the smaller local villages before finding his way to the bustling city of Bacău where he could hide in plain sight, staying in hostels and houses, pushing the owners into giving him board, reminding them every night not to tell anyone who he was or where he'd come from.

He damaged some people and helped others, but felt little emotion either way. Like the harsh winter, he was cold and unforgiving to the people he met.

Victor found his talent was growing and he had no difficulty in getting what he wanted, but he was empty of purpose. He wandered aimlessly during the days, eating when he could and watching the world roll by. The revolution had caused chaos, but that was a good thing as it turned out. Victor lost himself in the reshaping. The whole country, not just Victor, was haunted by the past.

The months turned into years. Every morning Victor expected the soldiers to arrive. To point him out and tell everyone what he was. They'd capture him, put him in the back of the truck – the one with the huge tyres and green top – and drive him away.

He woke in sweat every night, seeing Laura's face staring up at him from the courtyard. He saw every child who had died, and they all stared at him. They hated him for not saving them. 'How could I?' he asked them. 'I am one of you, no different.' His dreams ended with the stomping of feet, boots thumping over stone and staircases, soldiers coming to take them into the mountains. Everyone knew what happened in the mountains.

They would capture him and take him back. The punishments would be severe. The other children would watch while he was beaten and drugged. They would watch while he was made to perform the experiments. The soldiers would look on and they would laugh at his inability to stop it.

But the soldiers never came and Victor realised he was truly on his own. Not even his enemies wanted him. Still he existed in a state of perpetual fear, but he began to turn his mind to the future, and wondered how he could begin to heal the chasm in his soul. The soul they'd tortured and maimed through his years at Comănești.

He also noticed worrying symptoms. They called it 'the fever' back at the orphanage. Victor had suffered on occasion in his younger years, but lately he'd been getting more frequent attacks. After every trance he would feel a thumping at the back of his head, throbbing, a pumping of blood that caused nausea and dizziness. If he pushed it too much he'd vomit and the shakes would start. He would go to bed for a few hours and recover, but it worried him. He couldn't survive without his talent, and therefore he couldn't survive without getting sick.

Romania changed. The revolution of '89 was just the start. Politicians and their laws threw opportunity to even the smallest of villages. Freedom of movement was on everyone's tongues. A relaxation in the rules saw many people leave the country, seeking a better life elsewhere.

Victor stayed put. He didn't know what life he was seeking so there was no point leaving. This was all he knew. Even when he turned sixteen, he maintained the same routine, the same hiding, the same ruthless manipulation of people's minds, in order to keep himself safe.

He considered getting an education. The city library was open to anyone, and he didn't need to force them into letting him stay. He turned up every morning at 10 a.m. At first he was wary of the old lady who nodded to him from behind her desk. He worried she was watching him, reporting him, getting the soldiers ready to take him away. But of course she wasn't, and he began nodding back, the brief acknowledgement that two unconnected humans can share in a familiar setting. An acknowledgement that said he was welcome here, even though they were strangers.

The library was fascinating to Victor. The towers of shelves and rows of books were unlike anything he'd seen before, and he read with hunger, not seeking anything in particular, although he found himself enjoying geography and travel. He gazed at maps and daydreamed of one day leaving Romania. But to do what?

He didn't find the answer to that in the library.

Every morning, Victor went to the library – apart from on Sundays, when he went to church. There he found the welcome even friendlier, although he shied away from the conversations the priest kept trying to start. The priest left him alone, but made an offer: Victor could tell him anything.

Victor knew this to be false. There was nothing about his life Victor could share, so he remained silent and walked away, sitting in the back pew, listening to the congregation make their promises, confess their sins and sing to their god.

He observed the regulars, and exchanged polite nods with some of them. A girl roughly his age attended the same services. She was accompanied by a younger boy. No parents. She caught his eye several times but always looked away. She seemed scared, but Victor paid it no thought. Many people came to church precisely because they were scared. He was one of them. He ignored the girl and her boyfriend. They were not his concern.

The church was modest but well maintained. The stained-glass windows around the outside told a story, and Victor played it to himself over and over. He broke his silence with the priest, asking the man to explain it.

'Why did he let them do this?' he said, one morning to the priest. He knew what he wanted to hear. What the priest said surprised him.

'He needed to,' said the priest. 'Saving himself wasn't as important as saving everyone else.'

Victor frowned. 'But they got away with it.'

'At the time,' said the priest, 'but ultimately not.'

'There was no revenge,' said Victor.

'No.'

'Then they got away with it.'

The priest explained again what he believed, and the core tenets of his faith. Victor listened to the priest justify why Jesus let his tormentors do what they did. If he had the power to stop it, why didn't he? Victor loved stories, but this one didn't make sense, and it angered him.

The priest continued. 'Forgiveness, child, is one of his messages. Do you understand?' He said it in a way that suggested it should be obvious – that by questioning it, Victor was naive, or worse, stupid.

Victor told him what he thought. He was disgusted by the story and the message it tried to send. The priest was stunned and tried to object. He gave Victor a lecture on forgiveness, repeating that it was the only way to salvation.

Victor was quick to anger. To suggest he should forgive his captors, his tormentors and torturers was tantamount to saying that what they did was OK, that they shouldn't be punished. His voice wavered and he shouted. He vented his anger and cursed the priest for being so weak, then sent him away with a mind full of instruction: to stop what he did and demolish the house in which he stood.

The priest backed away, his mind damaged, for Victor was careless in his anger. He'd taken control of the man in a rage and his instructions were confused and contradictory. Victor left the church, the priest kneeling on the stone floor, sobbing, pleading with Victor not to make him do the things he asked.

Victor spat his forgiveness at the priest and never went back to the church. He was thankful though. It had given him purpose, although perhaps not the purpose the priest would have liked.

A few weeks later Victor pulled out his last souvenir of the orphanage. The sheets were crumpled and yellow, torn at the edges, but the ink was still legible. A list of his captors and tormentors. Victor smiled for the first time since he'd walked away from the truck as a child, the snow blasting in his face.

Tomorrow he'd go back to the library. He had research to do.

The priest was right.

Victor did have people to forgive.

CHAPTER
TWENTY-SIX

Victor was free, yet he dreamed of captivity and his youth. He dreamed of the discovery, all those years ago, of his own particular brand of forgiveness. Forgiveness of those who had sinned against him, forgiveness of everyone who stood in his way.

He'd begun his story, but already hurdles were being raised to trip him. He cursed the God he didn't believe in, and the dead priest who had guided his hand. He cursed those in the prison who forced memories of his childhood captivity.

As he stared at the man in front of him, the prison guard he'd compelled to assist in his escape, he cursed again. The man was coming out of his trance naturally. Victor didn't have the energy to keep him deep under – his head was thumping – and there was no need. The man was bound and gagged and wasn't going anywhere fast. The guard had been useful, to a point.

Victor had followed the guard out of the prison exit then forced him to drive for several miles until they entered the sprawling suburbs. He picked a street at random, then a house. A bungalow, belonging to an old lady who answered the door with a scowl on her face.

'I don't buy anything at the door,' she said. 'Even religion.'

She wouldn't buy anything ever again, not after Victor forced her into the kitchen with his words, tied and gagged her and told her to lie on the floor. She choked on the rag he forced to the back of her mouth and stopped breathing a few minutes later.

Victor stared at the small body, hating himself for it, but knowing it was necessary. He couldn't let the guilt in. He had a job to do and she was an unfortunate consequence. There would be more. She'd start to smell soon, and then the flies would come, black swarms of them to finish her off. Not for a couple of days though. He still had some time.

The guard's car had been discarded several miles away. Victor had driven it himself and trudged back, his head worsening by the minute and his gut aching with acid. He paused to vomit and the feeling passed. His worry was put to one side as he focused on the task at hand.

Victor sifted through the guard's belongings. He found a mobile phone with an HMP logo stamped on the back. He pulled out the SIM card and stamped on the phone until it was dead. He found another phone with no official logos on it tucked into the man's pocket. It was unlocked so Victor reset and pocketed it.

Penknife, baton and belt were the only other useful items. He put them to one side and stared at the pathetic body of the man whose job it was to keep him caged like an animal, denied his liberty, and for what? They'd never understand, people like this. They pretended they did – this guard had even smiled and talked to him, before all communication had been banned.

The guard was coming round and his eyes opened, blinking and darting. He tried to understand his situation, lying on the floor, unable to move. His body twitched and he yanked his arms, struggling harder as panic took him.

Victor leaned forwards and sniffed. Detergent, or starch. What was it the orderlies used on the clothes after they boiled them? The smell clouded his thoughts and took him back. The dormitory, the laundry room, the weekly change of bleached fabric, thrown at them from the doorway. It sometimes burned the young children's skin. Unrinsed by mistake, or perhaps on purpose. It was another tool they used, those men and women of the orphanage, when the fear wasn't enough. Was it never enough?

Victor leaned back and watched. He didn't have the energy to force this one under again, not if he wanted to get moving with his other plans. Instead he hoped for a more traditional method. He searched in the kitchen, raking through the cupboards, throwing tins and packets of food on to the floor. The plates followed but the cupboards were soon empty. Upstairs, he found what he wanted. In the cabinet on the wall with the mirror and sliding doors were four packets of propranolol. The old lady had a heart condition. Not any more. He took them downstairs, retrieved a bowl from the floor, and emptied them into it.

On the garish green rug, in front of an ageing gas fire, Victor forced one hundred pills into the guard's mouth, making him swallow them in retches and gulps. He poured water into the guard's mouth periodically, ensuring the medication found its way into his stomach, then his bloodstream.

It didn't take long. While Victor's headache began to subside, the guard's heart began to fail. Erratic at first and with visible symptoms, the most obvious being his irregular breathing. He gasped and wheezed for twenty minutes before heavy convulsions racked his body. Victor watched on in fascination while the guard struggled, writhing on the floor. A wallet fell from a trouser pocket and Victor picked it up. He flicked through the contents – cash cards and loose change – wondering why the guard wanted life so badly. A photo poked out at him: a photograph of a young girl and a woman. Victor plucked it out, turning it in his fingers. The woman and child were smiling, innocence captured in a single moment. When the guard saw the photo his struggle increased. He kicked and moaned. Victor stared through the child in the photo before crumpling the thin card in his fist and throwing it into the gas fire.

The guard's eyes pleaded.

'*Te iert.*' Victor whispered forgiveness as he blocked out the sobs and gasps. The guard should know it wouldn't help. It never helped. Begging got you more punishment and more chores. It meant you were moved up the list, and if you were physically able, put on the stronger medications.

No, it wouldn't do. Victor told the guard as much. But it was right to forgive him.

It took all the energy Victor had left to drag the body of the guard through the house, across the back garden and into the alleyway. There was a patch of scrub several houses away that would offer some cover. The man would be found soon – cats were fiendishly good at honing in on the scent of death. Dogs even better. But he wouldn't be found for a while. And Victor didn't need long.

He'd be starting tonight. And what he had in mind would be over quite soon.

CHAPTER TWENTY-SEVEN

It was midnight. Victor watched the young carer from behind a large hydrangea bush at the side of the Georgian brick house. There were no blinds or curtains at the kitchen window. Everything was open to view.

The carer was female, perhaps early twenties. Pretty, with long blonde hair. Dressed in a T-shirt and short skirt, her feet were covered in thick woollen socks. She didn't appear to have a boyfriend with her, which was fortunate.

Her skirt rode up as she reached for one of the kitchen cupboards. He bit his lip and could feel his heart rate increasing, but not because of her. At the same time a deep discomfort gnawed at his gut. Something felt wrong. He knew what he had to do, but she was so young, so innocent. She wasn't part of his plan.

So what?

He watched the girl. His discomfort increased. Nausea and panic churning in his stomach, the acid seeping into his throat as blood pumped around his body.

She wasn't in his plan.

The girl picked up a tray of food, balancing it in one hand as she turned off the kitchen light and walked through a door, out of sight. When he could no longer see her, the discomfort eased, fading into the background. The nausea subsided and his heart rate dropped. He felt calm again. He shook his head, disappointed at the distraction.

He pushed her out of his mind. He would leave her alone. He had to. She wasn't the target. The target was upstairs. The owner of the house. The woman.

The doctor.

He approached the kitchen door, pulling out a small screwdriver. He was quick, jamming the lock, causing the door to creak open – a skill he'd been forced to learn in his younger years in Romania. He grabbed the handle and listened, picking up the faint sound of laughter through a set of expensive TV speakers. Good. The carer must be in the lounge. He hoped she wouldn't come back again, distracting him. Confusing him.

His shoes were silent on the kitchen tiles. There were two doors off the kitchen – one towards the back of the house, living room and study. She was through there; he could hear the TV. The other door led to the huge hallway and staircase.

At the top of the stairs he took several deep breaths and unslung the rucksack, preparing his equipment. Fourth doorway on the left.

There was no sound from the woman's room and no light escaped under the door. He clasped the handle and turned, easing the door open just enough to slide his head in. It was a large bedroom with two wardrobes, a desk and a double bed in the middle, perpendicular to the doorway.

The woman lay on her side, facing away from him. The duvet rose and fell with her breathing. It was slow. She must be asleep.

He slipped the plastic bag out of his rucksack and opened it up, making it ready. She might wake up, and he didn't want her screaming. She wasn't allowed to scream; those were the rules for this one.

The moment was right. With three strides he reached the bed and slipped the bag over the woman's head, down to her neck. There, he tightened and clamped the bag against her wrinkled skin, pulling it taut.

He straddled her body and waited the few moments it took for her body to register that something was wrong. The bag filled with breath and emptied again as she breathed back in. Her breathing became quicker as the carbon dioxide built up in her blood.

She woke up.

Victor climbed off and spoke into the woman's ear, whispering a few words of comfort and a string of relaxing instructions.

Her breathing slowed and with both hands she reached for the bag. She felt around in the dim light and grasped the edge, pulling it above her eyes to her forehead. She turned and faced Victor, unable to hide her horror, but unable to move her body.

'Who . . .?'

'Doctor Stevenson,' said Victor. 'Dr Emily Stevenson. You supervised my treatment in Comăneşti Orphanage in 1985. I'm number thirteen.'

The woman's lips trembled and she stuttered something incoherent. Victor whispered again to her. 'Sit up,' he said.

The woman lurched upwards, the speed belying her age. She swivelled around to face him on the edge of the bed. Victor remained standing, some three feet away.

'I have come for you,' said Victor. 'Some are already dead. The rest will be soon.'

Again the doctor stuttered. Her hand spasmed as she tried to reach out to him.

'I didn't . . .' she began, but her brow furrowed. She searched his eyes and he saw the recognition appear.

Victor was satisfied, and whispered to her, indicating the plastic bag, still held by the fragile fingers of her left hand.

'I forgive you,' he said.

Her eyes objected but her body didn't. Her hands slipped the bag down again, over her face, tight around her neck. She held it to create a seal, and the suction as she tried to draw breath dragged it into her mouth.

She thrashed. Her body was fighting but her mind held fast. The more she convulsed, the harder she held the bag tight around her neck. She was old, but still strong enough to fight and make a noise. She lashed out with one arm, catching the lamp on the bedside table. It teetered and fell, knocking over a glass of water as it went. Both smashed and the thud and crash of broken glass echoed in his ears.

Still Victor watched. He tilted his head, whispered again, and the arm withdrew, pulling the bag tight. Victor leaned in, studying the frantic battle between her mind and body, the confusion of wills. Only one could win.

Her movements began to slow, her breath laboured. He wished he could see her eyes, but the bag obscured them, the condensation blurring the inside. A few seconds more and she stopped breathing, her body giving up.

Her life extinguished by her own hand.

Victor paused to savour the moment, but he was aware of the noise she'd made. He needed to get away. Getting caught again would cause too much delay. He had no wish to go back to a cell and his symptoms would start again soon. He dreaded the onset. It made him weak and angry. He must go.

He made it as far as the top of the stairs.

'Professor?' It was faint. The carer, her voice high-pitched and concerned. 'Emily,' she called again, 'are you OK?'

Her voice wafted up. From where? He couldn't see her. The only escape was the stairs, so that's the way he had to go. Down he crept.

'Professor?'

He froze as he saw the carer slip across the hall in her socks, approaching the banister. An outside lamp by the front door cast enough light through the window to show her silhouette. Slow motion as she turned at the bottom of the stairs to face him. He was still eight or nine steps up, rucksack on shoulder. Unfamiliar and dressed in black, he must have looked like a nightmare.

She didn't scream at first. The situation took two or three seconds to register in the dim light.

Victor shouted, no longer frightened about the noise. But he was too late. She screamed at the same time, drowning out his instructions. The trance didn't take hold and she ran.

He dropped the rucksack, jumped the remaining steps and sprinted after her. The bag tumbled down the stairs, coming to rest by the front door.

The girl screamed as she reached the kitchen, slamming the door in his face as he pursued her. He barged through, splinters of the door frame scattering on to the floor as he lunged at her. She scrambled back, slipping on the tiled floor and falling into a seated position against the kitchen cupboards. She screamed again.

'Please! Don't hurt me.'

It's too late, he thought, advancing on her. He couldn't leave her.

He spoke again, trying to grab her with his instructions, but she was talking over him, pleading, screaming. Her wails prevented him from finishing his sentences. He was out of breath from chasing her, and the thumping intensified in his head.

He didn't have long. He'd soon be too sick to fight her.

He leaned over, hand in his pocket, searching for his penknife. He couldn't find it and took his eyes off the girl, peering into the recesses of his jacket.

She took the opportunity and jumped up, thumping past him, heading towards the hall. He swore as she caught him off balance, but before she reached the door the girl trod on a piece of splintered door frame, the sharp wood digging deep into the sole of her foot. Crying out, she staggered sideways, her socks causing her to slip and twist her ankle.

His heart raced and the headache deepened – a yawning background thump, signifying a much worse pain to come. The girl was trying to get up, hobbling, weeping loudly, blood pouring from her foot. He grabbed her by the hair, dragging her back to the kitchen and throwing her on to the floor. Her head cracked on the tiles and her eyes rolled. She coughed and tried to lift her head, begging. 'Please. Please let me go.'

He stared at her, confused and unsure. This wasn't in his plan. She shouldn't die. Or should she? What would the instructors say? They would tell him to finish it. He had no choice. It was sad, but it had to be. He looked around, keeping one eye on the girl, wary she'd run again. She screamed and his ears filled with pain.

His eyes settled on the knife block, but it was empty. Next to it sat a pot of utensils. He picked the biggest thing in there: a mallet with a metal head, used for tenderising meat. It was heavy and the metal looked sharp. His mind raced and the nausea took hold, the elephants in his head stamping their feet.

The girl was conscious, but dazed. She saw the mallet and gasped, putting both her hands up. 'No,' she repeated, over and over. 'No. Please no.' He frowned, feeling sorry for her. She was so pretty. It was a shame.

Hefting the mallet in the air, he hit her as hard as he could. She lashed out with her hand and deflected the blow. There was a wet thud as it hit her shoulder, the metal cutting the skin. He grunted and lifted it again for another go.

The screams were louder now, desperate and uncontrolled. No words, just noise. He couldn't have that. It might alert the neighbours, who might call the police. Police would be bad. He wasn't finished yet. He couldn't get caught again so soon.

Straddling the girl, he put his left hand over her mouth and hit her again with the mallet, on the side of her head. He wasn't sure what to aim at, but this time she went limp. He felt the heat of her blood on his hand as it raced out of her scalp, the skin broken. Her screams cut out, replaced by a weak muttering. At least it was quieter. He took his hand away from her mouth.

He raised the mallet again but something stopped him. Her eyes were open but vacant, her lips parted, trickles of blood running down on to her lips. Was she dying? He didn't know. He didn't need to hit her again. He'd just wait.

It was only 1 a.m. There was plenty of time. He looked around into the hallway. His bag was still there, where it had tumbled down the stairs after him. He mustn't forget it.

Turning back to the girl, his breathing slowed. He placed the mallet on the wet tiles and moved his face closer to hers.

Why did the guilt tug at him so?

He leaned back and stared at her body. She was still moving: small, gasping breaths. Her head injury must be severe. A cough or two as her body struggled. Her top half was a mess, covered in blood.

He stared at her face, watching her lips tremble as she struggled to breathe. She fought to keep her eyes open, trying to keep Victor in her sights. She looked so young, so innocent, but he could see the terror in her eyes. Terror he'd put there. He gasped as memories began to flood over him, and closed his eyes against the growing stampede in his head. He could see the past; he remembered. The dormitories. The young girls, so many of them. Laura was one of them, crying herself to sleep at night, trying to hold her breath to choke back the tears, hoping that the dormitory supervisor wouldn't hear her. The supervisor would stand at the doorway, watching for dissent, waiting until the children appeared to be sleeping before she left.

Victor had tracked the supervisor down. In his teens, many years after the soldiers had taken them away and he'd escaped. He roamed the city and grew into a young man and discovered his talent made it easier to live undetected.

She wasn't hard to find. She was old and careless, retired and showing no regret for what she'd done. She didn't care that all the children had been taken away to their deaths. She said she did, but she didn't. He could tell by the way she screamed.

Victor told her she'd pay for what she did. She didn't have a choice.

He'd followed her, back then. At a cafe, he'd lent her correct change for the vending machine and she'd bought a coffee with it. She smiled and joked and hadn't recognised the boy she'd abused.

It was in a parking lot. Dark. Underground. He didn't want to put her in a trance; he wanted her to watch, just as he'd been forced to. He found a quiet spot, pinning her to the floor.

She screamed and he clamped his hand over her mouth. He ripped her clothes and hit her until his fist swelled and his knuckles bled. He twisted her bones and dug at her nerves. His mind spiralled as he looked down on the monster, willing himself into action.

Cars raced by overhead and the occasional headlight lit up the concrete wall behind him. He waited, and remembered, and waited. He pictured those nights when she had hit him, punishing him for showing even a shred of emotion, a hint of the child within. He remembered the sick satisfaction she had taken in exerting her power, reducing him to a snivelling, grovelling wreck. He imagined the other children, night after night.

He held her head as she'd held his, forcing her to stare at him. He released his hand but she shouted and raged, hitting and scratching, calling him scum, even laughing at him. He was the first to break eye contact and he turned away, hiding his tears. He couldn't do what she did, and he hated himself for it.

Instead he forgave her in the only way he knew how. He pushed a knife through her throat and whispered his forgiveness into her right ear. He pulled her dress back down to cover the bruises and left her there.

He cried all the way home, his actions consuming him then for many months. However, it was foolish to think he could do such a thing without repercussions. The police swarmed all over the city and his face was known. Gathering his few belongings, he set off and travelled for years on end, never staying in the same city for long. Eventually age brought a change in his appearance and the authorities stopped looking.

Now, in the home of another tormentor he had forgiven in his own special way, he opened his eyes and saw the young woman in front of him, her skirt hitched up, helpless. His stomach tensed at the sight of what he'd done. The nausea surged and his headache thumped, masking the churning in his stomach, low down where his body knew something was wrong.

He reached for the girl's skirt and pulled it back down, covering her underwear. He patted it on to her legs and tried not to let the sorrow overcome him. Hitting her had been necessary and he had no choice. But he didn't need to do anything else. He didn't need to forgive her. This wasn't what he wanted. It wasn't what Laura would have wanted.

This young girl could live. She'd done nothing wrong.

He checked her pulse and then he left. His ability was spent and he needed sleep and painkillers. He must recover quickly, for he had so much to do.

CHAPTER TWENTY-EIGHT

A tall woman stared at Victor's crouched body from her vantage point in a garden across the road. She and her friend observed in silence, and it was some moments before she released the breath she was holding. Child thirteen, one of the puppet masters, was displaying what he could do. The boy who'd walked away into the Romanian village of Sălătruc and whom Natalia hoped she'd never see again.

Natalia's own number was fifty, and her life had been hard since Comăneşti. She had no doubt Thirteen's had been too, but Natalia had come in from the cold a long time ago. She had purpose, if little choice in what she did.

Her face twisted in disgust as she watched Thirteen bending over the young woman. She hissed and recited her words but was held back by Freak. He placed his hand on her arm to calm her.

'He didn't kill her,' said Freak, always one to state the obvious. 'Did you see that, Natalia? He let her live.'

'He killed the professor,' said Natalia. 'Upstairs somewhere. You saw it.'

'Yes,' said Freak, raising his eyebrows. 'Do you care?'

'Yes, I care, Freak,' she said, using his name from the orphanage, which she only did when angry. He flinched.

'Perhaps he has it right,' said Freak. 'Don't pretend they don't deserve—'

'Why are you being like this?' said Natalia.

Freak held his tongue.

Natalia put her hand on his arm. 'This is our job. Our purpose . . .'

Freak looked at her, his eyes troubled. They both knew he was never destined to be anything. He was within an inch of being discarded when Natalia found him.

'Thirteen was—'

'I know what Thirteen was,' said Natalia. 'He didn't have a choice then. But he does now.'

Freak nodded, as he always did when Natalia insisted. She believed in their mission. Whether Freak believed or not, it didn't matter. She was in charge. She had to endure her fake existence, her play-acting and fruitless attempts to figure out their prey.

'You think it'll be easier now he's out of prison?' Freak closed his eyes again.

Natalia knew she was taking her time. She didn't need Freak reminding her.

'I hope so,' she said, although she was far from sure. She felt her own anxiety bubbling up at the chaos in front of her.

Freak also knew how hard it had been for them both over the last few weeks, since Thirteen had reared his violent head and things got noisy here in the UK. The people Natalia and Freak worked for didn't like noise. Their organisation relied on a quiet, delicate approach, and they wanted this mess tidied up – fast. Thirteen needed to be dealt with, and Natalia was the one to do it. So far, it hadn't gone to plan.

'We were sent to put a leash on this dog,' she said, wishing it was that simple.

'He wasn't supposed to get away, was he?'

Natalia threw Freak a dirty look. She feared Thirteen and Freak knew it.

They watched Thirteen stagger from the house and away. Neither fancied confronting the man, not yet. Not until he was weaker, or he made a mistake. There were always cracks, and Natalia and Freak were practised at looking for them. Their talents – Freak's ability to run interference and resist control, and Natalia's to take it – complemented each other if used well, and they'd been encouraged – forced – to make it work. They had brought in no less than four products of the Romanian experiments so far, and two more from Russia. This was their mandate, as the fallout of that period of history was slowly but surely brought back under wraps. For what purpose, Natalia had her suspicions, but she couldn't air them. Her masters did not negotiate.

But Victor was their seventh and most lethal target by far, the strongest they'd ever been sent to hunt. When she made her move she'd need to be absolutely certain of victory. The alternative didn't bear thinking about.

'They might not wait much longer,' said Freak. 'Might they?' His eyes gave away his fear. They knew they were on a tight leash themselves.

'What choice do they have?' Natalia knew there was always a choice. Put a bullet in Thirteen, and both of them. The thought was never far from her mind, always left unsaid. 'They'll wait,' she said, convincing herself. 'They've waited this long for him. Big-game hunting is dangerous; it takes time.'

'Whatever you say.'

'Exactly.'

And it wasn't like they had another plan. After Thirteen's escape from prison, she'd asked to be brought back in and they'd refused.

Figure it out, they'd told her. *Don't come back until you have him.*

CHAPTER
TWENTY-NINE

Alex woke to the sound of Jane in the shower. She finished up and returned to the bedroom, dressing quickly in silence. The familiar smell of Cerruti perfume wafted over him. Grace had often worn that fragrance, and the thought of her caused a stir in Alex's stomach, another pang of regret.

Jane grabbed her bag from the dressing table and made to leave. 'I'll be late tonight, OK?'

Alex lifted himself from the pillow. Jane smiled. Their eyes met, but she turned away, perhaps not having the energy to deal with him this morning. He couldn't blame her.

Alex slumped back into the pillow. His neck and shoulders ached all over. He felt his forehead and glands but there was nothing to suggest he was ill. Just tired.

Jane left, the front door slamming slightly harder than it needed to. Alex slid out of bed, heading straight to the kitchen. He filled the coffee machine with water and rubbed the sleep out of his eyes while it spluttered into life. Checking his supply of Xanax, he popped one and made a mental note to call Mikey, his pharmacist, at the earliest opportunity.

Before he'd fallen asleep last night he'd had an idea, and now he mulled it over, trying to think above the noise of the dripping coffee and the incessant buzzing of his phone on the table. He huffed, feeling a headache coming on, pulled his shoulder joint until it cracked, then shuffled his feet on the cold tiles towards the phone. Grabbing it, he headed for the bathroom.

'Yeah.'

'It's me,' said Sophie.

'Hi. It's early.'

'I wanted to check . . .'

Alex rubbed his eyes, in need of caffeine, or perhaps just proper sleep, undisturbed by his frantic anxieties. 'I haven't heard anything. You?'

'No.'

'Are you at Whitemoor?'

Sophie hesitated. 'Are you worried?' she said. 'That Victor might come after you?'

Alex stared at himself in the bathroom mirror. 'No,' he said. 'I met him. Talked to him. He didn't wish me harm.'

'He might.'

'I'm safe, Sophie. Don't worry. I'll be in soon. Meet you there?'

As he hung up and turned the shower to scalding hot, he watched the water stream down the shower screen. He wondered if he should have been a little more honest with Sophie, because in truth he had no idea what Victor would do. He didn't think any of the staff at Whitemoor were in danger – Victor had been given ample opportunity to wipe out half of them if he'd wanted to – but who could say for sure?

However, Alex needed to accept that Victor might not have a plan, that he might be taking the opportunities where he found them. It would be a bad outcome, because it would be increasingly difficult to predict his behaviour.

Alex knew what he needed to do next.

'Bucharest?' Sophie stood in the prison parking lot, leaning against her Golf, hands in pockets. Alex had asked to meet her there. He thought he should tell her before he disappeared for a few days and he didn't want her to object to his idea in front of Robert and Hartley.

'I need answers,' he said. 'More than I'm getting now. Back to the source, as one of my tutors used to say. Bucharest is a short hop. I'll be back in no time.'

Sophie's eyes narrowed. She looked away. 'For how long?'

'A day or two,' he said.

Sophie nodded, appearing to consider it. She shuffled her feet, kicking her toes into the concrete.

'Just there and back?'

'That's the plan. Look, I—'

'To see Dr Petri? Just him, or anybody else?' One of her shoes caught a discarded drink can and it clattered off under a car.

'Just him,' said Alex, watching the path of the silver metal can, puzzled at the questions. 'Look—'

'OK,' she said. 'When do we go?'

Alex shook his head. 'Sorry, that's not what I meant. I'm going. You need to stay here, provide Hartley with assistance while I'm gone. Robert doesn't seem up to it. You know what I mean.'

He'd thought about it, of course he had, but in a rare moment of common sense he'd decided to go alone. Alex needed to be professional and, above all, focused. In his current state of mind he needed to remain undistracted by both Jane and Sophie. Grace would never leave his mind – but he didn't want her to.

Sophie kept her face twisted to one side, her shoulders slowly rising and falling. When she turned back to face him he thought he saw a flash of fear in her eyes.

'It would be better for me to join you,' she said. Her face relaxed. The fear disappeared and was replaced with a wry smile. She nudged herself away from her car and closed the distance between them.

'I can help,' she said. She reached out and placed her hand on his arm.

Alex paused. He watched Sophie, how her body language had morphed from anxious to seductive in three steps. He felt his certainty slipping.

'I'm from that part of the world,' she said. 'I'll fit in better than you. This would be a great experience for me. For both of us, perhaps.' She finished the sentence in a whisper, her smile growing. Alex felt his throat close up. She was close enough to touch, but he remained motionless, caught in the moment.

A couple of days away with Sophie. That wouldn't be so bad. And it was her idea, not his, so nobody could accuse him of being inappropriate. Not that he cared much if they did, but still, it had the potential to get awkward. He tried quickly to weigh up the pros and cons, but as Sophie cocked her head and kept her eyes fixed on his, the cons were fast disappearing. Her perfume wafted over him and he breathed it in. Her cheeks were flushed. She flicked her hair to one side, revealing the soft skin of her neck.

What would Jane say? It didn't matter – he wouldn't tell her. Besides, there was nothing innately wrong about going away with a work colleague. What would Grace say? Nothing. She wouldn't care. She'd made it quite clear that what he did was his business. She couldn't stop him when they were married; she wasn't going to try after they divorced.

The thought of Grace jolted Alex back to reality.

'I, er, do you think it's a good idea?'

'I do,' said Sophie. Her face remained locked in a smile. Her eyes took on a strange quality, her pupils dilating. Alex wondered if she'd taken something, but she didn't seem the type. And Alex didn't care to think that women only liked him when they were high or drunk.

No, he decided. Not high. She was coherent and stable. She wanted to come with him, and whether that was professional or personal, it didn't matter. Part of Alex hoped it was the latter, but he'd settle for whatever he could get. Going away with Sophie would be interesting and worth it. His mind was made up.

'OK,' he said. 'Why not?'

Sophie beamed, spinning around and heading for the entrance.

'I'll check flights,' she said, whipping out her phone and disappearing through the door.

Alex watched her leave, his body relaxing. He paused for a few moments, pleased with himself. What the hell. He'd made the right decision. Now it was time to tell DCI Hartley.

He doubted she'd be quite so supportive.

CHAPTER THIRTY

'You want to go where?' Hartley looked quizzical but not altogether angry. They were back in the office with several colleagues. The police were working their way through interviews with the remaining prison staff.

'You heard what I said last time?' said Hartley. 'We're considering all prison staff at risk.'

'They're not at risk,' said Alex, still not sure if he believed it.

'You don't know that,' said Hartley. 'If you leave the country, we can't protect you. We don't have many friends in Bucharest.'

'But Victor can't leave the country, can he?' said Robert. His usual grey-white shirt had been replaced with a faded black one today. The top button was missing.

Alex raised his eyebrows and gave Robert a few moments to consider this.

'Of course . . .' said Robert. 'How foolish of me.'

'But why would he?' said Alex. 'I think he came to the UK to exact his revenge. Professor Dumitru, Professor Florin, maybe others. You don't know any more than that, do you?'

'But his behaviour here has been—'

'Violent, erratic and unpredictable. Yes, I know. But you're no closer to catching him if I stay.'

Hartley frowned, tapping her pencil. 'I can't have you running around conducting formal interviews. The CPS has already screwed up the relationship with the Romanian officials.'

'I won't be. Patient background is a fundamental part of my assessment process. This is what I do, Detective.'

What I did, he thought. *I haven't done this for years.*

'This is strictly research,' he said. 'Background on the subject. I can't get what I need from a rushed phone call over a crackly international line. It needs to be personal, face-to-face, doctor-to-doctor. That's how my profession works. I'll pass on anything relevant to you and your team.'

Hartley looked thoughtful. She knew Alex's background, and hopefully she'd be intelligent enough not to treat him like a tabloid quack, as some of the others seemed to.

'And you think this . . .' – Hartley referred to her notepad – 'Dr Petri will help you? If we let you do this?'

'I think he knows more than he told me on the phone,' said Alex. 'Something catastrophic was inflicted on Victor back in his childhood. His appearance here in the UK is not random, we know that. But there is more to this than just the two professors. Victor is an aberration, a violent force, but you can't treat him like a normal fugitive. He's not going to pick a fight in a bar for the sake of it and get caught. He's looking for something or someone, and he may not even know what it is yet. This whole situation in the UK is one big mess for him. He's probably withdrawing now, looking to apply order. I need to get one step ahead. If I can find out what happened to him, we may stand a better chance of figuring out his next move.'

Alex paused. He realised his excitement had caused him to start lecturing his colleagues. He checked his elevated heart rate, a familiar sensation. It was getting more frequent. It was years since a patient had made him feel like this. He forced himself to relax.

Hartley glanced at Robert, who shrugged – unhappy, but devoid of any better suggestions. He looked under pressure and troubled, the bags under his eyes straining on his pale skin.

'What other leads do you have?' Alex insisted. 'If I do nothing, this man will disappear and you'll either be following him from crime scene to crime scene, or he'll be gone for good.'

'OK,' said Hartley, hands open in submission. She glanced around the room at her other officers and checked the screen on her phone. 'If you must, make your trip. Keep it clinical, please, and keep it short. If I get any complaints across from the Met that you're pissing off the Romanians you're off this case for good. Agreed?'

'Agreed,' said Alex with relief, although he wished he felt happier. He was chasing a dangerous man. Was the reward worth it?

'Our flights leave tonight,' said Sophie, hunched over her keyboard. While Alex talked, she'd been busy on her phone then on her laptop. She glanced up and nodded.

'You too?' Robert looked perturbed, and his eyes flicked between Alex and Hartley.

'I need an assistant,' said Alex, 'and it'll be good experience for Sophie.' He ignored the looks on both Robert's and Hartley's faces. They didn't appear altogether happy, but they had no good reason to stop her.

Alex's and Sophie's eyes met. Whatever had been worrying her in the parking lot was gone. All he could see now was her familiar warmth. It would do her good to get out of the prison, Alex thought. He tried to push aside the other thoughts.

Those would only get in the way.

CHAPTER
THIRTY-ONE

The young girl slept surrounded by cushions and soft toys under a colourful patchwork duvet. A white bunny lay on her chest, rising and falling, pinned there by her arm. Her face was illuminated by a faint pink nightlight, showing her petite features and ash-blonde hair, which had fallen over her cheek.

Victor studied her from the bedroom doorway. He glanced across the landing before flicking on his torch, scanning the bedroom walls. It was a pretty room. Pastel colours. Decorated for a younger girl than the one in the bed. Covered in posters of princesses and ponies. He'd never seen a room like this before. The girls he knew as a child slept ten to a room, the only thing on the walls was mould, and princesses didn't exist at all, not even in dreams.

He paused as she stirred and rolled over. She stretched and the bunny fell to the floor. A deep breath. He could smell lavender, soft and gentle.

The girl caused an unease deep in his gut. It upset him. He tried to ignore it, but the feeling persisted, like he'd swallowed a rock. It lay on his stomach and wrenched back and forth as he moved.

He'd seen so many young girls die. She didn't need to be one of them.

He pulled away, leaving the girl asleep, and crept back out of the room to avoid making a sound.

Further along the landing towards the master bedroom, Victor paused. He'd observed the occupants from across the street, watching them intently through the open curtains. She was middle-aged, a brunette with short, bobbed hair. Her husband was much older, but muscular and tall. Victor had watched, and left them to it. That was yesterday. Today it was time.

He'd entered the house through the French doors and tiptoed across the thick living room rugs and parquet hallway, stepping in time to the ticking of the grandfather clock under the staircase.

He paused as a woman's voice called out from behind the master bedroom door. Sweet nothings to a husband, wondering when he'd be finished in the shower. A reply, deep but muffled, confirming the husband's presence.

There was no need to delay. Pulling the thin knife out of his backpack he grabbed the bedroom door handle, turning and pushing hard. It was unlocked and offered no resistance, flinging open to reveal a brightly lit room. He squinted as the light hit his eyes, panning around to the bed on the far wall. The bed was occupied and the woman's eyes widened. She was dressed in a silk slip, her hands resting on the floral duvet.

Before she could find her voice, Victor whispered across the room. He repeated himself several times as the words seeped into her psyche, relaxing her, controlling her.

Her arms fell limp to her sides, and she slumped, seated, staring forwards with a vacant gaze.

Quickly now. Speed was of the essence. *Do it and leave.*

The door to the en suite swung open. The husband walked through, wet, with a towel wrapped around his waist, rubbing moisture out of his eyes. He didn't register Victor, who was stooped in the shadows by the door. He addressed his wife, looking puzzled at the sight of her dressed seductively in thin lingerie, but gazing, mouth open, and dribbling out of the left corner of her mouth.

He moved towards her, his brow creasing with worry.

Victor also moved, and whispered again, this time at the man he'd come to kill.

The man turned and opened his eyes wide in surprise. They flickered before coming under control, relaxing as Victor spoke, insistent and calm, relaying his instructions.

It took a while, but Victor waited for the glimmer of recognition from the man who had tormented him as a child all those years ago.

Victor held his knife by the blade, outstretched towards the man. He pushed and whispered. And it took.

'Do you remember?' said Victor.

The man reached out and took the knife. He hesitated, his eyes searching Victor's face.

His terror was absolute.

'Do you remember handing me a knife like this one?' Victor tilted his head, whispered and stood back.

The man opened his mouth but could only manage a croak.

'Marcu died on that day. Do you remember him? Twenty-nine?'

The man tried to shake his head but his eyes betrayed him once again.

'Do you remember Catina, Clara and Beniamin?' said Victor. He paused. 'You know their numbers. They were children. I can see that you do. And that's enough. I'm here to forgive you.' Victor whispered until the man was completely under, stooped, head hanging, eyes glazed. Open to instruction. Open to anything.

Victor whispered his final instruction.

Without hesitating, the man lifted his arm high and stabbed hard with the knife, downwards into his own chest from the side. The knife made a wet sound and struck a rib. Wrenching it out, the man adjusted his grip, then stabbed again, higher this time. The knife entered more cleanly into his neck, sinking deep, missing bones and cutting through muscle and ligaments.

The man's body reacted, even if his mind couldn't. Too late, but basic motor instincts took hold. A scream. A deep groan which ended with a gurgling sound as the blood gushed into the man's throat.

He staggered back into a dark oak wardrobe. The knife was stuck in the man's neck up to the handle, his severed artery spraying the mirrored doors in blood.

Victor glanced at the woman in the bed. She remained staring straight ahead, her eyes witnessing the carnage but her body unable to act.

The man slumped back against the wardrobe doors, blood pumping out of his throat and mouth. Knees folded and arms limp, his face like a goldfish out of water, gasping and gulping, unable to draw breath, unable to understand what was happening.

He died so rapidly that his eyes remained open, staring waist-height across the room towards the far wall, unfocused, flickering and empty.

Victor was still, watching as the mist descended, signalling his exhaustion. He didn't move for several minutes, motionless, just watching, before he was roused by a young girl's voice, calling for her mum.

He turned and left, passing the young girl on the landing. He didn't stop. Seeing the girl made the rock in his stomach heavier, and the nausea gripped him. He rushed past and down the stairs, before exiting the house by the front door.

The young girl's screams followed him out into the night, across the city and into his sleep.

Pain. Victor woke in pain every day. The stampede in his head began before his eyes opened. It continued for hours before seeping away, lurking beneath the surface, ready to return at a moment's notice.

Victor dreamed. Vivid and lucid, he dreamed of his parents, of what they might have been. He dreamed of a childhood by the lakes, the mountains casting their shadows. The shadows never reached him because his parents kept it at bay.

It was a dream, of course. It never happened. Not like the other dreams, the visions where he relived his real childhood, relentlessly, repeatedly, until the stampede woke him and reminded him the pain would never go. Not while he lived. Not while others lived.

It had taken him this long, and he was angry at himself. He had confused things, delayed and spent his efforts in the wrong place. But they deserved it, didn't they? Didn't everyone share some responsibility? How dare they live without the pain, if he must live with it?

He sat up, the bed creaking in protest. He sniffed and scrunched up his nose. Another house, and the bed smelled of its owner, a frail lady who'd opened her door and stared at him with innocence as he'd barged his way in.

She'd looked poor, her clothes tatty and worn. Scared, she had pleaded with him to leave. Victor held her by the shoulders and peered into her eyes. He saw honesty and fear, but no anger.

She reminded him of one of the cooks at Comănești. Local women, farmers' wives, visiting only for an hour or so a day, seemingly oblivious to the treatment of the children, or at least they pretended to be. Memories bubbled to the surface and Victor forced them back down. He couldn't find it in himself to hurt this woman; her eyes were innocent and so was her soul.

He'd sent her away, out of the house and into the street. She'd wander and roam until somebody found her. A son or daughter, perhaps? No husband, not by the look of the house.

She would live. He'd killed more people than he needed to, although still not enough to repay what they'd done. If he had any doubts, he thought of Laura. The memory of her face was enough to cause his throat to catch. He swallowed but the pain of her memory stabbed him through the chest.

You saw what they did to her.

You saw what they did to all of us.

Take your revenge, Victor, or die trying.

That was his promise, and those who got in his way could never understand.

CHAPTER THIRTY-TWO

The seat-belt sign blinked off and Alex finally saw Sophie's hands relax. She'd been gripping the armrests of the small economy seat all the way since take-off. Taking a deep breath, she stared out of the window. Her eyes were glazed and for the second time in as many days Alex wondered if she'd taken something. If so, he couldn't judge. His own private sourcing of benzodiazepines was hardly rare among members of his profession, and he'd been using the same source for years since they'd studied together at UCL. His friend Mikey was a pharmacist and a gambler. Good at the former but poor at the latter. He welcomed the opportunity to bring in some untraceable cash in exchange for untraceable prescription meds. It was a neat arrangement and one which meant Alex could avoid facing up to his own habit.

They'd been delayed for an hour at London Stansted Airport. They were flying budget and their promised three-hour non-stop flight was turning into something rather more tedious. While waiting in the lounge, trying to ignore the bustle of other travellers and the frequent announcements, Alex tried to get Sophie to open up a little. He worried that he still knew hardly anything about her. Robert had been next to useless on the matter.

'Robert doesn't know anything,' said Sophie. 'I'm not sure he even remembers my name half the time.'

Alex remembered Robert's comment that had confirmed as much. 'What brought you to the UK?' he said.

It turned out that Sophie hadn't been in the UK for long – only a matter of months, in fact.

'Germany was a lovely place,' she said, 'but . . . I had to leave.'

She described her childhood. Born in Germany to working-class parents, her mother was a care assistant and father a plumber. Life had been unremarkable until she was fourteen, at which point her normal family life had unravelled. Her dad, a timid and otherwise kindly man, left her mother. He'd been living a double life of sorts. The separation was swift and brutal.

'It must have been awful,' said Alex, his face flushing, knowing the effect that it must have had on a young girl. He avoided the usual plummet into self-pity and anger. His own situation was too far gone. But he saw himself in her story.

Sophie said that her mother had coped for a short time until the cracks had widened. She had found herself pregnant, a parting gift from a deceitful spouse. It could have brought the family back from the brink, and for the next eight months it almost did, until the birth. Fate had held a further wicked surprise in store for the family, and in this case it was chromosome 18q- syndrome in the newest member, Dieter. Dieter suffered from multiple serious developmental issues, both physical and psychological, and had required intensive support from day one. Dieter had got the support he needed, but his mother hadn't. She'd hidden it well, but her grief triggered depression and by the time anyone thought to address it she was two bottles into her stash of sleeping tablets.

Alex's eyes widened at this point. He didn't know what to say or how to say it. Sophie had revealed a deep insight into her personal life. When he'd asked, he hadn't meant for her to tell him her darkest secrets.

He stared at her and watched. Her eyes darted as she told the story – up and to the left. A slight chill washed over him. She was lying, or embellishing. The story came out ordered and logical. Rehearsed? He put the thoughts to one side. *Too much caffeine*, he decided. His judgement was off when it came to Sophie. She was getting under his skin, seducing him and causing him to lose himself.

Sophie continued. She said she had discovered her mother after the overdose, unconscious on the kitchen floor. Her mum had been admitted to hospital and then remained under residential psychiatric care for some time. Sophie had not been expected to look after her brother Dieter, despite her protestations that she could. He was taken into a specialist foster home for children with severe disabilities in Munich, and remained there still.

Sophie said she had suffered a nervous breakdown soon afterwards, despite the best efforts of all the professionals and friends around her.

'I saw my whole family and life disintegrate before my eyes within eighteen months,' she said. 'I was lost. The foster home was my rescue.'

Sophie described the rest of her teenage years with a smile. She had excelled in the final years of school and joined Munich University as an undergraduate in psychology at nineteen. She pursued the clinical route and had headed to the UK earlier that year on a European placement scheme. It was all arranged at an international level, which was why Robert didn't know much about what was going on.

'He thinks I appeared out of thin air,' said Sophie.

Alex was taking this all in, but his discomfort persisted. The hairs on his neck prickled. Sophie had told him a story. A fabrication, perhaps part truth, but mainly lies.

It was a relief when their flight number flicked on to the overhead screen. They gathered their things for boarding and Alex considered Sophie's behaviour. He didn't fool himself: most people lied about their childhood, himself included.

He watched a young family up ahead, queuing, the children playing while the parents searched for boarding passes and passports. Alex refused to believe that any family was perfect, but he knew from experience that some fared better than others. Stability in childhood was hugely important – having a strong foundation on which to build everything else offered a secure platform for a child to launch themselves into the world, knowing they could always fall back and start again. It was why Alex desperately wanted to mitigate the damage his divorce had wrought on Katie. By offering her stability, even if not within a traditional family unit, she could still have the foundation she deserved.

Sophie, regardless of her story, clearly hadn't had that. He again felt a connection to her in the way she felt compelled to fabricate such a tale. Whatever failings she felt, and whatever blame lay on her or her family, she tried very hard to mask it and live her life regardless. He considered Sophie's response and used it to reformulate his assessment of her. Something traumatic had happened, probably in her formative years. He could relate to that, and the fact that she'd headed into the same profession said a lot about her motivation. Her anxiety around her patients made Alex think she might also have suffered a professional misadventure similar to his. But she was possibly too inexperienced, and besides, that should have shown up on her background checks by Robert.

Personal, then. Her story was a cover. Alex wanted to tell her that whatever she had survived did not have to define her, that it might end up being a good thing. The best psychologists are often the ones who've experienced, not just read about, the symptoms they treat.

Alex was tempted to ask if Sophie was in regular contact with her mother or brother back in Germany, but he held his tongue. He didn't know whether she'd answer truthfully or not, and he was thankful he'd learned even a snippet more about her. Perhaps in time he'd learn more, if she'd let him.

With a certain amount of concern he realised all of this only increased his feelings towards her.

The tyres jolted on the runway. Alex opened his eyes. He'd fallen asleep and the harsh deceleration caused his book to slide off on to the floor. It triggered a memory of Katie's first holiday to the Canary Islands with him and Grace. Katie had only been four. She'd refused to put her seat belt on and had screamed during departure, take-off and for the first hour of flight, finally falling asleep for the rest of the journey. Grace had shrunk into her seat, embarrassed and upset. Alex had found the whole thing quite amusing, apologising to the surrounding passengers before ordering a second, then a third glass of wine.

Alex apologised now to the person in front as he shook their seat, rummaging around his feet to retrieve his book. He grabbed the cover as the pilot announced their arrival at Bucharest Henri Coandă International Airport. He slid his bookmark into the wrong page and stuffed everything into his hand luggage.

The weather was confirmed as a pleasant eighteen degrees and windy, which would explain the bumpy landing. Either that or the pilot was asleep, as Sophie suggested when she packed her own book away. Alex guessed her comment was to imply she was not a frequent flyer, but that didn't seem to tally with the ease with which she gathered her belongings and made ready to leave. She glanced at Alex several times. He rubbed his eyes and followed her through the cabin towards the exit.

They passed through immigration towards the baggage pickup. As they walked, Sophie kept staring at a number of other passengers until they stared back with hostile expressions.

'Do you travel much?' Alex looked on in amusement.

'No.' Sophie continued to stare at a man in the distance. Alex's smirk faded and he wondered if he'd done the right thing.

'You don't have to stay,' he said. 'I thought it would be good for you.'

'I'll stay,' said Sophie, as the man she was staring at turned around and walked in the other direction, pushing a brown trolley suitcase.

Alex followed her gaze. 'Victor isn't here,' he said, noticing the man with the case was similar in appearance and build to their fugitive.

'Let's go,' said Sophie, as her tatty grey bag rounded the carousel and bumped its way towards her. Alex already had his and they headed through customs to the exit.

'We're staying at the Grand Boutique Hotel,' Sophie told the driver as they clambered into the next available taxi. Alex had insisted they wait in line for a licensed one. 'On Strada Negustori.' The driver nodded.

'It's close to the university,' Sophie told Alex, 'and very reasonable.'

'Wonderful,' said Alex, watching the way Sophie stared at the back of the driver's head, flicking her hair behind her ears and chewing her lip.

She relaxed as they settled into the thirty-minute trip into the city. 'Has Dr Petri even agreed to see us?'

'Not exactly.' Alex had left a voicemail with the doctor suggesting he would like to speak again about Victor Lazar. He left out the part where he was coming over to Romania and would be there in person later that day.

'I checked his lecture timetable online,' said Alex. 'He's running lectures until five thirty.' Alex looked at his watch. 'Which gives us an hour to check in and dump our stuff.'

Sophie nodded and appeared to relax a little further. 'You don't think this is a wasted trip?'

'No, I don't. Whatever happened to Victor has its roots here, and Dr Petri knows or can find out. Everybody leaves a trace, even in this country, even in the eighties. There must have been state records, documents, fragments. I can't believe someone as incredible as Victor is unknown here.'

'You're determined.' Sophie smiled at him. 'That's a good thing.' Her eyes once again sparkled with humour. 'For someone in our profession, I mean. I said you were good at this.'

Alex returned the smile, realising his determination had increased day by day. Their progress was minimal and the challenge great, but he felt positive. If Romania could give up some of its secrets, they might get a step closer to stopping Victor.

He caught a wave of nausea as the taxi lurched across lanes – the travel-sickness pills must be wearing off – and stared out of the window. He'd never been to Romania before, or even to this part of the world. He hadn't known what to expect. The highways were wide and new, but fewer cars adorned the roads than he was used to in the UK, and those that did moved across lanes as if the white lines didn't exist. American-style gantries hung across the road at intersections, signals controlling the light traffic.

The built-up industrial area near the airport gave way to trees and a huge park to their left as they crossed the river. The Dâmbovița was a tributary of the Danube, but its waters were slow here, coasting under the road and through the city.

As they approached the inner city, both he and Sophie stared through their windows, taking in the impressive architecture and the contrast between blocks – some spotless and clean, others tarnished by graffiti and with crumbling brickwork. The mixture of old city and post-Communist buildings was unlikely to win any awards for beauty or style, but the streets looked modern and vibrant.

They crawled into the centre and queued at several sets of traffic lights before the driver stopped, cursing, and pulled over.

'Grand Boutique Hotel,' he announced, without moving from his seat.

Alex paid him in cash and they both stared at the rather grand hotel entrance. It was a substantially restored old building, with original features and ornamentation on the walls. The sandstone finish was old but clean.

'Very reasonable, you say?' said Alex. 'You sure?'

'This isn't London,' said Sophie, dragging her small wheeled suitcase up the steps. Alex noted that she travelled light, perhaps one other outfit in there, in addition to the old jeans and vest she was wearing. He found it endearing, after months of Jane's exorbitant shopping habits. Jane wouldn't be caught dead travelling with anything less than a full wardrobe.

The hotel reception was warm and functional, as were the two single rooms Sophie had booked for them. They were on the first floor, overlooking a walled park, but after a cursory look around, Alex left his suitcase on the bed and locked his passport in the room safe. He checked his wallet, keys and Xanax, and headed back out again, rapping gently on Sophie's door. She appeared, notepad in one hand and laptop in the other. She'd changed into a black skirt and blouse.

'I'm the note-taker then,' she said, eyeing his empty hands. Alex had his MacBook in his bag, but decided to leave it there. Today was for talking. They might not get anywhere, in which case they'd be straight back on a plane the following morning. If it turned out Dr Petri was in a collaborative mood tomorrow, he'd start documenting their findings then.

They avoided another taxi in favour of the walk. It was warmer than in London and the fresh air helped to quell the growing unease in Alex's gut. Like at the airport, Sophie was behaving strangely, staring at passers-by until they stared back.

'Should I ask what's wrong?' said Alex.

She turned to him. 'It's nothing,' she said, 'I feel a little groggy. The flight.'

'Could be,' said Alex, not mentioning she'd been behaving like this before they'd even boarded. He couldn't help glancing at her as they approached the university buildings. She noticed his gaze but didn't say anything, and a wry smile on her lips suggested she didn't mind. Alex took it as permission to let his mind wander and imagine the possibilities of being away for a night or two with Sophie.

As they approached a crossroads and waited for the lights to change, Sophie turned to him.

'Tell me something you love,' she said.

Alex was surprised but found himself answering quickly. 'My daughter, Katie.'

Sophie nodded. 'Another thing.'

'My ex-wife. Grace.' He paused. 'But . . . I just want her to be OK. Happy. Am I making sense?' Alex knew that wasn't the truth. He loved Grace in every way possible, but saying that would change nothing and possibly spoil whatever he was creating with Sophie.

Sophie nodded, turning her eyes back to the road. 'Do you love your girlfriend?'

'No.' Alex's response was quicker than he thought it should be. 'Jane and I are not . . .'

'OK.' Sophie crossed the road without waiting for him. He hurried to catch up.

CHAPTER
THIRTY-THREE

The psychology faculty building was on Panduri Street. It was a grand four-storey, stone-faced building in need of repair. Graffiti marred much of the lower walls, although attempts had been made in the past to wash it off.

Sophie tilted her head to look up. 'You know in the seventies psychology was outlawed in Romania? As an academic discipline?'

Alex was pleased Sophie had done her background. He knew little of the history of this place and hadn't had the time to read up.

'The regime was worried any practical study of the mind would undermine Communist propaganda,' she continued. 'The Communist leader at the time – Nicolae Ceaușescu – decided to prohibit both the teaching and practice of psychology nationwide.'

'Thank you, Doctor,' said Alex.

'I have a point,' said Sophie, her face flushing. She looked puzzled by the graffiti.

'Sorry.'

'Psychologists were transferred out to other departments. It wasn't until 1990 that psychology was reinstituted as a discipline.'

'So?'

'I thought it worth pointing out. Dr Petri said the university was sponsoring orphanages for the purposes of research. But there wasn't a psychology department in the eighties. Not anywhere in Romania.'

Alex frowned. Until now he'd assumed the university would know all the details, however buried. But perhaps they wouldn't. Perhaps Victor was a ghost from a deleted past. But it didn't explain who had created Victor. If not the university psychologists, then who?

There was no security on the building entrance and they followed the signs for the lecture theatres, of which there were two. They paused outside number one while Alex checked the lecture details on his phone.

'He's in here, finishing shortly,' said Alex, checking his watch. 'Shall we?'

The door creaked open. The hall was large, half-filled with undergrads all facing a small wiry figure at the front, who was gesturing wildly at the projector screen. The slide changed to show a bulleted list of reference material, prompting a good-natured groan from many of the listeners near the front. Dr Petri said something Alex didn't understand and the same students erupted in laughter. The doctor had the respect and attention of his group, and Alex's mind drifted to his own postgrad days and thoughts of lecturing himself. It was never too late – with his specialism he'd have no trouble getting slots as a visiting lecturer.

Sophie cleared her throat and a few faces in the back rows turned towards them, but snapped back again to the front when Dr Petri spoke.

Alex massaged his wrist. It was aching. He rummaged around in his pocket for some painkillers but remembered he'd left them in the hotel room. He and Sophie slipped into a couple of empty seats near the back.

Dr Petri didn't notice them and continued his lecture. Alex saw a familiar face on the large screen at the front – a Russian psychologist named Ivan Pavlov, famous for his work in classical conditioning. In an accidental discovery, Pavlov was looking at salivation in dogs in response to being fed when he noticed that his dogs would begin to salivate whenever he entered the room, even when he was not bringing them food. This was an important behaviourist breakthrough and Pavlov devoted his life to it until his death in 1936. 'Pavlov's dogs' became a famous experiment, used to illustrate classical conditioning and taught in all undergraduate study.

Alex's own behavioural therapies had their foundations in some of Pavlov's work and he followed the slides – labelled in a mixture of Romanian and English – on conditioning, control and suggestion with interest. Although modern psychology followed strict ethical guidelines, the history of the discipline was somewhat murkier.

Dr Petri finished his lecture, staying to chat to a couple of students afterwards, two male and one female. When the theatre was empty, Alex and Sophie stood and made their way to the front.

Dr Petri narrowed his eyes as they approached. Alex pulled his warmest smile and stretched out his right hand.

'Dr Petri? Dr Alex Madison.'

Dr Petri paused for a second before the recognition appeared on his face. His eyes darted to Sophie and back to Alex.

'What are you doing here?' Dr Petri shook his head and shuffled his papers together, unplugging his laptop from the projector lead and sliding it all into a large battered leather bag.

'I said I'd—'

'You didn't say you were coming here,' said Dr Petri, fastening the clasps on his bag and straightening up.

'My apologies. I thought it might be best.'

Dr Petri considered this for a moment. 'Who told you?' he said. 'Was it my secretary, Magda? Was it Dr Franks? It's really not his area.'

Alex was confused. 'Tell me what? What do you mean?'

Dr Petri shook his head. 'You can't pretend this was a coincidence,' he said, 'what we found. Then you turn up.'

'What you found?' said Alex.

Dr Petri held Alex's eye for several moments, searching for the truth. 'I see,' he said. 'Well, I guess you've forced my decision. I wasn't sure whether to call you or not. I wondered whether I needed to pass it up the chain. It's rather serious stuff. You're sure you don't know? It would be unprofessional to hide that sort of thing.'

Alex glanced at Sophie. Her eyes gave nothing away, but his pulse jumped. 'If it's related to a clinical assessment of Victor Lazar,' said Alex, choosing his words with care, 'I'd appreciate a professional agreement to share it. I'm not the law. I'm merely charged with providing a psychological assessment. That's in both our interests?'

Dr Petri examined Alex again. The doctor's manner changed, his initial resistance softening, although he still appeared uneasy.

'Very well,' he said, 'although I don't think you'll like what we found. It doesn't paint you in a very good light.'

'Me?' Alex was surprised.

'You British.' Dr Petri beckoned them to follow him as he made his way to the theatre exit. 'Come. The project I talked about on the phone, at the orphanages – it was run by the British. Not us.'

Even after Sophie's history lesson outside the university, this revelation came as a bit of a shock. It made sense: UK psychology departments had plenty of funding back then, and it wasn't inconceivable to think that the ethically dubious projects would seek to carry out their experiments abroad in a politically unstable regime. It would be much easier – clearly – to cover their tracks afterwards.

They entered a large office with Dr Petri's name inscribed on the door. The office was lined with bookshelves. They held neatly ordered textbooks in hardback and bundles of yellowing journals held together with thin string. A smudged bay window at the far end overlooked the street and the park opposite, while the wooden desk was positioned off-centre, with utilitarian-looking chairs to either side. An old Dell laptop, a couple of folders and an old brass desk lamp sat on the scratched surface.

'Please, sit.' Dr Petri indicated the chairs. He walked over to the folders on his desk and spread them out. They looked fragile and decaying, the thick paper stained with age and torn around the edges.

Dr Petri paused and turned to Alex and Sophie. 'This doesn't make for pleasant reading,' he said, tapping one of the folders with his finger. 'I have an appointment with the chancellor tomorrow morning.'

He passed a folder to Alex who glanced at the front of it, his eyes widening with surprise as he read the title.

'It's in English,' he said, showing Sophie.

'Some,' said Dr Petri. 'Our archivist found them. They should have been in the original information request, but they'd been incorrectly filed. The archivist noticed the irregularity and dug them up. She came to me yesterday, rather shocked.'

'Project Trancework,' said Sophie, reading the faded grey lettering. Her eyes moved to the lower edge of the cover and she traced a handwritten note. 'Marionetă Masterat, Section . . .' Sophie trailed off. She closed her eyes, her face flushed. When she opened them she looked distant, distracted.

'You OK?' said Alex.

Sophie nodded. 'Fine.'

'Puppet Master,' said Dr Petri, eyeing them both with concern. 'That's the literal translation. No reason to suggest it wasn't exactly what they meant, when you read the contents. This was one of two folders found. Nothing else.'

He let Alex open the folder and browse the contents.

'What am I looking at?' said Alex, staring at the text, some typed, some handwritten. There were twenty or so pages.

'Clinical observations,' said Dr Petri, pointing to the top of each page. There was a date, a reference of some kind, and the name of a clinician. 'Some are incomplete. They aren't following any sort of protocol, as far as I can make out. It is quite informal, rather opinionated.'

'But what does it say?'

Dr Petri beckoned for one of the sheets, and he leaned against the desk. 'Dr Marius Petrescu,' he said, reading from the top. 'Fifth August 1985. End of day obs. Lot 6. An initial source of conflict in the team is playing out as expected. There can be little doubt, from our latest trial, that the conditioning works. Some of my colleagues – Dr Brovak in particular – are reluctant to give up the traditional view that we should be using hypnotic suggestion, but our work at the orphanages is proving this approach to be flawed. The disagreements are becoming less intractable, and we are reaching consensus on the next phase.'

Alex glanced at Sophie, who looked increasingly uncomfortable. She stood and paced, taking a bottle of water from her bag. Dr Petri continued.

'Our new methods, with the narcotic boosters applied to the master, are showing rejection of control stoppable, or at least delayed. It is too simplistic at this stage to claim this applies in all scenarios, or with all patients, but Lot 6 – the youngest ones in particular – are showing promise. This is not full control yet, but we'd be foolish to ignore its potential applications.

'Now we have proven the principle, our focus should be on delayed interpretation of suggestion. Dr Brovak believes that planting suggestions upon which they will later act – perhaps hours or days after the control session has finished – is too dangerous, but he was out-voted, and our sponsors agree with me.

'We have tested this so far with three children, using the older ones – sometimes siblings – as subjects. After the unfortunate incident with young Emilia we must review the dosage of LSD-25, but I am loath to return to nitrous and more primitive substances. Such progress will require difficult decisions. We are lucky to have the support of the university, even if at arm's length.

'The ethical challenge is ever-present in my mind, but the price of progress has been agreed. The project will continue.'

Dr Petri paused and put the sheet on his desk.

'There are several others like this,' he said, 'plus several cover sheets detailing the orphanages involved – four in total – and the dates.'

'Puppet masters,' said Alex. 'A sick joke?'

'Not a joke,' said Dr Petri, 'but perhaps it doesn't translate well. I think that's what the psychologists called the children.'

Alex considered the callousness of the term. These were children, for Christ's sake. He thought of Katie, her innocence and goodness, and the sheer delight she brought to the world. When Katie laughed, he laughed. When Katie hurt herself, even a minor graze on the knee or bruise on the arm, Alex felt the pain too. Seeing his daughter's distress triggered a primal response in him, as it should in all people. To imagine Katie suffering what these children suffered sent chills down Alex's spine and he felt physically sick.

'Do any of the accounts say exactly what they were doing?' said Alex. 'What were the lots? What were the drugs? You say it mentions LSD. This is gross child abuse.'

'Which is why I'm meeting with the chancellor,' said Dr Petri. He cleared his throat. 'And there are a couple more things. First, this.'

He handed over a handwritten sheet containing a list of names, thirty or so, on the left-hand side. On the right were references to Lots – most of the names had Lot 5 or Lot 6 next to them. Alex ran his finger down the list.

'Victor Lazar,' he said, pointing with his finger. Sophie nodded. Her jaw was clenched. 'Number thirteen,' she whispered.

'What?'

'Number thirteen. Victor's number.'

Alex frowned. He suggested Sophie photograph it all. She took her phone out of her pocket and switched on the camera.

'Do you mind?' said Alex.

Dr Petri shrugged. 'Depends.'

'I either take a photo or take notes.'

Dr Petri stood back so that Sophie could photograph the page. 'So there we have your man. He was nine years old at this point.'

'Comăneşti Orphanage,' read Alex from the top of the sheet.

'Yes. It's in Bacău County. The orphanage doesn't exist now, of course. These places were from darker days.'

'But he's listed as being part of . . . whatever this was.'

'It looks that way.'

'He was experimented on by these doctors, or whatever the hell they thought they were.'

'Yes.'

'So where are they now?'

'I beg your pardon?'

'The children,' said Alex. 'You won't give me their details, but I assume you know.'

Dr Petri cleared his throat. 'We don't. It's not uncommon for orphans to change their names and identity once they come of age. I'm embarrassed to say there was, and still is, a certain stigma attached. I doubt anybody knows where they all are now.'

Sophie walked away, facing out of the window. She held her bottle of water and took a swig.

'You said this paints the British in a bad light,' she said. 'Why?'

Dr Petri pulled out the second folder and sifted through the contents.

'There are a couple of reasons why,' he said. He handed Alex a crumpled sheet of what looked like a bank statement. On closer inspection it appeared to be a bank transfer agreement, detailing six separate amounts ranging from £3,000 to £12,000. It was stamped at the top with the Barclays logo – a UK bank.

'This doesn't mean anything,' said Alex, although he was puzzled at the stamp at the bottom – originally in red ink, now faded to pink. It said CONFIDENTIAL – DO NOT FILE.

'It shows funding from a UK bank into a department here in Bucharest. This next item is rather more damning.'

Dr Petri handed Alex another sheet, thicker and glossy. It was a photo. The black-and-white image had faded over time, but the people in it were clear enough. A group of ten men and women in white clinical coats, standing together for a group photo. One of the men, in the foreground, had a logo emblazoned on his coat. It had been circled in red biro. It was the name and crest of one of the most famous universities in the world.

'Didn't you go to Cambridge?' said Sophie, squinting at the blurred but unmistakable writing.

'Yes,' said Alex. 'King's College. And my father before me, and his before him. Something of a family tradition. It wasn't a choice,' he added.

Dr Petri snorted. 'Then you won't pretend this isn't a British project.'

Alex stared at the photo. Three women and seven men. One of the men at the back had thick, bushy hair and round glasses. He looked familiar. Alex racked his brain but couldn't place him.

'Only one has the Cambridge logo,' he observed. 'Do you recognise this man?' he said to Sophie.

Sophie studied the face for a few long moments. She shook her head and turned away.

'No names?' Alex glanced at Dr Petri.

'Some are in the reports,' he said. 'But they are Romanian names. So perhaps not this group. I don't know.' He shrugged.

At Alex's request, Sophie took more pictures. 'We can take a look' he said. 'The British police will help.'

Dr Petri frowned. 'I should clear this with the chancellor. We need to investigate this further.'

'We wouldn't dream of stopping you,' said Alex, 'but if these are British people in the photo then we need to find out who they are.'

'You think they're in danger?'

Alex nodded slowly. 'If that's who Victor means by "them", then yes, any who are still alive and connected to this work are in great danger.'

The trio took a few moments to consider the significance of what they'd discovered. Hartley needed to see this, but Alex wanted to be there when she planned her response.

'Do you object to us taking copies back to the UK with us now?' said Alex. 'We need to talk to the police. The Romanian handwriting – could you translate it for us? It'll speed things up.'

Dr Petri looked troubled but didn't object. Alex thought he looked worried enough about his own meeting with the university chancellor the following morning. This no doubt had the potential to seriously damage the reputation of the university, as well as international academic relations. The reverberations would be felt for many years to come as the history of the university's operations was examined in detail, and the orphanage records were resurrected from the archives.

Alex and Sophie left Dr Petri with the agreement they'd come back in the morning, after Dr Petri had spoken to his superiors. Sophie was studying the student building guide, printed on a wall in the foyer.

'What's on your mind?'

'The archives,' said Sophie. 'I think we should poke around. There's a good chance once their university chancellor gets wind of this we'll be cut out.'

'You don't think he showed us everything?' said Alex. 'He seemed pretty shocked.'

'Maybe,' said Sophie. 'It doesn't hurt to ask.' She shuffled her feet and gave him a small shrug.

'I'll come with you,' said Alex.

'No,' she said. 'The archivist is male.' She pointed to the department and the name of the contact. She smiled and tilted her head.

'I see,' said Alex. 'You'll have more chance without me.'

They agreed to meet back in the foyer in forty-five minutes. Alex decided to head outside. He needed some air. Once in the fresh air he paused and looked back at the building. His phone vibrated and a glance at the screen tarnished his otherwise good mood.

'Jane.'

'When are you getting back?' Her voice was firm but laden with hurt.

'When I've finished,' he said.

'You didn't even tell me you were going. I had to find out from the police administrator.'

Alex bit his tongue. He'd been avoiding Jane over the last few days, it was true, putting off the inevitable break-up. He should have told her.

'I wanted to talk about Katie's visit,' she said.

'What's to talk about?'

'Do I still have to cancel our trip?'

'We never had a trip, Jane. I told you I was busy.' He paused, and then in a softer tone said, 'You should go.'

Alex knew it would upset her, but it was for the best. Before she could respond he said goodbye and hung up.

Alex stared at his phone for a few seconds, half-expecting Jane to call back or text. She did neither. The nausea returned and he put it down to the flight and the excitement. He sat on a public bench and closed his eyes, enjoying the warm air on his face. He'd wait until the nausea passed then he'd go for a stroll.

CHAPTER
THIRTY-FOUR

Dr Petri stood behind his desk, staring at the city through the window, the grubby panes still streaky after yesterday's rain. It was unlike him to feel anxious – his position was remarkably stress-free and he enjoyed lecturing. This current situation with the British prying into their history was unfortunate and he considered himself unlucky to be caught in such a scenario. He intended to get out of it as soon as possible.

He glanced at the two folders on his desk. He'd gathered the papers together and arranged them for the chancellor. It could go one of two ways. If the chancellor wanted to unveil the truth, there would be a scandal, no doubt. The university's name would be dragged through the mud. Most of the mud would be made to stick on the psychology faculty and its overseas sponsor, although it could backfire. He doubted his own university carried much weight against the University of Cambridge.

Or, the chancellor could pick the other option, which would be to destroy the files and deny their existence. It was something they should have done years ago, but histories are complicated things, and Romania's was murkier than most. He should have stopped the British photographing some of the papers but they'd caught him off guard. The woman had been intriguing and distracting. He decided it didn't matter. He hadn't shown them everything, and it was easy to deny if the original was lost.

He was disturbed by a knock at the door.

'*Intră*,' he said, frowning at the clock. Most of his students should be gone by now. Perhaps the British had forgotten something. He waited but nobody entered. Another knock, softer this time.

'*Intră*,' he called again, more loudly this time, and headed for the door. He swung it open and stood back in surprise. The corridor was empty. Puzzled, he stepped forwards into the doorway. He turned his head to the left and felt the slightest of breezes to his right, not even a movement of air, but more an awareness – a subconscious sensation of somebody else sharing the same space.

He didn't get a chance to see who. A thin rope was placed around his neck and pulled tight so fast his breath wasn't even forced from his lungs. He tried to turn but the rope yanked backwards and he stumbled to the left, back through the doorway into his office. The door slammed and again he tried to turn to see his attacker but the rope was pulled tighter and his eyes watered. The pain in his neck was excruciating now, and he could feel a crunching sensation as his windpipe was crushed. His hands pawed at his throat but the rope was thin and dug into his skin. He couldn't grip it, even if he'd had the strength to do so.

A whisper, a hiss, then nothing.

His heartbeat was audible now, thumping fast in his ears, hot and disconnected. His diaphragm contracted and he convulsed, falling to his knees, unable to bend over because of the pressure holding him back.

His vision faded at the edges, a grey curtain beginning to close on the show, his part in it extinguished. He opened his mouth twice but his jaw locked. The same sensation of losing the ability to move his muscles spread through his neck and into his body. His hands fell away and his legs folded at the hip. Face down, the brown wooden floor faded to grey, then black.

Then it was gone. His heart stopped a few seconds later.

CHAPTER THIRTY-FIVE

'OK?' Sophie emerged from the faculty building. Her hair fluttered in the wind as she bounced down the steps. It brought a smile to Alex's face, in spite of the nausea. He was surprised. She hadn't been gone long. Sophie paused at the bottom. It looked as though she was catching her breath. Alex thought he saw pain in her eyes.

'Why so quick?' he said, puzzled. 'No luck?'

Sophie glanced at her watch. 'I've been gone twenty-five minutes,' she said, giving him a blank look. She paused, staring up at the sky, stretching her neck.

'But no,' she said, 'no luck. Despite giving the archivist a verbal tour of my life, followed by a tour of his life in broken English, he wouldn't budge. No access without Dr Petri or the chancellor.'

Alex checked his watch. He felt as though he'd just sat on the bench five minutes ago, the sun and warm air permeating his anxiety and calming his body. His daydreams had begun as complicated puzzles, picturing mind experiments on young children, wondering what they had managed to achieve. Was Victor Lazar a success or a failure in experimental terms? What were they trying to create, and for what purpose? Victor was deranged. Confused and corrupted. Full of vengeance and hatred. A victim of abuse, could he be blamed? Where was the line drawn?

The puzzles had faded and the daydreams had turned to Sophie. He didn't need her here. He shouldn't have brought her. Why had he?

'So perhaps we'll come back tomorrow,' he said.

Sophie shrugged.

'Until then—'

'Dinner,' said Sophie. 'First thing to do in a new city, apart from work, is eat.'

'Done,' said Alex. Their eyes locked again and this time neither of them broke it.

'But I thought you didn't travel?' he said.

Sophie looked surprised, caught off guard. Alex noticed but didn't react.

'I don't,' she said. 'Still a good idea though?'

'It is.'

'OK then,' said Sophie. 'There's a place not far from here. Good reviews. Authentic.'

They ordered quickly, following recommendations from the waiter. Alex's dish turned out to be a grilled spiced sausage, while Sophie was given a stew of some kind. She thought it tasted like pork, but couldn't be sure. Alex insisted on French wine despite the hefty mark-up. With all that had happened he at least needed something familiar. The restaurant was busy and full of locals, which was a good sign. They paid little attention to Alex and Sophie, who asked to be tucked away in a corner, away from the main bar.

Dinner was good but the conversation was strained. Alex tried to talk about the orphanage, but Sophie withdrew and kept glancing at

Alex when she thought he wasn't looking, searching his face. When he made eye contact she looked away.

'Why did you stop for so long?' Sophie asked, sipping her wine. 'Working criminal cases. What happened?'

Alex sipped his own wine and studied Sophie. Given what she'd told him about her background, however untrue, he felt he owed her an explanation.

'I combined some of my techniques,' he said. 'It didn't go so well.'

Sophie leaned in but didn't answer.

'I was asked to consult on a case. Fratricide – a man's brother had been murdered in a violent attack and he was prime suspect. He didn't deny it, but sat tight and let the police run all over him. He was confused, withdrawn, crying out for help. The CPS insisted on a psych evaluation.'

'Did he do it? Kill his brother?'

'Oh, he did it, but the police investigation was full of holes and mistakes. They were getting nowhere – no evidence, nothing. As part of my assessment process I added hypnotic regression to my standard neuropsychological evaluation.'

'He agreed to that?'

Alex cleared his throat. 'Not exactly. He was confused. It was a fine line. That wasn't the issue.'

'Then what was?'

'I tried to take him back to the date of the murder. I got a complete blockage. No way through. He'd done it, as was discovered much later, but he had no recollection of it.'

'So?'

'While he was under he went back much further, to the birth of his daughter and before. Several years of regression.'

'Which revealed?'

'Nothing at the time. But the case collapsed soon afterwards and he was released. He went straight home and murdered his wife and daughter. He stabbed each of them ten times. I was shown the crime scene photo. It still haunts me.'

Sophie put her glass down, picking at one of her fingernails.

'He was caught a few hours later. And do you know what he did? He asked the police to thank me.'

Alex took several deep breaths. He hadn't talked about this for a long time, and he was finding it harder than he'd anticipated.

'He killed his brother for having an affair with his wife. He discovered it when he caught them in the act. What he didn't know was the affair had been going on for many years. Right back, in fact, to before the birth of his daughter.

'During our session he regressed and unearthed memories that should have stayed hidden. Memories of conversations between his brother and his wife around the time of his daughter's birth.'

Sophie gasped. 'She wasn't his daughter?'

'She wasn't. They confirmed it post-mortem.'

'It isn't your fault.'

'He never knew until I put him under. He never realised. I forced his mind to surface thoughts and memories that should have stayed hidden. His psyche had hidden them for a reason. Because of what I did, he killed his wife and her child.'

Alex drained his glass. He placed it on the table and twisted it in his hands, pausing before continuing. 'After that case I realised the destructive power of my profession when we get it wrong. We understand so much, yet so little. Delving into people's minds is an immature science, even for those of us who have studied it for years. I was wide of the mark and couldn't risk it happening again. That's why I stopped working for the CPS and entered private practice.'

'I'm so sorry,' she said, extending her hand across the small table.

Alex took it. Her palm felt soft, her fingers fidgeting, but she used them to caress the back of his hand.

'But it didn't solve anything,' he said. 'Private work is lucrative, sure, and sometimes interesting, but it's not where my heart is. I went a little self-destructive afterwards. I'd always been emotionally distant from Grace, never able to commit myself in the way I knew I should. Does that sound odd?'

Sophie shook her head. Her eyes dropped to the table. She examined his hand as she traced her finger lightly over the back of it.

'I always looked at my parents and saw such a disaster. I guess I never really believed that, coming from them, I could make a normal family of my own. My training should have told me otherwise, but it's much easier to dish advice out than it is to take it oneself.' He paused, wondering why he was telling Sophie all of this. Wondering why he felt so comfortable doing so.

'My vision became self-fulfilling. I collected all of my stresses and insecurities and destroyed the perfect family I could have had. I was aware of the damage I was doing, but ignored it, throwing myself into work and pretending things would work out.

'After the failed case, well, that was the final straw. I shut Grace out and did things I'm not proud of, searching for an escape. I was unfaithful and spiralled into self-pity for a good few months, drinking myself into such a mess I would sleep in my office rather than go home. It wasn't long before Grace asked me to leave.'

Sophie nodded, holding his hand, not talking or judging, just listening. Alex breathed, feeling a weight lifting from his shoulders. A brief confession of sorts, and good for him. His unease at Sophie's behaviour loosened and his anxiety dropped. He realised he'd been hunched, tense in the neck and back. As he gazed up he thought he saw the same relaxation in Sophie's eyes. She looked exhausted, but comfortable with him. Her own frequent anxiety seemed spent, if only for now. Alex felt himself wanting to prolong this moment for as long as he could. He put his other hand over hers, not wanting to say anything for fear of breaking the spell.

It had been his turn to open up. Something he'd hardly ever done with Grace, and never with Jane. The act of doing so was therapeutic in itself, but with Sophie it felt intimate. Whatever haunted her, she related in some way to what he'd said. The trauma he'd experienced triggered not just empathy but something deeper in her. Understanding. It gave Alex comfort – to have broken through whatever wall she put up. She was letting him in.

It should have been like this with Grace. He should have taken the help she offered. But he had been too raw – the pain too recent, too intense – and he'd pushed her away, seeking comfort from other sources. It had been nothing but a cheap high, an ego boost. His marriage, already on shaky ground, had not been able to withstand it.

Sophie left her hand in his and downed her wine before topping it up again, almost to the brim. She did the same to his glass. Alex felt his stomach flutter.

His strange attraction to Sophie was at tipping point. He felt on the edge, ready to commit either a misguided betrayal of trust or a leap into a strange new relationship. Alex felt lost, and she seemed to know it.

'Let's go,' she said, draining her glass. Alex tried to do the same, as Sophie led him away from the table.

They left the restaurant barely talking. The night was just getting started as far as the city was concerned, but they headed away from the noise. Alex scanned for a taxi as they walked, avoiding growing crowds of people out for the night. Laughter seeped out of nearby bars and the odd drunk barged past. Alex focused on his thoughts and slid a Xanax into his mouth to combat the growing anticipation in his gut.

The taxis were plentiful and they hailed one within a few minutes. They sat close in the back seat of the taxi, their legs touching. Sophie made no move to separate. Alex felt his excitement surge. He tried to read her eyes, but it was impossible. They sucked him in and made him feel lost, insignificant, as if she had the universe on her shoulders.

She bit her bottom lip, the corners of her mouth flaring. Her eyes were darting between his eyes and his lips. She flicked her hair back from her shoulders, her hand lingering, playing with a few strands. Her eyes didn't leave him.

In the hotel they climbed the stairs, silent on the thick carpet. Alex's heart pounded, his thoughts lingering on the brief touch in the car. He had a few seconds before they reached their rooms. He opened his mouth to speak but his voice caught in his throat. He swallowed and the moment was gone.

But Sophie stopped outside her room and rested her head against the door before turning towards him. Her eyes were wide and her lips parted.

She opened the door to her room and held it open. Alex raised his eyebrows and she nodded, a small smile escaping before she slid inside.

As the door closed behind them, Alex reached out and took Sophie's hand.

'Look, I—' he began, but Sophie shook her head, putting her hand on his cheek and pushing her mouth against his. Alex didn't resist and they kissed. She tasted warm and unfamiliar, her smell sweet and musky. He pushed his tongue into her mouth and she put both arms around his neck, exhaling as he pushed her back against the wall.

Their mouths remained locked as he yanked at her skirt until it was hitched around her waist. His breathing was heavy and his hands shook as he held her, heart racing. Her physical attraction was seductive, but this was something more primal. She pulled at something deeper in him. He felt the need to hold her and protect her. He was overwhelmed with lust and her willingness thrilled him.

He caressed her with more care but still with urgency, and they undressed, gently at first but with more aggression as the moment took them.

Naked, they manoeuvred themselves around the small room and towards the bed. Sophie slid on to it with Alex in front of her. Without pause he climbed on to the bed and they embraced. He held her and she gasped, emitting a low groan, before rocking her hips, urging him to follow her lead.

As Alex moved and she responded, their eyes never broke contact and he felt closer to her than he had ever felt with a woman. He wasn't sure how long he would last, the taste and smell of Sophie driving him to the verge, not helped by the gasps of air escaping from her mouth. He could feel her breath coming in fits and starts.

They moved in sync for several minutes, eyes locked, until Sophie threw her head back, rocking her hips ever harder. Finally she trembled, while Alex was forced to slow, stopping every second or two. In response her movements intensified until she shuddered violently and gasped, letting out a cry, reaching up and digging her nails into Alex's chest. She held her position for several seconds, before falling back and taking several large breaths.

Alex climaxed and didn't try to stop it. When he opened his eyes, Sophie kissed him gently on the lips.

He put his head on her shoulder and panted into her neck for a few moments. 'I, uh . . .' he whispered. 'That was . . .'

Sophie shushed him and sat up, pulling the duvet over her legs. Alex leaned over and picked up her blouse and skirt from the floor. She pulled her hair back into a ponytail and they faced each other.

Sophie stared into space. The tension in her jaw was gone, but replaced with a look of longing. She looked sad. Alex shifted towards her. She glanced up.

'Are you OK?' he said, thinking it was a stupid question. Sophie looked flushed. He thought he saw disappointment in her eyes. Regret?

'I'm fine,' said Sophie. 'I'm fine.'

'You're amazing,' he said, then, struggling for words, 'I'm sorry if it was a bit . . . Perhaps it was inappropriate.'

She shook her head. A soft smile appeared. 'No, that's not it. It was lovely. It really was.'

Alex remained silent, worried he'd already spoiled the moment. He thought they could both do with a drink, and looked around for the fridge, when his phone buzzed, still in the pocket of his trousers on the floor.

He checked the time before he picked up. Nine thirty. He sniffed, cleared his throat and answered.

'Hartley,' said Alex. 'I wasn't expecting you to call. What's up?'

Hartley sounded distant, the phone connection crackling as she breathed heavily into the other end. 'I need you to come back, right away.'

Alex shuffled on the bed, attempting to cover himself. Sophie frowned, questioning.

'We'll be back tomorrow or the next day,' said Alex, shrugging at Sophie. 'Why—'

'Try to get a flight tonight if you can,' said Hartley.

'But we've discovered some startling information,' said Alex. 'We need to follow it up.'

Hartley sounded interested. Alex gave her a brief summary of their conversation with Dr Petri and what they'd found, reluctantly focusing away from Sophie and on to work. He offered to email some of the images across.

'You've poked a wasp's nest there,' said Hartley. 'You think you've learned as much as you can?'

'Maybe. Depends how much they'll open up to us.'

'I'm afraid my request is the same. Robert agrees. We need you back here.'

'Why?'

'We've had two murders in the city. The connections with this case have just been made. We think it was him.'

'Suicides?'

'I can't tell you over the phone, that's why I need you back here.'

Alex glanced at Sophie, who was watching his face. When she heard the word 'suicides' her expression changed. Her shoulders tensed and he saw the muscles in her face clench, her jaw go rigid. The relaxed Sophie had disappeared in an instant to be replaced with her former self. As Alex talked she looked at both palms, turning her hands over and examining her fingernails. She clenched two fists then relaxed them again. Her legs shuffled nervously.

Alex looked at his watch again. 'I guess we could get a late flight out?' He said this more as a question to Sophie, who paused before sliding off the bed to find her phone. A flicker of frustration crossed her face as she searched the airline website, but after a few moments, she nodded and mouthed 'Eleven p.m.'

'We'll be back in the UK early morning,' Alex said to Hartley. 'I'll call you then.' He hung up.

Sophie stared at her own phone for a moment before she stood, still naked, to gather her clothes.

Alex turned away, searching for his own. An awkward few minutes passed as they dressed in silence. 'We'd better get our stuff together,' he said, pausing at the foot of the bed.

Sophie came up next to him. She placed her hand on his chest, her eyes searching his face. 'I don't regret it, Alex,' she said. 'If that's what you think, you're wrong.'

Alex shook his head. 'I—'

'But we must go,' she said, turning away. She started throwing her few belongings into her suitcase. 'We'll talk later, I promise, when we get back to England.'

Alex let it go. There was something not quite right, something he was missing, but it must wait. They'd both stepped over the line, for better or worse, and it would run its course one way or another.

CHAPTER THIRTY-SIX

Alex ran his finger over the handle of his coffee cup. His heartbeat was a slow thud and his eyes were blurred. It was 5 a.m., the earliest he could get to HMP Whitemoor. Sophie was with him, slouched in a chair. She looked exhausted. Neither of them had managed to get any sleep.

Hartley looked expectant after Alex had given her a fuller account of their visit to the university in Bucharest. He'd forwarded some of the photographed copies of the documents by email, showing Hartley the other sheets now. She scanned the hastily scribbled translations by Dr Petri, putting the rest to one side.

'The lasting damage would of course depend on the nature of the experiments,' continued Alex, 'but these findings are damning. Victor was made this way. For lack of a better term, this is mind control, created through extreme drug and conditioning therapy. A cruel and irresponsible practice, and for what end? Some of the reports talked of unfortunate events. The translations of the others would no doubt reveal more.'

He paused to sip his coffee. 'That's it, I'm afraid.'

'Does Dr Petri know you're back here?' said Hartley.

'I left a message. He wasn't picking up – but it was the middle of the night. I'll try him again later today. I wanted to see him after his meeting with his chancellor.'

'And that's important to you, I understand. But, and forgive my bluntness, all I want to know is whether this gives us motive and targets – more targets, I should say.'

'Of course it gives you motive,' said Alex. 'The man was abused for years at the hands of the very people entrusted to protect and nurture him. He was an orphan, for Christ's sake. More than that, abuse by clinicians ranks as one of the worst abuses of power you can possibly achieve.

'Victor is driven by hatred, revenge and whatever damage was inflicted on him. He's far worse, in a clinical sense, than a psychopath. He's unclassifiable. I don't understand what brutal conditioning he was put through, but we should consider him deranged and unpredictable, and he has an incredible talent that he will use to exact his revenge. He has the ability to change people forever and they might not even know it.'

Hartley sighed long and hard. She pinched the bridge of her nose. Her clenched jaw revealed the face of a woman under pressure.

'As for the targets – you have the papers. You have names,' said Alex.

Hartley nodded. 'We've already matched some of them.' Their eyes met. 'Your connection to Southampton was corroborated,' she said, 'assuming this isn't all fabricated. Both Professor Florin and Professor Dumitru were mentioned in the accounts Dr Petri unearthed. There are more.' She reached for her bag and pulled out her phone. She sniffed, wiping her nose with the back of her hand, then swiped through some emails. 'I've been assigned two murder cases. The ones I mentioned on the phone. Separate, but connected. We've had confirmation of the victims' identities.'

Alex glanced at Sophie. Her face was blank, closed.

'Dr Emily Stevenson and Professor Nathan Peers. Both identified from the photo. She'd aged a lot, but it was her.'

'The circumstances,' said Alex. 'Suicide?'

'Yes, but we have witnesses from both.'

'And what did they see?'

Hartley cleared her throat and flicked through some notes on her phone.

'The first – a carer employed by Professor Stevenson. She was also attacked, we assume by Victor, but left alive.' She raised her eyebrows.

'Attacked how?' said Alex.

'Well, that's the weird bit. She was beaten and left unconscious. Left for dead.'

'That's not Victor's MO,' said Alex. 'He's not a physical man. Why didn't he control her?'

'I don't know,' said Hartley. 'She's traumatised. The fact we got a statement from her at all is a miracle.'

Alex muttered under his breath. 'But why—'

'He came at me but his eyes were strange,' read Hartley from the witness statement. 'He looked surprised. He kept repeating something, over and over, but I was screaming, I couldn't help it, and I couldn't hear what he was saying.'

Alex raised his eyebrows. Hartley nodded.

'And the professor?'

'Suffocated herself with a plastic bag. At least that's what the pathologist said. She didn't quite believe it – says it's impossible to kill yourself like that. You can't grip hard enough, not once your oxygen drops below a certain level.'

They shared a glance.

'And the other one?'

Hartley described the scene to Alex and Sophie. 'We barely got a statement. The wife claims she witnessed a man entering her bedroom, who handed her husband a knife. She watched him stab himself twice before collapsing.'

'When did these happen?' Alex had his eyes closed and was trying to contain the anxiety. The waves of it were increasing. He'd need more Xanax within the hour.

'Both in the last three days.'

'But no positive ID of Victor.'

'Nothing definite. And no DNA.' Hartley narrowed her eyes before flicking through more notes on her phone.

Alex leaned back, stretching his arms, trying to slow his breathing. He wondered where Robert was. The man had been acting increasingly erratically. The stress of this case was evident from the start, but Robert seemed overly vulnerable. Alex wondered if he should have mentioned it to the CPS, who could have had a word with the prison governor. But it was probably too late now. The police would lead on Victor, and Robert could take a back seat. Even more of a back seat than he had already.

'Does the description match for both?' he said to Hartley.

Hartley shrugged. 'Male, slight build, anywhere between five foot six and five foot ten. It was dark in both cases. We showed the witnesses photos of Victor but they couldn't be sure.'

'So you don't know if it's the same person.'

'The carer heard him speak. We can't be sure about the second, but who else has motive?'

There was a silence while each of them considered the implications. Hartley spoke first. 'We must assume this is Victor. Do you agree?'

Nods all around.

Alex glanced at Sophie. She was staring at her feet and didn't look up. Her eyes were bloodshot. Just tiredness. Perhaps.

'We must work on the assumption he's going after anybody involved with his childhood. Anybody linked to the orphanage and his time there.'

'Which is why I wanted you back here.' Hartley scratched her head, then picked at her fingernails. 'We're struggling to match anyone, or track them down. The dean of King's emphatically denied knowing any of the people in the photo. He circulated it to his management team and they all agreed. Their position is anybody could buy a lab coat with their logo on it, even thirty years ago. Some post-docs did just to impress colleagues. We've put an email out to psychology faculties in every university in the UK. So far, all deny knowing anything about any programmes in Romania.'

Alex raised his eyebrows. Could he blame them? Who involved in such a hideous – not to mention illegal – programme would own up to it? 'They'll know their lives are in danger, the people involved. Admit it or die.'

'Perhaps,' said Hartley. 'That's not what they're doing though. There are twelve people in the photo, but the only ones we can identify are the four who are dead.' She left the number hanging. Eight more murders was not an outcome anybody was willing to comprehend.

Alex examined the photo, feeling the thick paper, rough with age. The faded faces stared back at him, blank and sinister. These were men and women of science who had chosen a particular path. What caused people to pursue a goal even after the boundaries were broken and the consequences known? What pushed them to immoral and unforgivable experimentation on human subjects – and children at that?

The man at the back of the photo with bushy hair . . . The memory teased at the edge of his thoughts. Where had he seen him before? The lab coats were standard, but the particular cut and trim was niggling at him.

Alex had his own whites, of course, from his training and clinical days. Hung somewhere in his wardrobe, he doubted he'd ever wear them again. Not if he could help it. It reminded him too much of his hospital days, when his teachers and mentors led and he followed, through the depths of the wards and the humans who inhabited them, if only for a short time.

The photo reflected the light overhead and he tilted it in his hands. The man's face was humourless, but friendly. He held his chin to one side, not just for photos. Alex had seen him do it before. 'Him,' he said.

Hartley frowned. 'What?'

Alex tapped the photo. 'This man . . .'

'Who is he?' said Hartley, flicking though her notepad.

'I don't know his name, but I know somebody who does. Can you give me a day?'

Hartley narrowed her eyes. 'If you have an idea, I need to hear it.'

'Nothing concrete,' said Alex, swallowing. He was starting to feel nauseous. He needed to get out of there. 'I need to speak to somebody. It may be nothing.'

Sophie gave him a piercing stare but Alex held his tongue.

He wanted to be sure before sharing the revelation he'd just had.

Alex stood in the corridor, checking over his shoulder, anxious not to be overheard. He checked the time on his phone before he dialled. It was mid-afternoon and he hoped they were in. One of them would be, for sure.

'Alex.' His father's voice boomed down the line.

'Dad,' said Alex.

'Another call so soon,' said his father. 'To what do I owe the pleasure?'

His father's voice was still firm, but Alex detected a change in pitch. A slight catch in the throat that betrayed him.

'Why didn't you tell me you were connected to this, Dad?' said Alex. 'Why didn't you tell me you were in Romania?'

CHAPTER THIRTY-SEVEN

Elena was pretty. She was thirteen when Victor was eleven. They played together. She taught him tic-tac-toe. He looked up to her. She was one of the nice ones. Not like the boys. She was his first, after the treatment. It took several tries, but on the fifth attempt he did it.

She hanged herself from the swing set in the yard, just as he'd asked her to. It was his task, after all, and he would be punished until he succeeded. He still bore the scars on the soles of his feet from the beatings. Every night before bed, ten whacks with the bar. Heels mostly, but sometimes the arches. It meant he often crawled for days. The pain was terrible, but it faded in contrast to the other things. But it was her or him, at least that's what he told himself. He'd even resigned himself to death, not believing he could do it. But he did.

Repeatedly, over a period of several weeks, he whispered and let the words lie. At first his technique was poor, but he listened to the doctors and the therapists. He moulded the words into the poetry required to grab hold of her. And once he took hold, she had lost.

They found her in the morning. Her younger sister woke everyone with her screams. She vomited on the playground floor and was dragged away and beaten. Victor appeared with the others to stare at the limp, lifeless body of Elena, hanging by the rope he'd given her.

He'd won. She'd lost. That was the game.

There was no respect for what he'd done. The other children looked at him with empty eyes and hollow souls, knowing it could have been him up there, swinging with a white face and swollen purple lips.

He'd won, she'd lost, but the pain never stopped flowing.

Victor opened his eyes and rubbed away the fading image with his fists before sitting up and reaching for his glasses.

His mind was clearer today. The confusion that had reigned for many days was subsiding. To do what he was doing with such regularity was killing him. The sheer effort involved, to reach out and plant such a toxic seed, was the reserve of only the most talented and the most trustworthy. Victor had achieved such status before he left Comănești, and once learned the skill never left him. Victor could do what most of the other children could not, and his ability had festered and grown throughout the years.

It had drained him so much he'd been powerless for days. It caused the elephants to stampede in his skull. It caused fever and delusions, and it caused him to hear the screams of the dead.

Or were they his screams?

The pain would continue, for those who deserved it. The pain would be appropriate to their particular involvement.

The next one would pay for Elena. The doctor would feel what it was like for the young girl to lose her mind and lose her soul. To commit suicide, not because she wanted to, but because she had no choice, no control, and no other possible outcome.

It was simpler this way. Suicide was easy. To whisper across the void and watch while the other person lost control. To stay and pick up any stray thoughts was important. More than once a trance hadn't taken hold, and the subject had escaped, only to be driven insane by the messages dancing in their head. Many children had thrown themselves at the mercy of the doctors, pleading for the voices to stop. Unable to kill themselves and unable to continue living. An outcome as bad as death, for they never recovered. Those children were taken to the mountains. The echo of the gunshots lingered in his head, even now.

The stampede came on in waves. He laid his head back on the pillow, and made his plans.

CHAPTER THIRTY-EIGHT

The darkness was cold that night. It seeped through Victor's skin and he shivered, swallowing to keep the nausea at bay. There were few cars on the roads at this time, and he made good progress across the city.

He'd left his temporary lodgings behind and sought out a new place. Never stay in one squat too long – he'd learned to move fast in the first few months after escaping Comănești. He knew where he wanted to go next, and was pleased to find what he was looking for. The building was listed online, but was derelict and condemned. No matter. It would do for him, temporarily at least. The place held a certain fascination, even though it summoned memories best suppressed.

He drove and he dreamed. He dreamed of the prison. He saw the other prisoners with their foul mouths and confrontational eyes. He saw them again, lying in their own blood. He allowed himself a brief smile before the image faded, to be replaced by a long corridor with a concrete floor. It was grey and smelled of bleach. He could hear shouts in the background, boys and girls in pain. He drifted along the corridor, stopping at a metal gate. A woman to his right looked at him and slapped him hard in the face. He turned to look but no matter how far he turned, her face was too far around to see. She said something and it made him shiver. He knew her and she knew him.

The woman was gone and in her place somebody else stomped along beside him. Heavy footsteps and a jingling of metal, perhaps a keychain. A muffled voice whispered before the footsteps faded away into the distance, leaving him alone, facing a single grey metal door. It looked like the door to the medical room.

The hairs on his neck prickled as he touched the door. It was cold and smooth. It wouldn't move. He struggled, pushing it with both hands, but it remained locked and he didn't know where the key was. He took his hands away and closed his eyes.

The sirens woke him from his daydream.

His heart stopped and he straightened in the car seat as the blue lights appeared, flashing in his rear-view mirror. He held his breath long enough for the single police car and fire engine to overtake him and speed off into the night. His heart recovered, back to its thumping, reverberating around his skull like a kettle drum.

The car he'd stolen from the old lady worked well, but if the police were looking they'd find it. Although he'd made some minor alterations, swapping the number plates with a different car, it was a poor disguise and wouldn't last. He gulped with relief.

He slowed and stopped the car near the playground under a large oak tree, shielding it from the nearby lamp post, which was bright, despite the misty air. He checked his watch. Good. Two thirty-seven. Plenty of time.

He dragged the sleeping body of Professor Branson from the boot of the car across several feet of damp grass before dropping her on the soft surface of the playground. He went back for the rope and his bag. He touched the ground with his hands, marvelling at the forgiving rubber. It was an alien scene, for he'd never experienced a playground like this as a child. *People will do anything to protect their children*, he thought as he stood staring at the metal frame of the swings. Except for some children, who were forsaken before they ever set foot in a playground.

Professor Alice Branson had followed Victor out of her house and into his car on instruction. She'd slept when he told her to, and nobody was there to miss her. She wouldn't be discovered missing. She'd be discovered dead.

The swing set had two seats, attached by chains to a single thick metal bar which was sunk into the ground on each side. He sat on one and judged the height.

He wanted the scene to be accurate. It wasn't for the people who discovered her, although they would wonder why. It was all for her. She'd know. He wanted to see the realisation in her eyes before he gave her the final instruction. Every detail had to be correct.

First, he removed one of the professor's shoes from her sleeping body. He placed it under one of the swing seats, its laces loose. Next, he took the rope, measured out the correct length, and threw it over the top of the bar, so that the noose fell halfway towards the seat.

He left the rope and unpacked a dress from his rucksack. It was floral and vintage-looking. Simple white cotton patterned with faded yellow roses. He struggled to get the professor out of her pyjamas, storing them in his bag. He pulled the floral dress over her head. It reached her knees.

He lifted her into a seated position and sat behind her, pulling her hair back into a ponytail and securing it with an elastic band.

Floral dress with yellow roses and a ponytail. That was correct. That was how she needed to look.

He sat in silence for a moment, a stab of fear pushing at his stomach. Why did his head hurt so much? His doubts caused even more pain. His thoughts were sharp daggers in his temples. He held back the vomit but knew he must get on with it. It was the only thing that would make him feel better.

'Wake up, Alice,' he said. Barely a whisper, but he was close enough for the words to seep into her consciousness. She'd respond without delay.

The professor coughed and opened her eyes. She saw Victor's face and her mouth opened.

'Calm yourself,' said Victor. He whispered a combination of short phrases. The professor closed her mouth and looked puzzled for a few moments, her eyes searching.

'It is Alice, isn't it?' said Victor, standing up, giving her room to move.

She stood and stared at him, taking in the dark night, the playground. She glanced to the rope and back again. Victor could see she was struggling to comprehend the scene.

'Elena called you Alice once, do you remember? Forty-five.'

The professor took a few moments. She stared at the rope for several seconds before turning to Victor. Her eyes were wide now, the realisation surfacing.

She remembered.

Victor smiled. 'She was beaten for that. She was beaten for calling you Alice. Alice was her dead mother's name. Did you know that?'

Professor Alice Branson didn't move a muscle. Her body was paralysed and her mind was gripped in a vice, but her eyes betrayed everything.

'She was beaten and then she was killed. You made me kill her. You.' Victor walked towards the swings and checked the rope. 'She wore a small dress on the day she died.'

The professor looked at herself, at what she was wearing. Her eyes begged. Victor allowed her to find her voice.

'Please,' she said. 'It was . . .' Victor yanked the rope. It tensed and held tight.

She shook her head. 'I beg you—'

'And we begged you. Didn't we? I begged you. Do you remember?'

'I . . . I remember,' the professor stuttered. 'But we didn't know what we were doing. I was ambitious, I—'

'Enough,' shouted Victor, his rage surfacing. She had no right to provide any argument or excuses. She had no right to anything.

'Sit on the swing, Alice,' he hissed.

The professor moved as if led by an invisible chain. She climbed on, awkward in her dress and given her age. *She must be eighty years old,* thought Victor. He was happy he'd managed to find her before she died of natural causes.

'Do it, Alice,' whispered Victor. For the next thirty seconds Victor spoke, describing his wishes, pushing and prodding at the professor's mind, exploiting the gaps and the crevices, planting the seeds.

With eyes full of tears, the professor eased the rope over her head and tightened it. The other end was already knotted to the frame, creating a gallows. She must sit upright on the swing, knowing that if she fell, the rope would tighten. Her legs weren't long enough to touch the ground. It was a delicate balance, keeping her upright and seated. She sat motionless for several seconds as the swing wobbled beneath her body.

Standing a few feet away, Victor scanned the ground and the swings. It was nothing like the playground at Comăneşti but it would have to do.

'Swing, Alice. Swing,' said Victor, watching as the professor edged herself over the rim of the seat. 'I forgive you.'

Victor watched for three minutes. The two seats hung limp in the still air. The professor swung alongside, by her neck, her lips swelling as her body failed. Her eyes never leaving Victor.

It was the way he wanted it.

CHAPTER
THIRTY-NINE

In an alleyway across the street, Freak turned to Natalia.

'You were right. We couldn't have stopped it,' he said.

Freak had initially suggested going for Thirteen in the middle of the night, sneaking in and catching him by surprise, but she'd refused. She hadn't forgotten the children who'd tried that at Comăneşti. It happened, on occasion, and you had to be certain of victory.

Surprise was not enough to catch a talented master like Thirteen, and it could backfire. Thirteen could wake in shock, unleashing a torrent of damaging words, catching them both unprepared. She couldn't risk it. Her bosses wouldn't allow it.

It would be much safer to wait. She'd waited this long, watching, coercing, willing him into a controllable situation. She'd put in a Herculean effort over the weeks, existing in a world in which she would never live, but her efforts had so far resulted in failure.

She'd called her boss. He was unimpressed at her progress, issuing a string of Russian expletives over the phone, but didn't offer any further help. The idea of putting a bullet in Thirteen's head was still not acceptable. It would create more problems than it solved, and besides, he was valuable. She must handle it in her own time, so long as she didn't drag it out for too long. She'd pleaded with them and they'd shouted back, knowing her talent, knowing if she tried anything they had their own forms of punishment. The threat was ever-present.

The Russian – Nikolai was his name – taunted her. The man who'd approached them both when they were lost and roaming the cities, surviving, but nothing more.

He knew all about them, about Natalia, about Comănești and the failed experiments. He knew all about the group of psychologists and doctors who were hurriedly covering their tracks, paying their bribes and disappearing under their rocks in faraway countries. He was from the old world, he said. The stable Romania, under Russian control, before the usurpers ruined it. Before the revolution that destroyed their future. He explained what would happen to them in the new world, no longer protected by the Russian government and its allies. He told them they'd be hunted and killed. There was no place for people like them in the new Romania.

He had presented them with a way out and Natalia had no choice but to become a recruit. Their new boss had offered protection and the chance to participate in something greater than the botched experiments of Comănești. Away from the influence of the cowards in British scientific establishments and their governments. Free to make real progress.

But progress requires sacrifice, and in exchange for this opportunity – for that's how it was presented to Natalia – she would belong to them. She became one of them, and from then on she did their bidding. Her future suddenly had prospects. Dangerous and full of threats, but with prospects nonetheless. At least they'd live.

If the experiments continued then Natalia was not part of them. Their masters knew her capabilities and knew where things had gone wrong. They were merely tools now, and must be used or discarded. Freak was another matter, perhaps, but for now he was her ward.

'I know that look,' said Freak. He shuffled closer and held her arm. She didn't resist, and her body relaxed. There was no romance between her and Freak, not even friendship, not in the traditional sense. But they had comradeship: a solidarity obtained by suffering together, many times, and over many years.

'I'm tired of these stupid games,' she said.

'At least you get to meet people,' said Freak. 'I live in a car.'

She smirked, despite her growing despair. He was right. And it was better than being back there, with the Russian and his demands. He had her, mind and body, whenever he pleased. At least being on assignment gave her distance from that. At least, for these short few weeks, she belonged to herself.

'And they should be pleased, after the university.'

Natalia nodded, not without a hint of sadness. 'They seem keen on burying our history.'

'I don't object.'

'Let's hope they don't bury us with it,' she said.

They headed away from the park. Freak announced he was hungry and they found an all-night cafe on the high street. The neon sign said coffee, and the waiter behind the counter smiled. Freak took a table in the corner, away from the two other patrons, both overweight men, scruffy and disgusting, who looked Natalia up and down. One of them licked his lips and Natalia tried to shrink herself, appear unattractive. Freak often told her this was impossible. He said she had chiselled features, a button nose and piercing eyes. Men liked that sort of thing, he said. But she pulled a hood over and on to her forehead. At least she gave the appearance of someone not to be approached.

'Hi,' she said, walking up to the bar.

'Hi, yourself,' said the waiter. His smile was genuine, but he was greasy and ran his eyes too easily over Natalia's body, resting on her chest.

'Coffee, two,' she said, 'and two full breakfasts. No beans with one, extra tomatoes with the other.'

'Sure,' the man said, his smile disappearing at her cold manner.

'We've already paid,' she said, nudging him, her words and expressions doing the work. His face ruffled in confusion and she whispered to him, assuring him there was no problem. The money was already in the till. He'd put it there himself. He'd count it later, when his shift ended, and realise she was right.

'Oh,' he said. His face showed that the information still didn't quite compute and Natalia pushed again. She was too tired and on the verge of giving up when the cracks appeared.

'Sure. Thanks,' he said. 'Take a seat. It'll be right with you.'

Natalia sighed and shuffled over to Freak. He looked worried.

'You'll need to do better than that.'

'I'm tired, OK,' she snapped. One of the fat men glanced over. She glared until he turned back around.

'I mean it,' said Freak. 'What are we going to do with Thirteen if you're struggling this much?'

'I said I was tired.'

'You're acting like we've failed,' said Freak. 'You need to pull yourself together.'

'Shut up,' she said, and pushed the chair to one side, looking for the toilets. The ladies' room was cleaner than she had expected. The floor was ninety-nine per cent bacteria, but the toilet bowl had seen a cup of bleach in the last twenty-four hours. She closed the cubicle and leaned against the door.

Freak was right. She needed to sort herself out. For weeks she'd been watching their prey, either unable to do anything, or too scared. Both would see her fail, and she shivered at the thought of what might happen then.

Natalia imagined life alone, in hiding and being hunted. She'd been there before and had no desire to return to the cold mountains of her homeland. As teenagers she and Freak had struggled through the winters, practising their skills but failing many times. She remembered watching the snow fall, looking enviously at the warm lights of a house. Knocking on the door had always been her job, while Freak lurked in the shadows. They'd ask for refuge, Natalia nudging with her language while Freak waited, ready to jump in if needed. Several times the person who answered the door simply slammed it again in her face. Other times they announced they were calling the police, which sent them both running. On the rarest of occasions, Natalia was successful and the inhabitant would open their door wide, puzzled, but accepting. Then Natalia would go to work, planting the seeds, widening the cracks, attempting to manipulate for as long as she could.

But her skills were incomplete and fragile back then. In the face of somebody such as Thirteen, that would have been fatal. It had taken her many years to build herself up to where she was now. Still, she worried.

But she would obey their orders. She would come through. More time, that's all. More time. Thirteen would slip up soon, and then they'd pounce.

She hoped she was right. There were no alternatives.

CHAPTER FORTY

'I wasn't in Romania,' said Rupert, 'not at first, anyway.'

The two of them were sitting in Rupert's study, having refused lunch from Catherine, who had fussed around Alex and expressed concern over his weight. She left a tray of drinks and went to lie down, with a promise to make tea as soon as she had the energy.

'I don't believe you,' said Alex. 'These people,' he tossed his father a copy of the photo from Dr Petri's files, 'they're your people. At least one of them was. The guy in the top left, I recognise him. He used to come here when I was young. He brought me a book once. A hardback. Enid Blyton. He's a friend of yours.'

Alex's father examined the photo for several moments before placing it on his desk. He closed his eyes and bit his lower lip. He pushed back from the desk and stood, pacing to the shelves, scanning the books.

'Do you know what it was like back then?' He paused at a particular book and wiped some dust off the top of it, frowning. 'It wasn't enough to earn your degree. It was good, of course, but not enough. Not for King's. Those who had higher aspirations . . . Well, there were other things to be done. There were demands.'

Alex kept his anger in check. He didn't want to listen to one of his father's stories, but he needed something.

'This research was state-sponsored. Did they tell you that? I doubt it. It wasn't going anywhere here though,' said his father, 'nor in the

US either. You can guess why. But the breakthroughs – accidental, of course – couldn't be ignored.'

'They could if they were inhumane.' Alex bit his tongue.

'Don't be so small-minded,' said his father. He looked genuinely troubled. 'Advancement has never been achieved by the meek. We needed to be brave and bold.'

Rupert shook his head as if Alex was the one who should be apologising. Alex wanted to object, but let his father continue.

'I would have thought your first reaction to this would have been excitement, not disgust.' Rupert studied his son's face, and Alex prayed he wasn't giving anything away. He cursed his father yet again for being right. Of course Alex was excited. If he was honest, excitement was what drove him to continue with Victor's case. But it didn't mean he was devoid of a conscience.

'Professional curiosity,' said Alex, 'of course.'

'Please, Alex,' said his father, 'be a man and admit it. If you'd been given the chance to study this phenomenon, as part of a funded programme, you'd have taken it. As we did. The first experiments were incredible, centuries of old theory thrown out the window. It was control, pure and simple.' He searched Alex's face. 'We've always tried to govern the physical. We can capture people, imprison them, force them to do certain things with physical threats. But we discovered the holy grail in our research. Controlling a person's thoughts through suggestion, nothing more. It's not crazy and it's not magic. We proved that. Advertisers have been doing a very basic version of it for decades. They know how to make people do things, buy things, and behave in a particular way, although they clearly fall far short of what we achieved. We distilled the theory, purified and concentrated it. We developed subjects with the ability to use language in ways we didn't think possible. They could grab the mind of another and manipulate it, completely and utterly dominate it, removing conscious control and passing it to the subject.'

His father's eyes were sparkling. 'I know what you're thinking – why such extreme experiments? Couldn't we use it to persuade people to obey the law, or buy more cars, or something quite mundane and harmless? Maybe, but mediocrity wasn't the point. The point was to explore the boundaries. The extreme. How completely could you control another person?'

Alex shook his head. 'It doesn't justify . . . The kids were competing against each other. We've got some of the trial notes. And it doesn't say what happened to them. Where did they all go?'

'I know that what you found may shock you,' said Rupert, 'but that wasn't the whole story. Most of the research was nothing like that. There was one project . . . the orphanages . . . yes, it may have got out of hand. But the programme as a whole was not—'

'They were killing each other!' Alex shouted. He bit his tongue and forced his breathing to slow. 'And they all disappeared. Where did they go?'

'I told you,' said his father, 'most of the programme was not like that. Believe me when I tell you this. What we did in Comăneşti wasn't what we set out to do. But by the time we'd reached a certain point, there was no going back. It was out of our hands; the government was running the show. They dictated the tests and we had no other option. The competitions were part of the training. The only way to develop such strong ability was to fight the mind of another with the same ability.'

'You're trying to distance yourself from it now?' said Alex.

'I'm trying to explain. My days in this field may be over, but yours aren't. You could continue. I—'

'Why children?' Alex couldn't help himself. 'Orphans? What's wrong with the normal test subjects? The military, adult volunteers, anything?'

'Ah . . .' His father waved a finger at him. 'It didn't work with adults. We tried, of course, but it didn't take. The phenomenon we studied must be developed in the formative years of brain development – certainly before the prefrontal cortex matures, and the speech centres in the cerebral cortex. They are vital for the persuasive language development.' His father cleared his throat. 'The younger, the better.'

Alex observed his father's excitement and passion, but the reality of Victor Lazar tempered his own mood. He calmed himself.

'That doesn't justify using foreign orphaned children,' he said. 'You say it was just one element of the programme. How did it come about? Why them?'

'Ah, that's where we can't venture, I'm afraid.'

'Can't?'

'We swore, and more than that, we signed. State secrets, so they say. We were just a group of like-minded scientists, above the petty tugs of politics. Science must maintain that, or we're all doomed. The Romanians offered something the Russians couldn't. The US was out because of its irreconcilable differences with the Kremlin. And of course the Warsaw Pact meant we couldn't discuss it above board. All the politics was above us, or beneath us, depending on what you value.

'The Romanian revolution changed all that, but we struggled to maintain contact and the Foreign Office thought it best we cut all ties and disappear until things had settled. It wasn't good for the British to be associated with a regime that had just been terminated. Our government was very pleasant about the whole thing, but made clear the penalty if we ever spoke about it. Sorry. I can't say any more. Not even to you, Alex.'

His dad stood, impassive, scratching his chin.

'Why did you get me involved?' said Alex. 'Why did you recommend me for Victor's case?'

'I didn't know it was connected. Not at first. As far as I knew, all of those subjects disappeared in the winter of '89. The revolution left very few stones unturned. I didn't know what happened to them . . . at first. That wasn't my choice, I should add. Their military got worried, twitchy. They decided to eradicate some of the undesirable elements of their previous government. We had no way of stopping it.'

Alex watched as his father talked impassively about the disappearance of dozens of children. He knew his father was cold, but had never dreamed of the depths of his detachment.

'I wondered though,' his father continued. 'There may be others in another project, elsewhere. If you got involved – it couldn't be me, you see – we might salvage something from the old research. You might have learned something and we could have . . . perhaps together . . . pursued it again?'

His father looked wistful, his eyes glazed. Alex, with a horrific realisation, saw the signs he'd been trained to look for.

'You're obsessed,' said Alex, standing up and stepping back towards the shelves, away from his father.

His father whirled on his feet. 'It's not obsession. It's called dedication. Use your skills, Alex, for God's sake. We could have had it, before the Russians. Before anyone.'

Alex shook his head. 'If this was an arms race, you lost. I hope the Russians did too.'

His father's stare was piercing. 'It wasn't a game, Alex. Not like your pathetic little practice, treating people who have no right to use talent like ours. We are destined for greater things, son.'

Alex turned and breathed out, counting to ten, then to twenty. He walked over to the sideboard and the tray his mum had left. He poured two glasses of iced water from a jug.

Facing his father, he tempered his anger and resisted the urge to tell Rupert exactly what he thought. It was typical of the man. The arrogance was always there. Inbuilt? Perhaps, although maybe his dad had no choice. Nurture is a powerful mould, and Alex's grandfather had always been distant. But what did that say about Alex? Was he doomed to follow? Alex always thought he possessed the emotional intelligence his father so clearly lacked, a result of watching and caring for his mother during his early years. But he'd already managed to ruin his own family, albeit in a different way.

Alex closed his eyes and drew several large breaths. It was time to change tack. He'd achieve nothing if they fought. He needed to be the bigger person – prove he had the skills to do that.

'I need to know what he's capable of,' said Alex, handing his father one of the glasses. 'Background aside. I can't change that. But what can he do now?'

Rupert put his hand to his mouth. He took a quick sip of his water, his hand trembling. Alex had never seen his father shaking like this before.

'I accept you don't approve,' he said, deep in thought. 'There are limits. There are cracks – I think. You might be able to . . .'

'What?'

'Catch him in the weak hours. Afterwards.' His father screwed his mouth up. 'We found many of the children suffered after using their ability – after a difficult session. They'd complain of headaches, nausea. Some of them vomited immediately. A handful were bedridden for days with fever. We could never pinpoint exactly what caused it. Tests revealed severe serotonin imbalance; it fluctuated for days. Temporary, but quite debilitating. Akin to severe anxiety or panic disorder.'

'Which would explain his capture and stay at prison?'

'It might.'

'But even if it does, what is it he can do now? What damage can he inflict before we catch him again?'

His father put his glass on a shelf. He nodded, looking thoughtful. 'He may be able to control people, physically and mentally,' he said. 'But it's not absolute.' Rupert frowned, looking for the right words. 'He can't read people. They can't read thoughts, or conjure up memories, or persuade people to give up information they don't want to. That was out of reach. We never figured out where to look . . .' Rupert's voice faltered. 'But physically . . . that was where the real power was. We got them to a point where they could grasp another mind and treat them like a puppet.'

'Hence the name in the files,' said Alex.

His father just stared.

'But Victor can do more than that,' said Alex. 'He walked right out of HMP Whitemoor. Nobody remembers him leaving. What did he do to the guards?'

His father's face hardened. 'Hard to say. The persuasive technique leaves little footprint in the target's mind. Sometimes the subject would remember, sometimes not. It's possible, if Victor has had decades of practice, he knows how to remove the traces.'

Alex thought back to his own encounter in Victor's cell. The memory was clear as could be.

'That's not reassuring,' said Alex. 'How can we know who he's spoken to, who he's controlled?'

'I don't think you can,' said his father. His eyes narrowed. 'Although I think he would need to be close to the person to control them. The experiments confirmed that early on. It's not all verbal, you know. His facial expressions, body language – it all contributes. He can't do it remotely, on the phone or suchlike. At least . . .'

'At least what?'

'I don't know, of course. The experiments were out of our control by that point, but—'

'For God's sake, spit it out,' said Alex. He was losing his temper again.

'There were a few cases. Not many, but a few. The results went beyond our wildest expectations. We saw things we didn't understand – results that defied logic, not to mention science. There was one particular child . . . He had an inexplicable ability. Something altogether different. He . . . It was intriguing, but I don't know what happened to him.'

'What could he do?'

Rupert frowned, and again his hands shook. Alex didn't know whether it was nerves or excitement at recalling his precious experiment.

'That's the thing,' said his father. 'He couldn't do what the others could, but he knew when they were doing it.'

'Explain.'

'I can't. One of the youngest subjects, a boy, had a sixth sense, although we'd never categorise it as such – we'd have been laughed out of the faculty and our careers. But he gave us all the creeps. He was able to sense when the other children were being tested. I read the reports. He'd cry out from his dorm – the other side of the orphanage from where the trials were taking place. There was something . . . I don't know. It went wrong. We stopped his treatment early.'

His father turned away.

'There were others. Identical twins. Girls. The mirror sisters, the staff called them. They could cause hallucinations, forcing daydreams and extreme paranoia. One would start and the other would finish. They seemed to enjoy it. They were . . . not evil, but uncontrollable. They had to be . . .' His father cleared his throat and shuffled away.

Alex decided not to press the matter. Of all the monsters his father might have created, and the atrocities he'd been party to, Alex only cared about one right now.

'So there's no telling exactly what Victor Lazar can do?' said Alex. 'Is that what you're telling me?'

His father scanned his bookshelves and huffed. 'You're familiar with the method of loci?'

'Memory palace,' said Alex. 'Yes. A technique for improving memory. The creation of a spatial framework – mentally storing items in rooms, then walking through the palace to remember them.'

His father frowned and pulled out a thin journal. It had a plain blue cover. 'The trance – if that's what we call it – can be at different levels, from waking dream to deep torpor. You know this. We were experimenting with ways to walk oneself out of a deep trance using a similar loci technique.'

Alex recalled his own trance at the hands of Victor. He had been physically handicapped, yet his mind had remained clear. 'Victor's victims weren't all in deep. Some of them knew exactly what they were doing. You could see it.' He shivered as he remembered the prison CCTV. An inmate, terrified, as he slit his own throat.

His father shrugged, handing Alex the journal at an opened page. 'Same technique. Read it. I'm not saying we made much progress.'

Alex glanced at the page. It was untitled, with his father's name printed at the top.

'Try it though.' His father frowned again. 'I could never master it myself, and I left before I had to.'

He walked over to his safe in the corner of the room. He crouched and spun the combination lock back and forth until it clicked open.

'I have something else,' he said. 'Blunter. Classified. But I suppose it doesn't matter now.' He rummaged through several folders until he found what he was looking for.

'The staff working with the children were at risk, obviously. In the early days we relied on obedience, but as the children's abilities grew, we realised obedience wasn't enough. We had a separate research strand focusing on drug resistance. It was partially successful.'

'Drug resistance to being controlled?' said Alex.

'Yes. It requires a specific combination. Benzos and two others. They act to inhibit the precuneus – the area of the brain that can be captured and controlled. We found it successful around sixty per cent of the time.'

'Sixty? That leaves a lot of room for error.'

His father didn't respond, but scribbled the name of the drugs on a sheet of paper.

'You might have a hard time getting hold of this last one,' he said. 'It's not in vogue at the moment.'

Alex took the list. His face flushed as he read the first item: 'Alprazolam or similar fast-onset benzodiazepine'. Xanax was the brand name for alprazolam. On its own it didn't help matters. He read the other two drug names: sumatriptan and clozapine. He thought the first was a painkiller. The second was an antipsychotic, hardly used these days.

He tucked the list away and studied his father, who was looking increasingly uncomfortable, sweat beading on his brow.

'You didn't think to give me this when you recommended me for the case? When you first heard why Victor had been arrested? You didn't think to tell anyone?' Alex was aware his voice was raised again.

'It would have raised too many questions. Why would I approach the CPS with this? What do you think they would do?'

'What they'll do now anyway,' said Alex. 'The story is out. You can't hide this.'

His father turned abruptly and paced. He reached for his water glass and clenched it in his hands, draining it in one gulp.

Both men stood with their thoughts. Alex thought his father looked old. Whatever greatness he thought he'd achieved was coming back to haunt him. He still couldn't see it. He still believed his work could continue.

'He's going after you,' said Alex. 'All of you.'

Alex's father shook his head. 'He doesn't know about us. He couldn't.'

'He's found four already,' said Alex. 'If I could find this information, so could he. I've met him. You must have guessed this might happen?'

Alex's father frowned and looked again at the faded photo of his colleagues. 'It was never meant to leave King's. I don't . . .'

'The orphanage journals and trial data,' said Alex. 'It was discovered in the university archives. How do you know he hasn't got your names?'

Alex frowned at his father's lack of concern. Rupert's face was still one of superiority, of denial.

'He is going to kill you if he finds you,' said Alex, raising his voice, the impatience creeping through, reinforced by an increasing sense of urgency. 'Do you realise? You're not safe. Mum's not safe. I—'

There was a knock at the study door and his mum popped her head around. 'Are you two OK in here?' she asked, her voice trembling, as it often did when Alex's dad was around. 'I could hear raised voices. Talking about work? Do you want some drinks? Food? You might be more comfortable in the living room.'

His father turned away and stared at the window. Alex shook his head, his anxiety bubbling up. 'We're OK, Mum.'

She slipped out, backing away.

'You must leave,' said Alex. 'Both of you. And you need to help the police identify the others – anybody else involved in this.'

'They won't . . .' His father eased himself into a hardwood chair tucked against the bookshelves.

'Won't what?'

'Admit any of it.' He studied his fingernails. 'Even if I did tell the police their names. They'll deny everything. They won't come with you.'

'They will if they think they're being hunted. Or do their egos prevent them from admitting they could be in danger?'

'These were great men and women, Alex. Thinkers ahead of their time. They were—'

'Child abusers,' said Alex. He shook his head as his father tried to protest. 'Save it. They made a breakthrough – astonishing. But it doesn't change what they did, and what they were party to. Perhaps it might be better to let Victor have them, but I have a conscience, even if you don't.'

It felt good, lecturing his father like this, even if he didn't believe in his own conviction. He wanted to stop Victor, no doubt about that, but he wasn't sure he could have cared less about his dad's precious colleagues. His father though . . . Well, they were still related, and his mother needed him.

Alex was distracted as his phone buzzed. 'We need to get you and Mum safe,' he said to his dad, before answering. It was Hartley on the phone. 'Yes?'

'Do you have anything for me?'

Alex paused. His father's eyes met his. 'I might,' he said.

'Good,' said Hartley. 'Because things are getting messier.'

'How?'

'We found Damian Reed, the prison guard. He's dead. Overdose.'

Alex hadn't anticipated any other outcome for the poor guard. It was shocking nonetheless.

'The bodies are stacking up, Alex,' said Hartley. 'And we don't know who's next. The information you gathered in Bucharest isn't enough. We're coming up with blanks. If you know anything, we need to talk.'

Alex agreed to come in. He hung up and told his father to start packing. 'I don't want to hear it,' he said, over Rupert's objections. 'If you don't care about yourself, please do it for Mum.'

He left with a promise to be back again as soon as he was able. He suspected Hartley might want to talk to his father.

Alex wasn't done with him yet either.

CHAPTER
FORTY-ONE

Victor watched from across the road, several houses down. He hid himself behind a large Transit van as he watched the young man speed away in his Porsche.

He was confused. The man walking away, he'd seen him at the prison. Dr Carter? Why was he here? Victor felt his control slipping. Like fragile china, his plan was cracking. What did the doctor know? What had he been told?

'Can I help you?' A voice in his ear. A young man appeared by the van. He wore a brown uniform and held a parcel under his arm. He looked suspicious of Victor, who was inches from the driver's door, peering through the windows at the Madisons' house.

Distractions, all the time. Why couldn't people leave him alone? His concentration was being ruined. Victor examined the list etched into his head. He saw the stained paper and the faded serif print, detailing the names of staff and their places of work. He saw the soldiers, laughing at him, their laughter tinged with fear. He remembered the promise he'd made to himself.

His head thumped. He forced himself to look at the house, the normal, modest brick that held the devil.

The man who lived here was top of the list. He was the fiend who played the fiddle and made his minions dance. There were others but this man was evil, and Victor reserved a special hatred for him. He was not here today to take this man's life and forgive him. He was merely passing, ensuring that when the time came, he would strike with the same wickedness he'd been shown as a child.

But the presence of the prison doctor was concerning. What were they doing together? Were they laughing at him, taunting him for his weakness?

'No, you can't help me,' Victor said, turning to stare at the young man. 'You should get into your van and stay there. When you leave, in ten minutes' time, you won't remember me.'

Victor continued to stare at the man and whispered several phrases, his voice clear and concise. Pushing, gently at first, then with more urgency. The man nodded, slowly, before opening the van door. He climbed in and sat, facing forward, his arms resting on the wheel.

The headache hit like a thunderclap and Victor cursed in his native tongue. The delivery driver didn't flinch. He sat, dribbling out of the right side of his mouth, eyes glazed.

Victor staggered away, around the corner of the street into the main road. His car was unlocked and he crawled in, rummaging for painkillers. A police car cruised by, neither of the uniformed officers glancing his way. Victor's heart missed a beat as the car slowed, but then sped up, passing the turn-off to Dr Rupert Madison's house and continuing on the main road, headed out of the city.

He would allow himself two hours' rest, after which his next visit was due. He had a feeling he must speed things up. He hoped, for Laura's sake, the next person on his list was ready, waiting for their death.

Victor parked in a bay marked 'Visitors'. UCL hospital was undergoing renovations. It looked as if the old concrete façade and slit windows were being replaced with an abundance of glass walls. Victor hid his disgust as he entered the emergency room, pausing to study the map and several of the corridors leading to other parts of the hospital.

He sauntered through a set of double doors, heading for a grouping of departments in the mental health wing. He found himself in a long grey corridor with direction markings on the floor. To each side were wards, labelled with letters.

He approached one and listened. There were beeps and hisses, overlaid with the squeaking and banging of staff going about their business: nurses checking on patients, cleaners dusting around the beds. It was like any other hospital ward, except that the sounds unearthed flashes of memory that sprang into his consciousness for seconds before disappearing again. He crept into the ward, mesmerised. He glanced at the walls and the ceiling. It was all unfamiliar. His own treatment had never warranted the safety of a real hospital.

He touched the end of a vacant bed. Cold metal. There was a table next to it, extendable over the bed, so patients could eat, or rest a book. Victor had a flash of a plate. It had cold bread on it with a lump of salted butter. A doctor had leaned over and told him to eat it.

He shook his head and backed out of the ward. He'd never stayed in such a place, but he remembered the sick ward at Comăneşti. The metal beds and the sounds. It was all tucked away in there. Victor struggled to forget.

Heading for the next ward, Victor paid more attention to the people he saw. The face was etched into his memories. The professor would be older, much older, but Victor would never forget him. The professor worked here as a consultant psychiatrist, with hundreds of people under his care. Victor knew how caring the man could be. He'd remind him of it.

Victor kept his head down and shuffled along. He was practised in keeping to the side, using the posture and mannerisms that guaranteed nobody noticed him. They wouldn't see him come or go, and few would remember he was ever here. He'd persuade people if he had to, but his energy was best saved.

Pausing to take his bearings, Victor leaned against a row of chairs. They were empty, and he sat on one, swallowing the frequent acid that insisted on forcing its way into his throat. He couldn't shake the feeling something was wrong. He pictured the house of Dr Madison again. He saw the other young doctor leaving in his grotesque sports car.

What if the devil had some other plan? Did he know all about Victor and his journey? Surely he must know righteousness would prevail? There was no avoiding fate. And yet, something tugged at Victor's gut. He'd had all the time in the world. Now, he sensed the distant urgency of a countdown.

He stood, lurching forward, barging into an elderly couple. They apologised. He didn't. He shuffled off towards what he knew to be the correct department. If time was running out, he needed to be faster, more efficient. He could do it. Swallow the pain and just do it.

Victor was seething now, furious his hand was being forced. How dare they? How dare they make him feel rushed? He was executing what he knew to be the correct course of action. There was no option other than to forgive these people. Why couldn't they see that?

He turned a corner and stopped in his tracks. At the far end of the corridor was a reception desk, quiet, with one lady behind it, peering over her glasses at the two people in front of her. Victor gulped back his anger and frustration. The two people were police officers. They were uniformed and looked alert, capable. One talked to the receptionist and the other stood to the side, one hand on his hip, the other on his radio. Victor's eyes were drawn to the side of the corridor, where a third officer appeared. This one wore a bulletproof vest and a cap with a chequered strip and carried a firearm on his belt.

Victor's jaw clenched and he let out a stifled breath. He backed away behind a cleaning cupboard, giving himself just enough space to see that the police were serious and here in force.

He glanced back, observing their movements. All three were twitchy, anxious. They knew they were dealing with something unpredictable and dangerous, but how much had they been told? In Victor's experience, not enough.

In previous years this wouldn't have bothered him. Police, soldiers, customs officials. Many carried guns and many were much stronger than he. He'd passed borders, walked through checkpoints, even escaped the prison.

In his early twenties Victor had faced six officers in Romania. At a random checkpoint, they had wanted Victor to identify himself and his intentions. Why was he passing through the area? What was his job? Who was waiting for him in the next district?

It had been easy. Armed or not, the officers bowed to his will, one by one, dominoes rattling into place as he whispered to them. He didn't need to identify himself or his intentions. It wasn't important and nor was his destination. Nobody waited for him. They would let him pass and they would have no recollection of it. It worked, and he smiled, and back then only the murmurs of a headache disturbed him. He'd feel unsteady, tired, as if he'd drunk too much red wine at too early an hour. But he recovered quickly.

Never was he in any doubt of his ability.

But Victor knew things were changing. In the last few years, the crucial years during which he'd defined his purpose, he had changed.

The pain was more frequent and never left him. It pulsed and soared, from the top of his head, deep into his neck. It pervaded every crack in his being. His eyes watered and his ears rang. The tinnitus diminished in the early morning, but was back again by lunch, dampening his hearing, driving him to distraction, irritating his every move.

He had constant nausea, every waking hour, and no longer tried to suppress it. His gut wrenched and convulsed, and his teeth were starting to yellow from the bile and vomiting.

He knew he was rotting inside, and suspected the end wasn't far off.

Glancing down the corridor, he judged the impact he'd need to make if he was to take on all three of the police before they reacted. With anger and dejection, he realised he couldn't. Not if they were expecting him. Not if they knew his face. They would overpower or kill him.

Victor wasn't scared of death – far from it. But he couldn't die yet. He owed Laura and the others. He had people to repay, people to forgive. If the police were already here, his plan was ruined. His carefully memorised list was over. He was back to being nothing more than a fugitive.

He had no choice but to leave. They'd kill him on sight.

If this was the end, Victor knew what he must do. Given a chance of one more, Victor had no doubt who it must be. He cursed the fact that he hadn't taken the opportunity earlier, but that wasn't the order on his list. Without order he got confused.

One more. Then death. He was comfortable with that.

He left the hospital, reversed out of the parking space and headed back the way he'd come, towards the house of Dr Rupert Madison.

It was the devil's turn to dance, and Victor would be playing the fiddle.

CHAPTER FORTY-TWO

Victor's head throbbed as he stepped out of the car. The pain in his neck and shoulders forced him to stoop. He was crowded with noise. Any clarity was gone. His ability surged and waned. He was sick, a deep damaging disease, countered only by his anger, the burning rage ignited all those years ago and never extinguished.

It was this rage he used to force himself into the front garden and along the driveway towards a garage, offset from Dr Madison's house. A large garden lay at the rear.

He then waited for a reasonable time but the police were absent. Surely they knew about this one. If not, they would soon. He didn't have much time.

He paused at the back door and checked his bag. He'd brought no props along this time. For this one, he simply needed to look the man in the eyes and see the recognition. Recognition was what he craved, what he demanded. There was never any escape for this man. He was the worst and the most deserving of the lot.

He'd show them. He'd kill the devil himself and then they'd see what he could do. Then he could go to his death and know he'd be forgiven.

The door opened; it was unlocked. He found himself in the kitchen. There was an old lady staring at him, but she didn't scream or shout.

She looked confused and held a tea towel in one hand, a handful of knives in the other.

Victor smiled and whispered to her. He was gentle and polite. He needed to save his energy. She nodded and turned, walking out of the kitchen, into a reception room at the back of the house. Victor tilted his head and listened. Footsteps from the front of the house: a creaking of floorboards.

He crept along the hallway, although he had little fear of being caught this time, such was his fury and his physical pain. He remembered creeping along so many corridors and hallways in his life. This one, at least, was short and there was no threat at the end of it. Nothing he couldn't deal with.

The study door opened and the man at the desk looked up. There were several moments of silence as Victor eased himself in and closed the door behind him.

It was the doctor who broke the silence. He trembled, but remained seated. 'So you've come,' he said. 'He was right.'

Victor ignored the thump at the back of his skull.

'I came,' he said.

'I don't remember you,' said the doctor. 'Should I? Did we work together?' The old doctor twisted his face into a smile. Conciliatory. Pained. Fake.

'Work together?' Victor screwed his own face up. 'That was not what we did.'

'My colleagues, then? They didn't behave as they should have done. I know this. We could have treated you much better than we—'

'You know what you did,' said Victor. 'You know what you are. Save the pitiful attempts. I was one of the best. And I was treated the worst.'

The doctor's hand shook again. He scratched his face, picking at the skin on his chin. He was scared, but it wasn't enough. He pretended not to remember Victor. Unacceptable.

'You presided over my injections,' hissed Victor. 'Mondays. Monthly at first, then weekly. They hurt. I screamed. You watched. Look at me – I'm Thirteen.'

The doctor strained his eyes but they were cold. No flicker behind them. The hand stopped trembling.

'It doesn't need to end like this,' said the doctor, straightening up. 'I know what I did. I won't apologise and I won't explain.'

Victor bared his teeth and stepped closer to the desk. The doctor flinched but kept talking.

'You were one of the best. A puppet master.' The doctor paused, searching Victor's face. Victor tried not to show any emotion at hearing that title.

'There is a future for you. You can come in from the cold. Work with me. I can't promise you won't be punished for what you've done, but I have influence. We might be able to work together again . . .'

Victor let out a cry of surprise. 'You can't promise I won't be punished?' he shouted. 'You?' He turned away in anger. It wasn't supposed to be like this. He shouldn't be letting the man talk, let alone make him angry. Even now, the doctor was trying to manipulate him.

'My son is also an expert in this field,' said the doctor. 'You've already met – he assessed you at Whitemoor. We can both work with you. I was talking to him just now, as it happens.'

Victor paused. 'Your son?'

Of course. It hit him. A sickness in his gut as the realisation dawned. They looked alike. The recognition in the prison was because this old man had looked the same many years ago. He should have pieced it together. The father sent the son. To continue his work. To continue his torture.

How could he have been so stupid? They were plotting against him all along. The devil's son was after him and he didn't even know it.

Victor reeled in anger. 'You sent him?'

The doctor shook his head. Surprised, his face creased. 'No. Not . . . No. That's not what—'

Victor screamed. 'Your son caved in an instant.' He saw the surprise on the doctor's face. 'He didn't tell you that, did he? I plucked his mind from him and made him cower in front of me. I told him to stay away from me. Your *son?*'

Victor seethed at the thought of having this man's son in front of him and letting him go. Why couldn't he see it at the time? He could have killed him then and there. That would have been enough, wouldn't it? To kill this man's son would have healed so much; it would have made up for such a great number of deaths.

But he'd been cheated.

'He's way ahead of you,' said the doctor, shifting backwards in his chair. 'The police know what you are. You have limited time left. Why not stop now? My offer stands.'

Victor shook his head and closed his eyes. He blocked the lies and focused on his purpose. This cowering, snivelling man in front of him wouldn't live to make any more offers, and he wouldn't inflict any more of his pain on others.

And that wasn't all. Dr Rupert Madison had just offered up his son. And Victor would take great pleasure in taking him.

Whispering, Victor planted his first words, watching the doctor's face as his suggestion took hold. The shaking returned, and the panic on the doctor's face satisfied Victor.

'I won't beg,' said the doctor, his voice wavering. 'I did what I thought was right.'

Victor responded. He cultivated his phrases and hissed them across the air between them. The words hung in the air and the doctor shook his head, trying to ward them off. But he did it without hope. He knew he couldn't stop it.

'Stand, Doctor Madison,' said Victor. The man stood, mechanically, jerking to his feet. The panic in his eyes increased. It was one thing to create the puppet masters and oversee their development, it was quite another to be controlled by one. Victor doubted the doctors ever anticipated this outcome – one of their children hunting them down.

But Victor wasn't finished. Not by a long shot.

'It's time, Dr Madison. Time to die. Take off your belt.'

The trembling increased and the doctor pulled his leather belt from his trousers, staring at the buckle.

'You'll die today, Dr Madison,' he said. 'And so will your son. He's next. He's the only one I want now.'

It hit home. The doctor's eyes were wide and the terror was complete. He opened his mouth to plead but his voice was cut off. He gasped and failed.

Victor was satisfied, and he smiled as he issued his final command.

Victor staggered out of the driveway and into the street. A truck passed and the driver eyed him with curiosity, but Victor ducked his head down and headed towards his car. He struggled into the seat and allowed himself a few seconds of deep breaths. The throbbing behind his eyes was unbearable; the back of his neck felt as if it was caving in.

But he smiled, for he had a renewed purpose. He forced aside the nausea and the bile. He had taken the devil, and now the child of the devil was within reach. A prize above all else.

It would please her. Laura. If she knew, she'd cheer him on. He'd take the weak, scheming doctor's son and show him what the devil had created.

Victor turned the key and winced as the engine roared into life. He drove slowly, along backstreets, focusing hard on the road, squinting as the pain caused his vision to blur. He allowed himself to stop when he was several miles from the Madisons' house, at which point he opened the door and vomited on to the street.

CHAPTER
FORTY-THREE

Natalia and Freak had watched Thirteen's departure from the home of Dr Madison, senior. They sat at a bus stop, inconspicuous, smiling at anybody who approached them. She waited for the next bus to leave, waving it on, before turning to Freak.

'Did you see what I saw?'

Freak nodded.

'Is that good?'

'He's struggling,' said Freak in a small croak. 'He's got the fever. He may be too far gone. Good for us, but not good for . . . Well.'

Natalia turned to her companion. He looked like a freak, of that there was no question. Short, malformed and with a crooked face. They called him other things too at the centre, during their training. The Russians didn't hold back in their insults, and Freak soon became accustomed to being the joke. There, but for her grace. She had enough sway – not much, but some – to keep him from being retired. He was not retarded, not in the way they said he was. Damaged, yes, but no more than she was. No more than any of the children who found their way out of Comănești or one of the other orphanages. He'd suffered a reaction to the drugs they pumped into him week on week. A gross overdose of psychotic drugs and conditioning. Comatose for three days then kicked back into the dorm, reeking of urine and sweat.

At Comăneşti he was treated with cautious disregard. He couldn't do what they wanted, which meant he was low value. Ferried back and forth between examination rooms and testing scenarios, the other children largely ignored him. He wasn't considered a threat, but if anything had saved Freak back then, it was his kindly nature. He wasn't aggressive, even after weeks of invasive testing. He was scared of the staff and friendly towards the other children.

Time moved on and the pressures at Comăneşti refocused the experiments. Freak was cast aside for later investigation. He and a few others were put in a dorm of their own and locked down for twenty-three hours a day. The numbers in that dorm fell swiftly as children disappeared. Taken away for 'relocation'. Natalia and the other children knew what that meant. Freak was one of the lucky ones.

Natalia was pleased he had survived. It was only later, after their escape, that Natalia encouraged Freak to explore his mental talent, considered useless by his peers at the time. They practised together, perfecting his interference of her own suggestions and influences, careful to avoid the damage that Freak had inflicted on subjects in the past. It was the only way he'd survive. To be valuable to their masters was paramount. Low-value assets tended to disappear.

Freak's curious ability interested the Russians enough to keep him alive and assigned to her. Together, with her ability and practice, they had a not insubstantial capability. Was it enough?

'You think we could do it soon? Together?'

'Maybe,' said Freak. 'Do you want to wait?'

'Not much longer,' said Natalia. 'He's raising his profile, which could raise ours. He's going to do something stupid soon.'

'Like killing more of those people?'

Natalia looked at Freak in dismay. He cowered away. Thirteen was making a complete mess of things – of course it was stupid. If the killings continued it wouldn't take much to tip the balance and her masters might well decide to get rid of them too. Freak should know better.

'Of course,' Freak added, seeing her face. 'Of course.'

'I do wonder about you sometimes, Freak.'

A bus turned the corner and slowed as it approached them.

'You're not making much progress elsewhere,' said Freak, cringing, anticipating her response. 'When are you going to give that up?'

'When I decide to,' she said, sounding more in control than she felt. 'Come on. I'm hungry. Once we've eaten we'll head back to where he's staying.'

Freak frowned.

'I don't like it either,' she said, recalling her reaction when she'd first seen where Thirteen was hiding out. She'd read the faded sign over the building's entrance with interest.

Freak narrowed his eyes.

'Look,' said Natalia, smiling at the bus driver as he opened the door. 'When the time is right, we'll take him. And our job is done. OK?'

If only it were that simple, she thought. Rumours were growing and the Russians were gathering momentum, bolstering their medical staff back at base. If anybody wondered what happened to the children of Comănești, the Russians had the answer. Her masters' true intentions were unknown, but Natalia began to worry again about her future and that of Freak. Once she had dealt with Thirteen, she had no idea what awaited them. She'd made several mistakes so far, but one of them bugged her more than most. Using people to achieve their ends was natural. Getting too close to them wasn't. She'd gone too far, let her guard down. She couldn't let it happen again.

She turned to Freak, who simply shrugged again, turning away.

'I've got to go,' she said, checking her watch, before dismissing the bus driver, who gave her an annoyed look before driving off into the traffic.

CHAPTER
FORTY-FOUR

Sophie stood behind Alex, her hand resting softly on his shoulder. He felt her withdraw it as Jane strode into the room. She'd called Alex to say she was rushing straight over. That was an hour ago, and Alex noticed the fresh change of clothes – there was no end to her designer suits – and waft of perfume. Her make-up was immaculate, and he noticed not a single teardrop had blemished it.

'Alex,' she said, her heels clacking on the floor as she brushed Sophie aside with a smile and embraced him. 'I'm here.'

Alex stiffened at her touch, but didn't have the energy to do anything. Not in front of the crowd who were gathered in the living room of his parent's house. Hartley stood to one side, talking to a couple of uniformed officers. Sophie eyed them both cautiously. His mum was still in her bedroom. They were waiting for the doctor to finish up.

Jane swivelled around to face him.

'It's terrible,' she said, shaking her head. She glanced over to the officers. Neither of them looked back, which seemed to irk her. 'Have they caught him?' said Jane, raising her voice. 'The person who did this?'

'Jane,' said Alex, wishing she'd leave and let him deal with this, 'it's nice you came, but I've got a lot to do. I need to talk to the police, the doctors. I need to sort out where Mum will stay—'

'I can do that,' said Jane. 'I'll put her up at Rivers. The manager knows me. I—'

'She needs care, Jane,' said Alex. 'Constant care. She can't stay in a hotel.'

'Oh,' said Jane. She looked genuinely concerned. 'Well, I guess I can—'

'Please,' said Alex. 'Your support is sweet, but we've got it taken care of. Perhaps we can talk later?'

Jane stood, her face twisted. She glanced around the room, as if unsure what to do. Alex saw the distress in her face and wanted to say something. She controlled most aspects of her own life. Alex figured it must be hard for her when she couldn't control his. All he managed was a weak smile. He offered to meet her back at the house later.

Jane's heels made even more noise on the way out, and Alex slumped in his chair. She'd only tried to be supportive and he'd thrown it back at her. He'd fix it later, but for now his mind whirred, second-guessing his every move and conversation for the last two weeks. What could he have done to change this?

Everything, he suspected. He could have been better at his initial visit. Better at assessing the background Robert had shown him. He could have admitted what Victor did to him in his cell – his heart raced and his cheeks flushed at the thought. But why hadn't his dad been honest from the beginning? One conversation was all it would have taken. His dad could have admitted his past and what he'd done. He could have told Alex the man in the cell was in fact a monster and needed special treatment. Victor should not have been allowed contact with anyone. They could have taken precautions.

Instead, his father had strangled himself with his own belt, noosing it over the corner finial of a heavy antique bookshelf. He was dead when Alex's mother found him and started screaming. The neighbours called the police, but nobody saw what happened. Nobody saw Victor Lazar enter Alex's parents' house and kill his father.

'Dr Madison?'

Alex turned to see the family GP, a young woman who offered her sincerest condolences. She looked genuinely shocked. A social worker trailed behind her, scribbling on a notepad. The social worker's phone rang and she withdrew from the room, offering an apologetic look.

'Your mother is resting,' said the GP, 'but she's OK. Confused, but she understands what's happened. She's asking for you.'

Alex nodded. 'I'll be right with her.'

He turned to Sophie. 'My father's study. We need to search it.'

Hartley's ears pricked up and she stepped over. 'Again, I'm so sorry,' she said. She looked troubled.

'It's not your fault,' said Alex. 'I should have pieced it together, his involvement . . . He pushed me towards this case and I didn't see it. I was too slow.'

'It's not your fault either,' said Hartley. 'Even if you'd managed to get hold of me, I couldn't have guaranteed we'd be able to protect him. You said he refused to leave – we couldn't have forced him.'

'But the rest of them.' Alex's eyes found Sophie again. 'The rest of the doctors, the psychologists and psychiatrists. My father was the only one, apart from Victor, who knew who they all were.'

'We know more than we did,' said Hartley. 'We've connected another couple with the photo. They are already under protection.'

'But the rest will never admit it. Even if we put it out on the evening news, they may well remain silent. Until . . .'

'The reason I've been distracted,' said Hartley, 'is that we found another. Confirmed identity.'

'Who?'

'Professor Alice Branson. Eighty-one years old. She was found in a playground in Greenwich Park, on the swing set. Two morning runners spotted her and called us. When the first responders got there the runners had cut her free.'

'Same scene?'

'Suicide. Brutal and cruel. Hung from the frame by a rope.'

Alex winced, but couldn't find any energy to mourn her. He was still figuring out his feelings towards his father. He had a professional suspicion he was bottling it all up, and once the Xanax wore off he'd come down pretty hard.

'Is my father? I mean, has his body . . .'

'Your father's body's been taken away. You can see him at the morgue. I'll take you.'

Alex nodded. 'Not yet. I need to speak to Mum, and we need to search his things. I need to get you a list of his colleagues.'

'I'll start searching the study,' said Sophie.

Alex headed upstairs, pausing near the top to assess his nerves. He was worried to find his packet of Xanax almost empty. He added a reminder on his phone to pick up some more – and he needed to have a conversation with Mikey about the other items too.

CHAPTER
FORTY-FIVE

Alex entered the front bedroom, glancing around at the walls. It smelled stuffy, of lavender soap, and it evoked strange memories of his childhood. Not an event, but a time. He wondered at what age he'd stopped going into his parents' room. He wondered at what age his father had moved out into the back bedroom.

'Mum,' said Alex, pulling up a chair. He gave her a peck on the cheek. Her skin was wet from tears and she reached out to him. He embraced her, but still couldn't find his own tears. He was in pain, no doubt, but he wasn't distressed. Not like he should be. He wondered at what point in his life his love for his father had departed.

'I'm here, Mum,' he said, thinking that she was smaller and thinner than he remembered. Seeing her so distraught, weak and confused stirred anger in Alex and he clenched his jaw. Whatever his father's deeds, this had got personal. His father didn't deserve to die for what he did and his mum didn't deserve to be left a widow.

Alex struggled with the fact that he'd been face-to-face with his father's killer and let him get away. He'd failed at every step in this case so far and couldn't see the light at the end of it. Even if they caught Victor, he'd failed his family. His dysfunctional, distant and broken parents. Family all the same.

'Did the man leave?' said his mum. Her eyes were searching. They closed again as tears welled up.

'Did you speak to him?' said Alex. 'The man who was here.'

His mum sniffed. 'Yes. I asked him why he was in the kitchen.'

'What did he say?'

'He told me to go into the living room and stay there. I did. I wasn't worried. He seemed nice enough.'

'Did he say anything else to you? Did he tell you to do anything else?'

'I went into the living room. I sat. I think I might have dozed off.'

Alex examined his mother's face. Could he be sure Victor hadn't tried to harm her? Place some suggestion, no matter how small, into her already fragile mind?

'OK, Mum,' he said. 'Perhaps get some rest.'

'Did he hurt your father?' she said. Her jaw trembled. 'Did he hurt Rupert? Did your father die at his hands?'

Alex held his mother's hand tight. He closed his own eyes. 'Dad died of a heart attack. There's nothing anybody could do, including you.'

'Oh.' His mum's hand relaxed a touch. 'I thought the man had hurt him. A heart attack? His brother went the same way. He was older, mind you . . .'

Alex squeezed his mum's shoulder, promising she wouldn't be left alone in the house. He'd speak to the social worker before he left and arrange everything. She had her own money, but Alex could pay for the best care he could find. She deserved nothing less.

'I need to look through the study,' said Alex. 'Is that OK?'

His mum pulled a faint smile. 'Of course. There's nothing in there for me. You might make sense of it.'

Alex paused. He found himself short of words. He had nothing to describe his sense of frustration and loss. They were a messed-up family unit, but he loved them – in his own way, which he supposed was the same excuse his father had used.

'Zero eight, zero six, two zero zero zero,' said his mother.

Alex frowned. 'What?'

'The safe combination. You'll need it. If you're going through his study.'

'How on earth—'

'The date of your graduation. Your father was so proud. He uses it for all his passwords. I saw him once. He never knew.'

Alex didn't know which amazed him more, his mother's sudden clarity of memory, or his father's use of his graduation date. The date he'd embarked on his career, following in his father's footsteps. His father had never once told Alex he was proud. Why couldn't a man who studied emotion for half his life exhibit even an ounce of it when he was alive?

Alex left the room and headed back down the stairs, pausing at his childhood bedroom. The colour was gone and it was now used for storage. He saw suitcases and three chests of drawers.

'Alex,' Sophie whispered up from the hall.

'Anything?'

'Nothing,' said Sophie. 'Your dad has some fascinating journals on his shelves. I haven't seen some of them before.'

'Is the safe locked?'

Sophie nodded.

'OK. Let's take a look.'

Alex felt awkward in his father's study. He'd never been allowed in here alone, and even now he was reminded of his childhood, searching for interesting things to poke or steal. Sophie had been neat and tidy, putting things back where she'd found them. It looked exactly as it had on his last visit, all evidence of his father's suicide already removed by the police and coroner.

Alex skipped over most of it and headed straight to the old Yale safe in the corner. The combination was correct, and the door clicked open.

It was a small safe with two shelves. Four folders and an envelope rested on the top shelf. Several passports were scattered on the shelf below, most of them expired. Out of interest he flicked through one of his father's oldest ones, going back to the eighties. Sure enough, the stamps of several eastern European countries were in there. There were too many Romanian stamps to count.

One of the envelopes contained his father's will. Alex put it to one side – he'd need it for probate, although he didn't care much what was in it. The other three envelopes contained a selection of academic papers. Alex didn't recognise the titles – he was familiar with all his father's publications – and sat at the desk for a closer look, stacking the papers next to him.

They were all yellowed with age, and Alex's eyes were drawn to the dates first. All of them were written in the eighties; not a single one was current. Nor were they in the correct format for a proper peer-reviewed research paper. They were formal but clearly not intended for academic review.

He frowned, handing Sophie the first one.

'*Neural and psychological control interventions for physical pain and distress in children and adolescents*,' she read. 'Nineteen eighty-three. No author.'

'I think we know who the author was,' said Alex, reading the second in the stack. '*Suggestive control as a core construct and clinical utility*.'

He scanned the others. They all concerned treatment for behavioural conditions using drugs and therapies – many of which he'd never heard of. All of them summarised their test group as children of less than sixteen years of age. Alex wasn't surprised to see the locations of the experiments listed as several cities across Romania.

'He must have known these would be read on his death,' said Sophie, flicking through hers. She was fidgeting again, her eyes narrowed. Alex thought she looked angry.

'That's what I thought,' said Alex, putting the second down and taking the third, not bothering to read the front sheet. He skipped to the end and saw what they were looking for.

'Here it is,' he said, pointing at a list of names, all prefixed with Dr or Prof. 'Are yours the same?'

Sophie flicked through her paper and several others on the desk. 'Yes.'

She looked at him, eyebrows raised. 'This could be your list of doctors. Victor must have it too. What do you want to do?'

'Give it to Hartley,' said Alex. 'What else can we do? They may have heard what's happened so far, or they may not. Whether they agree to be protected, well, that's up to them.'

'You don't sound too concerned.'

Alex paused. Should he be concerned? His father had died only hours ago, and he was in shock. But Sophie was right. He had little sympathy.

'Look what they created,' said Alex. 'What do you expect?'

Sophie nodded but narrowed her eyes again. She took the list and offered to talk to Hartley.

'You should . . . you know.'

'What?' said Alex.

'Organise some stuff. Whatever it is you need to do. Victor is . . . beyond you now.'

Alex slumped as Sophie left the room. She used an odd turn of phrase, but she was right. The police needed to take over and protect the remaining doctors – the scientists and psychologists in the photo and any others they could trace. Alex had no idea if Victor would be caught, but Alex's job was over, and he'd failed at it. Until Victor was back in a cell, he had no role to play, and even then it was unlikely they'd let him near Victor again. The rules had changed. Victor wouldn't see a normal prison, if a prison at all. He'd be sedated, confined and kept in solitary forever. Alex wouldn't be told where, and he'd be thanked for his time and given his pay cheque. Told to go home to his private patients. As if nothing had happened. Just like his last case.

That was if the police had their way. What if Victor had other plans?

Alex looked around the office, looking for alcohol. He found none and cursed, taking the remaining two Xanax from his pocket, crunching them dry.

He needed to call Mikey, and pulled out the crumpled note with the drug combination he'd got from his father. He might as well still get them. Better to be prepared.

He checked the study door and the hallway. The various visitors were busy and most of them were leaving. He nudged the door shut and pulled out his phone. It rang for ten seconds or so before a cheery voice answered.

'Alex, buddy. How the hell are you?'

Under other circumstances Alex would smile. Mikey was an old friend and he owed him a drink and a catch-up. Today, however, Alex needed his fix.

'I can't talk, Mikey,' he said. 'I need a repeat of the usual, plus a couple of others.'

'Others?' Mikey sounded worried. 'Look, fella. I know we have an understanding, but it's not as easy as that. You sure you don't need to talk to somebody? Me, for starters?'

'Nothing's changed,' said Alex. 'And the other drugs aren't for me. Trust me. OK?'

There was a pause, and a sniff. Alex hoped he wasn't damaging this relationship with his brash approach. He needed his source of Xanax.

'OK,' said Mikey. 'The usual for Xanax. What are the others?'

Alex read out the names of the two drugs. 'I don't know what dosage,' he said, aware it would probably cause even more angst. 'Just give me what you can get.'

There was silence on the other end for several moments.

'Clozapine might take a day or so,' said Mikey. 'We order it in on demand.'

'Is it a problem?' said Alex, nervous. His father had said all three in combination. The other two on their own were unlikely to help, should he need them.

'Not a problem, buddy.' Mikey's voice sounded cheery again. 'And the dosage is in the patient info document. Be careful. That's quite a combination. You . . . I mean, whoever takes it might be woozy and dozy for hours. Best not to drive, OK?'

'They won't,' said Alex. 'And thank you for this, Mikey. When things have settled down a little we'll go for a drink. Catch up. You know.'

'Sure thing, bud,' said Mikey. 'I'll drop them off to you when I have them. Along with your invoice.'

Despite the circumstances, Alex smiled. 'Of course. Add ten per cent for your trouble.'

'Oh, you pay way more than ten per cent, Alex. I'm absolutely fleecing you, my friend.' Mikey laughed and hung up.

Alex put his phone away and paused, narrowing his eyes. There was a creak by the study door. He walked over and yanked it open.

'Oh,' he said, relieved, 'it's you.'

Sophie tilted her head and looked surprised. 'You look like you've been caught,' she said.

Alex looked past her into the hall. 'Is everyone—'

'Going or gone,' said Sophie. 'DCI Hartley has nipped back to the station. She needed to act on the list ASAP and trace any who are in the UK. She wouldn't tell me what they were doing but I think she wants to bring them all in – she'll need to contact other forces if they aren't in

London. She said to call when you're ready, although she might not be able to see you until tomorrow.'

It was a relief, as Alex didn't fancy visiting the morgue.

The Xanax was kicking in and he relaxed, pulling Sophie into the study and nudging the door shut.

'I want to apologise again,' he said, his hand not leaving her arm. She didn't pull away and they found themselves close.

'No need,' she whispered, drawing him towards her. They paused, faces close, mouths almost touching. Her breath warm on his lips. She smelled sweet and fresh. His mind embraced it and his desire for Sophie surged to the surface.

Their lips touched, featherlike for a moment, but she pulled away. 'You should tell her. Jane.'

'Tell her?' Alex frowned. He tasted her lip balm. 'About us?'

'There is no us.' Her face twisted with a flash of disappointment. 'It's not about us. Tell her you want to break up. That it isn't working and you're not happy with her.'

Her head dipped. Alex studied her face. She was right.

'I will. Tonight.'

'OK,' said Sophie, disentangling her arms from his.

'Then we'll talk?' said Alex, letting her hands go.

'I'll be back in the office tomorrow at Whitemoor,' she said. 'I have other work. Study. Call me?'

Sophie stared at him, her deep eyes troubled and darting to and fro. Her foot shuffled and her left hand was fidgeting, scratching nails against her palm.

Alex nodded and watched her leave, the study door creaking shut behind her. His mind, dulled by the Xanax, was still a whir of confusion, emotion and anger.

Alex arrived home late that night. He'd felt guilty about leaving his mum, even though the carer was there. He thought it funny how guilt pervaded every thought after a death in the family. He was sure he should feel some, and his mother should feel none. His father, however, had gone to his grave without atoning for any of his crimes. Alex would struggle to forgive that.

Jane had waited up, which surprised him. She didn't even try to seduce him, which was out of character. Instead, she played a good supportive partner, to a point. The point where she mentioned that Grace had popped round.

'Oh,' said Alex. 'I, er—'

'Asking after your mum,' said Jane. She couldn't help pouting. 'I told her everything was fine. She didn't need to stick around.'

'Fine?' said Alex. 'Everything's fine?'

Jane's eyes widened. 'Not what I meant,' she said. 'I meant she didn't need to be involved. I would take care of you. She said something about Katie staying too. I said I wasn't sure if it was still a good idea, given the circumstances.' Jane pulled a rather insincere concerned look. Practised, but badly executed.

Alex stared at her, suddenly weary of her insecurity. Was it his fault? Of course it was. Who else could be to blame? It didn't take a therapist to figure it out. Alex's passive aggressive behaviour was bound to leave its mark, whoever he was with. To make matters worse, he was still sleeping with her, keeping her hanging on. No wonder she was confused. If she were a little more cold-hearted she would have left him long ago.

Sophie was right. They must break up. Today was as good a time as any to do it.

'Jane,' he said. 'We need to talk.'

Jane's phone buzzed and she picked it up, waving a finger at Alex. 'Of course. In a minute.'

'Now, Jane.'

'Shh,' she said, walking off, phone glued to her ear. Alex sighed and went to the kitchen, pulling open a bottle of red, selecting a glass and filling it to the brim. He gulped it back, feeling the warmth sloshing into his stomach.

Jane's grief was perhaps over, although Alex didn't seriously expect her to mourn for Rupert. He'd never introduced her to his parents and was pleased his father had never had the pleasure. He would not have approved.

He was distracted as the front door slammed. Several seconds later he got a text message from Jane:

Cara's having problems. Gotta nip round to hers. Talk tomorrow?

x

Alex held his phone in a vice-like grip and counted to ten. He finished his glass of wine and went to bed. He was out of patience and out of ideas.

He fell into an uneasy sleep, a cacophony of voices echoing in his mind. Victor's voice rang in his ears more than once, and another voice, female, but not one he recognised. He heard his father shouting, but at whom he wasn't sure. He woke and sat up in bed more than once, peering into the darkness, but all he could hear was his heartbeat. Eventually the Xanax and alcohol got the better of him and he succumbed.

CHAPTER FORTY-SIX

Alex woke, groggy and with an ache in his spine. It was morning. The TV in the bedroom was on, and Jane was perched on the end of the bed, phone to ear, gossiping about the news.

'I know,' she said. 'I know.' She glanced around at Alex and smiled. 'Speak later,' she said into the phone, and placed it on the sheet. 'You won't believe the news. That was Kat on the phone, over at the *Mirror*? You know she's on the night desk? She gets all the best gossip. Well—'

'Shh,' said Alex, tuning her out as the TV came into focus. It was BBC One, and there was a red banner across the bottom of the screen, signifying breaking news. The ticker read something about an escaped suspect on the loose. A man wanted in connection with five murders.

'Shut up!' he shouted, as Jane continued to talk. She stopped abruptly, jaw dropping.

'There was no need . . .' She trailed off as Alex grabbed the remote and turned the volume loud enough to drown her out.

'Police won't comment on the activity at Holborn Police Station,' said the newsreader, 'but inside sources say several university professors have been taken into custody during the night. It's not clear if they are suspects or connected in any way to the recent murders of several prominent scientists in the UK.'

Alex listened as the newsreader repeated various facts, guesses and lies. Hartley had warned him that it would hit the news, but Alex was surprised it had happened so soon. Alex hoped Hartley was prepared. If Victor was tracking these people – and they had every reason to suspect he was – a few police weren't going to stop him. They'd need to get those men and women into hiding pretty damn quick – at least those who were willing.

His own phone buzzed on the bedside table. He answered it.

'Are you watching the news?' It was Sophie. 'No mention of us or HMP Whitemoor. Victor's name hasn't been mentioned.'

'What do they have?' Alex was interested, not that it mattered. It was nothing they could control.

'Details of the murders so far, including Southampton. No connection to the inmate murders here. The police have an unnamed suspect on the run. That's it.'

'Who leaked it?'

'The police. They always do. It's hard to keep a murder investigation under wraps for long, especially when it's linked to an escapee.'

'You seem to know a lot about it.'

'I read a lot. And I watch a lot of telly.'

Alex smiled, but deep down the uneasiness hadn't gone. Bringing in Victor's targets was risky. Victor was unpredictable and unfathomably powerful. If he saw this news, there was no telling what he'd do.

Alex tried to call Hartley but got a constant engaged tone. He left a message urging Hartley to move the doctors as soon as possible. Victor must not know where they were. In the meantime, armed police should be positioned at Holborn Police Station. Hartley would understand why, even if the rest of the police force, the reporters and the public didn't.

Jane walked off. Alex thought about stopping her but heard a light tapping at the back door. In the time it took for him to pull on some trousers and head downstairs, the person had gone, but in the rear porch was a small package wrapped in brown paper. Alex glanced back inside before picking it up. He locked himself in the toilet and unwrapped it.

Inside were two of the drugs he'd asked for, with double his usual dose of Xanax. He rummaged around in the brown paper and found a handwritten note on a post-it. It said:

Sorry. Couldn't get Clozapine, distributor was out of stock. Maybe next week. £100 for what I did get, if you please. Usual method.

Alex transferred the money online. His friend had tried his best and Alex paid his debts. He thought for a few moments and popped one of each of the pills out of their foil. No use buying and not trying. He had no idea if two out of the three would have any effect whatsoever, but he popped them into his mouth anyway, along with an additional Xanax to get him through the morning. He wanted to have the chat with Jane, and he might as well do it while she was already mad at him.

He hoped the drug cocktail wouldn't send him straight off to sleep, but he did hope it would at least partly dull the pain of the conversation he was about to have.

CHAPTER
FORTY-SEVEN

In another part of town, a mobile phone displayed news snippets from the BBC. Nothing new had appeared in the last half hour, but still, Victor read and sneered.

He was in a metal bed, devoid of mattress but padded with rugs and scraps of carpet, where he'd remained since his visit to Dr Madison's house. Nearly out of painkillers, Victor had little choice but to wait for the stampede in his head to subside.

It pulsed and pounded. Waves of nausea tore through him and he had given up trying to reach the bathroom in time. The stench of vomit had been unpleasant at first, but had receded into familiarity and it no longer troubled him.

He read the news with interest and contempt. He wondered how the police had learned about the list of doctors so fast. He wasn't fool enough to think that only he knew, but time and distance had buried most of the records relating to his childhood. He should know, for he'd spent many years searching and chasing, bribing and persuading those who had the information. The list of conspirators was not in the public domain and it would have taken them a long time to track down everyone.

But they were too late. The other doctors, those snivelling vermin, held no interest for Victor any more. They could shrivel and die on their own terms. Victor only had one target now: Dr Alex Madison.

He'd laugh if he didn't feel so sick. His head throbbed and he closed his eyes. He leaned over the side of the bed and stared at the bucket, but his stomach was too dry. He didn't even heave.

He would make them all pay. A generation ruined. Just like his.

Bile rose into his throat, his stomach contracted and the thumping in his head made him cry out in pain. Time, he thought. That's all he needed. A day or two. It would take a lot of effort to get to the doctor, and he couldn't risk failure. He'd be bundled back into a cell, and he was under no illusions what would happen next time. They knew him now. He'd been careless, messy, and they knew what he could do.

Time. He'd waited this long for a prize he didn't even know about. He could wait.

Alex Madison could wait.

CHAPTER FORTY-EIGHT

Alex tried to placate Jane, but she wouldn't sit still and insisted on pacing up and down the stairs, pausing only to throw either an insult or an object at him.

'Who is she?' Jane said for the seventh time.

Alex shook his head, pausing to grasp the handrail on the stairs as his vision caught up. His head was light and detached, floating above his body. *Must be the drugs*, he thought, trying to focus.

'That isn't the reason, Jane. Can't you see? We're nothing alike.'

'Alike enough for you to screw me,' she retorted. 'Morning, night and whenever you want it. We're alike enough for that.'

'But that's all we do,' he said, his own voice rising to a shout. 'Sex is great. I'm not complaining about the sex. But it takes more than that.'

'More?' Jane shrieked with laughter. 'What are you? Christ. Most men would kill for a relationship like this. I try and I try. You've obviously got a lot of shit to deal with. I get it. That's why I've let you treat me like dirt for the last three months. All my friends say you're not worth it. I persevered because I thought you were. So I do nothing but please you. I play the meek girlfriend and let you take out your stupid aggression. And this is what I get. It takes more?'

Alex bit his tongue. He closed his eyes but his balance was off and he forced them open. He felt drunk. 'Perhaps . . .'

'What?' Jane was red-faced. Tears streamed down her cheeks.

'Perhaps we can take a break for a bit.' *No*, he was screaming inside. *Don't give in.*

Jane's face softened, but her chest still heaved. 'A break?'

Alex realised his mistake. 'No, I didn't mean . . . I mean, we need to break up. But perhaps we can talk. In a week or so.'

Her jaw cocked to the right. 'Break or break up, Alex? You don't seem so sure. What's the matter, haven't quite hooked your new slut yet? Not sure if she'll have you?'

Alex shook his head again and wished he hadn't. He sunk into a chair and waited for the dizziness to pass.

'That's it,' said Jane. 'Give up. Ignore me.' She grabbed her bag from the hallway and wrenched open the front door. 'You are such a bastard,' she yelled as the door slammed.

Her car roared off and he slumped even further, wondering if he'd expected it to go any better than that. Not really.

He sighed without an ounce of pleasure. At least he'd done it.

CHAPTER FORTY-NINE

Victor staggered and fell into the side of the car. He dropped the keys and crouched, fumbling in the gutter until he retrieved them. Despite eating, drinking and pouring the last of his maximum-dose ibuprofen down his throat, his symptoms wouldn't subside. He screamed inside. Outside he was pasty and his body stank. He didn't care.

He'd had enough rest. He knew where to go and what to do. Then he could rest. Only then.

The directions were on his phone, the address in Harrow. It wasn't far to the young doctor's house and he drove with enough care to avoid drawing attention. Slowly and clumsily, he manoeuvred the small car around the tight corners as he searched the streets. Road after road of unremarkable and tasteless houses. All of them held enemies. Only one of them was worth forgiving.

He opened the window and let the air rush over his face, waking him, keeping alive the anger, stoking and stirring it until he recovered. A car swerved and beeped as he drifted over the centre line. He swore and wrenched the wheel back the other way, drifting into a side street, checking his map.

A red light appeared ahead. He was forced to stop at a set of road-works. The light was temporary and it threw his map reading off. He checked the address and cursed. The house was here, in this street. Suddenly alert, he peered ahead, counting the houses from his position, checking the lights, inspecting the pedestrians. There were a few parked cars and he checked them all, one by one.

A Volvo, black and empty. A Mini, white, also empty. Then a BMW. Large, parked one door removed from Alex Madison's house, marked clearly with police insignia. Victor's breath caught in his throat as he saw movement in the car. His windscreen was dirty and he wiped it with his sleeve. Sure enough, there were two figures in the vehicle. He couldn't make out the details, but they looked to be dressed the same, in uniform, which could only mean one thing.

He slammed his fists on the steering wheel and rested his forehead on top. He butted his head against his fists in rage. Too late. He was too late. The police bastards were here and they wouldn't let him kill the devil child. If they knew the truth they might, but they wouldn't listen to him.

The sound of a horn startled him. He checked his rear-view mirror and saw a man gesturing to him. Rude and unnecessary, the man was swearing at Victor to move. Victor looked up. The traffic light was green, but he paused. It was a narrow street and if he carried on he'd pass close to the police car. They were obviously looking for him and he couldn't risk it.

The motorist beeped again, and he was joined by another. Victor turned the engine off, tapping several times on the wheel. He took four deep breaths and opened the door.

'What are you doing?' shouted the man behind. He'd opened his window and was looking at Victor with disgust. His eyes took in the dirty figure of the sick-looking man.

'You can't stop there,' he said. 'I can't get through.'

Victor ambled towards the man in his car, wincing as his footsteps compounded the stampede in his head. It was an Audi, long and sleek with large wheels. He kept his head down until he was right next to the car. He leaned in so his face was level with the man.

'Stop,' said Victor. His face changed and he locked on to the man's eyes. He clenched his jaw and changed his expression several times in rapid succession. He whispered a few words to calm the man. As he waited for the suggestions to permeate, Victor closed his eyes against the pain.

More honking, this time from the next car along.

'I need your car,' said Victor, hushing the man with more reassuring words as the inevitable objections were raised. The man looked puzzled now, his mind caught between the real and the planted. He struggled. Victor pushed.

The man opened the door from the inside and stepped out. His arms hung loose as he glanced around, lost, like a small boy staring at the stars.

'This is my car,' said Victor. 'Yours is over there.' He indicated the small hatchback he'd arrived in. Stolen, but serviceable. The other man would believe it was his, and he'd tell it to anyone who would listen until he went mad as the memories conflicted and bounced around in his head. He'd survive it, or he wouldn't. Victor couldn't worry about that. Wrong place and time. The man was in Victor's way.

'Hey!' Another shout. The drivers of two other cars were getting angry. The traffic light turned red again and one of them swore, beeped his horn three times and slammed his car door.

Victor peered up the road. His time was up. The police car's internal light was on and one of them stepped out, staring towards the commotion. Victor ducked in time, sliding into the stranger's car, putting it straight into drive and jamming the steering wheel hard to the right until it locked. He didn't look towards the police or the devil child's house, he simply stood on the accelerator and the car lurched forwards and to the right. The turn took him on to the opposite kerb but he kept going, ignoring the honks and the shouts, yanking the wheel back as the tyres gripped the tarmac and powered the car into the main road and away.

CHAPTER FIFTY

Alex was vaguely aware of his phone ringing. He assumed it was Jane, and made to throw it on the table, when he noticed it was caller withheld. It could be a client from his private list, or the police switchboard.

'Dr Madison,' he said, his own voice sounding distant, like an echo. He swallowed. Pressure popped in his ears.

'It's Hartley. How are you?'

'I'm, er—'

'Sorry, stupid question. Forgive me. I haven't been getting much rest. My social skills suffer first.'

'Don't worry about it,' said Alex. His ears popped again and his hearing cleared.

'Anyway, listen, I've managed to get more resources. The press leak means this case is going high profile. Normally that's bad news, but it means I have more manpower and more cars.'

Alex wondered if Hartley had been the one to leak the news to the press. He sniffed. 'For what?'

'Firstly, protection. Because of your father you're getting a watch put on you and your house.'

'I really don't—'

'Save it,' said Hartley. 'It's not up to you. In fact, there's a patrol car outside your house already. I know what you've told me, but if there's any chance Victor heads your way, we want to be there. There'll be a visible presence outside your house at all times. An armed response vehicle.'

'Great,' said Alex, wondering why he didn't feel reassured. 'But I think you're wasting your people. Victor doesn't care about me.'

'I hope that's true,' said Hartley. 'But for now, do me a favour and stay at home?'

'For how long?'

'Just a few days.'

'How can you possibly—'

'Sorry, I've got to go,' said Hartley. 'Just do it, please? Be nice to the officers. Make them a cup of tea or something.'

'Nice,' said Alex, hanging up.

He checked through the blinds and sure enough, a marked BMW sat outside. He saw two officers, one in the front and the other in the back. One of them pulled out a thermos and poured a cup of something. The other glanced over to the window. Alex, embarrassed, raised a hand and gave them a wave, before feeling stupid and ducking away.

He grabbed his phone and called Sophie.

'Yeah?' She sounded abrupt.

'I wondered what you were doing.'

'Oh,' she said, her voice softening. Alex heard shuffling in the background and the slamming of a car door. 'Nothing.'

He told her about his police protection and orders to stay put.

'For how long?'

'No idea,' he said. 'But if I'm stuck here, do you want to come over?'

There was silence and Alex thought maybe it was a bad idea, inviting Sophie here so soon after breaking up with Jane.

'Yes,' she said, 'actually I do. We should talk.'

'Good,' he said, trying to push away his gnawing doubts. Sophie wouldn't help his anxiety. Their relationship was a complication he shouldn't invite on top of everything else. But still, he couldn't pretend the attraction wasn't there, or deny what they'd done.

Sophie arrived an hour later. Alex had showered and dressed casually, but with attention to detail. He realised he was dressing to impress, in spite of the circumstances. He examined himself in the mirror and frowned, still not sure of Sophie's feelings for him. He might have it all wrong. Perhaps Romania was just a one-off: a workplace affair destined for disaster. It felt more meaningful than that, but his judgement wasn't exactly spot on lately.

Thankfully, Sophie didn't arrive in a hoodie and jeans. She was dressed in tight black trousers and black top. Sleek, not exactly what he'd been expecting. Alex's eyes tried to take it all in without being obvious, but Sophie brushed him aside with a quirky smile. She glanced around.

'You alone?' she said.

'Yes,' he said. 'Apart from my bodyguards. Did you give them a twirl?'

She frowned. 'Don't joke. Hopefully they won't be necessary.'

'I agree,' said Alex, watching Sophie survey his hallway and saunter through into the kitchen.

'You look great,' said Alex. 'I feel like a bit of a slob.' He indicated his immaculate polo shirt and slim chinos.

'You look it,' she teased, but it was strained. She didn't look like she was here for fun. She leaned on the worktop, shuffling her left foot and biting her lip, which in the last few days had been her standard resting position, always nervous, always fidgeting. Alex was troubled at the sight. Was this case too much for her? Was he being selfish by keeping her on it? Or was it just him?

'You heard Robert's been put on administrative leave?' said Sophie.

'I hadn't heard,' said Alex, 'but he looked worn out last time I saw him. He was as out of his depth as the rest of us, and with the added responsibility. Where has he gone?'

'Nowhere. He called in. Told us all to be careful. He told me no patient was worth this strain. He gave me a message for you. Told you to stay away and leave it to the police.'

'Which is exactly what I'm doing,' said Alex.

'A bit late,' said Sophie. 'You could have left it alone the minute you saw what Victor could do.'

Alex nodded. 'I could. Coffee?'

'Sure.'

'If I had – left it alone, I mean – then we wouldn't have . . . got to know each other.'

'Had sex, you mean.'

Alex spluttered. 'That's not what I meant. What's got into you?'

'Nothing,' said Sophie, shaking her head. 'Sorry. But that is all we've done. We don't owe each other anything.'

Alex was taken aback. He'd thought he was making progress with Sophie, breaking down whatever barriers she had. Clearly he was wrong. He had a sinking feeling about where this conversation was headed.

'I know that,' he said. 'Jane's gone,' he added. Was that the right olive branch? What Sophie wanted to hear?

'For good?'

'For good.'

Sophie accepted the coffee and held it with both hands towards her mouth. She blew the steam away and sipped, pulling a face. 'Sugar?'

'It's bad for you,' said Alex, helping himself to three lumps before passing it to Sophie.

'We can't do this,' said Sophie. Alex stared at her, but her face was downcast and she refused to make eye contact.

Alex gulped the hot coffee and put his cup on the worktop.

'Do what?'

'I'm sorry. I really am. We should never . . .' Sophie paused and took a deep breath. He saw a battle in her eyes. 'It was great getting to know you. You've been helpful, really. But I can't—'

'Tell me why,' he said. Alex wanted desperately for her to tell him what it was that bothered her, what demons caused the hurt. The story about her family was false, he knew that much, but he couldn't say it.

Something ate away at her, something that caused her to disappear into a troubled state of mind. She wasn't his patient, nor was she his partner. Were they even friends?

'I'm sorry if we did things wrong,' he said. 'The sex. We don't need to . . . We can start again. If you want to.'

'You didn't do anything wrong,' she said. 'I did . . .' She raised her head and he could see her eyes were puffy. A single tear rolled down her left cheek.

'What?' Alex moved to put his arm around her but she stood and backed away. Wiping her face with her sleeve, she picked up her bag.

'I shouldn't have done this. You need to concentrate on your family.'

'Done what?' he said. 'What did you do?'

Sophie shook her head. She wiped the tear from her eye and threw her shoulders back. Alex saw the confident Sophie trying to break through, her eyes sparkling. She backed out of the kitchen.

'I'm sorry, Alex. Look after yourself,' she said, and strode towards the front door.

'Wait!' Alex shouted after her, frustrated and confused.

Sophie looked around once as she opened the door.

'I mean it,' she said. 'Take care.'

The door closed and Alex was left alone in the hall. He didn't pursue her. He didn't know why she'd picked today to break off a relationship that hadn't even started, but there was nothing to be gained by shouting in the street. He'd wait – perhaps until after Victor had been caught. He couldn't switch off his feelings for Sophie, but they were new and embryonic. He didn't know what he really felt against the background of the situation with Victor and the prison.

Alex headed back to the kitchen, downcast, second-guessing his moves and conversations with Sophie, but failing to reach any meaningful conclusions. He threw his coffee away and grabbed a bottle of red. His day couldn't get any shittier, and he was stuck in his house. Getting drunk wouldn't make things any worse.

CHAPTER
FIFTY-ONE

Victor lay on the tiled floor for several hours until he could stand. Furious, he splashed water on to his face from a metal pail. He wasn't willing to fail now. He'd had the devil child in his sights, only to be forced away.

He knew he couldn't get to the house. Victor had seen enough police in his time to know they were waiting and they were prepared. He'd be done for the minute he approached. He'd kill one, maybe two officers, but there'd be more. Hiding, waiting.

He had to find a way of luring Alex Madison out of his lair and into the open. He must tempt the precious young devil child to him, and Victor would show him what happened to the children who thought they could escape punishment.

Victor was precious, they'd told him, over and over. So precious. What is more precious than a young child? Innocent and trusting of anything. That's how they arrived at Comănești. They didn't stay innocent for long. None of them. Not even Laura.

Victor stared at his blurred reflection in the twisted metal and asked himself the question again. It came to him, slowly, but the answer was correct. He knew Laura would question it, but he would tell her the ends justified it. How else? She would understand, he thought. She'd come round, given time. She'd give him her blessing when she saw what it meant.

Victor knew what would lure his prey to him. Innocence must be spoiled.

It didn't take Victor long. He'd forced himself up and out of the house. It hurt, but he had no choice. His fury dragged him through. He had no qualms about what he was going to do next.

A series of phone calls was all it took to locate both the mother and the child. Pretending to be Dr Madison loosened the lips of every school receptionist in the area, and it wasn't long until he found the right one. Even if one of them reported his suspicious phone call, it would be too late. He was now parked across the street and a few buildings away from the school Alex Madison's daughter attended. Sipping a bottle of water, he watched the coach slow and pull into the entrance, creeping along the narrow road, turning at the end. With a hiss it stopped and the driver jumped from the cab, welcomed by the crowd of eager parents waiting for their children. As they unloaded the bags and camping gear, Victor kept watch.

He didn't know what the girl looked like, but he had a photo of the mother, and the car registration. He'd spied the Saab convertible already and was parked facing the same direction, ten or so cars back. He'd watch and wait.

For ten minutes Victor watched parents and their children. It troubled him to see the relationships and the obvious love between them. So protective and yet so trusting. It was complicated and Victor didn't understand. He had no comparable reference with his own parents. He had a vague picture of them in his head, but the image came along with feelings of pain and anguish, not love and tenderness. He clenched his teeth and his fascination turned to hate. Why did these people have the right to such happiness? At least for two of them, their happiness would soon be over.

He straightened as the woman crossed the road, dragging a large black holdall and trailing a young girl. The girl was still yelling back to her friends. They all shrieked and danced around, while the parents patiently ushered them into cars, throwing mud-covered bags and rucksacks in behind them.

The Saab pulled out into the road and Victor followed.

A fresh wave of nausea hit as he drove through the suburbs. Images of Laura, his childhood friend, popped into his head and he dismissed them, distracting himself by imagining the pain on Alex Madison's face when he found out what had happened.

As he drove, his mind whirled with hate. His mood was blackened further by the constant pain in his temples, and his anger flared with every bump in the road.

He would destroy them. The Madison family was about to reap what they had sown. Victor wouldn't blink at adding one more orphan to this world.

They drove for less than ten minutes before pulling into a plain-looking cul-de-sac filled with large detached houses, the sort built to last a lifetime, with cellars and outbuildings. Perfect. The Saab coasted into the driveway before stopping. The girl jumped out first.

Victor knew her name was Katie. She was blonde and skinny, dressed in jeans and a patterned T-shirt, her hair pulled back into a plait. She bounced towards the front door and waited.

Her mum, Grace, followed. She had mousey brown hair and was short. Her face looked kind, but strained. The stress of raising a child, perhaps, with an absent father. Victor acknowledged these things in a cold and mindless way. He resisted the urges at the back of his head to stop. He resisted the look on Laura's face, asking him what he'd become. He wanted to scream he was doing this for her – because of her. Her face disappeared as the front door slammed, and Victor prepared to move.

He reversed out of the road and parked in the main street. It was busier here and his car wouldn't draw attention. He slumped in the seat, took another couple of painkillers, and downed the last remains of a bottle of water, cursing himself for not bringing more.

Should he wait for nightfall? He watched the entrance to the quiet road. A thought came to him. Perhaps there was no need to take them anywhere. It would certainly be easier for him. But no, he dismissed the idea as quickly as it came to him. His other location was far more appropriate, and the significance surely wouldn't be lost on Alex Madison.

Victor made his decision and got out of the car, smoothing his grubby shirt and adjusting his glasses. He zoned in, channelling his anger as he'd done so many times before. He used it to counter the sharp throb in his temples, the dull ache in his skull, and the shards of pain stabbing through his neck.

For the last few years he'd recited his list in his head every morning – his tormentors and abusers. Now he'd added one more to the list. An opportunity missed, but he wasn't going to get away twice. This time Victor's vengeance would see the final conspirator put in the ground where he belonged.

The cul-de-sac was quiet. A dog barked and the birds sang back in return. No sign of neighbours or cars. Victor shuffled along the road and up the driveway, scanning his surroundings and settling on the path along the right-hand side of the house. He didn't need to break in, but his entrance would be better out of sight, just in case.

The back door was solid oak with frosted glass. Fortunate. Victor thumped three times and waited.

He heard calls inside from mother to daughter, footsteps across the kitchen floor. The locks were unfastened and the door creaked open a foot or so.

'Yes?' The mother, Grace, answered, peering at Victor. They were a similar height, and he probably looked unthreatening, if a little sloppy and dirty.

'Grace Madison?' As much as Victor's hate carried him, he mustn't get the wrong people. Laura would never have approved – and besides, it would slow his plans.

'Yes, I—'

'Is that your daughter Katie I heard?'

Grace stiffened and closed the door a fraction.

'Who are you?' she said.

'Let me in, please.' Victor whispered his suggestions. It didn't take much; she was standing in front of him and didn't know she ought to resist.

'I, er . . .' Grace let the door swing open. She backed away, her brow furrowed. She made to speak but looked as if she'd forgotten what to say.

'I'll come in,' said Victor, stepping into the kitchen. He eased the door shut behind him, locking it.

The kitchen was grand, with a stone floor and marble worktops. An Aga stood proud along one wall, a faded pine table in the centre. Grace backed against the table and waited. Her eyes darted but she was confused.

'Call Katie down here,' said Victor, watching her eyes, crafting his words, whispering and coaching. Grace was completely under. She called, once, loud and mechanical, for Katie to come to the kitchen. There was a protest from upstairs, a shout followed by a reluctant stomping of feet.

'What now?' called Katie. 'I'm busy.'

Victor waited until Katie walked in. She stopped and stared at her mum, then at Victor. Her eyebrows went up, hands on hips.

'What?' she said again. 'Hi,' she said in an offhand manner in Victor's direction.

Victor paused. Up close, Katie was younger than he'd thought, no more than twelve or thirteen years old. He stared at her hair, at her skin – unblemished, so young and innocent – and memories flooded over him.

Laura was younger than this girl when she died, but not much. Laura had blonde hair too. All the girls were young. So many of them disappeared. Victor had tried not to make friends with too many of the new ones because they didn't last long.

But the biggest difference was the spark in this girl's eyes. The girls at the orphanage had looked dead inside. Only Laura had a spark, despite the terror and the abuse. Despite the midnight beatings and the drugs. Laura had looked at Victor with a spark in her eyes, as if one day things would be different. She could imagine a future beyond the orphanage and the experiments, beyond the cruelty and barbarism. She was naive but at least she had dreams.

Victor was shaken back into the moment by Katie's voice.

'I said who are you? What's wrong, Mum?'

Victor pushed aside his memories and the guilt tugging at his gut. Why should this girl live when Laura had to die? If it was true about bad apples this one would be rotten anyway, the product of her father and his father before him.

His anger grew. He tempered it before turning to her.

'Katie,' he said, whispering a mild set of instructions. It wouldn't take much for a young mind such as hers.

Katie's face blanked and her eyes glazed over. Her shoulders slumped. She was under.

'Grace,' said Victor, raising his voice. 'Where is Katie's coat?'

'By the door,' said Grace, her voice calm but mechanical. She glanced at Katie, at Victor, then at the clock on the wall. 'What time is it?'

'It doesn't matter,' said Victor. 'Get the coat. Bring it back to the kitchen. Katie will stay here. Do you understand?'

Grace nodded. 'Yes.' She reached out for Katie's hand.

'No,' said Victor. 'Do as I say. Katie stays here.'

Grace nodded, her face anxious, but walked out of the kitchen into the hallway. Victor waited until she returned. She was in a simple trance but showing signs of resisting. It would get much harder once she did.

She stood with two coats. A small one for Katie and her own. Her eyes were troubled.

'Where are we going?' she said. Her eyes were panicky now, and Victor sighed. She wasn't going to be as easy as he wanted. She was shifting into what they called a waking trance. Over half of people hit this point within seconds with the methods they taught them at Comănești. It was the most terrifying state to be in, from the target's perspective. Conscious you'd lost control, but confused and anxious. Your body was no longer your own, and the panic it caused was immense.

Once in a waking trance, it was all or nothing. Victor couldn't afford to be gentle. He whispered a harsh set of commands focused at a more primal level. It would confuse and probably damage her, but it was necessary.

'Please,' she said, as her body jerked.

'You're staying here, Grace,' said Victor. 'Over there, in the corner. Sit on the floor. Katie, you're coming with me.'

Grace sat obediently, but started crying, a low moan. Her small shoulders shook as she sobbed, unaware of why she felt such anguish. She asked again where Katie was going, but Victor bound her to the spot before exiting out of the back door. Katie followed him, oblivious to the turmoil in her mother's voice.

Victor saw Katie to the end of the driveway, where he walked next to her. They reached the main road without any prying neighbours approaching them. Victor unlocked his stolen car and opened the back door, swinging it wide.

'Get in,' he hissed. Katie shot into the car and sat upright, staring forwards at the back of the driver's seat, still deep in her trance.

'Where are we going?' she asked. Her voice was distant and relaxed, as if she didn't really care.

'Shh,' said Victor. 'Sit and be quiet. We're going for a little drive.'

He turned, slammed the door and climbed into the driver's seat. He started the engine and pulled into the traffic. It shouldn't take more than twenty minutes to get back to Battersea, although he was already suffering after-effects. He fought the pain and the nausea for several minutes, opening the window wide for fresh air. He swallowed two more painkillers dry, and tried to ignore his symptoms. It wouldn't be long now.

Victor only relaxed when he pulled up outside the building he'd been hiding in for the last few days. Before exiting the car, he reached for his mobile phone.

He had an important call to make.

CHAPTER
FIFTY-TWO

Alex paced and festered. He finished the wine then drank strong coffee heaped with sugar, stopping every couple of hours to take more Xanax. He felt exposed and anxious, and Sophie's visit had pulled any confidence he had left from under his feet.

Jane called. They fought. He knew he was being awful but it was best in the long run. Best for Jane, anyway. They were done. He felt guilty. He'd been unfaithful, even to her. But he knew Jane would move on. People like her had no difficulty finding admirers, lovers and partners. He stood firm and the shouting stopped. Jane ended the call with a string of cutting insults. She had the reserve not to mention his family, and for that Alex was grateful.

Hartley had told him to sit tight, and he intended to do just that, but his chest ached and he realised his heart rate was elevated. He took an extra Xanax to counter it and sat, not knowing what to do. He thought of Hartley frantically locating the remaining doctors, trying to place them out of harm's reach, not knowing for sure when or where Victor would strike next.

Alex was struggling and he knew it. Catapulted out of his stable private practice, Alex's life was in chaos and he saw no easy resolution.

He had failed. All these people were dying at Victor's hand, and his own father had borne the brunt of this, even if he'd had it coming.

Alex had always been one step behind Victor, distracted by his own screwed-up personal life and catching everything too late. Eleven people already slain. Had he saved the rest? Perhaps. Perhaps they would have been saved without him. He'd never know.

The news repeated on the BBC, but it was already relegated to the fifth and then sixth story. By the afternoon it was out of the top ten. Their source in the police had probably been silenced, and without fresh details it got sidelined in favour of party politics and interest rate rises.

Alex poured himself another coffee, but the smell was making him feel sick and his gut couldn't take any more. He went back to the wine, uncorking a cheap bottle, rinsing out his coffee mug and pouring it into that.

He rested on the breakfast bar and watched his phone buzzing on the counter. He didn't bother checking the caller. Would it be Jane? He gulped back the wine and headed back to the lounge.

The home phone rang. Alex cursed but picked up the handset from the coffee table. Jane would never call the landline. It must be somebody else.

'Hi.'

'It's me.'

'Sophie.' Alex pulled himself up. He thought Sophie was done with him.

'Are you . . .' Sophie trailed off. She was breathing heavily.

'What's the matter, Sophie?'

'You haven't . . . I mean . . . dammit.'

Alex's mind was clouded by the wine and he couldn't make out what Sophie was trying to say. 'Did you call my mobile a few minutes ago?' he said.

There was a pause.

'No.'

Another pause.

'I've got to go. Alex?'

'What is it, Sophie?'

'Just . . . take care. We'll get through this.'

'I don't understand. Sophie?' But she'd hung up.

Alex cursed and paced back into the kitchen. The last thing he needed was Sophie screwing with his head. If she was through with him, fine. If she wasn't, she could at least talk sense. He'd had enough.

He poured another cup of wine and his mobile vibrated again. This time, he answered it.

Thirty seconds later, Alex's mind was a mess of swirling panic. He reached to his pocket and pulled out two Xanax, running to the sink for a glass of water. He gulped it back, repeating Victor's call to himself word for word.

He had Katie. The bastard had his daughter.

There was no negotiation, no small talk. Victor sounded sick, desperate and deluded. Alex had no way in, and was forced to listen to the simple demand.

Drive to an address in Battersea – a derelict building, the site of St Joseph's orphanage. Alex had scribbled it down. Drive there and call Victor back from the courtyard on this number. Victor was waiting for him. He'd called him the devil, and the devil's child. He was ranting, insulting Alex over and over, furious at him. Alex had listened, rigid with fear and sick at what he'd heard.

If he failed to show, his daughter would die – as an example, in the way so many children had died at Comăneşti. The words chilled Alex to his bones. He stuttered and begged but Victor wasn't listening.

Call the police, and she dies. If Victor heard a siren or saw a uniform, all Alex would find was her mangled body.

Those were Victor's instructions and Alex had no doubt he would obey them.

He had an hour, no more. He poured his wine into the sink and watched it swirl into the plug, mixing with the water until it looked like blood. He shivered and ran the tap. He drank. One cup, then another. He needed a clear head. He cried, struggling to keep down the waves of terror. He slumped against the kitchen counter and begged the air for an answer. There was none.

In his right hand he still clasped his mobile phone. He checked it, but there was just a cryptic text from Sophie saying she'd be in touch. Alex didn't have the time to figure it out.

Twenty minutes passed. He stood and paced the hallway, on the verge of a panic attack. His breathing was uncontrolled, his hands were shaking and he was in no fit state to negotiate for the life of his daughter. He had made a mistake, he was sure of it. Why hadn't he called Hartley yet? Surely he must? They could go round there and . . . And what? What would Victor do? He couldn't overpower all of the police, but it didn't matter. All he needed to do was hurt Katie and . . . the thought caused a fresh wave of panic.

He'd taken four Xanax now, and even with his high tolerance threshold, built up over many years, he was beginning to feel lethargic and unfocused. He forced himself to drink more coffee. The filter jug was cold so he heated it in the microwave. The liquid scalded his throat, but he needed the caffeine. He rummaged around in the kitchen cupboard and found some Pro Plus tablets. He popped one of them, aware he was causing a ridiculous play-off between Xanax and caffeine. Neither would win; he would lose.

He fingered the packet and tried not to descend into despair. He was aware of the psychological cycle and knew what to say to other people in this situation. Dire circumstances required careful dissection of the component parts and a coping strategy for each. But Alex had no time and few options. His patient of interest had turned on him in the most merciless fashion possible.

Victor had no clear plan. It made him completely unpredictable, even if Alex was able to talk or negotiate. He had no guarantee Victor would let either him or Katie go. He might kill them both. He'd feel no remorse – not yet, anyway. Remorse for somebody like Victor would come much later, when his task was over. Until then, he'd be indiscriminate and callous.

As always at these times, Alex couldn't help but think about his last criminal case. Mother and daughter. He couldn't help it, the similarities were striking. His bungling of the case then had killed them both. His misunderstanding of the evil lurking within otherwise normal people had caused their deaths. Whatever the official outcome, he still blamed himself. Now he risked knowing the pain at first hand.

His phone buzzed with a message. It was from Hartley and he read it with confusion: Dr Petri found dead. The day after you left Romania. We need to talk. I'll call later.

Alex's mind whirled but he didn't have the time to think about Dr Petri now. He could barely cope with what Victor had dealt him. He gulped back the bile and breathed, shoving the phone into his pocket and grabbing his wallet and coat. His deadline was approaching. He had to go.

Pausing at the front door, he checked through the side window. The police protection was still there, the dark BMW resting in place, two figures inside. It meant he couldn't take the Porsche. They'd either follow or stop him, and he couldn't risk either. Instead, he slipped the keys back on to the stand and pulled out the garage keys. He could take the Alfa. The garage was at the back of the house, leading to a private alley and joining the main road at the end of the row.

He slipped out of the back door, heart thudding in his throat, praying this day wouldn't end the way he feared.

CHAPTER
FIFTY-THREE

The derelict building of St Joseph's orphanage loomed on the right as Victor hung up the phone. It was old, a nineteenth-century brick mansion, crumbling at every corner.

Half the tiled roof had caved in, leaving much of the front of the building open to the elements. Victor had chosen a couple of rooms at the back – old dormitories near the bathrooms, which still had running water. It was a sick attraction, coming to one of these places again, but he felt it necessary, given his current task. St Joseph's wasn't Comăneşti – far from it – but the echoes were the same. He could walk the corridors and feel the pain of the children who'd walked them many years ago. He didn't suspect for one moment that the children here shared the same torment he had, but he had no doubt they'd experienced pain. After all, they were at the mercy of their orderlies, their doctors, their nurses. Victor knew there was a universal evil in the treatment of unwanted children. He felt it in his toes as he trod the shower room and pulled at the metal-framed beds.

It was to this place he'd invited his enemy. The man who should have let Victor be. The doctor who insisted on treading in his father's footsteps. The devil's child. He would pay for his interference. It was only by this route that Victor could forgive him.

There was no noise from the back seat. He had given clear instructions to sit and be quiet. The girl had started off easy – she wasn't old enough to resist or suspect anything was wrong, but she was sweating now, her face pale and her eyes watering. She wasn't aware of the trance, but she knew something was wrong, and her conscious mind was fighting itself, tying itself in knots trying to understand the physical binding preventing her from controlling her own body.

'Out,' said Victor, waiting until the street was clear and the traffic was light. 'Follow me.'

He ducked through a hole in the high brick wall surrounding the building. The girl followed and they made their way around the side, weaving through overgrown segments of ground covered in bricks and roofing tiles. Rubbish littered the earth and weeds tore through holes in the concrete. A dead rat lay off to one side, the body half-eaten, its mouth open.

Broken glass crunched underfoot as Victor shouldered open the door. Once through he pushed it back again into its frame.

Victor glanced at the corridor. The flashes returned. Unwelcome, but necessary. Peeling paint and damp corners, the huge iron radiators still lining the walls next to the wafer-thin glass windows – several of them cracked or shattered.

He picked his way along, ordering Katie to follow him. She tripped over a concrete block and fell, grazing her knee and ripping her jeans. Blood oozed out. She didn't notice and pulled herself up, staring straight ahead. Her eyes darted about but she wasn't clear what had happened.

'Where's my mum?'

'Silence,' said Victor.

He led them further into the building, past doors hanging off their hinges, leading to dormitories and communal rooms, perhaps classrooms. Victor paused and stared at one. His vision grew hazy and he heard the distant shouts of his fellow children. Some happy, most sad. Shouts of anguish and terror. Shouts of the staff ordering them around, ushering them into private rooms, telling them they were ready for the next stage.

Victor clenched his teeth. That was another time, another orphanage. But he was here because of it. He was making his story heard in the only way he knew how.

'In there,' he said, pointing to a small room. It was one of the few with intact windows and a solid door with a working lock. It still smelled strongly of vomit, and he screwed his nose up. Katie walked to the centre of the room without a word.

'Sit on the bed,' he said, producing a rope from a rucksack on the floor. He tied her to the metal frame by her hands. It would be enough. She wouldn't struggle, and she wouldn't try to escape – he'd told her not to. Despite his debilitating symptoms, he still trusted his ability to hold her.

'Where's my dad?' said Katie. Her body was rigid.

Victor allowed himself a smile. 'He's coming,' he said, but his smile vanished as he studied her face. She was too innocent, too pure. She looked too much like Laura.

It was nearly time to wake her up. He wanted her awake and lucid when Alex Madison arrived. He couldn't have the burden of controlling two people at once, and he wanted to see the fear on both their faces.

'Stay here,' he said, unnecessarily, forcing his thoughts away from the girl and leaving the room. He closed and locked the door with the rusty key. He needed some time to himself. To sit and get his head under control. He'd taken too many painkillers already, so he must push through it himself. If Alex Madison had followed his instructions, he should arrive soon. This time, he would not escape.

CHAPTER FIFTY-FOUR

Natalia shuffled uncomfortably on the plastic chair. She risked another glance up at the heavy-set man standing in front of her, across the table in the backroom of a grotty Ukrainian restaurant not far from Clapham Junction. She slid her hands together, cracking her knuckles in turn.

Her attendance had been demanded via a short, sweet telephone call, and the penalty for not showing up was laid out to her in a few choice Russian expletives.

'We're doing our best,' she said in a small voice, for the fifth time, wondering if this man would be susceptible to her. She doubted it. They wouldn't send anybody to meet her or Freak who could be influenced. He would be trained and protected, just like the others. She wondered how long he'd been in the UK. He'd made no attempt to soften his thick Russian accent when he'd called. In person he looked every bit the Soviet-era thug. Natalia's eyes darted around the room, her nerves on end.

The waft of cooked meats hit her nostrils. She was hungry and hadn't eaten all day, but the man didn't look as if he was going to offer her dinner.

He'd kept her here for thirty minutes so far, asking why she'd screwed up so badly, why things were so noisy, and why the police were all over it. Her protests were met with deaf ears.

'You've had a long run at this one,' said the man. His huge frame was draped in a seasonally unsuitable coat and he had a slovenly appearance, his long black hair swept to one side. He scraped one of his boots on the tiled floor and sniffed.

'Perhaps you'd do better yourself?' said Natalia, rising to the bait but instantly regretting it. The man frowned. He leaned in and put his fists on the wooden table.

'It has been discussed, believe me,' he said. 'Your position is precarious.'

Natalia bit her lip. The man breathed heavily, his stale breath washing over Natalia's face, mixing with the smell of meat, causing her to screw her nose up. Noises from the kitchen seeped under the door, which had been closed and locked by her companion.

'You are not unique,' he continued, 'but we thought you were able, you and your dog. You are well thought of. Praised, on occasion. If we were mistaken, I can recommend we review your status.'

Natalia tensed. This man was not a thug. He spoke with clarity and eloquence. She knew what that meant. Would she be protected by her man in Russia – Nikolai – the man who had brought her in? She doubted it. Not if he'd sent one of his men all the way here. She sensed she was within a hair's breadth of being retired.

'We are able,' she said, her tone soft. She smiled through her racing heartbeat. 'I meant no offence. It's just frustrating, and I'm sorry not to be able to give you what you want yet. What we both want.'

The man nodded, keeping his eyes fixed on hers.

'I want nothing more than to solve our current problem,' she said. 'Thirteen is dangerous and a threat to us. But we can deal with him. I can deal with him. There's no need to bring in anyone else.'

The man sniffed again and nodded. He backed away and paced, staring through a dirty window out into the alleyway behind the restaurant, towards the stacks of cardboard and wheelie bins. Natalia had spent a lot of her youth hiding out in such dark and secluded places, where a body could be discarded with ease. She shivered. Her throat felt dry.

'So many chances,' the man said. 'You children, we gave you everything. Some of you are so . . . ungrateful.' He shook his head.

Natalia remained seated and silent. She glanced at her watch and felt an almost overwhelming surge of guilt and desperation. She had failed so far, she knew that, but still had time to put it right.

'I leave for Saint Petersburg next Tuesday at noon,' the man said, nodding to himself. 'If the matter is taken care of, then you will return with me and enjoy our hospitality and thanks. There is a place for you on the programme, training the newest subjects.' He paused, scratching his nose.

'But if I don't have good news to take with me, you will be recalled. Your services will be terminated. You and your friend will be sent to Volgograd. I think you know what awaits you there.'

He walked over to the door and unlocked it, swinging it wide open. He looked sad, but resigned. 'I have nothing more to say.'

Natalia pushed herself to her feet, the threat echoing in her ears. She left without a word, not daring to look back.

Natalia joined Freak twenty minutes later. She'd paced up and down in the street, glaring at pedestrians for a few minutes, mulling over her options, before Freak had called. He babbled something about Alex Madison's daughter and then sent her a text message with a location.

Natalia walked the short distance, deep in thought, controlling her heart rate. She was angry at herself and her masters, but terrified with it. She'd screwed up. It was her fault. Would it be better just to cut and run?

She found Freak huddled uncomfortably under the shelter of a large shrub in an abandoned garden in Battersea. The garden bordered the property where Freak said Thirteen was hiding out: a decrepit and rambling old building on a side road, the inhabitants long since departed. The road was full of potholes and the pavements were cracked, weeds everywhere. This place had been forgotten.

Natalia listened as Freak recounted the last hour, following Victor's kidnapping of Alex's daughter and subsequent journey here.

She took it all in calmly, still reeling from her meeting and still trying not to picture their shared future if she failed. The man's words rang in her ears. She'd been to Volgograd before, in the beginning, and it meant death for those who didn't comply, but not before they'd taken every ounce of life from you. She couldn't go back, and she couldn't let them have Freak either.

All the more reason to pay attention and do her job. They couldn't run. For one, they wouldn't get very far. Her masters had a way of finding people and they'd be tracked. Others would be deployed. Others like them, capable of a violent and protracted hunt across the globe. They'd never be safe.

Two, they couldn't leave that little girl in the hands of Thirteen. Natalia would never forgive herself.

This would be their only chance. They would take Victor today, or die trying.

'Where is he?' said Natalia, dropping her bag down next to Freak and peering through the windows of the building. She couldn't make anything out. The windows were intact but many were boarded over or obscured with grime.

'He's there,' said Freak, his lips parted as he drew breath, in and out, hissing into the undergrowth. 'At the back,' he continued, pointing to the rear of the building. 'I came out here to wait.'

'And the girl. Still with him?'

'I guess,' said Freak. 'I didn't get close enough to see. I'm not facing him alone.'

Natalia nodded. She sympathised. He'd suffer far worse than she if they failed, for she was the only thing that had protected him over the years. He wouldn't be missed by the world.

'Tell me what you think,' she said. An olive branch. He'd only ever been a loyal companion, following her, protecting her, and now being failed by her. If he died it would be her fault, nobody else's. 'Your assessment. What should we do?'

Freak hesitated. He breathed out and closed his eyes. 'He's desperate,' he said. 'Thirteen is in pain, and confused. The kidnapping of this girl was impulsive and idiotic. He is weak. Possibly as weak as he's likely to get.' He sniffed deeply and screwed up his face. 'I think he's near breaking point,' he continued. 'If we do anything, it needs to be soon.'

Natalia nodded, preparing herself, feeling her stomach turn. If Thirteen was desperate and suffering, he would be unpredictable, but Freak was right. They needed to strike now.

She understood why Thirteen had targeted the doctors, and why he had killed Dr Rupert Madison. The doctor was a part of her history too, and she could find no sympathy for him. But when Freak told her about the young girl, well, that was a different crime altogether, and entirely impossible to ignore.

She couldn't watch Thirteen butcher an innocent girl, his madness outdone only by his brutality. It wasn't – shouldn't – be what they were all about. Her kind had a destiny far nobler than butchery and pain. It was never supposed to end like this. She'd got far too involved and let her feelings cloud her judgement.

But their time had come. It was today or never. Callous, cold and amoral, her actions over the years had built a debt she wanted to repay. If this was it and it led to her death, so be it. To return to the Russians, leaving Thirteen behind, would be worse. They'd made that clear.

She patted Freak on the shoulder. He opened his eyes and gave her a small smile, then huffed and looked around.

'Why is Thirteen here?' said Freak. 'At an orphanage, of all places?'

'Why does Thirteen go anywhere?' she said. 'He's deranged.'

Freak nodded. 'They say that about me.'

Natalia gave him a weary look. 'You are. But not in the same way.'

'Great.' Freak's smiled widened, but faded as he read Natalia's face. 'I know that look.'

'You're right. We have to go in,' she said. She wished, on one level, that she'd managed to shed her own morality and empathy during her training. It would make life so much easier, to be able to observe a situation like this, deal with the problem and to hell with the lives lost.

But she couldn't. The child, Alex Madison's daughter, was innocent of anything, as far as she knew. Of course, there was the possibility she was evil in some other way, some humans just are, but Natalia doubted it, and couldn't convince herself it was a possibility worth killing her for.

No, this was the time and the place. Determined by Thirteen; determined by her masters. They had no choice.

Silencing Thirteen was paramount.

'A few more minutes,' she said. She needed a few deep breaths to prepare herself. 'Then we're going in. And we're gonna do our thing.'

She looked around at the building and into the road. They had a clear view. They'd see if Thirteen left, or anybody else approached.

Freak just nodded and sat on the bare concrete. 'Whenever you're ready.'

CHAPTER
FIFTY-FIVE

Alex followed the satnav, hurtling through outer London as fast as he dared. His driving was erratic and dangerous but he kept going until the robotic voice announced that he'd arrived. He screeched to a halt in the road, beside a high brick wall. Faded lettering above the arched gate confirmed it as St Joseph's. Looking beyond, he shivered. This place was darker than HMP Whitemoor and more foreboding. His daughter was captive and helpless; he was her only chance. He thought of Grace and a rush of emotions hit him. He'd ruined his family once already, and now he was exposing them to this.

He tried not to think of the reasons why Victor had chosen such a repressive place to hide out. The significance of the building was not lost on Alex, but it must hurt Victor too, reminding himself of an abusive childhood. The man was tormenting himself, as well as Alex and Katie.

He pulled over and turned off the engine, which ticked and popped as it cooled. Fumbling his phone out of his pocket, he checked for messages. Nothing yet from Sophie, so he sent her one, with his location. I had no choice, he wrote.

He sent it and stared for a few moments, before bringing up Hartley's contact details. His thumb hovered over the call button but he resisted. Victor had been clear. If the police screamed up with sirens blaring and lights flashing it would condemn Katie. Instead he crafted a text message and saved it. It outlined his intentions and where he was. If things went south and he had the chance, he'd send it. If not . . . it would be a record of his last thoughts, and the police could do with it what they wanted.

With a deep breath, he viewed the last caller ID. Pausing briefly to get his thoughts in order, he dialled.

It rang for twenty seconds or so. Alex was on the verge of hanging up when the call connected. Silence at the other end.

'Victor, it's—'

He said no more, for Victor's voice came loud and clear. Not from the phone, but from a gap in the wall, where the face of a madman twisted and snarled. Alex didn't make out the words, but the world turned grey. His eyes glazed over and he slumped.

CHAPTER
FIFTY-SIX

It seemed misty to Alex. Thick. Or was it fog? What was the difference? He vaguely remembered fog being wet, like walking into the bathroom after his mum had showered, the large mirror covered in microscopic droplets, begging to be drawn on with a finger sketching a snake or a snowman. His mum would call out to him – *Get my pills, would you? Oh, and pass me my towel. No, not that one, the small one.* She'd yell if he got the wrong towel. She'd yell until the pills kicked in. Then she'd hug and forgive him.

But she called him by his pet name. What was it? He grasped at fragments of memory, willing the name to appear. But like the mist, his memory was hazy and insubstantial, disappearing as he closed in on it. Try as he might, his memory failed, and he couldn't recall it any more than he could name a stranger in the street.

He stood in silence for a moment, listening, tilting his head, imagining he could hear a voice, but the wind was picking up and it drowned out everything except the rustling of the trees at the edge of the walled garden. He slammed the car door and glanced at the starless sky. It felt strange, to have the wind on his face yet at the same time a mist all around. Was that right?

His mind spiralled in confusion and the anxiety hit him like a fist. He groaned as pain shot through his forehead and panic cut through his stomach, making him retch. He vomited on to the pavement, bent double. His breath came in short gasps and the dizziness increased as he hyperventilated.

Then he heard the voice.

It told him to crawl through a hole in the wall. Alex saw, through the mist, a ragged break in the bricks. He ducked and shimmied through. Standing straight, he walked several paces to the building. It was grey, like rain, and whispered to him.

The whispering washed over him. He looked around but there was nobody there, yet the inner voice calmed him. He focused his breathing, slowing it and breathing out more than he breathed in. The pins and needles in his face gradually faded and the nausea disappeared.

Closing his eyes, he smiled, listening to the man who was whispering to him. He didn't catch any of the words but it didn't matter.

The grounds were still foggy but punctuated with bursts of sunlight, bright and overwhelming. Everything was unkempt and overgrown, the grass ankle-length, hiding daisies in their hundreds. The walls were in need of treatment, covered in climbing plants: clematis and something thicker he couldn't identify. Perhaps a type of ivy. A cherry tree at the end was coming into bloom, the white petals giving way to baby pink as they opened. It all felt familiar, but brighter, as if it had come to life.

He walked along a concrete path made of square paving slabs cut into the mud. A dead rat appeared on one of the slabs, and he stepped over it. The rat was long gone, dried up and half-eaten. Alex shivered but kept walking until he reached the end, staring at a large brick porch and wooden door.

The door stood open.

He found himself in a corridor, following the voice. His eyelids drooped, his pupils dilated and the corridor stretched into the infinite distance. It was grey and smelled of bleach.

He could hear shouts in his head, and clangs as metal-rimmed doors hit their metal frames. He drifted along the corridor, stopping at a metal gate. A woman to his right smiled and slapped him on the shoulder. He turned to look but she vanished into the fog.

He was through the gate and it shut behind him. The woman was gone and in her place somebody else stomped along beside him. Heavy footsteps and a jingling of metal, perhaps a keychain. A muffled whisper in his ear followed by footsteps fading into the distance, leaving him alone, facing a single grey door. It looked like the door to a cell.

The hairs on his neck rose as he reached out. The door was cold and smooth. It wouldn't move. He struggled, pushing it with both hands, but it remained locked, and he didn't know where the key was. He took his hands away and closed his eyes.

'Wake up, Alex.'

Alex opened his eyes and the dream ended. He was back in the real world.

His surroundings sharpened into focus. Immediately, he was hit by the stench. The room he was in smelled revolting – the waft of vomit and excrement was overwhelming. The floor was broken, tiles scattered and bare concrete exposed. The walls weren't much better. Some peeling paint remained but age had stripped everything else.

His few days at the prison had conditioned him, but this place was worse. Light filtered through a dirty window, illuminating Victor, who sat between the legs of an upturned trolley, stiff and upright. His plump frame rose and fell with his breathing and he didn't look at Alex. He adjusted his glasses and cleared his throat.

'You get used to it,' said Victor, his voice barely a whisper. 'But I won't apologise. As I doubt you'll apologise for smelling of perfume.'

Alex paused and couldn't help but sniff. He might have brushed against Sophie earlier; he detected the slight floral musky odour. Victor had a better nose than he did.

'They often wore perfume,' said Victor. 'I suppose it made them feel like normal people, with lives and boyfriends and romance. Even while they were doing what they did.'

Alex touched his nose, aware the stimulants had set his heart racing.

'Dad!' The voice tore through him and he yanked his head around. Behind and to the left, on an iron-framed bed, was Katie, bound at the wrists. She had pure terror in her eyes.

He tried to stand but found his hands tied behind him, securely fastened to a metal shelving unit.

'If you struggle, it'll hurt,' said Victor.

'Please,' said Alex. His head felt awash and his heart thumped. It hurt to breathe.

'Let her go,' he said. 'Where's Grace?'

'Your father killed a lot of people.' Victor sniffed and picked his nose, wiping his finger on his trousers.

'I can't answer for my father,' hissed Alex. 'Please, let—'

'What is your relationship with your parents like?' said Victor. 'I mean, what *was* it like? Don't you hate them for what they did to you?'

Alex narrowed his eyes, checking his heart rate. Victor might be close to the truth, but now was not the time. Could Alex afford to play Victor's games? Answer his questions? Could he afford not to?

'We're not talking about me,' said Alex. He tried to keep the emotion out of his voice but failed.

'But of course, you know I didn't live with my parents.' Victor sniffed again.

'I know you suffered in the orphanage,' said Alex. He saw the reaction he was looking for. Victor stiffened, his left fist clenching.

'They mistreated you, Thirteen.'

Victor closed his eyes and shook his head. 'They created me, Dr Madison.' He let it hang for a few moments.

'They abused you, tortured you. Did despicable experiments on you and your friends. I get that,' said Alex. 'But what's to be gained by involving my daughter? By dragging this out? Where's Grace?'

'Dragging it out?' Victor's manner switched. He bared his teeth. His voice lowered in tone. 'I spent ten fucking years at Comăneşti. Dragging it out? I will drag it out as long as I fucking like, Dr Madison. That's the point. You don't know who is next. You don't know what role you'll be asked to play.' He spat on the floor and wiped his mouth on the back of his palm.

Alex looked again at Katie. Her eyes were wide with fear. She wept, her chest trembling and shaking with each breath.

'Why now?' said Alex. 'This . . . whatever happened to you, it happened when you were a child. Why are you doing this now?'

Victor glared at him.

'I'll tell you where they are,' said Alex. The desperation caused his voice to slur. 'I'll find out from the police. They trust me. I'll give them all to you in exchange for my daughter. You can keep me.'

Victor turned on his heel. Alex saw him wince in pain, clenching his teeth. Alex thought he looked like a wounded animal. The most dangerous kind.

'Begging,' said Victor. 'You're begging me for your life?'

'Not for mine,' said Alex, his eyes welling up. 'For hers.'

Victor winced again. 'Do you know how many times I begged?' he said. He stood over Katie's bed, looking down, not at her, but through her. 'I begged until they made me bleed, until they knocked me to the floor, until I was drugged and unconscious.'

He cocked his head and examined Katie's face. 'I begged while I watched a friend die in front of me. Do you know why?' He paused but didn't wait for an answer. 'I begged because I didn't believe people could be so evil. Not deep down. Not in their hearts. I thought if I cried hard enough or long enough it would stop.'

Alex met Victor's eyes. He saw them burning.

'Who did I beg, Alex?'

Alex shook his head.

'Which makes this little party all the better, doesn't it?'

Alex's eyes flicked to Katie. Through the fear she looked puzzled, her eyes questioning.

'How long have you been part of this, Alex Madison?' said Victor. 'How long have you and your father hidden the torture and the lies? You know I came for him.'

'I wasn't part of it,' said Alex, gasping. Victor was spiralling out of control and Alex knew he couldn't pull him out of it. He couldn't convince Victor of his own innocence – the man was in a fury, reason was out of the window.

'Your father was a most evil man, as it turns out,' said Victor. 'And you know what they say – they don't fall far from the tree.' He turned to Katie again. 'Which makes what I'm doing necessary. Do you see that? I can forgive you all, but you must pay.'

'No!' Alex shouted. Then, softer, 'My father, yes. But not me, and not her. She is as innocent as you were.'

Alex watched for the response, desperately seeking common ground. Victor believed he was an innocent, corrupted. To a great extent he was right. Alex needed to paint them all in the same way.

'I saw you in the prison,' said Victor. His face was pasty and full of pain. He shivered, as if bolts of electricity were hitting him. 'And I saw you at your father's house, right before I killed him. How can you protest your innocence? You're one of them. Part of it. You came to continue what he started.'

'You're wrong.' Alex regained some of his composure. 'And you know my daughter is innocent. As innocent as all the children were back then. You know it, Victor.'

Victor paused and Alex continued. 'I'll give you the location of the other doctors – my father's colleagues. The ones who created this programme and tortured you and your friends. I have no obligation towards them, Victor. I'll give you their location and I'll take my daughter in return. I swear I wasn't part of this.'

His eyes pleaded with Victor, but he saw no change in the fire behind Victor's eyes. Alex had been right about him – there was no rationality there, not at the moment. The man was a whirlwind of hate, wrapped in his mutant ability. He was a damaged, tortured soul.

'No,' said Victor, finally. 'Those despicable people are beyond reach now, but it doesn't matter. You're the ones I need. You and your daughter. You're my redemption.'

Alex gulped. 'You're wrong, Victor. I can help you. Let me help you.'

Victor closed his eyes and shook his head. He reached out and touched Katie's head, cradling her face in his hand. He looked sad. He fingered her hair, trailing strands between his fingers.

'I forgive you, Dr Madison,' he said. 'It's time.'

The fog returned. It crept around the edges of Alex's vision as he drifted away. The voice echoed in his head, friendly but insistent. It explored and burrowed, grasping parts of him and tying them together, dangling them out of reach.

He was aware of his arms moving. His wrists were free and he held them up. His hands were missing, and in their place were two bottles of drugs. Brown glass with white plastic caps. Both said ALEX MADISON on the front and they rattled. He didn't know what was in the bottles – he had no way of opening them. He shook his arms left to right and the bottles disappeared.

The room dissolved and he walked. A long corridor with a bed at the end. There was somebody in it, facing away. The person called to him in a soft, feminine voice. He walked faster then ran, but the bed remained at the same distance away. He stopped and the figure turned over. It was Sophie.

She smiled and pulled the sheet away to reveal her naked body. She writhed and beckoned to him with her finger. He smiled, but Sophie shook her head.

'I'm sorry, Alex,' said Sophie. Tears streamed down her cheeks as she wept. Alex blinked, and when he opened his eyes Sophie had gone.

His mother lay in the bed. An old lady, frail and weak. She opened her eyes and spoke to him.

'Alex,' she said. He leaned in closer. 'Please don't do this.'

Alex recoiled. His mother hissed and slid under the covers. Alex pulled them away but the bed slid away into the fog.

He could still hear the voice, but muffled, in the distance. It was high, firm but scared. He couldn't make out the words.

His unease deepened as the fog gave way to darkness. His heart thumped and tendrils of panic snaked at the edges. Something was wrong and he shuddered.

A silhouette appeared, several feet away. He couldn't make out her face, but she had long, flowing hair. She backed away from him and he followed. Her hands came up in defence and she tripped, falling backwards. Alex rushed forwards and she screamed. He paused, but didn't stop. His hands appeared in front of him, covered in blood. He held them to his eyes and saw the dark liquid seep through his fingers.

The woman screamed again. A third time. She was pleading, begging.

Alex felt a slam at the back of his skull. A noise, as loud as an explosion; pressure popping his ears. Then a familiar voice, shouting at him. The fog cleared, seeping downwards, bright light flooding the area above.

He gasped.

His trance was broken. He was back in the room with Victor and Katie. How or why, he didn't know, but he was hovering over Katie, who lay on the bed, her eyes streaming with tears. She was screaming and pleading, repeating the word 'Dad' over and over. He glanced at his hands. The right one held a kitchen knife. With horror he twisted the knife around in his hand and looked back to Katie. Hurling the knife to the floor he staggered back, trying to make sense of the situation. His body was still resistant, still partly under. He couldn't move his feet properly; it was like wading through deep water.

Victor remained in the corner, his face masked with menace and confusion. He glanced around the room, eyes darting into the corners and to the ceiling.

Alex struggled. Katie's screams echoed in his ears.

Victor hissed. 'How did you do that? How did you break it?'

Katie's sobs subsided. Alex turned to her but had no words to explain what had happened. Katie was shaking and hyperventilating, staring at Alex in fear. He couldn't keep her gaze. His world was caving in, shattered by the man who was leaning against the far wall, holding his own head.

Victor looked to be in excruciating pain. He banged his head backwards into the wall and bent double. He gasped and groaned, holding his temples. He panted for several moments before staggering over to a bucket in the corner. He vomited, retching violently before stumbling to his knees. After several moments he raised his head.

Alex's eyes were bleary with tears. Victor's eyes were pained and full of hate.

'You,' said Victor. 'You are forgiven. Both of you.'

Alex tried to move – his arms, legs, anything – but he was still under Victor's spell.

Victor approached him, trying to speak, but the words caught in his throat. He stuttered and turned to the window. His eyes narrowed and Alex saw uncertainty in the man's face.

Puzzled, he followed Victor's gaze. Through the grimy cracked window he saw a man – short, dark-haired and wild. His crooked head was tilted, and his eyes were focused on Victor. He was muttering under his breath, the whispers seeping through the broken glass.

For the first time, Victor looked scared.

CHAPTER FIFTY-SEVEN

Natalia and Freak were still waiting in their huddle behind the bush. They had watched Alex arrive at the front of the orphanage, ditching his car in the middle of the road.

'This makes things more complicated,' said Freak, picking his ear and examining his forefinger.

Natalia nodded. Natalia wondered how many of the people in that building would die today. Perhaps all of them. Perhaps her. Not the little girl, she hoped. Not an innocent.

Natalia felt the familiar anxiety wash over her. Her time at the prison had been uncomfortable but manageable. Dr Madison, though, had been a factor she hadn't predicted. Alex could have been useful. That was her plan. It was always the plan. But faking it for so long confused her. It gave her glimpses of a normal existence, with people who also experienced terrible things and still managed to live. She felt attracted to the man, who treated her as an equal – so unlike her experience of men before. Against her better judgement she'd followed that attraction and found herself falling, experiencing emotions that were forbidden, punishable in the harshest way.

Alex had been a mistake, professionally, but one she'd always remember, long after she left this place or departed this world, whichever came sooner. She'd been honest with Alex at the time, on that matter at least. She didn't regret it.

Natalia watched Alex now for several moments, sitting in his car outside the orphanage walls, talking into his phone.

'He's under,' said Freak, his eyes darting around. 'Thirteen must be close.'

Natalia frowned.

'He's going in,' said Freak.

'We need to get closer,' said Natalia, as Alex disappeared behind the front wall, 'so you can do what you do.'

Freak sucked in a breath. 'Now?' he said. 'Are you sure?'

'Now.' Natalia caught his eye and tried to look confident.

Freak straightened up. She saw the fear in his eyes but also the determination.

'I will try,' he said, then stood and strode towards the orphanage.

Treading across the broken concrete, they both avoided the rubbish and crumbling stone, creeping along the side of the huge brick monstrosity, avoiding the section where Alex Madison had entered, instead heading towards the rear of the building where Freak had spotted Victor earlier.

They stopped in a walled courtyard with a rusty swing-set at the centre. The actual swings were long gone. Broken tarmac suggested other playground equipment had once adorned this place, no doubt providing some distraction for the children who lived here. Natalia looked wistfully at the swing. She never got to play as a child. She was always late with her chores or punished and made to do extra. Her dormitory supervisor had at least spared her the alternative, perhaps because she was plump as a child, clumsy and unattractive. She took the chores and was thankful.

'Where are they?' she hissed.

Freak cocked his head. He shrugged and moved closer to the building, stopping every few steps and listening.

'Well?'

Freak put his hand up to silence her. 'He put the girl somewhere around here. Ground floor. If you keep talking I'll never find him.'

Natalia bit her tongue and crouched next to a pile of bricks. She knew she was on the verge of panic. They were out of time. Thirteen's murderous rampage was unique among the targets they'd acquired over the years, and only caution would keep them alive. She watched Freak searching along the outer wall, peering in through the cracked and splintered windows, searching for their prey. He paused to listen, ear against the crumbling bricks, pacing to the next window. Underneath one he froze, ducking down. He pointed upwards, keeping his head below the sill, tilting his head to listen.

He looked over to Natalia, eyes wide, finger to his lips.

Natalia crept over, careful with her feet not to snag any twigs or trip on the broken concrete. She approached the window and risked a look inside, peering in from the bottom right corner. It was broken, a jagged triangle of glass missing. She took in the situation and swore several times.

'Shit,' she said, under her breath. Natalia closed her eyes for several seconds. When she opened them, she had determination in her eyes.

'Background noise,' she whispered to Freak. 'As strong as possible. Can you do it?'

Freak raised his eyebrows.

'Can you?'

Freak nodded. 'But . . . what about Thirteen?'

'You have to.'

'He might not be good for anything afterwards.'

'I'll take the risk,' said Natalia.

'If it works, that is. I said I haven't—'

'Just do it, Freak. Snap the doctor out of it. Block what Thirteen's doing. Do it now.

I'm going in.'

CHAPTER
FIFTY-EIGHT

Alex's eyes darted from the man at the window and back again to Victor. The man at the window had his eyes locked on Victor, and was speaking. The distance dispersed the sound, but Alex recognised it as the technique Victor used when attempting control.

Victor sneered but the worried expression remained. His mouth dropped open and he shouted some words Alex guessed were Romanian – curses, perhaps. He doubted they were greetings. Victor ran towards the bed, grabbing the knife from the floor in a quick sweep of his hand.

'No,' yelled Alex, but Victor grabbed Katie's hair in one hand and yanked her head back. She screamed as he reached behind her and cut the rope that bound her to the bed. He dragged Katie by her hair, off the bed and towards the door. His right hand still held the knife, which he pressed to Katie's neck, breaking the skin. A thin trickle of blood ran on to the collar of her T-shirt.

Victor kept the knife where it was but flinched, his eyes once again darting to the window, where the wild-looking man still stood.

'Please,' begged Alex.

'Stay where you are,' Victor said, his voice hammering into Alex's forehead. 'You've had your time, Dr Madison. It's over for you. Remember, with your dying breath, this is personal. Your father, you and then this little girl. Three generations of yours in exchange for countless innocents on my side. I forgive you all.'

Alex froze, his body jerking as Victor muttered under his breath. Victor raised his hand towards Alex and shouted several words in quick succession. Alex tried to turn away, to block his ears, anything, but he couldn't.

There was silence. His nostrils flared as the air got colder.

Alex found himself staring at his mother again. It was her bedroom in his childhood home. She lay on the bed, sheets tucked under her chin. He reached out but she shied away, scared.

'Leave,' she said. 'Leave. You know how to.'

Alex didn't know what she meant, but he backed away. His footsteps echoed and the room expanded. No matter how far he walked, the bed remained right in front of him. His mother turned over and he saw the back of Sophie's head.

Something was wrong. Alex had been here before, and he grasped at the edges, trying to recognise where he was. He was on the edge, but in a dream. Victor. He knew what was happening to him. He knew he was under, within his own mind. He knew it wasn't real.

He tried to spin around but the room spun with him. *Focus, Alex.* He stopped trying to move and instead decided that he wanted to be somewhere else. Outside the room, on the landing.

The room disappeared and Alex found himself in a corridor. Dark and cold. Concrete floors and orange brick walls. The distance was still hazy, but there was a door. He walked towards the door but with every step it got further away. The fog descended again and his heart thumped. Wrong. He was doing it wrong.

He closed his eyes and willed the door open. He grabbed the door handle and pulled himself through. His heart sank as the silhouette of Sophie strode away from him. *Don't try to catch her up*, he thought, glancing around the prison office.

Where do you need to go? Think. Alex examined the structures around him. His mother, Sophie and his family. Images of his failures – mother and daughter lying on the floor. His worst insecurities building themselves around him, in danger of creating a dream he would circle forever until released or ordered otherwise.

But Alex was aware. He understood the method, and could battle it. All it took was a journey in his head. Find his way out and he'd be free. Locations mattered. He needed to find the path.

His mind resisted, his thoughts were slow. The drugs dispersed into his bloodstream.

A dark corridor appeared. It extended forever, without a single door in its black walls. Alex's feet felt heavy as he forced himself to walk. Faster he paced, until he broke into a run, the walls skimming past as he raced towards the darkness. He heard voices, screams, muffled in the distance. He recognised Katie's voice in an instant. She was calling for help. A second voice snarled.

The prison flashed into existence. The corridor became clear, the cell doors shut and locked, all except one, facing him. The grey door swung open, revealing an empty cell. Victor's cell. Alex lunged forwards but he found Sophie inside the cell, sitting on the edge of the bed. She stared at the wall. His gut heaved. Sophie's face kept flickering, changing and morphing into someone else. She smiled and turned, then disappeared.

The cell dissolved, his vision jolted.

His mind swirled and he screamed for release. Spiralling downwards, the fear seared through his throat and into his stomach where it convulsed and wrenched. His back ached and his legs tensed, the muscles jarring and jerking in protest. The pain travelled through his veins, a pulse throbbing into the back of his skull and waiting, building up pressure with every heartbeat.

Still, he couldn't escape. Trapped and floating, Alex's head spun with vertigo.

Move, Alex, move, he told himself.

His ears screamed with pain. Somebody was calling him. The words hit him like a hammer but he didn't understand them. They dug and chiselled away, causing his thoughts to break apart. New thoughts wouldn't form – they were too insubstantial, and the voice swatted them away like flies.

It persisted. Calling that tugged at the corners of his trance. Primal and cutting, this voice was different. It was familiar and grasped his mind with an equal force, giving him a moment of clarity. He was under, but near the surface. He must break free. Follow the voice.

He saw his car, abandoned in the street, a derelict building behind it. He recognised it. The orphanage where Katie was being held. He forced himself towards the crumbling brick wall and through into the garden. He heard the voice again. Female and calm, it was increasing in intensity, a warning. Alex willed himself through the door and into the bleak interior. He listened for her voice, blocking out everything else.

The walls floated, grey and marked, the plaster falling around him. A door stood open. Two figures silhouetted against the light, struggling. Katie wept but Alex couldn't reach her. He walked as if underwater, his strides failing to reach the room before the silhouettes faded and disappeared.

Alex entered the room. This was where he needed to be. The voice called to him again. Once more before cutting off.

Wake up, Alex.

A scream shot through the fog. It cut the trance and Alex rose up, lifted and carried out of the darkness. It found him, and dragged him into consciousness. He heard her. Not in a dream, but here and now.

His trance was broken. Somebody had led him out. Alex opened his eyes and found himself in the same room, kneeling at the foot of the bed.

But the bed was empty.

'Katie.' His hands were shaking. He was in shock, hyperventilating, his face hot and breath shallow, gasping for air. His panic was boiling over.

'Victor!' he shouted, his voice hoarse. He pulled himself up, dazed and uncoordinated. His vision was crooked and he blinked hard. He instinctively reached into his pocket. He must call the police. But his hand met nothing but his car keys. His phone was gone.

'Katie,' he whispered. 'Where are you, Katie?' He stared at the doorway where he'd seen her last. There was nothing but the scuffmarks of shoes on the dusty concrete. Victor and Katie had gone.

'Alex.'

A woman's voice, clear and calm, met his ears. The figure of a woman appeared in the doorway. He was unable to hide his surprise.

'Sophie?' he said, with a mixture of desperation and relief, squinting through his tears and the shadows. 'Is that—'

Sophie emerged into the light. Alex shook his head and blinked. His mind spiralled in confusion.

'Hi, Alex,' she said.

'I don't . . .' He tried to refocus, but it was like an illusion. One second it was Sophie, the next she transformed into a stranger. His eyes flickered and his brain struggled to keep up.

'You were on the precipice,' she said, leaning forward, looking into his eyes, 'but I think we got you out in time. You scared me.'

She whispered to him. Her features changed, subtly but surely. Her face danced and his recognition shifted. His head spun.

'My name is Natalia, Alex.'

'I'm sorry, I—'

'We don't have time,' said Natalia, nodding upwards. 'Katie. She's still here. Upstairs, somewhere.'

Alex struggled to find his voice. 'Natalia? I don't understand.'

The woman shook her head. Her eyes were familiar and sad; the troubled depths remained.

'I'm sorry, Alex. It was the way it had to be.' She frowned, then called out. 'Freak. Hurry up.'

Alex backed away and found himself against a wall. He heard glass breaking as the rest of the window smashed, followed by a grunt and the appearance of the short, wiry man. The same man who'd stared through the window and caused Victor to run off.

The man shuffled across to her. He glanced at Alex. 'Upstairs.'

'I know that,' she said.

'He's weak.'

'Weak enough?'

'Maybe.'

'Did you manage to?'

'A little,' said the man, shuffling off again, heading around the corner.

Natalia paused. 'Follow us,' she said to Alex. 'I think your daughter . . .'

'Katie?' Alex swallowed, his eyes darting around the room. There was nothing here except the scattered remains of Victor's squat. Food, drinks and some old clothing.

'Which way?' said Natalia.

Alex didn't remember coming in. He remembered being outside, calling Victor, and then . . . he had woken up in this room. He stared at the woman in front of him, still groggy and weak. He didn't understand, but Katie was his focus and he lurched past her into the corridor.

Outside, the corridors opened out and around into an L-shape, with rooms feeding away from it. He ran into a couple – classrooms with the odd desk lying around. A few chairs tossed here and there on the floor, several missing legs. No sign of Katie or Victor, but he thought he could hear footsteps. A girl's voice echoed.

Natalia began to run. Alex, startled, picked himself up and ran after her. He staggered, confused, unable to process what was going on.

They shot around the corner, through a set of double doors and into a stairwell. The concrete staircase was crumbling but intact, with rusting handrails, winding up to the next floor. It smelled stale and earthy. The dust caught in Alex's throat.

'Up,' she said and climbed the concrete stairs, two at a time. Alex followed, avoiding the cracks and newspapers. Shards of broken glass crunched underfoot.

Two flights up, Natalia jolted to a stop. She put her hand out and crept forward. Alex followed. He could hear voices, both male, both speaking Romanian, or that's what he figured.

The top of the stairs opened into a huge dinner hall. The sun streamed in from the south, and reflected off the steel beams. The floor was thick wood, black after so many years, strewn with broken tables and chairs. Many of the windows were broken and the wind blew in, swirling into the corners where paper and other rubbish piled restlessly.

In the centre of the room stood Victor. He leaned against one of the steel beams that supported the ceiling. Scattered lumps of plasterboard and bricks surrounded his feet. His face was pale and he wheezed, but the fury still burned in his eyes. He held Katie by her hair. She was sobbing, on her knees.

Alex tried to run forwards but Natalia stepped into his path.

'No,' she ordered. Alex watched the stranger who called herself Natalia. He was surprised at the authority in her voice.

She walked forward, issuing a stream of Romanian and broken English. Alex wasn't sure who she was talking to. Her voice was calm, but wavered slightly. Alex felt her fear.

Victor winced. He slapped his right hand to his temple and screamed, his eyes darting around. With his other hand he still had Katie gripped by the hair. A figure emerged from the shadows near the stairway. The man Natalia had called Freak crept around Victor, staring at him, whispering. Freak stood barely three feet away, moving his face left and right, tilting his head in a way that sent shivers down Alex's spine. The thin man was light on his feet and darted in until his face was within an inch of Victor's. He said something and Victor screamed again, falling to his knees.

He wrestled Katie closer to him and Alex gasped as he saw the knife. Victor held it to her throat.

'No!' Alex shouted.

'Wait,' said Natalia. She spoke again, as did the man. Both of them, whispering in concert, alternating as they projected their voices towards Victor. Victor's face contorted and he scrambled around on the floor.

'You can't do this to me,' said Victor. 'Why would you?'

Both Freak and Natalia stopped; they looked at each other.

'We don't want to,' said Natalia.

Victor's pained expression met hers. Something passed between them.

He shuffled into a seated position. 'I remember you. You're Fifty.' He turned to Freak and spat something in Romanian.

'Please, let her go,' said Alex. His voice sounded feeble in the huge room. Victor threw him a look of hate and held Katie tighter. The knife nicked her neck and another bead of blood appeared.

'I am Natalia,' said the woman. 'You have a choice, Thirteen.'

Victor breathed heavily for several moments. 'You sound like them.'

Natalia looked hurt. 'You're wrong.'

'Then leave me be.'

'I can't.'

'This is the child of the devil,' said Victor. His face was dripping with sweat and his breathing laboured.

'You are misguided, Thirteen.'

Victor pointed at Alex. 'They must pay. Don't you see? I have them.'

He winced again and opened his mouth as if his ears were popping. 'Your friend . . .' He turned to Freak. 'He . . . What is he doing? If you must kill me, then do it, but not until I am finished.'

'We did not come to kill you,' said Natalia. 'We came to rescue you, comrade.'

Freak smiled. Alex backed away; his eyes darted to Katie and back to Natalia. Alex's mind churned as the pieces began to match up.

'Sophie . . .?'

Natalia raised her hand towards Alex. Her eyes softened as she addressed him. 'I didn't know, OK?' she said. 'About who your father was. That bastard. I didn't know. We didn't piece it together until it was too late . . .' She trailed off, her eyes darting to Freak, who looked away.

Alex staggered back.

'Everything you did,' said Alex. 'It was all to get him . . .' Alex indicated Victor. 'This man is a monster.'

Katie whimpered, but Victor held her fast.

'I didn't lie about everything, Alex,' said Natalia, giving him a weak smile. 'And it wasn't easy.' She raised her eyebrows, the battle behind her eyes clear to Alex. He saw the familiar anxiety he'd watched in Sophie. But it didn't make it any less of a betrayal.

'I confess,' she said. 'You know my motive. But please believe me when I say I didn't have a choice. This,' she indicated Victor and Freak, 'is bigger than you or I. I'm sorry you got dragged into it. Truly I am.' She turned away for a moment, then sniffed and threw her shoulders back. 'But we have him now.'

She turned to Victor. 'And you, Thirteen,' she said. 'You thought we were coming to kill you? You've screwed up, and death is nothing more than you deserve, but that's not my call. We're here to bring you in. From the cold.'

She pointed at Katie. 'And let the girl go. You know she's innocent. You know you're wrong. Killing her won't fix anything. Killing her will only deepen the chasm. It won't bring back Laura, or any of our friends.'

Alex's heart thudded. He watched Victor wrestling with her proposition.

'Please,' said Alex. Victor looked up. 'Whatever happened to you, she had no part in it.'

Victor looked again at Natalia. Alex watched her leg shuffling as she held his gaze. She was nervous, desperate. 'Let her go, Victor,' she said. 'It's time for us to leave.'

Freak leaned in once again and whispered in his ear. Victor clenched his jaw and groaned in pain, the knife falling to the concrete with a clatter. Whatever Freak was doing, it was eating away at him. With a roar he writhed on to his side, causing Katie to fall back on her hands. She scrambled away and into Alex's open arms. He grabbed her tight and backed away, his heart leaping.

'Freak,' said Natalia. 'Don't break him.' She moved quickly, bending to retrieve the knife from the floor, along with a loose brick. She trembled but didn't hesitate. She ran at Victor and brought the brick down hard on his forehead, the crack echoing across the hall. She released it as if her hand had been shocked, and stepped back as Victor's screams turned to gasps. The thin man remained close. He was still talking, repeating a phrase to Victor, even as blood poured from his head. Then he did a strange thing. He pulled his shirt off and made it into a bandage, tying it around Victor's forehead, applying pressure to the wound.

Natalia placed her hand on Victor's shoulder. She turned to Alex, who was standing protectively in front of Katie. She whispered under her breath and nodded to Freak. He nodded back.

Alex felt her words rather than heard them. They spoke to him in a whisper. Warm and sensuous, they seeped into his mind and he relaxed. The room became bright and airy. The sun broke through the panes, casting rays of light on to the dark concrete. He listened as a second voice joined her. It snuck and twisted, jolting parts of him and grabbing at his stream of consciousness, even as he saw it unravel before him.

They both spoke to him, and he listened until all he could hear was silence.

'Alex.' Her voice was loud and clear. He opened his eyes and stared at her.

Their eyes met and held. In that moment he saw the loss, the sorrow and the regret. A single tear ran down her cheek, drawing a line in the dust. She mouthed the words to him, 'I'm sorry,' before wiping the tear away and raising her voice.

'Leave!' she shouted at Alex, grabbing Victor under one arm. Freak grabbed the other.

'Leave, and don't look back.'

CHAPTER FIFTY-NINE

Alex closed his eyes and willed sleep, but it eluded him. His mind wasn't ready to relax and neither was his body. He ached, but his muscles twitched and he couldn't get comfortable. Stretching didn't help. His head was foggy and hazy. Whenever he tried to shut off, the visions hit him, and they woke him with a start.

He saw images, floating, of a woman. He could make out her eyes but nothing more. They were deep, but terrifying. The more he searched, the more he became aware they were searching for him in return. They reached into his soul and pushed it down, warning him to stay away.

After a few hours Alex could take no more. He grabbed the plastic cup from the bedside table and emptied the water into his mouth. Glancing over, he watched Grace and Katie.

Katie had her own hospital bed – her physical wounds were superficial but the trauma was real. She'd been there, next to him, ever since they'd arrived in hospital. Sedated, but only mildly. The doctors said it would be useful to get her through the first few days. Until he and Grace recovered enough to look after her.

Grace had insisted on staying in hospital too. She had no physical injuries of her own, but as Katie's mother, the doctors didn't object.

She wasn't medicated, but the offer was there. Alex knew the mental wounds would take a long time to heal. He hadn't even attempted to discuss their experience yet. His relief at discovering Grace alive was all he needed for now. That and Katie by his side.

Five days, so far. Five days of hospital and police interrogations, following their ordeal at the abandoned site of St Joseph's orphanage in Battersea. During those five days, Alex had tried to piece together the chain of events – what exactly had happened to him and his family after he had left his house and driven to Battersea, abandoning his Alfa in the middle of the road. Everything went dark after that.

The Alfa, as luck would have it, had been reported within thirty minutes, tagged outside the orphanage by a passing police patrol. It was unusual for such a valuable classic car to be sitting there in the middle of the road. By the time the police had realised the significance of the vehicle and connected it with Alex, and then with DCI Hartley's case, nearly an hour had passed. Alex was glad they hadn't arrived sooner.

He wanted more water but the jug was empty. He considered calling for a nurse but thought it would be lazy. For he wasn't injured either. Physically and mentally, he felt as solid as he'd ever been.

But they wouldn't discharge him. They wouldn't discharge any of them.

PTSD was the first diagnosis he'd heard, whispered by a young psych to the matron, when they thought he was asleep. He knew they were wrong. Katie, perhaps, might suffer such effects. It was too early to tell. She was young enough to receive the right help and get through things. Alex knew what the plan would be for her, and he didn't object, apart from a few details, which puzzled him.

Grace's condition and treatment hadn't been discussed with him other than when he asked her directly. They weren't married any more and it wasn't his business. Grace was distant, but not hostile. Her eyes were tired and full of fear, but she was tough. She'd had to be, dealing with Alex and his behaviour. Her terrifying experience at the hands of

Victor would leave a unique stamp in her memories, but Alex hoped no lasting damage was done. Victor had not hurt her in that way. He didn't know why. Perhaps all of Victor's hate was directed elsewhere.

Alex did know, when it came to PTSD, that he was suffering no such thing. He was an expert, after all, which he told the consulting psychiatrist repeatedly. They assured him he would be fully consulted on all of their thoughts and plans, but he knew it was a lie, because he'd been in the other chair in similar situations before. The patient rarely knows best when it comes to psychological trauma.

The doctors concerned him, but it was the whispers and hurried meetings with police that gave rise to his anger and confusion. The police agreed with the doctors – all three of the Madison family would stay in 'for observation' until further notice. It was not a request, and Alex saw – even though he suspected he shouldn't have – the police officers standing guard outside, changing shifts, glancing into the room with the three beds and no other patients.

Alex had shown his anger at first, but then relented. Although confusion reigned, he was overjoyed to have Katie and Grace with him and safe, so he tried to forgive the furore and the misunderstandings.

Hartley visited every day. Alex was pleased at first, but it rapidly became tiresome as Hartley's motivation revealed itself. She might be concerned for Alex's wellbeing, but her primary aim was not in ensuring Alex's recovery.

Hartley asked the same questions, every day. And every day she was dissatisfied with Alex's answers, to the point where she shouted, stood and paced. Her frustration was ushered out of the door by the nurses and their matron, who suggested she return another time, minus her temper.

Alex, for the life of him, did not understand the source of Hartley's frustration, and tried to be as helpful as possible. He told Hartley what he remembered, what had happened.

What he knew to be the truth.

Victor had taken Katie. Had Hartley stopped this? No, she hadn't, and so Alex had little choice but to slip his guard and do what Victor wanted. He had headed to the location he'd been given – the orphanage in Battersea – to offer Victor his life for his daughter. What choice did he have? Calling the police would have been too risky. Victor might have panicked. Katie might have been hurt. Hartley nodded at all of this. She agreed it was the truth.

But Alex's recollection after this point became hazy, although he was clear on the main details. Victor held Katie at knifepoint in a derelict room of the building. He remembered only too well, for it still caused his heart to miss a beat, seeing his daughter captive, panicking, and at the mercy of a psychopath.

What had they spoken about? He couldn't remember. It was a high-stress situation. Of course he couldn't remember every word. Victor had blamed Alex. He blamed Alex's father, and he blamed the others. He was full of hate and desperation. Alex had talked to him, reasoned with him, but to no avail.

Victor got spooked and fled, taking Katie with him to one of the upper floors. Alex had given chase and confronted Victor. The man was sick, desperate – dying, by all appearances. He had reached the end and they both knew it. Victor had let Katie go and collapsed to the floor. Alex hadn't stopped to help Victor – why should he? His first priority was Katie. The two of them had run down the flight of stairs, outside and into the street, straight into the path of the first responding police officers. Victor was left in the building, easy to recapture.

Where was Victor now? Why had Victor let them go? Hartley couldn't understand it.

But he was sick; he looked pale and pasty, sweaty and feverish. He knew it was over. In his final moments, he relented. His anger had been misplaced anyway; he saw it was the right thing to do.

That's not what happened, insisted Hartley.

Grace had been found an hour later, huddled on her kitchen floor. She was out of her trance, but too weak to move, in shock and with mild dehydration. The paramedics had brought her in and the hospital psych spent some time with her, helping her recover from her confused state. Grace remembered little about her encounter, and Alex urged them not to push her. It would come out, in time. Physically she'd recover quickly. Mentally, she had an expert on hand to help.

Hartley pinched the bridge of her nose and repeated the questions again, phrased differently, in a different order. Alex gave the same answers.

A different inspector arrived on day four. A man, older, sterner and more abrupt. Hartley accompanied him for the first round of questions, then left him to it. He had no personal connection to Alex and was ruder, less compromising. Alex knew the man didn't believe him but he didn't know why.

He told his story to the nurse and to the psychiatrist who was tasked with the psych evaluation. He didn't understand why his explanation was causing so much trouble.

No, he repeated until he was blue in the face, *there was no one else there. It was Victor, Katie and me.* It was an abandoned orphanage. Besides, who else knew about Victor? Only the police.

Knife? Yes, there had been a knife. He didn't know what had happened to it. Didn't the police find it? If not, why not?

And that was what troubled Alex the most. That was what caused the confusion to spiral into anger. That was what caused him to call out for Xanax – which he was being refused – and caused the sleepless nights.

The police had failed to catch Victor. He wasn't there.

They had searched the building, the block, even a five-mile radius. The first responders were bolstered by a fresh wave of specialists. Forensics were early on the scene, and so were a bunch of suits. They were all too late. Victor had fled. Once again, he was a fugitive.

But Alex felt, deep down, that something was missing. He didn't admit this to anyone, for he worried it would affect his chances of being listened to and reasoned with. But Hartley was right about something. Alex tried to remember the last few minutes with Victor, but whenever he tried to picture Victor in the orphanage, either in the squat room downstairs, or upstairs in the dining hall, he became confused. The mental image blurred. He was dizzy. His head swam and his ears popped.

He was sure that was where he'd last seen Victor. Wasn't he?

He spoke to Grace and Katie, late in the evenings when the police and medical staff were reduced in numbers and busy on other things. Their stories corroborated his. Katie was still shocked and sedated, and couldn't recall what building she was in, but she was clear: Victor had released her. No, there was nobody else there. Like who? Of course she would have remembered.

After Katie went to sleep, Alex painstakingly walked Grace through the case so far – Victor's history, why he was involved. Grace sat patiently and listened, interrupting only when Alex skipped over certain details. For example, he neglected to talk about his drugs, or his first trance under Victor's control. Otherwise though, he was straight with her. He didn't bother considering confidentiality. Not after what had happened. Grace could keep a secret.

'Who is Sophie?' Grace had said, on the second or third day.

Alex thought long and hard. He didn't know a Sophie. He asked why she mentioned it.

'Hartley keeps talking about Sophie,' she said. 'To me. She asks if I ever met her. She says you worked with this woman at the prison.'

Alex frowned. 'I'm sure I'd remember,' he'd answered, and no more was said on the matter.

But it troubled him. The missing details, the fragments of memory, the behaviour of the police. He studied his own behaviour but could find no inconsistencies.

But his condition worsened.

Not in waking hours, but at night, when he tried to sleep. He thought of those moments at the orphanage and the name Sophie, and he let his mind wander. It conjured up images of darkness, wisps, fragments, but nothing substantial. He called the nurse and he spoke to Grace. They both suggested Alex should get more rest.

Sophie, whoever she was, had gone missing the same day as Katie's kidnap. Hartley described matters with obvious care, her eyes working on Alex's face, looking for a reaction. The woman worked for the prison, that much had been confirmed, although, much to Hartley's frustration, hardly anyone there remembered her either.

Whitemoor's governor said Sophie worked in Robert's office, but Robert was unavailable for comment. Within days of Victor's escape Robert had spiralled into severe anxiety and panic disorder. His wife had found him at the weekend, confused and incoherent, babbling 'Thirteen' into his pillow. He was now under the care of his own mental health team and signed off indefinitely.

One of the guards said he thought he knew the name Sophie, but he might have her confused with another agency worker.

There was no doubt she existed. Hartley had requested CCTV footage from HMP Whitemoor and satisfied herself. But she didn't get much more than that. Whoever Sophie was, she hadn't left much of a mark. They were tracing her through the academic exchange programme, but that would take time, and they weren't holding out much hope.

Hartley stressed over and again that Alex must remember Sophie, but her frustration became too loud. She said Sophie was a suspect. Dr Petri was dead. The nurses urged Hartley not to press the issue. Alex apologised but remembered nothing.

The conclusion, if tentative, was that if Alex was suppressing memory, it was a defence mechanism driven by trauma. He needed time, the doctors ruled. Hartley and her team, with a great degree of frustration, withdrew.

All of this was a puzzle, and it concerned Alex, but he didn't let it overwhelm him. He recalled enough about his case to know he'd had a lucky escape. Katie was safe, which was all he truly cared about. He and Grace spoke into the early hours and he saw that the spark in her eyes hadn't been extinguished. When she looked at him he felt the tug at his heart. He knew he loved her still, and he knew what he wanted. He didn't ask if it was possible, but the moments they shared reminded him of the millions of moments they'd shared years ago, before he'd screwed it all up.

He hoped, and he could see that Grace shared that hope. His family was back together in this room, just the three of them. He dreamed it could continue beyond the hospital ward.

Would Victor come back? It was possible, but Alex didn't think so. Victor's last act was in St Joseph's. Whatever his choices and motivations from this point on, Alex felt oddly certain he was safe, that Victor Lazar would never darken his future again.

He watched Grace and Katie, listening to the ever-permeating noise of a hospital at night. Beeps and hisses, footsteps and shouts. A door closed along the corridor and a trolley knocked into the wall. A nurse laughed and a child cried. It all faded as sleep finally found him.

Alex dreamed again that night. He dreamed of a beautiful woman, dark and tall, lithe and sensual. She excited him and made him nervous. She approached his bed and whispered in his ear in a foreign tongue, then fell away laughing. She was familiar. Alex knew her, but he'd never remember her again. She put a finger to her lips to silence him, touched him softly on the cheek, and waved goodbye.

Don't dream too hard, she said, as she disappeared into the mist. *It will be better for you, and the family who love you. Trust me.*

Some things are best forgotten.

ACKNOWLEDGMENTS

Writing *Trance* was a hugely challenging and rewarding experience, made possible by a select few, influenced by a great many. I thank them all.

The groundwork laid by my parents should be up first. My childhood was a delightful and nurturing experience and, importantly, full of books. Being born to a teacher and an editor was enormous good fortune, and I really can't take all the credit. I'm still not convinced my semicolon usage is correct, but they tried their hardest. Having a seriously bright older sister helped too – a lot of her influence found its way to me during my early years, as well as the contents of her bookshelves. Thank you to Mum, Dad and Lucy.

A generation on, my wife and daughters provide the rock from which I launch myself every day. My writing is possible only because they tolerate my long hours in the study as I tap away, pausing only to stare blankly at whoever dares enter. My family provide me with the constant inspiration, fun, love and understanding necessary to propel me through from first draft to finished product. Thank you to Kerry, Isla and Daisy.

But a finished manuscript is never finished. When I thought it was, things got serious, albeit in a wonderfully exciting way. My agent, Julie Fergusson, took a gamble on me and I'm eternally grateful she did. Julie worked tirelessly to get *Trance* publication-ready, providing all the guidance and expertise a top agent should. It paid off, so thank you, Julie.

Finally, in the hands of my publisher, my good luck continued with Thomas & Mercer. Jack Butler and the Amazon team (Laura, Martin, Monica, Shona, Emma and Bethan, among others) threw their substantial skills and experience behind *Trance* and managed to make every stage of publication professional, exciting and, above all, fun. They are a delight to work with and I couldn't ask for more.

Thank you.

ABOUT THE AUTHOR

Adam Southward is a philosophy graduate with a professional background in IT, working in both publishing and the public sector. He lives on the south coast of England with his young family.